T0145334

Editors
Federico Cabitza
Department of Informatics, Systems
    and Communication
University of Milano-Bicocca
Milan, Italy

Massimo Magni
Department of Management
    and Technology
Bocconi University
Milan, Italy

Carlo Batini
Department of Informatics, Systems
    and Communication
University of Milano-Bicocca
Milan, Italy

ISSN 2195-4968   ISSN 2195-4976   (electronic)
Lecture Notes in Information Systems and Organisation
ISBN 978-3-319-90502-0   ISBN 978-3-319-90503-7   (eBook)
https://doi.org/10.1007/978-3-319-90503-7

Library of Congress Control Number: 2018946932

This Springer imprint is published by the registered company Springer Nature Switzerland AG
The registered company address is: Gewerbestrasse 11, 6330 Cham, Switzerland

Preface

'Organizing' is a broader term than management: it entails the understanding of how people and machines interact with each other, and how resources, data and goods are exchanged in complex and intertwined value chains, as well as how lines of action and activities can be articulated according to exible protocols and often ad-hoc processes in situated practices of use and production.

This book contains a collection of research papers shedding light on these phenomena and the related practices from both an academic and a professional perspective. The plurality of views that this book offers makes it a relevant contribution to the understanding and appreciation of the complexity of the digital world at different levels of granularity, focusing on how the individuals, the communities, the society and the coopetitive societies in the new global and hyperconnected world produce value and pursue their objectives and ideals in mutually interdependent ways. The content of the book is based on a selection of the best papers (original double-blind peer-reviewed contributions) presented at the annual conference of the Italian chapter of AIS which took place in Milano, Italy in October 2017.

Milan, Italy
May 2018

Federico Cabitza
Massimo Magni
Carlo Batini

Contents

Organizing for the Digital World: An Overview of Current IT Solutions to Support Individuals, Communities and Societies

Federico Cabitza, Massimo Magni and Carlo Batini

This book collects some of the best contributions to the 14th conference of the Italian Chapter of AIS (ItAIS), which was held at the University of Milano-Bicocca, in Milano, on October the 6th and the 7th. ItAIS is an established forum for scholars, researchers and practitioners involved in the Information Systems (IS) field and akin scholarly disciplines where both Italian researchers and scholars from all over the world gather to present and discuss the most important trends in their domain of studies and applications. More precisely, this books collects the revised and extended version of the papers that were selected for their contribution to the more technological and IT-oriented side of the broader conference theme, which was: "Organizing for Digital Economy: societies, communities and individuals". This main theme, which this book inflects along the IT dimension, acknowledges the opportunity, as well as the responsibility, of the researchers and practitioners involved in the IS community to conceive, develop and present technologies, in the broadest sense of this term (and hence including also infrastructures, platforms, classification schemas, organizational constructs, protocols, architectures, tools), to enable, support and foster the fluid *organization* of the socio-economic context in which organizations, communities and individuals work, act and interact.

The term "economy" mentioned in the conference's title should not be considered an anachronistic legacy of the past, but rather a sign of responsible awareness that the main challenges currently faced by those who develop Information and Commu-

F. Cabitza (✉) · C. Batini
Department of Informatics, Systemics and Communication,
University of Milano-Bicocca, Milan, Italy
e-mail: federico.cabitza@unimib.it

C. Batini
e-mail: carlo.batini@unimib.it

M. Magni
Department of Management and Technology, Bocconi University, Milan, Italy
e-mail: massimo.magni@unibocconi.it

© Springer International Publishing AG, part of Springer Nature 2019
F. Cabitza et al. (eds.), *Organizing for the Digital World*, Lecture Notes in Information Systems and Organisation 28, https://doi.org/10.1007/978-3-319-90503-7_1

nication Technologies (ICT) in organizational settings (i.e., the traditional scope of IS research) *do not* regard the mere automation and optimization of bureaucratic and administrative procedures, nor the establishment of an all-monitoring Panopticon that includes a wider and wider portion of our interactions as workers, consumers and citizens, as many dread [4, 6], but rather the *renaissance* of a new kind of Homo Economicus, not seen any more as a "flat conception of the human as a cold, unemotional" [3] agent, but rather as a collective and embodied network of individuals who are augmented in their social and communicative dimensions, as well as in their cognitive and emotional ones, to build and maintain communities of practice and knowledge, both within and across institutional and organizational boundaries.

In the main mold outlined above, this book focuses on how IT and IS can contribute to this vision concretely, to create a "digital world" in which technology helps individuals, seen as both single users of their applications and tools, and as members of networked communities [5] of increasing complexity, up to the whole global society of which the more local societies (which we belong to) are tightly interconnected parts, to collaborate, coordinate their activities, and have knowledge circulate [1] in heterogeneous and multiple forms, adapted to the context. To this aim, the volume collects 18 contributions, which were selected from the ItAIS Conference papers and extended to make them chapter contributions to this book after a standard blind review process in order to guarantee theoretical and methodological rigor.

The book has been organized into two sections covering (a) the relationship between ICT and people; (b) the relationship between ICT and organizational change.

The first stream covers the relationship between the users and their tools in the broadest meaning of these both terms, so that even speaking of human-computer interaction would be limiting if with this common phrase one denoted only the dimension of use. In the first stream, this book considers the main themes of the IT adoption, IT adaptation, IT-mediated decision support and IT-enabled networking and collaboration [2]. Indeed, the article by Cremona, Ravarini and Jan Vom Brocke applies a qualitative approach to several case studies to focus on the dimension, of increasing importance, of the human-data interaction in organizational settings, that is how different Business Intelligence tools allowing managers and executives to visualize and explore large datasets, the so called big data, can impact typical managerial tasks like trend interpretation and decision making. The paper proposes four types of roles that current data visualization tools can play, also according to their level of customization, and gives guidelines for a larger and more effective adoption of these tools.

In a similar line, Fernandez-Marquez, Francalanci, Mohanty, Mondardini, Pernici and Scalia aim to show the feasibility of integrating social media analysis with crowdsourcing. They describe a system, called E2mC, which aims to improve the quality and dependability of the information that is made available to the members of Copernicus, a network established by the European Union to provide professional users with information services that are based on satellite Earth Observation and other georeferenced resources. In this contribution, the tool is considered part and parcel of a methodology that is proposed and validated in a real-life scenario to extract data from social media, to involve the "crowd" in the task of cleaning and validating the data (mainly pictures), and to visualize these data in an appropriate way for the task of rapid mapping.

The human contribution to data analytics is a central theme also in the contribution by Bednar and Welch, who describe a scenario in which Business Intelligence (BI) and Artificial Intelligence (AI) converge and merge in a new class of powerful, and partly autonomous, data analytics and decision support systems. In their conceptual yet refreshing contribution, Bednar and Welch advocate an open systems approach in the design of these new systems, which recognizes the role of human creativity as well as of praxeology (i.e., the notion that humans engage in purposeful behavior) and axiology (i.e., the consideration of ethical or aesthetic dimensions).

Also Cabitza, Ciucci, and Rasoini focus on the hybridization of BI and AI, AI in terms of machine learning predictive models, and on its application to the challenging organizational domain of hospital work and medicine. In their paper, they expose one of the main drawbacks of these models, that is information bias, seen in terms of the reliability of the input data of these models, especially when data are extracted from real-world records and registries. The authors argue that it is difficult to get more accurate medical data from the context where these are produced (i.e., care processes), also because often data just mirror the ambiguity and uncertainty of medical phenomena. For this reason, the interaction between the decision support systems and the human decision makers who use them must be developed within a broader socio-technical appraisal of the potential and shortcomings of machine learning, in which users have to become more aware of the intrinsic limits of computational tools in medicine and embrace uncertainty as an important key to interpret and cope with medical conditions and situations.

In the same application domain, Hanseth, Masovic, and Mørk report on their analysis of a new high-tech medical procedure called transcatheter aortic valve implantation (TAVI), seen through the conceptual lenses of Assemblage Theory. In their descriptive and analytical contribution, the authors show how complex innovations like TAVI can be seen as sociomaterial assemblages whose continuous evolution is affected by the combination and interaction of stabilizing and de-stabilizing processes.

Complex sociomaterial settings are also studied by the contribution carried out by Spagnoletti, Me, Ceci and Prencipe, who focus on Electronic identification (e-ID) infrastructures, and recognize their role of key enablers for the development of e-services in both public and private sector. The authors conducted a measurement study on identity theft and discuss some key features of three black markets within the darknet and in the Tor network, more in particular. In doing so they also show how data collection from the darknet can complement more traditional data sources for the analysis of new forms of crimes.

Also Cox and Bednar focus on Forensic Investigations but from a socio-technical perspective regarding the spread of Solid State Disc (SSD) and with a more qualitative approach grounding on interviews with an experienced Forensic Investigator. The authors scrutinized a number of themes to identify how specific characteristics and features of this increasingly common technology can impact and limit investigations.

Simone, Locoro and Cabitza, following a similarly qualitative approach, report about two adoption experiences of an Enterprise Social Media (ESM) within a big international corporate: the former process occurred at one mid-size business unit of the corporate, and the latter one was undertaken later at global level in the rest of the same corporate. The authors observe how the scaling up of the positive experience carried out at local level had been challenged by a number of factors (like the coexistence of multiple legacy technologies, different expectations and local work practices) and how the results achieved in the first adoption process were not replicated at global level. Their chapter discusses some lessons learnt from this experience, which regard how ESM should be introduced in complex organizations and across different communities of practices.

The complexity of real settings is also a theme discussed by Longo and Zappatore, who in their chapter make the point of the need to redesign transportation services by adopting a multi-dimensional framework and systemic approach, in order to improve the Quality of Service (QoS) as this is perceived from multiple perspectives (i.e., service providers, service customers, additional stakeholders). In this chapter, the authors report about a case study in the Apulia administrative in Italy where their framework was validated both technically and methodologically to achieve QoS sustainability even when multiple expectations and different constraints have to be considered systematically.

As hinted above, the second stream of papers collected in this volume can be traced back to the relationship between ICT and organizational change. In particular, the evidence provided by several papers outline how the role of ICT has modified organizations and organizational processes in many industries. For example, the paper by Virili and Ghiringhelli investigates how the introduction of an automated parcel sorting system has effects on the configuration of roles within an organization. The authors point out the critical role played by industrial engineers to facilitate the change by balancing the several components related to the change process.

Along this line the paper by Mola, Kaminska and Carugati focuses on the role of practices in implementing a mandated technology within the organizational boundaries. In particular, by leveraging on a case study, the authors point out the importance of knowledge sharing and collaboration in dispersed settings, and how such a challenge is tied to the different strategies that organizations can embrace in the implementation of an IT system aimed at facilitating employees interactions. On the basis of the collected findings, the authors show that institutionalized practices, organizational silos as well as lack of time and incentives represent important factors that may hamper the change process and compromise the effective use of the implemented technology.

The previous findings are complementary to the study ran by Di Fabio, Roncagliolo, Avallone e Ramassa who analyze the diffusion of XBRL (eXtensible Business Reporting Language) and its mandatory use as iXBRL in the European Union. Because of the mandatory implementation of such kind of language, primarily adopted to exchange financial and accounting information, the authors aim to consider the point of view of preparers and key subjects in providing a better understanding of the potential drawbacks related to this change. The results of the paper outline that this transition is characterized by a trade-off between the need for innovation and the necessity to reduce administrative burdens to enhance the competitiveness of European companies. The evolution of information systems in the accounting domain can be also analyzed through a decision-making lens.

The paper by Di Vaio, Varriale, and Alvino looks at how Accounting information systems (AIS) and Management Control Systems (MCS) may facilitate the decision making process of several organizational actors in a complex organizational setting. In particular, by conducting semi-structured interviews, the authors outline the usefulness of AIS and MCS introduction for supporting seaports players (e.g. forwards and shipping agents) in dealing with their tasks. Taking a decision-making perspective in the IS literature has been widely adopted for facilitating capabilities development and to foster a more agile approach to organizational challenges.

By embracing a marketing capability lens, Moi, Cabiddu and Frau contribute to previous literature by outlining how IT and dynamic marketing capabilities evolve into agile marketing capabilities in order to meet the market challenges and customers' need. In particular, they develop a framework aimed at supporting managers and decision makers to better understand the competitive advantages tied to agile marketing capabilities development.

The widespread diffusion of information technologies and the changes that are rooted into their pervasive impact on organizational processes has lead the attention also to the challenges in terms of information security. Indeed, on the one hand is pivotal to effectively lead the change in terms of adoption and introduction; on the other hand is critical to lead these changes with a security perspective in mind.

The paper by Zellhofer looks at information security policies implementations and the challenge of compliance within the organizational boundaries. In particular, the paper offers a useful framework to better understand how HR practices may contribute to ensuring information security in organizations. Another important and critical issue of current ICTs can be traced back to the ethical values.

The paper by Poponi, Mosconi, Ruggeri and Arezzo di Trifiletti investigates how the transparency, integrity and responsible governance represent key factors in the crowfunding domain. In particular, the authors focus on B Corp certification (a voluntary certification system), and investigate how the Kickstarter Platform manages the ethical values of B Corp certification.

Furthermore, a critical aspect concerning the changes related to ICTs introduction is tied to the role of the leaders in supporting and facilitating the adoption processes. In particular, a critical role is embraced by the Chief Information Officer (CIO) and the Chief Digital Officer (CDO).

Locoro and Ravarini looks at how the interaction between these two actors may affect the alignment between the IT and business vision, and through a set of semi structured interviews they provide a picture of the possible future roles and configurations of CIO and CDO in organizations.

From such a perspective, the paper by Kirkham and Cox investigates the importance of inter-agencies collaboration by looking at Checkland's Soft Systems Methodology (SSM) and its impact in favoring change. Moreover, besides looking at the advantages of this approach, authors pointed out the challenges that need to be addressed during a cultural change.

The above necessarily cursory outline has been intended to intrigue the readers of this book, which we hope will supplement the existing body of literature and inform their readers on some of the current ways in which ICT can help us build a better and fairer world at various levels of description. Finally, as editors of this book we acknowledge the collective nature of this publication, which should be considered as the collective achievement of a group of people who contributed to it in various and complementary forms: for this reason, we are grateful to all of the Authors, the Conference Chairs, the members of the Committees and the Editorial Board, as well as to all of the Reviewers involved in the difficult task of supporting the authors in improving the quality of their contributions, for their competence, diligence and commitment.

References

1. Cabitza, F., et al.: The knowledge-stream model a comprehensive model for knowledge circulation in communities of knowledgeable practitioners. In: International Conference on Knowledge Management and Information Sharing, pp. 367–374, 21–24 October 2014. Scitepress (2014)
2. Cabitza, F., Simone, C., Cornetta, D.: Sensitizing concepts for the next community-oriented technologies: shifting focus from social networking to convivial artifacts. J. Community Inform. **11**(2) (2015)
3. Mutch, A.: Actors and networks or agents and structures: towards a realist view of information systems. Organization **9**(3), 477–496 (2002)
4. Myers, M.D., Klein, H.K.: A set of principles for conducting critical research in information systems. MIS Q. **35**(1), 17 (2011)
5. Mynatt, E.D., et al.: Network communities: something old, something new, something borrowed. Comput. Support. Coop. Work (CSCW) **7**(1–2), 123–156 (1998)
6. Sia, S.K., et al.: Enterprise resource planning (ERP) systems as a technology of power: empowerment or panoptic control? ACM SIGMIS Database **33**(1) (2002)

Automation as Management of Paradoxical Tensions: The Role of Industrial Engineering

Francesco Virili and Cristiano Ghiringhelli

Abstract In this paper, we explored the introduction of an automated parcel sorting system in a major company in the logistic and parcel delivery industry. Adopting a Grounded Theory approach, we carried out a study that highlighted profound and unexpected organizational implications and management challenges connected to the introduction of the new technology. Our analysis revealed the key role of the Industrial Engineering function as a change agent in devising and managing the introduction of the automated system. In particular, Industrial Engineering actually managed the organizational change by determining the right balance between several opposite dimensions (manual vs. automated; planned vs. emergent; local vs. global). Handling these tensions with a holistic approach may constitute a crucial factor for the change program effectiveness. Contrasting our findings with extant literature, we found resonance with latest works on ambidexterity, interpreted as a firm's ability to manage tensions. The resulting outcome is a substantive grounded theory of ambidexterity in an automation enhancement program.

Keywords Automation · Ambidexterity · Grounded theory · Industrial engineering · Change management · Tensions

1 Introduction

In this paper, we explored an automation enhancement program in a major company in the parcel delivery industry. This strategically relevant program was aimed at increasing volumes, reducing operational costs and enhancing operational flexi-

F. Virili (✉)
Department of Economics and Business Administration,
University of Sassari, Sassari, Italy
e-mail: fvirili@uniss.it

C. Ghiringhelli (✉)
Department of Human Sciences and Education, University of Milano-Bicocca, Milan, Italy
e-mail: cristiano.ghiringhelli@unimib.it

© Springer International Publishing AG, part of Springer Nature 2019
F. Cabitza et al. (eds.), *Organizing for the Digital World*, Lecture Notes in Information Systems and Organisation 28, https://doi.org/10.1007/978-3-319-90503-7_2

bility by shifting from a manual to an automated parcel sorting system. Our analysis investigated the initiatives carried out by the Industrial Engineering function aimed at managing this shift in two different European hubs. Compared to previous studies on automation and manufacturing strategies, two important differences emerged. First, we examined industrial (and not pure production) processes. Second, we know that successful automation needs to be aligned with manufacturing strategies [48], but we do not know how to actually achieve alignment. However, we found that change management was crucial to this regard. Typical automation projects are often regarded as mandatory choice aimed at preserving the organizational competitiveness as well as the alignment with technological evolution. Consequently, the switch from a manual process to an automated process could appear as a technical replacement, very poorly related to key dimensions such as organizational strategy and product/service innovation. In this perspective, the typical drivers of the advances in automation are cost reduction and imitation, as stated in Lindstrom and Winroth [26], instead of programs aimed at innovating the organizational strategy.

Similarly, also the program investigated in this paper—the development of an automated parcel sorting system—could appear too simple and ordinary. Thus, not so interesting from an organizational point of view. Surprisingly, our investigation has revealed instead that this a complex program which requires both to carefully manage relevant multiple dimensions and to deal with a challenging decision-making process related to numerous and very often conflicting issues. In particular, the switch from manual to automated approach introduces the need for finding and implementing the right balance between (a) manual versus automated, (b) planned versus emergent and (c) local versus global.

In Sect. 2, we discuss the methodological approach that we adopted when carrying out the case analysis. Then, we discuss the main findings (Sect. 3). In Sect. 4 we debate them considering the extant literature. Finally, in the last section we highlight the main implications of the findings, and we declare the next research steps.

2 Research Methodology: Grounded Theory Data Collection and Analysis

The aim of our research was threefold. First, to observe a remarkable phenomenon, potentially valuable when investigated in terms of organizational change management. Second, to obtain a thick description of the topic investigated. Third, to integrate our empirical findings within the current theoretical debate. Considering that the intent wasn't to empirically test an extant theory, we started from a "blank sheet" (instead of theory analysis), using a Grounded Theory methodological approach in order to build rich descriptions grounded in the observed empirical data. Our rich descriptions would gradually evolve towards an empirically grounded theoretical contribution. In particular, we started from a very broadly outlined explorative approach, aimed at opening the black box of the change management issues related to the automation of a core organizational process. The development of the research program has allowed us to clarify our goal step by step: what arose from the data collected during each research stages helped us to increase also our theoretical sensitivity [12] and, therefore, our understanding of the phenomenon itself. Of course, it has been necessary to accept the high degree of uncertainty at the former stages of the research program and leave both interviewees and data free of pre-defined theoretical frameworks [47]. Adopting this approach, we firstly developed a strong relationship with a key Industrial Engineer (Industrial Engineer 1) of the Company with some informal meetings and two preliminary interviews. In the first preliminary interview, the goal was to verify the chance of (a) sharing and specifying the purpose of the research program, (b) collecting data by a reasonable wide range of internal sources, including not only Industrial Engineering experts but also others key organizational roles involved in the AEP program. In the second preliminary interview, we started collecting data on the whole automation development process in the last three decades (1987–2017). This first data collection led us to focus only the last decade (2006–2017). In this period, in fact, the Company implemented the highest shift in terms of technological model, developing and fine-tuning the current organizational approach that, by promoting and managing AEP programs, apply automation to its organizational key processes.

A preliminary data analysis step followed, outlining the first research themes as discussed in the next section.

In the next research step, we carried out a telephone interview with the Chief Regional Industrial Engineer (Industrial Engineer 2), at the moment holding also the role of Plant Director at the plant Alfa. This interview was conducted with the support and participation of the Industrial Engineer 1.

In the following step we carried out a follow-up interview with the Industrial Engineer 1, aimed at discussing and refining what emerged in the telephone interview with Industrial Engineer 2.

After, we prepared an interview guide for the next step, in which we visited the plant Alfa.

Here, we carried out two interviews. First, a two-hour interview with Industrial Engineer 2, followed by a one-hour interview with two Hub Managers (Hub Manager 1 and Hub Manager 2). Moreover, we had the chance of two additional, unexpected and unplanned informal interviews with three supervisors.

The day after, we carried out a follow-up interview with Industrial Engineer 1 aimed at checking data gathered during the visit and collect additional information and documents.

An analysis step followed: here, we developed a first and temporary framework aimed at leading us toward the next research steps. In particular, we carried out a new interview with Industrial Engineer 1, aimed at sharing such a temporary framework as well as at discussing the purpose and the structure of the visit at a second plant. We chose a plant Beta and, finally, we organized the visit.

In a further step, we visited the plant Beta, carrying out a two-hour interview with the Plant Director (PM1), and a follow-up interview with the Industrial Engineer 1.

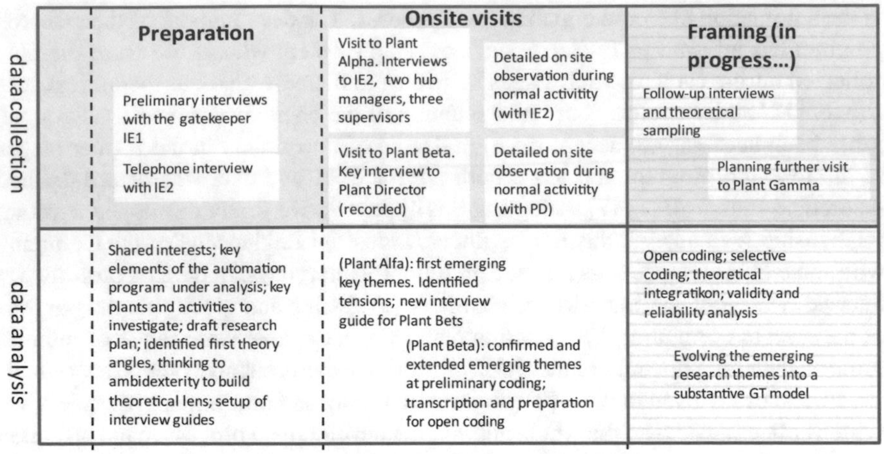

	Preparation	Onsite visits		Framing (in progress...)
data collection	Preliminary interviews with the gatekeeper IE1	Visit to Plant Alpha. Interviews to IE2, two hub managers, three supervisors	Detailed on site observation during normal activitity (with IE2)	Follow-up interviews and theoretical sampling
	Telephone interview with IE2	Visit to Plant Beta. Key interview to Plant Director (recorded)	Detailed on site observation during normal activitity (with PD)	Planning further visit to Plant Gamma
data analysis	Shared interests; key elements of the automation program under analysis; key plants and activities to investigate; draft research plan; identified first theory angles, thinking to ambidexterity to build theoretical lens; setup of interview guides	(Plant Alfa): first emerging key themes. Identified tensions; new interview guide for Plant Bets (Plant Beta): confirmed and extended emerging themes at preliminary coding; transcription and preparation for open coding		Open coding; selective coding; theoretical integratikon; validity and reliability analysis Evolving the emerging research themes into a substantive GT model

Fig. 1 An overview of the research work in progress

Afterword, we started our analysis of data collected, producing a more detailed set of research themes briefly explained in the following section.

Or work in progress is now at this point of development. We have planned the following steps: (a) textual transcription of the interview carried out at the plant Beta (now fully accomplished before paper resubmission); (b) detailed analysis and textual coding using Atlas.ti; (c) theoretical sampling; (d) iteration until theoretical saturation [47]. A schematic representation of the whole research program is provided by the following Fig. 1.

3 Emerging Themes: Automation Enhancement Program Ambidexterity

3.1 Thematic Coding with the Bottom-up Approach

Themes from the first interview with Industrial Engineer 1. In the initial part of the research (preparation and first on site visit in Fig. 1), during interviews, discussions and telephone calls, both the researchers took separate notes in parallel. Just after data collection, they revised, discussed and merged their notes in order to start building the main research themes grounded in observation. The quantity and quality of source data was not yet appropriate at this stage for analytic open coding. Therefore, a "thematic coding" was carried out with the bottom-up approach, as suggested and discussed in [47: 40]. The emergent research themes were identified, written down and then coded and linked (using the software application Atlas TI version 8) in order to build the thematic concept networks and graphics represented in the figures here.

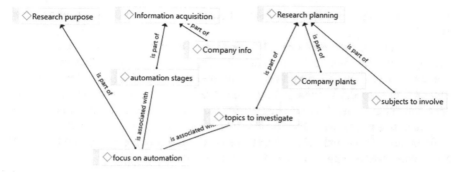

Fig. 2 Main thematic categories emerging from the first interview: research purpose, information acquisition and research planning. The related concepts and relationships discussed above are shown in the figure

The first interview with Industrial Engineer 1 led us to share the main purpose of the research program and an initial planning. We also collected a first set of general information about the Company and his development history. Further emerging themes: (a) a first classification and timing of the main stages by which the Company has applied the automation to its business processes; (b) the focus of the research; (c) both the specific subjects to put under investigation in the next data collection stage (in terms of interview strictly focused on the automation topic) and the Company's experts to involve in it; (d) choosing the Company plant to visit (Fig. 2).

Themes from the second interview with Industrial Engineer 1. In the second interview with IE1, the three main thematic categories were further specified. First, discussing the research purpose, *a shared interest on the organizational aspects of automation* emerged. We found Industrial Engineer 1 very interested about the organizational issues related to automation advances. Really, he was very persuaded that a research program focused on them would most likely be able to produce valuable findings. Second, we accomplished a better *focus selection*. The switch from the manual to the automated sorting process was identified as a promising specific field of investigation, by which to study the organizational dimensions related to automation advances. Third, we had a more in depth information acquisition with *an introduction to the sorting process*—a preliminary description of the sorting process was carried out by Industrial Engineer 1, bearing in mind three matters in particular: (a) the different types of sorting (primary, secondary, small parcel, non-standard shape, dangerous packages, etc.); (b) the different sorting challenges to deal with when operating within a ground hub versus an airport hub; (c) the stages of automation advances over the last decades promoted by the Company; (d) the need of adjusting standardized process (global dimension) reflecting specific traits of each plant (local dimension). Fourth, *visit planning*—first: plant Alfa (specific traits: very fine-tuned processes, automation well consolidated); second: plant Beta (specific traits: recent advances in automation, ongoing fine-tuning); third: plant Gamma (specific traits:

field of ongoing experimentation/test/validation of next advances in automation) (Fig. 3).

Themes from the telephone interview with Industrial Engineer 2. In the following telephone interview with Industrial Engineer 2, the main themes emerged are (a) clarifying and sharing with IE2 the research aim, plan, expected outcomes emerged in precedence with IE1; (b) the relationship between company's strategies/policies and the role of automation; (c) the role of Regional Industrial Engineering Department; (d) main traits of Plant Alfa and AEP programs in plant Alfa; (e) main organizational and HR issues; (f) the practicalities of the visit at the Plant Alfa and the interviews with two Hub Managers (Fig. 4).

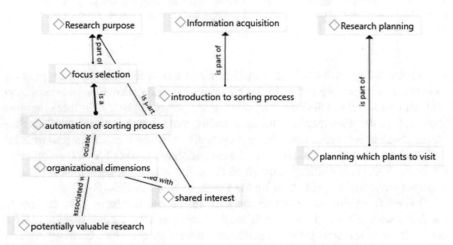

Fig. 3 Main thematic categories emerging from the second interview with Industrial Engineer 1, specifying and reinforcing the initial research direction and planning and widening the information basis

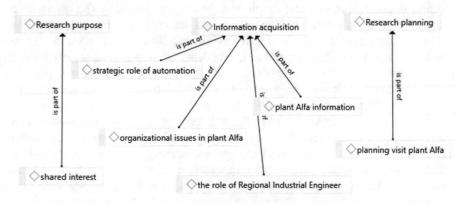

Fig. 4 Main themes emerging from the telephone interview with Industrial Engineer 2, in preparation of the visit to plant Alfa

Themes from the interview with Industrial Engineeer 2 during the visit at the plant Alfa. The thematic coding of data collected during the visit at plant Alfa (one official presentation, three interviews, informal talks—see Sect. 2) revealed the following themes: (a) the evolution of plant Alfa; (b) the production capacity index of the plant Alfa (and comparison with other plants); (c) the parcel journey analysis, focusing the need of synchronisation between plants; (d) the primary and the secondary sorting in depth; (e) a list of typical exceptions and mistakes within the automated process that require the human involvement; (f) a comparison between exceptions and mistakes made by humans and by the automated process; (g) (cited twice) the need for managing some trade-offs. At this regard, the coordination between the (still) manual actions and the (already) automated parts of the whole sorting process has been evaluated as the most challenging trade-off); (h) the small package sorting feed as the next area of automation advances; (i) the opportunity for automating the movement of shelters within the hub adopting self-driving trucks (Fig. 5).

Themes from the two interviews with Hub Managers 1–2 during the visit at the plant Alfa. Main themes emerged: (a) relevant differences on impacts produced by the automation on the unloading (no impact), the sorting (very high impact) and the outbound operations (high impact); (b) new key roles and competencies created by automation: control room operators and managers, operation supervisor (tasked with the control of processes), plant technicians skilled on cyber-physical devices and on teamwork; (c) the need for new training programs aimed at developing those competencies; (d) the role of the headquarter in the change process (relationship between global and local dimensions); (e) the high acceptance of change by operators, supervisors and managers rooted on both contextual and cultural factors.

Themes from the informal interviews with three supervisors during the visit at the plant Alfa. Main themes emerged: (a) a sense of pride and empowerment as

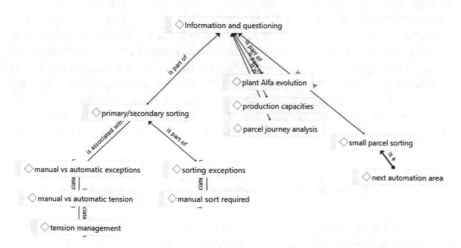

Fig. 5 Main themes emerging from the interview with Industrial Engineer 2, during the visit to plant Alfa

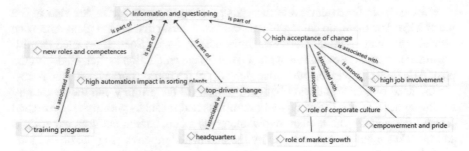

Fig. 6 Main themes emerging during the visit to plant Alfa and the interviews of hub managers and supervisors at the site

result of the work environment change after the automation advances; (b) a high job involvement perceived by employees rooted in deeply rooted organizational values; (c) the high acceptance of change by operators, supervisors and managers rooted on both contextual and cultural factors (Fig. 6).

3.2 Interview Guide Definition for Next Steps and First Theoretical Sampling

Among the most relevant concepts emerged in the thematic analysis, the recurrent mention of trade-offs by the interviewees and the informal talks occurred at the plant Alfa led us to adopt the ambidexterity perspective in the next research stage. As discussed in the next section, ambidexterity signifies a firm's ability to manage tensions between exploration and exploitation [10]. In particular, one of the more evident tensions frequently cited by interviewees is the copresence of manual and automated processes. Consequently, we have developed an interview guide structured in five investigation areas, as follows: (1) State A (the hub before automation) versus state B (the hub after automation); (2) the change management process from state A to state B; (3) finding the right balance between state A and state B: benefits, challenges and limitations of the automation; (4) relevant figures and roles: hub Manager, Industrial Engineering and others; (5) impacts on People and behaviours.

3.3 Insights on Emerging Themes on Data Analysis

The structure described above was used to interview the Plant Director of plant Beta. The interview, of about 2 h, was audio recorded in order to make it possible to fully transcribe it into text. The resulting text document is the primary source for open coding and micro-codifications, sentence by sentence and even word by word. This stage is still in progress, but we are already able to underline some emerging insights.

First, we found several paradoxical tensions related to an AEP: manual/automated; planned/emergent; local/global.

Manual versus automated tension. The manual versus automated tension refers to the fact that automation is not integrally and universally applied in all the areas of the sorting process. Manual and automated process areas actually coexist now. Such a coexistence needs to be explicitly addressed with managerial and technical integration solutions.

Planned versus emergent tension. The planned versus emergent tension refers to the contrast between the formal, explicit and rationally formed automation plan with well defined implementation phases, and the needing to take into account unexpected requirements and adaptations emerging during the implementation of the original automation plan.

Local versus global tension. The local versus global tension is related to a dual need. On the one hand, to adopt global standard solutions and best practices in the whole corporation on a global scale, eventually adapting them to local specificities. On the other hand, to take into account the possibility to standardize and unify local solutions to the whole corporation, when appropriate.

Second, the management of these tensions is important for AEP effectiveness. In the theoretical sampling, we are going to challenge this emerging theme by distinguishing tension management episodes with positive versus negative outcomes and the related factors. Industrial Engineering appears to play a key role in managing these tensions, while developing and maintaining positive relationships with other units.

Third, managing AEP requires a holistic approach taking into account, besides the technical and engineering aspects typically observed in classical automation studies, also organizational innovation and change management issues, investigating critical aspects of people management including culture, values, climate, competences, managerial and leadership styles, and communication. These aspects, now emerging from open coding, are going to be more deeply observed and analysed through further cycles of theoretical sampling, data collection and theoretical coding.

4 Discussion and Theoretical Integration

The notion of ambidexterity has been widely studied (see e.g. [3, 5, 7, 9–11, 13, 14, 21, 28, 30–32, 34, 38, 42]) and it is generally connected to the need of simultaneously achieving exploration and exploitation [10]. In particular, "Organizational ambidexterity refers to the ability of an organization to both explore and exploit—to compete in mature technologies and markets where efficiency, control, and incremental improvement are prized and to also compete in new technologies and markets where flexibility, autonomy, and experimentation are needed." [32, p. 324].

Table 1 Trade-offs in selected literature on ambidexterity [38]

Ambidexterity's trade-offs			
Authors (Ref.)	Study type	Sample and method	Tradeoffs
Duncan [10]	Conceptual	n.a.	Initiation versus implementation
O'Reilly and Tushman [29], Tushman and O'Reilly [45, 46]	Theoretical	n.a.	Incremental versus discontinuous innovation
Adler et al. [1]	Empirical	Case study (NUMMI)	Flexibility versus efficiency
Helfat and Raubitschek [18]	Conceptual	n.a.	Incremental learning versus step function (radical) learning
Sheremata [37]	Conceptual	n.a.	Centrifugal versus centripetal forces
Winter and Szulanski [49]	Theoretical	n.a.	Exploitation versus exploration
Katila and Ahuja [23]	Empirical	Archival study of 124 films in the robotics industry	Search depth versus search scope
Rivkin and Siggelkow [35]	Empirical	Agent-based simulation study	Search versus stability
Gibson and Birkinshaw [11]	Empirical	Interviews and surveys in 41 business units of 10 MNCs	Alignment versus adaptability
Kyriakopoulos and Moorman [24]	Empirical	Large-scale survey of 96 Dutch business units	Examines the complementarities between exploration and exploitation in marketing strategy
Rothaermel and Deeds [36]	Empirical	Archival study of 325 biotechnology companies	Exploratory alliances versus exploitive alliances
He and Wong [17]	Empirical	Large-scale survey of 206 manufacturing firms in Singapore and Fenang	Exploratory innovation versus exploitive innovation
Chen [8]	Theoretical	n.a.	Exploitation versus exploration
Smith and Tushman [39]	Theoretical	n.a.	Exploitation versus exploration; cognitive differentiation versus cognitive integration

(continued)

Table 1 (continued)

Ambidexterity's trade-offs

Authors (Ref.)	Study type	Sample and method	Tradeoffs
Jansen et al. [20]	Empirical	Large-scale survey of multi-unit firm	Exploitation versus exploration
Atuahene-Gima [4]	Empirical	Large-scale survey of 227 electronics firms in China	Competence exploitation versus competence exploration
Tiwana et al. [44]	Empirical	Field study of CIOs in 133 firms	Information systems alignment versus adaptability
Han [16]	Empirical	Case study of Merrill Lynch and Comdirect Bank	Pro-profit versus pro-growth strategies
Lavie and Rosenkopf [25]	Empirical	Archival study of 19,928 alliances from 1990 to 2001	Exploitation versus exploration
Gupta et al. [15]	Theoretical	n.a.	Exploitation versus exploration
Raisch [33]	Theoretical	n.a.	Exploitation versus exploration
Bierly and Daly [6]	Empirical	Survey of 98 SME manufacturing firms	Exploitation versus exploration
Andersen and Nielsen [2]	Empirical	Survey of 185 manufacturing companies	Central exploitive strategy processes versus decentralized exploratory strategy processes
Tarafdar and Gordon [41]	Empirical	Longitudinal case study of healthcare firm	Strategic vision versus operational excellence
Swart and Kinnie [40]	Empirical	Case study of a marketing agency	Exploitive learning versus exploratory learning; accelerated versus planned
Tiwana [43]	Empirical	Survey of 42 innovation-seeking project alliances	Alignment versus adaptability of alliances
Kang and Snell [22]	Theoretical	n.a.	Exploitative versus exploration
Im and Rai [19]	Empirical	Survey of company in logistics industry	Exploitative knowledge sharing versus exploratory knowledge sharing
Menguc and Auh [27]	Empirical	Survey of Australian manufacturing firms	Exploitation versus exploration

A widely recognized common trait of extant research includes the distinction of two research approaches to ambidexterity. On the one hand, the structural approach, showing how ambidexterity is implemented through using dual structures and formal organizational means. On the other hand, the contextual approach, showing how ambidexterity is pursued in informal ways, leveraging values, cultural systems and organizational behaviours [11].

Recent attempts to overcome the distinction of structural and contextual approaches on ambidexterity with an integrative view, taking into account both formal and informal means at the same time, like [3], have empirically shown that successful ambidextrous organizations are actually dealing with multiple tensions at the same time in finding the right solution to the exploration/exploitation dilemma.

An overview of the analytic classification of the literature presented in [38], tends to further underline the presence of a wide variety of dimensions in the typical trade-offs faced by ambidextrous organizations, as shown in last column of the following Table 1.

Our emerging concepts under analysis seem to suggest affinities with the literature on ambidexterity mentioned above, evidencing the presence of multiple dimensions in the handling and balancing of the exploration/exploitation dilemma.

A further direction of investigation and theoretical integration is the stream of recent research opened by works, like in particular [13], reinterpreting ambidexterity in the light of a wider theory of paradox. Such an approach could converge with the emerging outcomes of our data analysis. In our still emerging intuitions, the classical dilemma exploration/exploitation might be revisited within a wider view of organizational change as holistic management of multidimensional paradoxical tensions.

Our substantive theoretical constructs under analysis may therefore confirm and extend some of the latest directions of research on ambidexterity with a focus on management of multiple paradoxical tensions.

A further promising research stream may shed light on the inevitably rising questions: Are there specific directions to successfully manage multiple tensions? What are the relevant factors to take into account? Our ongoing analysis of actual decisions and actions taken on the field may find resonance in recent analyses of ambidexterity focused on the costs and benefits of shifts along the continuum between the opposite dimensions of ambidexterity: the recent study by Gulati and Puranam [14] may represent and important point of reference to this regard.

5   Conclusions

We are at an already quite advanced stage of a work in progress aimed at building a substantive grounded theory of ambidexterity in an automation enhancement program. Our emerging results are encouraging, suggesting us to proceed with open coding and theoretical sampling towards theoretical saturation. All in all, this study seems to recommend an evolving, multidimensional view on ambidexterity, possibly framed within a wider view of paradoxical tension management as the key of automation-enabled organizational change.

References

1. Adler, P.S., Goldoftas, B., Levine, D.I.: Flexibility versus efficiency? A case study of model changeovers in the Toyota production system. Organ. Sci. **10**(1), 43–68 (1999)
2. Andersen, T.J., Nielsen, B.B.: The effective ambidextrous organization: a model of integrative strategy making processes (2007). Accessed from http://openarchive.cbs.dk/bitstream/handle/10398/7424/2007-12.pdf?sequence=1
3. Andriopoulos, C., Lewis, M.W.: Exploitation-exploration tensions and organizational ambidexterity: managing paradoxes of innovation. Organ. Sci. **20**(4), 696–717 (2009)
4. Atuahene-Gima, K.: Resolving the capability—rigidity paradox in new product innovation. J. Mark. **69**(4), 61–83 (2005)
5. Benner, M.J., Tushman, M.L.: Reflections on the 2013 decade award—'exploitation, exploration, and process management: the productivity dilemma revisited' ten years later. Acad. Manag. Rev. **40**(4), 497–514 (2015)
6. Bierly, P.E., Daly, P.S.: Alternative knowledge strategies, competitive environment, and organizational performance in small manufacturing firms. Entrep. Theory Pract. **31**(4), 493–516 (2007)
7. Cao, Q., Gedajlovic, E., Zhang, H.: Unpacking organizational ambidexterity: dimensions, contingencies, and synergistic effects. Organ. Sci. **20**(4), 781–796 (2009)
8. Chen, E.L., Katila, R.: Rival interpretations of balancing exploration and exploitation: simultaneous or sequential? In: Shane, S. (ed.), Handbook of Technology and Innovation Management, pp. 197–214. Wiley (2008). Accessed from http://maryannfeldman.web.unc.edu/files/2011/11/Contribution-of-Public-Entities_2008.pdf#page=214
9. Du, W., Pan, S.L., Zuo, M.: How to balance sustainability and profitability in technology organizations: an ambidextrous perspective. IEEE Trans. Eng. Manag. **60**(2), 366–385 (2013). https://doi.org/10.1109/TEM.2012.2206113
10. Duncan, R.: The ambidextrous organization: designing dual structures for innovation. In: Killman, R.H., Pondy, L.R., Sleven, D. (eds.), The Management of Organization, pp. 167–188. North-Holland, New York (n.d.)
11. Gibson, C.B., Birkinshaw, J.: The antecedents, consequences, and mediating role of organizational ambidexterity. Acad. Manag. J. **47**(2), 209–226 (2004)
12. Glaser, B.G.: Theoretical Sensitivity: Advances in the Methodology of Grounded Theory. Sociology Press (1978)
13. Gregory, R.W., Keil, M., Muntermann, J., Mähring, M.: Paradoxes and the nature of ambidexterity in IT transformation programs. Inf. Syst. Res. **26**(1), 57–80 (2015). https://doi.org/10.1287/isre.2014.0554
14. Gulati, R., Puranam, P.: Renewal through reorganization: the value of inconsistencies between formal and informal organization. Organ. Sci. **20**(2), 422–440 (2009). https://doi.org/10.1287/orsc.1090.0421
15. Gupta, A.K., Smith, K.G., Shalley, C.E.: The interplay between exploration and exploitation. Acad. Manag. J. **49**(4), 693–706 (2006)
16. Han, M.: Achieving superior internationalization through strategic ambidexterity. J. Enterp. Cult. **15**(1), 43–77 (2007)
17. He, Z.-L., Wong, P.-K.: Exploration vs. exploitation: an empirical test of the ambidexterity hypothesis. Organ. Sci. **15**(4), 481–494 (2004)

18. Helfat, C.E., Raubitschek, R.S.: Product sequencing: co-evolution of knowledge, capabilities and products. Strateg. Manag. J. 961–979 (2000)
19. Im, G., Rai, A.: Knowledge sharing ambidexterity in long-term interorganizational relationships. Manag. Sci. **54**(7), 1281–1296 (2008)
20. Jansen, J.J.P., den Bosch, F.A.J.V., Volberda, H.W.: Exploratory innovation, exploitative innovation, and ambidexterity: the impact of environmental and organizational antecedents. Schmalenbach Bus. Rev. (SBR) **57**(4), 351–363 (2005)
21. Jansen, J.J.P., Tempelaar, M.P., van den Bosch, F.A.J., Volberda, H.W.: Structural differentiation and ambidexterity: the mediating role of integration mechanisms. Organ. Sci. **20**(4), 797–811 (2009)
22. Kang, S.-C., Snell, S.A.: Intellectual capital architectures and ambidextrous learning: a framework for human resource management. J. Manag. Stud. **46**(1), 65–92 (2009)
23. Katila, R., Ahuja, G.: Something old, something new: a longitudinal study of search behavior and new product introduction. Acad. Manag. J. **45**(6), 1183–1194 (2002)
24. Kyriakopoulos, K., Moorman, C.: Tradeoffs in marketing exploitation and exploration strategies: the overlooked role of market orientation. Int. J. Res. Mark. **21**(3), 219–240 (2004)
25. Lavie, D., Rosenkopf, L.: Balancing exploration and exploitation in alliance formation. Acad. Manag. J. **49**(4), 797–818 (2006)
26. Lindström, V., Winroth, M.: Aligning manufacturing strategy and levels of automation: a case study. J. Eng. Tech. Manag. **27**(3–4), 148–159 (2010). https://doi.org/10.1016/j.jengtecman.2010.06.002
27. Menguc, B., Auh, S.: The asymmetric effect of ambidexterity on firm performance for prospectors and defenders: the moderating role of marketing orientation. Ind. Mark. Manag. **37**(4), 455–470 (2008)
28. Mom, T.J.M., van den Bosch, F.A.J., Volberda, H.W.: Understanding variation in managers' ambidexterity: investigating direct and interaction effects of formal structural and personal coordination mechanisms. Organ. Sci. **20**(4), 812–828 (2009)
29. O'Reilly III, C.A., Tushman, M.L.: The ambidextrous organization. Harvard Bus. Rev. **82**(4), 74–81 (2004)
30. O'Reilly III, C.A., Tushman, M.L.: Ambidexterity as a dynamic capability: resolving the innovator's dilemma. Res. Organ. Behav. **28**, 185–206 (2008). https://doi.org/10.1016/j.riob.2008.06.002
31. O'Reilly III, C.A., Tushman, M.L.: Organizational ambidexterity in action: how managers explore and exploit. Calif. Manag. Rev. **53**(4), 5–22 (2011)
32. O'Reilly III, C.A., Tushman, M.L.: Organizational ambidexterity: past, present, and future. Acad. Manag. Perspect. **27**(4), 324–338 (2013). https://doi.org/10.5465/amp.2013.0025
33. Raisch, S.: Exploration vs. exploitation: a metaparadigm view of ambidextrous organizational forms. In: Annual Meetings of the Academy of Management, Atlanta, GA, Aug 2006
34. Raisch, S., Birkinshaw, J., Probst, G., Tushman, M.L.: Organizational ambidexterity: balancing exploitation and exploration for sustained performance. Organ. Sci. **20**(4), 685–695 (2009)
35. Rivkin, J.W., Siggelkow, N.: Balancing search and stability: Interdependencies among elements of organizational design. Manag. Sci. **49**(3), 290–311 (2003)
36. Rothaermel, F.T., Deeds, D.L.: Exploration and exploitation alliances in biotechnology: a system of new product development. Strateg. Manag. J. **25**(3), 201–221 (2004)
37. Sheremata, W.A.: Centrifugal and centripetal forces in radical new product development under time pressure. Acad. Manag. Rev. **25**(2), 389–408 (2000)
38. Simsek, Z., Heavey, C., Veiga, J.F., Souder, D.: A typology for aligning organizational ambidexterity's conceptualizations, antecedents, and outcomes. J. Manag. Stud. **46**(5), 864–894 (2009). https://doi.org/10.1111/j.1467-6486.2009.00841.x
39. Smith, W.K., Tushman, M.L.: Managing strategic contradictions: a top management model for managing innovation streams. Organ. Sci. **16**, 522–536 (2005)
40. Swart, J., Kinnie, N.: Simultaneity of learning orientations in a marketing agency. Manag. Learn. **38**(3), 337–357 (2007)

41. Tarafdar, M., Gordon, S.R.: Understanding the influence of information systems competencies on process innovation: a resource-based view. J. Strateg. Inf. Syst. **16**(4), 353–392 (2007)
42. Taylor, A., Helfat, C.E.: Organizational linkages for surviving technological change: complementary assets, middle management, and ambidexterity. Organ. Sci. **20**(4), 718–739 (2009)
43. Tiwana, A.: Do bridging ties complement strong ties? An empirical examination of alliance ambidexterity. Strateg. Manag. J. **29**(3), 251–272 (2008)
44. Tiwana, A., Bharadwaj, A., Sambamurthy, V.: The influence of interunit linkages on technology: an empirical study of the mediating role of knowledge integration. Soc. Sci. Res. Netw. (SSRN) Working Paper (2007)
45. Tushman, M.L., O'Reilly III, C.A.: The ambidextrous organizations: Managing evolutionary and revolutionary change. Calif. Manag. Rev. **38**(4), 8–30 (1996)
46. Tushman, M., O'Reilly III, C.A.: Winning Through Innovation: A Practical Guide to Leading Organizational Change and Renewal. Harvard Business School Press (1997)
47. Urquhart, C.: Grounded Theory for Qualitative Research: A Practical Guide. Sage (2012)
48. Winroth, M., Safsten, K., Stahre, J.: Automation strategies: existing theory or ad hoc decisions? Int. J. Manuf. Technol. Manag. **11**(1), 98–114 (2007)
49. Winter, S.G., Szulanski, G.: Replication as strategy. Organ. Sci. **12**(6), 730–743 (2001)

Visualizing Big Data: The Impact on Sense-Making and Decision-Making

Luca Cremona, Aurelio Ravarini and Jan Vom Brocke

Abstract Firms living in a digital disrupting world should continuously understand variables from inside and outside the organization and consequently act efficiently and effectively. This study aims at investigating the role of innovative digital tools to manipulate big data in transforming managers and executives activities, in particular their sense-making (how they interpret data) and decision-making (who is using data and to what extent). A qualitative methodology has been selected to explore how organizations use Business Intelligence (BI)/Data Visualization (DV) tools. A multiple case study approach has been adopted and interviews have been carried in companies belonging to different industries, to investigate how the decision-making process has changed and which benefits and issues have emerged from the use of BI/DV tools. Data collected have been analyzed using the most recent version of Nvivo and within-case and cross-cases analysis have been carried out. The paper suggests four types of roles that BI/DV tools can play, related to a set of organizational characteristics (such as innovation rate of the firm or level of customization of the solution) and provides guidelines for future adoption of these tools.

Keywords Business intelligence · Data visualization · Sense-making
Decision-making

L. Cremona · A. Ravarini (✉)
Università Carlo Cattaneo - LIUC, Castellanza, VA, Italy
e-mail: aravarini@liuc.it

L. Cremona
e-mail: lcremona@liuc.it

J. V. Brocke
University of Liechtenstein, Vaduz, Liechtenstein
e-mail: jan.vom.brocke@uni.li

© Springer International Publishing AG, part of Springer Nature 2019   23
F. Cabitza et al. (eds.), *Organizing for the Digital World*, Lecture Notes in Information
Systems and Organisation 28, https://doi.org/10.1007/978-3-319-90503-7_3

1 Introduction

Today firms are operating in a dynamic market where competition is more than ever based on managing information efficiently and effectively. Information, derived on a growing amount of data collected from processes, inside and outside the organization, needs to be managed in real time. Supporting decision making through insights developed by processing data collected has been at the core of rise the business intelligence (BI) tools, one of the most relevant IT trends of the last decade. BI tools can capture, store and organize data as long as create and present insights [25]. Seminal definitions of BI focus on "the ability to understand presented information and to subsequently use it to effectively guide business actions toward desired goals" [18]. With the advent of the recent digital technologies the definition has included "technologies, applications and processes for gathering, storing, accessing and analyzing data to help users make better decisions" [30].

Nowadays, the business world calls for the analysis, often in real time, of data coming from processes. A steady competition on the markets challenge managers to use these data both to understand the context and to take actions efficiently and effectively. Although BI tools are widespread and help firms in monitoring and controlling their activities, recent studies report that decision makers do not use BI to its fullest potential [3]. Specifically, managers use data coming from BI to take short-term decisions but most of the time they are not part of a data-driven strategy. In this light this paper aims at studying how managers can exploit recent BI tools, providing sophisticated data visualization (DV) features, to better understand the business environment (sense-making) and taking decision (decision-making). Given the novelty of the available DV tools, only limited research has been carried out to interpret their organizational impact [16].

As a first step of a research process, in this paper we studied how data are used and interpreted in different firms, who is using them, to what purpose and, eventually, highlighting benefits and issues arising. Given the exploratory approach, a qualitative methodology has been used to be able to generalize all potential results.

2 Background

Sensemaking can be defined as an ongoing socio-cognitive activity that organizational actors initiate when seeking to understand and control their environment (cited in Lewis et al. [17]). Organizational researchers claim that sensemaking has been helpful in investigating management practices [7, 11], supporting decision making processes [29], implementing information systems [13, 14], understanding communication channels [4], adopting information technology (Lewis et al. [17, 24]; Swanson and Ramiller 2004), managing processes [19, 20], and conducting organizational change. Sensemaking as a concept arose from the organizational theory context, but it has strong links with information processing and information quality, which have given it credence as an important research topic in information systems. Few studies, however, link BI and organizational sensemaking with BI research, which in its majority focuses on providing support for decision making [2, 6, 26].

In the past few years, IS scholars have been studying to develop theoretical frameworks enabling to understand the phenomenon of "big data and analytics" with which practitioners had already been dealing with for some time [23]. Amongst the different research lenses adopted, in a recent editorial of a special issue on the impact of business analytics on organizations, Sharma et al. [26] called for research efforts "to understand how organisations can create value from the use of business analytics" by studying, in particular, the resource allocation in organizational decision-making processes. In the same direction, Fosso Wamba et al. [10] through a systematic literature review, were able to develop a taxonomy of 5 types of value creation from "big data", among which they identified "replacing/supporting human decision making with automated algorithms".

In this paper we address this issue by exploring the general impact perceived by executives on business value generated by BI/DV tools.

RQ1: how can be quantified the value on an investment in BI/DV tools?

RQ1.1: what is the purpose to invest in BI/DV tools?
RQ1.2: how to correctly invest in BI/DV tools?

Secondly, exploiting we focus our attention on the recently developed BI/DV tools and on their decision making process.

RQ2: How does the nature of decision making change with the use of BI/DV tools?

Finally, we will investigate the individual and social implications of the use of these tools:

RQ3: What kind of competences are requested and what kind of people are impacted?

The following sections describe in detail the methodology and the domain in which the empirical study has been carried out, and the deriving research results achieved.

3 Methodology

A qualitative methodology, as reported in literature [8], aims at providing valuable insights into proposed interaction between constructs. A team of researchers collected all the data and analyzed them, to capture deeper findings and maximizing reliability. Following Yin [31] a case-study protocol was designed including the following sections: overview of the project (objectives and issues), field procedures, questions, and guidance for the report. Two criteria drove the choice of a case study research: the cost per subject and the potential for theory generation. In the empirical section of this research we used an exploratory case study whose aim is let the assess the impact of data visualization on sense-making and decision-making. A multiple-case study approach [31] was chosen for investigating the theoretical framework on how visualization of big data is impacting on sense-making and decision-making. The approach was appropriate to answer our research questions [1, 31]. Future research will be, wherever possible, in the direction of a longitudinal study to facilitate comparisons and draw better insights.

The unit of analysis chosen was the one of manufacturing firms. The case unit was analyzed through the collection of primary and secondary data. Primary data sources were interviews, direct observation, and informal discussions. Secondary data sources were mainly a set of documents of the firm, produced as a consequence of the transformation brought by data visualization tools. Before starting the collection of primary data [5], some preliminary background information was collected to help the interviewer during the data collection process. The preliminary information came from the Internet web site of the firm and some supplementary information was given by the interviewee. Together with a representative of each firm, the names and the positions of all the potential participants were identified and contacted for an interview [5]. The interviews were semi-structured interviews [9, 15]. To operationalize the theoretical constructs and ground the findings, whenever possible, key representatives of the firm (C-level Executives, Senior Managers, Entrepreneurs) were interviewed. The interview was focused on introducing the main themes and subthemes to discuss: at the beginning of each interview an introduction on the reasons and the subject of the interview was [21]. This explanation reduced the researcher effects at the site, which could bias the data collection [5, 21]. The interview guide was designed to gather the characteristics of the interviewee and what is his view.

The set of data produced by each interview was analyzed in parallel while the next interviews were taken, to use the content of the previous interviews as a source of questions to ask in the next interviews [21].

The context of the empirical study was a set of manufacturing firms with production plants in Italy and strong international presence. Thanks to this choice we could investigate on firms with a wide and exhaustive understanding on how analytics and data visualization tools could support people and processes upon a data-driven perspective. In these firms, data visualization tools are used for different purposes: production planning, sales forecast, energy costs optimization, marginal analysis, ... All firms subject of the study have created specific development centers to facilitate the spread and improvement of data visualization tools. All firms use Qlik software, specifically Qlik View but are slightly moving towards the adoption of Qlik Sense.

3.1 Data Collection

As a major source of qualitative data, interviews were carried out with a pre-defined interview guide. A questionnaire, originally designed in English [22] and later translated in Italian, was used to carry out interviews. Specifically we conducted 5 interviews with CEOs, senior managers and/or entrepreneurs in 4 firms among the criteria above mentioned, for a total of 270 min. To increase the validity of our coding and data analysis procedure, we aggregated multiple sources of evidence [31]: artefacts (i.e. extracts from the data visualization tools), documents from each firm and information from websites. The data were collected from both primary sources and secondary sources, including interviews, direct observations, participant observations, documentation, archival records, and physical artefacts [31]. All interviews were tape-recorded and transcribed: the transcripts from the 5 interviews were aggregated into a case protocol helping the researchers in organizing data. The projects were encoded and structured using the software NVivo 10, following a grounded theory approach that aims at finding properties or links between data [12, 28]. The coding procedure was done as follows: first, to mitigate potential bias, the junior researcher (first coder) who had not taken part in the interviews read and coded the interview transcripts by identifying text passages that included information about the constructs of the theoretical framework. For the purpose of literal and theoretical replication, the instances of the theoretical constructs were determined for each firm whenever possible. A purposeful sampling strategy was pursued in order to stay in line with the research objectives and the multiple case studies design. In order to control for potential bias of organizational culture, a pilot case study [8, 31], with aim to refine data collection plans and gain insights into the basic issues studied, was chosen (Tables 1 and 2).

Table 1 The firms subject of the study

	Industry	# employees	Turnover
Firm α	Textiles	63	7,9 mln €
Firm β	Consumer goods	3.600	1,3 mld €
Firm γ	Electric and electronic products	2.800	745 mln €
Firm δ	Design	400	75 mln €

Table 2 Demographics of the interviewees

	Age	Role
Firm α	44	CFO
Firm β	54	Senior manager
Firm γ	51	Industrial director
Firm γ	34	Analyst
Firm δ	50	Sales and marketing analyst

4 Discussion

In this section we discuss the most relevant results emerging from the data collection and we try to answer the research questions of our study.

The context subject of the study led to interesting insights in order to answer to the research questions. A first top-level research question was "how to effectively quantify the value on an investment in BI/DV tools?" From the interviews it emerged that the highest returns are in terms of time savings. The BI/DV tools makes it possible to managers to monitor and constantly check what is going on inside the business processes, allowing them to save time and identify errors. From firm γ: "before, to have the bill of materials of a class of products we had to create a request an upgrade in the software, and wait 3–4 days to have an answer. Today we have all bill of materials of all products in a unique web-based dashboard, in few seconds", and: "even in the case we have just one typo, within a cycle time we can recognize it, thanks to a tool easy to understand". Therefore there is a reduction of the costs deriving from a lack of data or errors that before could not be easily understood.

A sub-question of the first RQ was "what is the purpose to invest in BI/DV tools?" All firms agree that BI/DV tools are necessary and unavoidable to be competitive in a turbulent market. Firm α reports "Time ago the firm was earning a lot of money and we did not need to control all information. Today is different and where we have low margins and low volumes we need to better control all data. In this light DV software … helps in pulling off the dust from under the carpet". Nevertheless, the adoption of these tools often requires high initial investments and long implementation time while often they do not bring immediate positive feedback to the firm. It is important to underline that all firms object of the study positively supported the introduction of these tools.

The last sub-question to the first RQ was "how to correctly invest in BI/DV tools?" To have a real return on the investment is necessary that the firm exploits the full potential of the tool and understands its real utility. The advantage of these tools, as reported in the previous sections, is to facilitate data integration and leverage on interactive dashboards to visualize them. Nevertheless, a big risk is coming when several people in the firm are still using Excel files not updated or do not trust on reporting activities. What matters, then, is to change the mindset of the users and to create incentives for using BI/DV tools. This is not easy as firm γ reports: "To change 20 years of reports done in a certain way takes time. People, when you introduce a news system, search—systematically—to find something wrong. They say: 'data are wrong, the software is wrong'. But the software is not wrong! Either the data is wrong or you are saying something wrong!" To avoid this issue new intuitive dashboards have been developed and, by checking users log, was registered an increasing usage of them.

A second top-level RQ was "How does the nature of decision making change with the use of BI/Visualization tools?" Decision making is a complex and often time-constrained activity. The introduction of BI/DV tools does not lead to change the people in charge of (and involved in) the decision-making process, what changes is their speed of response. This result is due to the creation of a unique shared database that smooths the communication and facilitates information exchange along the decision process. In every firm, decisions are taken basing on data and measurable effects of sensations, perceptions and experiences that are extremely subjective. DV tools help people to combine personal experiences and intuition with real time data updated and represented dynamically within interactive dashboards. They can take better decisions and more efficiently, and finally they are able to control the whole business process in real time. As reported by firm β: "I have learned because I had an enlightened chief able to take decisions with his guts, he had that particular feeling coming from his experience and he was able to understand everything without data ... all those feelings were correct 100%. Using DV tools ... helped me in supporting with data those sensations". From firm γ we had supporting quotes: "It is not acceptable anymore that someone says: 'what about efficiency yesterday? All good, thanks'. The 'all good, thanks', is not acceptable anymore. We have to reply with numbers!". What is clearly emerging is that to take decisions, measurement is necessary as long as the collection of most information as possible.

A last top-level research question addressed by this study is: "What kind of competences are requested and what kind of people are impacted?". The whole firm is always involved in the usage of these tools and competences requested are typically the ones of management engineers, given their capability of work across several departments such as logistics, marketing, IT. Soft skills, such as creativity and curiosity, are necessary too. Quoting firm β: "When I search for new people to bring into my team I look for curious people, if she/he is able to see the big picture and then drill down. Being smart does not mean being able in maths but being able to see the reality around you and being able to change it. This is intelligence and you need to catch signals, connect dots, but if you have an issue arising you should be able to get it and understand it. Moving between horizontal and vertical, from a big picture to an atom is fundamental in a big firm like us". Some people tend to stay tied to traditional software tools for reporting, such as Excel, and they resist in adapting to a new system for treating data: there is a resistance to change mainly due to a low knowledge of tools and a lack of trust (especially about data consistency) often as a consequence of the age of the users. Furthermore we focused on answering to the sub-level question "Is the firm culture changing? If so, how?". Results from the study show that the whole firm culture is changing due a different approach in interpreting and managing data throughout the organization. As reported from firm β: "As long as we have fluidity on data and its management we need to have fluidity on organizational models. Data have to be managed, have to be timely and quality-assured and have to be consistently readable from everyone".

5 Conclusions and Future Works

This paper aimed at studying how managers can exploit recent BI tools, providing detailed data visualization features, to better understand the business environment (sense-making) and taking decision (decision-making). Data visualization, and the tools supporting it, proved to be crucial for each firm, leading to a better management of (big) data. Managers a/o Executives need to take effective decisions by transforming raw data into valuable information as shown in the Organizational Knowing Cycle (Sense-making, Decision-making, Knowledge creating). The empirical investigation showed that data visualization is an enabler of this process especially given its graphical representations that facilitate interpretation, exchange and transfer of data. Moreover, in a competitive and dynamic context such as the one in which the firms object of the study operate, the impact of these tools is on cost and time savings and this allows for errors identification.

In terms of contribution to practitioners, this study shows that the effective initiatives of adoption of data visualization tools started at the top level and then involved in the process the whole firm. The competences required are both those specific of a function (e.g. logistics, marketing, …) and the IT related ones. In fact, the people more involved and interested in the changes brought by these tools are management engineers. Moreover, skills and attitudes such as curiosity, creativity and smartness are fundamental. In terms of resistance to change we reported that some people strive to be tied to old tools such as Excel and struggle to adapt: this resistance is mainly due to a low knowledge of the tool and to a lack of trust (data reliability) that, most of the time, is correlated to the age of the Worker/Manager/Executive. To avoid this several training courses were held in order to change the firm culture.

The main limitations of the study are related to small number of firms interviewed and the variety of context/industries analyzed. The choice of qualitative methodology was done according to the availability of firms for data collection.

The future steps of the research will be: extending the set of firms to be studied (to include firm from same industry a/o firms with similar business models) and carrying out a survey to triangulate qualitative and quantitative methodologies.

References

1. Benbasat, I., Goldstein, D.K., Mead, M.: The case research strategy in studies of information systems. MIS Q. 11(3), 369–386 (1987)
2. Bucher, T., Gericke, A., Sigg, S.: Supporting business process execution through business intelligence: An introduction to process-centric BI. Bus. Intell. J. 14, 7–15 (2009)
3. Chen, H., Chiang, R.H.L., Storey, V.C.: Business intelligence and analytics: from big data to big impact. MIS Q. 36(4), 1165–1188 (2012)
4. Cooren, F.: The communicative achievement of collective minding analysis of board meeting excerpts. Manag. Commun. Q. 17, 517–551 (2004)
5. Darke, P., Shanks, G., Broadbent, M.: Successfully completing case study research: combining rigour. Relevance Pragmat. ISJ 8, 273–289 (1998)
6. Davenport, T.H.: Business intelligence and organizational decisions. Int. J. Bus. Intell. Res. IJBIR. 1, 1–12 (2010)
7. Drazin, R., Glynn, M.A., Kazanjian, R.K.: Multilevel theorizing about creativity in organizations: A sensemaking perspective. Acad. Manage. Rev. 286–307 (1999)
8. Dubé, L., Paré, G.: Rigor in information systems positivist case research: current practices, trends, and recommendations. MIS Q. 27(4), 597–636 (2003)

9. Emory, W. C.: Business Research Methods. Irwin (1980)
10. Fosso Wamba, S., Akter, S., Edwards, A., Chopin, G., Gnanzou, D.: How 'big data' can make big impact: findings from a systematic review and a longitudinal case study. Int. J. Prod. Econ. (2015) https://doi.org/10.1016/j.ijpe.2014.12.031
11. Gioia, D., Chittipeddi, K.: Sensemaking and sensegiving in strategic change initiation. Strateg. Manage. J. 12 (6), 433–448 (1991)
12. Glaser, B.G.: Basics of Grounded Theory Analysis. Sociology Press, Mill Valley, CA (1992)
13. Jensen, T.B., Kjaergaard, A.: Using Existing Response Repertoires to Make Sense of Information System Implementation. Scand. J. Inf. Syst. 22, 31–48 (2010)
14. Jensen, T.B., Kjærgaard, A., Svejvig, P.: Using institutional theory with sensemaking theory: a case study of information system implementation in healthcare. J. Inf. Technol. 24, 343–353 (2009)
15. Kerlinger, F.: Foundations of Behavioral Research: Educational and Psychological Inquiry. Holt. Rinehart and Winston. Inc. Wiley, New York (1964)
16. Kumar, O., Goyal, A.: Visualization: a novel approach for big data analytics. In: 2016 Second International Conference on Computational Intelligence & Communication Technology (CICT), pp. 121–124. IEEE (2016)
17. Lewis, M.O., Mathiassen, L., Rai, A.: Scalable growth in IT-enabled service provisioning: a sensemaking perspective. Eur. J. Inf. Syst. 20, 285–302 (2011)
18. Luhn, H.P.: A business intelligence system. IBM J. Res. Dev. 2(4), 314–319 (1958)
19. Maitlis, S., Lawrence, T.B.: Triggers and enablers of sensegiving in organizations. Acad. Manage. J. 50, 57–84 (2007)
20. Maitlis, S., Sonenshein, S.: Sensemaking in crisis and change: Inspiration and insights from Weick (1988). J. Manag. Stud. 47, 551–580 (2010)
21. Miles, M.B, Huberman, A.M.: Qualitative Data Analysis, 2nd ed., pp. 10–12. Sage, Newbury Park, CA (1994)
22. Namvar, M.: Using business intelligence to support the process of organizational sensemaking. Ph.D. Deakin University (2016)
23. Phillips-Wren, G., Iyer, L. S., Kulkarni, U., Ariyachandra, T.: Business analytics in the context of big data: a roadmap for research, Commun. Assoc. Inf. Syst. 37, Article 23 (2015)
24. Ramiller, N.C., Burton Swanson, E.: Mindfulness routines for innovating with information technology. J. Decis. Syst. 18, 13–26 (2009)
25. Sabherwal, R., Becerra-Fernandez, I.: Business Intelligence. Wiley, Chichester, UK (2009)
26. Sharma, R., Mithas, S., Kankanhalli, A.: Transforming decision-making processes: a research agenda for understanding the impact of business analytics on organisations. Eur. J. Inf. Syst. 23(4), 433–441 (2014)
27. Shim, J., Warkentin, M., Courtney, J.F., Power, D.J., Sharda, R., Carlsson, C.: Past, present, and future of decision support technology. Decis. Support Syst. 33, 111–126 (2002)
28. Strauss, A.: Qualitative analysis for social scientists. Cambridge University Press, Cambridge, England (1987)
29. Taylor, S.J., Bogdan, R.: Introduction to qualitative research methods: A guidebook and resource. John Wiley & Sons Inc (1998)
30. Watson, H.: Future directions for BI software. Bus. Intell. J. 13, 4–6 (2008)
31. Yin, R.K.: Case Study Research: Design and Methods. Sage Publications, Thousand Oaks, CA (2003)

XBRL Implementation in the European Union: Exploring Preparers' Points of View

Costanza Di Fabio, Elisa Roncagliolo, Francesco Avallone and Paola Ramassa

Abstract The wide diffusion of XBRL will reach another milestone with the mandatory transition to iXBRL in the European Union. This process involves all listed companies, as ESMA requires iXBRL for companies issuing IFRS consolidated financial statements from 1st January 2020. This paper explores the points of view of preparers, key subjects in identifying the potential drawbacks of XBRL adoption since they are directly involved in the transition. We analyse letters responding to the ESMA 2015 consultation paper and interpret them in the light of previous literature on the topic, also considering the positions expressed by other respondents' categories. This study contributes to XBRL literature by shedding light on preparers' positions before the mandatory transition. Additionally, it stresses the gap existing between subjects bearing implementation costs of a communication technology and its end users. We provide insights useful to European policy-makers to improve the process of transition to XBRL. Indeed, findings remark the trade-off between the need for innovation and the necessity to reduce administrative burdens to enhance the competitiveness of European companies. Our analysis could be of interest also for policy-makers of other jurisdictions considering XBRL adoption as well as for companies and consulting firms supporting them in the transition.

Keywords XBRL · Digital reporting · Preparers · ESMA · IFRS
European union · Comment letters

C. Di Fabio (✉) · E. Roncagliolo · F. Avallone · P. Ramassa
Department of Economics and Business Studies, University of Genoa, Genoa, Italy
e-mail: difabio@economia.unige.it; costanzadifabio@yahoo.it

E. Roncagliolo
e-mail: roncagliolo@economia.unige.it

F. Avallone
e-mail: avallone@economia.unige.it

P. Ramassa
e-mail: ramassa@economia.unige.it

© Springer International Publishing AG, part of Springer Nature 2019   33
F. Cabitza et al. (eds.), *Organizing for the Digital World*, Lecture Notes in Information
Systems and Organisation 28, https://doi.org/10.1007/978-3-319-90503-7_4

1 Introduction

After twenty years from its first development, nowadays XBRL is used in more than 50 countries around the globe. Thus far, the decision to adopt the XBRL format on a voluntary or mandatory basis has been taken by jurisdictions at the national level, often supported by regulatory bodies pushing for XBRL filings. The US, China, and Japan are notable examples of mandatory adoption, with a crucial part played by the Securities Exchange Commission in the US adoption of XBRL in 2008.

Within the European context, so far Member States have autonomously issued the rules on XBRL adoption. Only recently, the European Commission (EC) has addressed the issue of the reporting format at the supra-national level through the amended Transparency Directive (2013/50/EU) that mandates the preparation of annual financial reports in a single electronic format from 2020. Benefits expected by the EC seem high, but do not eliminate the trade-off between the need for innovation and the necessity to avoid jeopardising the competitiveness of European companies due to higher costs. The Directive charged the European Securities and Markets Authority (ESMA) to carry out an adequate assessment of possible electronic reporting formats and to develop draft regulatory technical standards indicating the electronic reporting format individuated and providing technological details on it. Accordingly, the ESMA undertook a cost-benefit analysis and launched a public consultation in September 2015, open to interested subjects until January 2016. The consultation was inspired by the idea that costs and benefits deriving from the adoption of a single electronic format, and specifically of an XBRL-based one, could be better assessed by understanding the positions of subjects involved in the information supply chain [1]. After the consultation, the ESMA individuated iXBRL as the appropriate electronic format for IFRS financial reports of listed companies.

Against this background, this paper aims at exploring the points of view of preparers that will be directly involved in the process of mandatory transition to XBRL, and at analysing the main issues raised by them. To achieve these objectives, we carry out a thematic content analysis of comment letters received by the ESMA in response to the 2015 Consultation Paper (CP) and we focus specifically on preparers' comment letters. These responses are particularly interesting as they reveal a variety of positions expressed by a wide range of stakeholders' categories and represent a critical input to be considered by European regulators. European policy makers need to understand issues that could arise as consequences of the implementation, to anticipate its potential drawbacks and be able to timely intervene improving and monitoring the process of transition to XBRL. Even companies and consulting firms that will support them in the transition need a clearer understanding of the incoming process. In fact, the European mandatory adoption of a single electronic format is expected to be overall beneficial, but prior implementations across the world reveal that adopters often deal with unintended criticalities arising especially in the early-adoption phase.

Our findings reveal that preparers are markedly sceptic on the benefits deriving from the mandatory transition. They oppose the regulator's view claiming that there is an extremely low demand for structured electronic reporting, that this format decreases the quality of issued information, and that the costs of implementation and maintenance of XBRL format will significantly exceed preparers' benefits. However, the majority of respondents belonging to other categories agree with the CP objectives, and highlight the considerably positive effects deriving from the adoption of an XBRL-based format.

The current paper provides insights that can be of interest not only for European policy-makers that are working to the success of this transition, but also for policy-makers of other jurisdictions that are currently evaluating the benefits and drawbacks of XBRL adoption. Finally, companies that will support preparers in the transition could benefit from a clearer understanding of this process, especially from a preparers' point of view.

The remainder of this paper proceeds as follows. The next section outlines the activity of the ESMA with reference to the XBRL transition (Sect. 2). Then, we present the literature focusing on the effects of XBRL on preparers (Sect. 3) and the methodology used in the analysis (Sect. 4). Section 5 presents the results of our analysis and discusses the findings in the light of responses by other stakeholders and of prior literature on XBRL effects. Finally, Sect. 6 provides conclusions, highlighting the policy implications and limitations of this study.

2 ESMA's Adoption of XBRL

The amended European Transparency Directive (2013/50/EU) requires that all annual financial reports are prepared in a single electronic reporting format with effect from 1st January 2020. The mandatory adoption of a harmonized electronic format is expected to be beneficial for issuers, investors and supervisory authorities, due to an easier reporting and to enhanced accessibility, analysis and comparability of annual reports.

In pursuit of these objectives, the Directive required the ESMA to undertake a cost-benefit analysis and to develop draft technical regulatory standards by the end of 2016 on the basis of open public consultations, a thorough assessment of the impact and appropriate field tests. In September 2015, the ESMA issued a Consultation Paper (hereafter CP) presenting: (i) policy objectives; (ii) an assessment of current electronic reporting; (iii) possible options in the light of technical developments in financial markets and telecommunication; (iv) the ESMA's preferred option; and (v) a cost-benefit analysis. The preliminary conclusions of the CP consider the overall context and use of financial reporting, taking into account the needs of retail investors, the facts that narrative parts of the annual report do not lend themselves well to transformation in a structured electronic format and the complexity inherent in the variety of sets of accounting standards applied by European companies. Based on these considerations, ESMA proposed a nuanced approach arguing that requiring the publication in a structured electronic format—in addition to pdf—is most beneficial for IFRS consolidated financial statements, and that the structured electronic format should be allowed (but not mandated) for individual financial statements.

The proposal of limiting this requirement to the parts of the annual reports that are most used for data analysis and to companies adopting the same set of standards is based on the idea of realising significant benefits without a considerable increase of cost for issuers. However, the ESMA itself acknowledges that the questionnaire of its cost-benefits analysis had a very low response rate, thus preventing a complete analysis representative of the views of all markets and actors of the information supply chain.

The CP invited comments from all interested stakeholders on the entire paper and on some final specific questions by 24 December 2015, explicitly asking for clear rationales for responses and alternatives to be considered. The questions (summarized in Annex II) regard the points covered by the ESMA in the CP as well as the cost-benefit analysis. They specifically consider XBRL and iXBRL as the two main options as a structured electronic format based on the cost-benefit analysis and on the wide diffusion of XBRL in other major markets (e.g. in the US). After the consultation, the ESMA went further in its agenda and specifically individuated iXBRL as the most suitable technology for the single electronic format. iXBRL is based on the XBRL, but it also enables a human-readable representation of information stored in XBRL and could be easily opened by standard web browsers. Additionally, it allows including extra annotations (tags) to the XHTML document, enabling the extraction of the tagged data from the reports (ESMA 2016). Then, ESMA decided for the mandatory transition to iXBRL of annual financial reports prepared under IFRS for all public companies with fiscal years starting on or after 1 January 2020.

3   Effects of XBRL on Preparers: Literature Review

This paper builds on the stream of XBRL literature [2, 3] focusing on the effects of the adoption of this standard.

From a theoretical perspective, XBRL adoption should largely affect financial reporting [4, 5], positively affecting the availability and the accessibility of financial reports, improving efficiency in investment decisions and facilitating business decision-making [6, 7]. Additionally, XBRL should enhance the standardization of financial information [8] and improve financial statement comparability and usability [9].

However, given the worldwide diffusion of XBRL, research has sought to understand the actual implementation costs and benefits, deserving particular attention to the opinions of preparers that usually face the main practical issues arising from XBRL implementation. In this respect, Pinsker and Li [1] interview managers of early-adopter companies from Canada, Germany, South Africa, and US, finding that in their opinion the main benefits of XBRL are cost savings due to lower data redundancy and the decrease in costs for bookkeeping. Similarly, interviews carried out by Robb et al. [10] in the Australian context suggest that preparers consider the improved efficiency (i.e. time and cost saving in preparing financial statements) as the main benefit associated with XBRL. These results are consistent with main findings of the UK-based survey by Dunne et al. [11], who highlight that XBRL facilitates the financial reporting process as it avoids to re-key information and improves data comparability.

Several studies support a positive effect of XBRL implementation on financial information quality. After the XBRL mandatory adoption, Chinese companies account for lower accruals [12] and obtain better performance [13]. Additionally, financial statements' comparability increases [14, 15], especially in the presence of a high compliance with the taxonomy [15]. XBRL adopters experience easier relationships with providers of financial resources, particularly banks, and obtain financial resources at a lower cost [16]. However, the reduction in interest rate spreads is more accentuated for voluntary adopters, as recently shown by Kaya and Pronobis [17]. After XBRL adoption, preparers also benefit from higher market efficiency. Archival research focusing on the US provides evidence that the XBRL adoption improves information efficiency [18] and reduces information asymmetry [19–22]. These effects are even stronger in case of voluntary adoption [23, 24]. The positive influence on market efficiency could also be expected to facilitate adopters to obtain financial resources at a lower cost of equity capital [25, 26], although some studies find higher cost of capital following the XBRL implementation [27]. Furthermore, adopters seem to obtain benefits in terms of improved corporate governance [28–30], mainly due to the improvement in the communication of corporate governance-related information.

Nevertheless, the benefits of XBRL adoption are associated with several costs. The main barrier to a widespread XBRL diffusion is a still limited awareness of its benefits among preparers, especially in the absence of a regulatory requirement [31], although this language is generally perceived as user-friendly [32]. According to the preparers' opinion, costs of XBRL initial implementation are mainly represented by the uncertainty of an unproven technology [1] and costs—in terms of time and money—needed for success [1, 11, 32]. Additionally, in XBRL initial implementation filing errors occur more frequently [33–35] and preparers state that the standardization due to XBRL adoption complicates the disclosure of voluntary information in the notes [14, 36]. Expected benefits from XBRL implementation should be assured by the adoption of a common taxonomy. Studies investigate the quality and the extensions of the XBRL taxonomy by exploring the quality of companies' disclosure [14, 15, 37, 38]. The development of a common taxonomy is a crucial issue to enhance a successful XBRL implementation [39–41], especially in order to balance the trade-off between the need to assure flexibility and comparability of corporate disclosure. European companies deal with the IFRS taxonomy [42] and research suggests that the IFRS taxonomy proposed in 2011 was not able to fully satisfy users' expectations, as the need of numerous extensions limits the comparability of financial statements, even if improvements have been introduced in the following releases of the IFRS taxonomy [43]. Valentinetti and Rea [44] suggest a general discrepancy between the financial items disclosed by the companies and the taxonomy tags and a loss of information unless the XBRL implementation system explicitly allows using taxonomy extensions.

Overall, literature reveals that perceived benefits and costs of XBRL adoption vary considerably depending on the level of awareness of users and preparers, and on the geographical setting, as regulatory actions are able to create a more favorable environment. In this perspective, this paper focuses on the European context to investigate the points of view of preparers facing the mandatory transition to XBRL and dealing with the practical issues related to the transition, and the main issues raised by them.

4 Methodology

To address the research objectives, this paper analyzes the comment letters to the CP posted on the ESMA website through content analysis, which is particularly suitable to codify text into various categories when qualitative information is particularly rich [45–48] and focuses on preparers' responses. Specifically, we analyze comment letters through thematic content analysis [49] that has been used by several studies on disclosure [50–52] as it enables individuating thematic units, identifying specific attitudes and drawing then inferences from them [51].

We articulate the analysis into three phases. In the first one, we analyze agreement and disagreement expressed by preparers on specific statements of the CP. At this stage, themes are represented by the issues addressed by the ESMA in its questions, and our units of analysis are responses to the CP.

In the second phase, first we exploit a meaning-oriented content analysis to extrapolate the main issues raised by preparers in the non-structured parts of the questionnaire, namely the 'introduction' to their responses and question 19 ('other'). Second, we use the meaning-oriented approach to analyze those comment letters that do not specifically answer the questions, but that de facto comment points made by ESMA. In these cases, our unit of analysis varies depending on the meaning of the message conveyed, but mainly it was the paragraph constituted by a certain number of sentences dealing with a single theme.

In the third phase, we extrapolate three main thematic areas, namely (i) the demand for structured electronic reporting; (ii) the usefulness of a structured format to enhance the quality of information; and (iii) the costs of implementation and maintenance of a structured electronic format. This phase of analysis (Sect. 5.2) includes also the discussion of issues raised by the 89 comment letters sent by French preparers; it discusses contents of comment letters in the light of responses by other stakeholders and of prior literature.

5 Results of the Content Analysis and Discussion

The CP received 161 responses from a wide range of subjects and their representative bodies, including accounting bodies and auditors (9), credit institutions (6), regulators, standard setters and governmental bodies (9), service providers (19), statistical bodies (4), users (9) and preparers (105).

5.1 Results of the Content Analysis on Preparers' Responses

Preparers were the most active group in responding. Our analysis focuses especially on their responses, to understand their view on the mandatory transition to XBRL.

It is worth noting that 89 comment letters were from 88 French preparers and their representative bodies. They do not specifically answer the questions formulated by ESMA but share a common template and use the same wording to address anyway points made by the CP and deemed relevant. To avoid a biased representation of results, we exclude these letters from the first two steps of the analysis but discuss them in Sect. 5.2 as they represent an organised contestation opposing the mandatory introduction of a single structured format.

Out of the other 16 letters, 2 have been sent confidentially to ESMA and the remaining available 14 comment letters are mostly from bodies representing an extremely high share of European companies. Associations at the higher level of representativeness cover all-sized enterprises across 34 European countries; additionally, there is a specific representativeness for 14 European countries, with German listed companies, small and mid-cap and large listed UK companies, FTSE 100 companies, Finnish companies, Swedish, Polish and Dutch listed companies[1]. These letters are the object of the first two phases of our analysis.

Results provided by the thematic analysis show that preparers strongly agree with the need of a wider assessment on the requirements of introducing a single electronic reporting format in Europe (64% of comment letters, namely 82% of preparers that responded to this specific question), while disagreeing with the description provided by ESMA of the policy objectives (50%). The preference for a non-structured form of electronic format (57% of comment letters, namely 80% of preparers responding to this question), the low relevance ascribed to XBRL format (50%) and the aversion to the creation of a European taxonomy (57%), explain the marked refusal of a further debate on audit for structured data (71%).

---

[1]Respondents are associations representing: (i) around 80% of the market capitalization of stock corporations listed in Germany; (ii) 9,000 quoted companies in 14 European countries, namely 8 billion euros of market capitalisation across the European markets; (iii) 60,000 Swedish companies with over 1.6 million employees; (iv) 152 small and mid-cap companies, below the FTSE 350, in the United Kingdom; (v) 345 investment companies managing £122 bn of assets and subjects to European directives; (vi) 16,000 Finnish companies; (vii) companies listed at Euronext Amsterdam; (viii) Polish listed companies; (ix) more than 550 IT, telecom, internet and office companies in the Netherlands; and (x) almost 90% of the market capitalisation of the FTSE 100.

Remarkably, preparers consider that the picture provided by ESMA on the current reporting scenario is not exhaustive; in their view, further elements are needed to depict reliably the extant reporting conditions and to enable regulators to implement useful policies at the European level (50% of comment letters, namely 78% of preparers commenting this point). In this perspective, preparers stress the urgency of a complete description of the existing technologies available for reporting purposes (64% of comment letters, corresponding to 90% of preparers answering the question), whose plurality seems to fit preparers' needs (64% of them disagree on a single electronic format composed of structured and non-structured data).

Although preparers do not agree with the XBRL format as a single European format, they overall support the ESMA's proposal to use the IFRS taxonomy for reporting under IFRS if a single and structured electronic format is chosen by regulators (71%), since uniformity in taxonomy should enhance comparability of information. Preparers reveal a limited interest in the application of the electronic format to financial statements of entities with securities listed on a regulated market in the European Union and applying third-country GAAP deemed equivalent to IFRS. However, 21% of the respondents agree with the ESMA, which proposed not to require them to prepare annual financial reports in a structured format and to allow them to use the XHTML format, as taxonomies do not exist for all the financial reporting frameworks adopted in their reports.

Finally, preparers find not appropriate a phased approach for SMEs, as they are out of the scope of the Transparency Directive.

The second phase of our analysis uses meaning-oriented content analysis to extrapolate the main issues raised by preparers in the 'introduction' to responses, in the scope of answers to question 19 ('other'), and in comment letters not specifically answering the questions posed but still touching relevant issues for the CP objectives.

The majority of preparers (79% of comment letters) felt the need to remark in the non-structured part of the questionnaire the relevant costs of the ESMA's proposal. Preparers stress the significant implementation and monitoring costs that could derive from the mandatory adoption of a single structured format in the European Union, without considering other practices already implemented in Member countries (57%) and running the risk of generating high implementation complexity (57%) and compliance risks that cannot be determined yet (36%). A major drawback of the mandatory transition would be an excessive burden for European companies, contrarily to the intention of the European Commission (29%) that is strongly willing to support their competitiveness. Moreover, preparers fear an overall decrease of perceived value of financial information (71%), as, in their view, the needs of investors and analysts would not be satisfied with this transition (64%). The interest of these users could be better met by preserving the richness of qualitative disclosure as allowed by the pdf format, and by following the development of technologies enabling a more efficient use of this format.

5.2   Discussions of Results

As revealed by the results of the first two phases of the analysis, preparers express a bitter criticism against the XBRL mandatory adoption. Overall, their positions contrast the opinions of other respondents' categories. Building on prior literature, we discuss findings focusing on three main thematic areas: (i) the demand for structured electronic reporting; (ii) the usefulness of a structured format to enhance the quality of information; and (iii) the costs of implementation and maintenance of a structured electronic format.

5.2.1   The Demand for Structured Electronic Reporting

Preparers perceive an extremely low users' demand for a structured electronic format. Some reveal a substantial criticism and believe that "it is not yet clear what the actual demand for structured electronic reporting really is" (EK 2015). In their view, such a format may limit the ability of some users to use financial information in their activities, especially considering that "not all the investors use the AFR [annual financial report] in the same way—especially when comparing private, retail investors and institutional investors" (European Issuers 2015). This point of view seems not always aligned to the financial analysts' positions. Some analysts do welcome the adoption of a structured electronic format, deeming it particularly useful. Indeed "analysts use it all the time" (CRUF 2016, p. 1) in different phases of their activity. Analysts exploit it as a source of secondary information when they require financial information about competitors of the target company, but they also considered it very useful in the initial phase of the coverage, since it allows avoiding time-consuming hand collection of data (CRUF 2016). However, consistent with preparers' opinions, analysts also maintain that a structured reporting is not sufficient to an in-depth analysis of the target company, which should be instead based on the comprehensive evaluation of financial information, therefore avoiding an automated processing of the information (SFAF 2016). Additionally, analysts fear the risk of discrimination among users, due to additional costs for training, equipment and software. The points raised by preparers seem also in contrast with evidence provided by literature supporting XBRL as particularly suitable just to a wide range of users in their everyday activities. Positive effects of XBRL are indeed documented in the case of both professional and non-professional investors [53–56] and financial analysts [57–60], although most of the literature on this topic investigates the US and Chinese contexts.

5.2.2   Structured Electronic Format and the Quality of Financial Information

From the point of view of preparers, the electronic format cannot provide qualitative information that users need to fully understand determinants of company results.

Such a format makes it fairly difficult to evaluate qualitative disclosure reliably, with negative effects on the comparability of financial information. This point of view is aligned with evidence provided by US-based studies investigating the effects of XBRL on users. This literature shows a decrease in comparability after the mandatory US filing of XBRL-based documents on the specific system [61]. In this respect, the IFRS Foundation underscores that comparability is not a matter of the reporting medium, since it "has the potential to facilitate comparability, because it can make it easier for a user to identify and analyse similarities and differences between entities and between periods (…) however, the extent to how well this is achieved depends on how electronic reporting is implemented (…) electronic reporting should facilitate analysis and accessibility of the complete set of financial statements" (IFRS Foundation 2015, p. 7).

According to preparers, investors prefer "human-readable format" (European Issuers 2015, p. 7). They strongly support the pdf format, already adopted by 13 European countries, due to some relevant advantages. Firstly, financial statements in pdf format seem widely appreciated by users, given a higher accessibility through the corporate website (Deutsches Aktieninstitut 2015). Secondly, there is a continuing evolution of the pdf format and of its mark-up technology, so that "a PDF is considered assured by investors, it is searchable, downloadable and portable (…) as annual financial statements can be quickly converted to PDF format (…) as soon as the annual financial statements are released" (AIC 2015, p. 5). If compared to the pdf format, the XBRL one would be less flexible. Additionally, preparers believe that XBRL has had a limited diffusion and it will suffer from the fast and growing evolution of information technologies.

Based on the UK experience, the Financial Reporting Council (FRC) believes "it is important to consider the application to structured and unstructured data separately" (FRC 2015, p. 4). iXBRL, which enables to embed the XBRL data into XHTML documents, is deemed by FRC as the most appropriate technology for structured information, and pdf as the best one for unstructured data. The iXBRL format seems particularly suitable to preparers, as "users can pick up an iXBRL and read it, versus XBRL, which displays as code" (Quoted Companies Alliance 2015, p. 8).

Preparers appear extremely reluctant to use XBRL when considering the peculiarities of IFRS financial reports. In their view, material and frequent amendments to IFRS may enhance the complexity and the costs for maintaining and updating the XBRL reporting format. Additionally, preparers argue that the IFRS Taxonomy is not complete yet (e.g. it does not include the alternative performance indicators constantly monitored by professional users). This position is shared by several users, maintaining that it is not "ready for immediate use. It is a starting point and require an extension" (KPMG 2015, p. 3). Nevertheless, the IFRS Foundation itself seems aware of the need to develop the taxonomy and expresses its commitment towards cooperation with stakeholders in the process of its extension and implementation (IFRS Foundation 2015).

5.2.3   Costs of Implementation and Maintenance of a Structured Electronic Format

Preparers' comments stress that the implementation costs and the costs of maintenance of a structured electronic language seem to exceed benefits. Preparers seem to contest the validity of the cost-benefit analysis run in 2014, deemed as not representative. If the complexity of the implementation phase has been remarked by literature especially in the first years of XBRL adoption [33–35], the skepticism of preparers on benefits deriving from XBRL contrasts the positive adopters' opinion. Literature remarks the improved efficiency of using an electronic format, as it reduces the time and the cost of preparing financial statements [10]. In their cost-benefit analysis, responding preparers do not take into account factors that, according to literature, represent substantial benefits for adopters. Following prior research, XBRL adopters benefit from a lower cost of debt [16, 17] and higher credit availability given that an improved accessibility of data improves relationship with banks and other creditors [16, 17, 62].

Moreover, preparers do not appreciate the ESMA's focus on the audit of XBRL financial statements. They argue that the auditing issue is premature until a single electronic format is not effectively adopted in the European Union. Anyway, preparers "reject in advance any increase in the audit expenses which it could involve" (VDI Group 2015). Even the letter sent by the FRC discourage from "a rush to standardise audit of structured data" (FRC 2015, p. 6).

The still limited knowledge of this reporting language among auditors and their still scarce experience is stressed by academic studies [63–65] and suggested by comment letters sent by audit firms. Audit firms' remark that electronic filing as proposed by the ESMA raises the questions of: (i) whether the audit opinion includes assurance on the structured electronic information, (ii) what auditors would be looking at, and (iii) to what extent existing audit requirements and standards should interact with the introduction of structured data (Deloitte 2015; PwC 2015). Auditors particularly emphasize the need for a standard for auditing and for a consequent discussion with the International Auditing and Assurance Standards Board (IAASB). Such a discussion should lead to new guidance and standards for auditors. In this perspective, it is an issue what assurance investors "want from structured electronic information (…) agreed upon procedures may be performed (…) but this approach will not be satisfactory (…) if investors seek the same level of assurance that they currently do with the 'paper' version (…)." (Deloitte 2015, p. 3).

6   Conclusions

This study illustrates the positions of preparers that actively participated in the debate on the mandatory adoption of XBRL for European IFRS financial statements by responding to the public consultation launched by the ESMA in 2015.

Consistent with prior literature, our analysis suggests that preparers' view contrasts users' positions, as users overall expect positive effects from XBRL adoption while preparers openly express criticism on the mandatory adoption. On the one hand, the actual benefits generated by a reduction of the cost of debt and by a reduction in information asymmetry seem still unclear. On the other hand, in the trade-off between benefits and costs [66], preparers explicitly stress the related costs, such as the cost of maintaining and updating the XBRL reporting system after the frequent amendments to IFRSs, the costs of implementation and maintenance. Their criticism could be explained also considering that the diffusion of XBRL could lead to a substantial opening of the firms' data to national enforcers and tax authorities, thus considerably reducing the room for a firm's opportunistic intervention in the external financial reporting process.

This paper contributes to XBRL literature by providing a picture of the views of European preparers, and by shedding light on the process of transition to XBRL as it is currently perceived by entities that will be directly involved in the preparation of financial statements in an electronic structured format. Our findings may be of interest for policy makers evaluating the foreseeable benefits and costs of XBRL adoption. In this respect, our analysis provides useful information to support future regulatory actions aimed at timely improving the process of transition to iXBRL, considering strategies to decrease the transition-related burden on preparers. Overall, findings suggest that European bodies should adequately address issues raised by preparers. Indeed, respondents are mainly highly-representative associations, covering 34 European countries and protecting interests of both listed and non-listed companies thorough the whole European Union.

Limitations to our study mainly concern the statistical generalizability of results, as the ESMA CP achieved an overall low response rate. Additionally, our sample suffers from a self-selection bias since respondents decided to express their opinion and we could not investigate the point of view of subjects that did not take part in commenting the CP. However, responding implies costs for respondents themselves; accordingly, subjects deciding to take an active part in the debate are those that deem their participation necessary to raise key issues.

References

1. Pinsker, R., Li, S.: Costs and benefits of XBRL adoption: early evidence. Commun. ACM 51(3), 47–50 (2008). https://doi.org/10.2308/isys-10258
2. Alles, M., Debreceny, R.: The evolution and future of XBRL research. Int. J. Account. Inf. Syst. 13(2), 83–90 (2012). https://doi.org/10.1016/j.accinf.2012.03.006
3. Perdana, A., Robb, A., Rohde, F.: An integrative review and synthesis of XBRL research in academic journals. J. Inf. Syst. 29(1), 115–153 (2015). https://doi.org/10.2308/isys-50884
4. Bonsón, E.: The role of XBRL in Europe. Int. J. Digit. Account. Res. 1(2), 101–110 (2001). https://doi.org/10.4192/1577-8517-v1_5
5. Debreceny, R., Gray, G.L.: The production and use of semantically rich accounting reports on the Internet: XML and XBRL. Int. J. Account. Inf. Syst. 2(1), 47–74 (2001). https://doi.org/10.1016/S1467-0895(00)00012-9

6. Doni, F., Inghirami, I.E.: Strategy management systems e XBRL: mutui rapporti e interconnessioni. In Zambon, S. (ed.): XBRL e informativa aziendale. Traiettorie, innovazioni e sfide, Part III, 286–311, Franco Angeli, Milano (2010)
7. Baldwin, A.A., Trinkle, B.S.: The impact of XBRL: a Delphi investigation. Int. J. Digit. Account. Res. 11(17), 1–24 (2011). https://doi.org/10.4192/1577-8517-v11_1
8. Wagenhofer, A.: Economic consequences of internet financial reporting. In: Debreceny, R., Felden, C., Piechocki, M. (eds.): New Dimensions of Business Reporting and XBRL, pp. 99–123. DUV (2007)
9. Vasarhelyi, M.A., Chan, D.Y., Krahel, J.: Consequences of XBRL standardization on finan-cial statement data. J. Inf. Syst. 26(1), 155–167 (2012). https://doi.org/10.2308/isys-10258
10. Robb, D.A., Rohde, F.H., Green, P.F.: Standard business reporting in Australia: efficiency, effectiveness, or both? Account. Financ. 56(2), 509–544 (2016). https://doi.org/10.1111/acfi.12094
11. Dunne, T., Helliar, C., Lymer, A., Mousa, R.: Stakeholder engagement in internet financial reporting: the diffusion of XBRL in the UK. Br. Account. Rev. 45(3), 167–182 (2013). https://doi.org/10.1016/j.bar.2013.06.012
12. Peng, E.Y., Shon, J., Tan, C.: XBRL and accruals: empirical evidence from China. Account. Perspect. 10(2), 109–138 (2011). https://doi.org/10.1111/j.1911-3838.2011.00021.x
13. Wang, T., Wen, C.Y., Seng, J.L.: The association between the mandatory adoption of XBRL and the performance of listed state-owned enterprises and non-state-owned enterprises in China. Inf. Manag. 51(3), 336–346 (2014). https://doi.org/10.1016/j.im.2014.02.006
14. Avallone, F., Ramassa, P., Roncagliolo, E.: XBRL extension to the financial statement notes: field-based evidence on unlisted companies. Int. J. Digit. Account. Res. 16, 61–84 (2016). https://doi.org/10.4192/1577-8517-v16_3
15. Fradeani, A., Panizzolo, D., Metushi, E.: Financial reporting in XBRL: first evidence on finan-cial statement notes of italian unlisted companies. Int. J. Digit. Account. Res. 16, 85–115 (2016). https://doi.org/10.4192/1577-8517-v16_4
16. Lai, S.C., Lin, Y.S., Lin, Y.H., Huang, H.W.: XBRL adoption and cost of debt. Int. J. Account. Inf. Manag. 23(2), 199–216 (2015). https://doi.org/10.1108/IJAIM-04-2014-0031
17. Kaya, D., Pronobis, P.: The benefits of structured data across the information supply chain: Initial evidence on XBRL adoption and loan contracting of private firms. J. Account. Public Policy 35(4), 417–436 (2016). https://doi.org/10.1016/j.jaccpubpol.2016.04.003
18. Efendi, J., Park, J.D., Smith, L.M.: Do XBRL filings enhance informational efficiency? Early evidence from post-earnings announcement drift. J. Bus. Res. 67(6), 1099–1105 (2014). https://doi.org/10.1016/j.jbusres.2013.05.051
19. Yoon, H., Zo, H., Ciganek, A.P.: Does XBRL adoption reduce information asymmetry? J. Bus. Res. 64(2), 157–163 (2011). https://doi.org/10.1016/j.jbusres.2010.01.008
20. Kim, J.W., Lim, J.H., No, W.G.: The effect of first wave mandatory XBRL reporting across the financial information environment. J. Inf. Syst. 26(1), 127–153 (2012). https://doi.org/10.2308/isys-10260
21. Kaya, D.: The influence of firm-specific characteristics on the extent of voluntary disclosure in XBRL: Empirical analysis of SEC filings. Int. J. Account. Inf. Manag. 22(1), 2–17 (2014). https://doi.org/10.1108/IJAIM-05-2011-0007
22. Liu, C., Luo, X.R., Wang, F.L.: An empirical investigation on the impact of XBRL adoption on information asymmetry: evidence from Europe. Decis. Support Syst. 93, 42–50 (2017). https://doi.org/10.1016/j.dss.2016.09.004
23. Geiger, M.A., North, D.S., Selby, D.D.: Releasing information in XBRL: does it improve information asymmetry for early US adopters? Acad. Account. Financ. Stud. J. 18(4), 66–83 (2014)
24. Efendi, J., Park, J.D., Subramaniam, C.: Does the XBRL reporting format provide incremental information value? A study using XBRL disclosures during the voluntary filing program. Abacus 52(2), 259–285 (2016). https://doi.org/10.1111/abac.12079
25. Zhang SS, Riordan R, Weinhardt C.: Interactive data: technology and cost of capital. In: Mancini D, Vaassen EHJ, Dameri RP (eds.): Accounting Information Systems for Decision Making. Springer, Berlin, Heidelberg, pp. 233–247 (2013)

26. Hao, L., Zhang, H.J., Fang, J.: Does voluntary adoption of XBRL reduce cost of equity capital? Int. J. Account. Inf. Manag. **22**(2), 86–102 (2014). https://doi.org/10.1108/IJAIM-11-2012-00 71

27. Liu, C., Luo, X.R., Sia, C.L., O'Farrell, G., Teo, H.H.: The impact of XBRL adoption in PR China. Decis. Support Syst. **59**, 242–249 (2014). https://doi.org/10.1016/j.dss.2013.12.003

28. Roohani, S., Furusho, Y., Koizumi, M.: XBRL: Improving transparency and monitoring functions of corporate governance. Int. J. Disclos. Gov. **6**(4), 355–369 (2009). https://doi.org/10.1 057/jdg.2009.17

29. Ahmadpour, A.: The improvement of governance decision making using XBRL. Int. J. E-Bus. Res. **7**(2), 11–18 (2011). https://doi.org/10.4018/jebr.2011040102

30. Yao, K.H., Xiao, S.P., Li, J.J.: XBRL and corporate governance. In: The 19th International Conference on Industrial Engineering and Engineering Management, pp. 403–412. Springer, Berlin, Heidelberg (2013)

31. Gray, G.L., Miller, D.W.: XBRL: solving real-world problems. Int. J. Disclos. Gov. **6**(3), 207–223 (2009). https://doi.org/10.1057/jdg.2009.8

32. Avallone, F., Ramassa, P., Roncagliolo, E.: The pros and cons of XBRL adoption in Italy: a field study. In: Mancini D., Dameri R.P., Bonollo E. (eds.) Strengthening Information and Control Systems—The Synergy Between Information Technology and Accounting Models. Lecture Notes in Information Systems and Organisation, pp. 157–170, Springer, Berlin, Heidelberg (2016)

33. Debreceny, R., Farewell, S., Piechocki, M., Felden, C., Gräning, A.: Does it add up? Early evidence on the data quality of XBRL filings to the SEC. J. Account. Public Policy **29**(3), 296–306 (2010). https://doi.org/10.1016/j.jaccpubpol.2010.04.001

34. Bartley, J., Chen, A.Y.S., Taylor, E.Z.: A comparison of XBRL filings to corporate 10-Ks—evidence from the voluntary filing program. Account. Horiz. **25**(2), 227–245 (2011). https://doi.org/10.2308/acch-10028

35. Markelevich, A., Shaw, L., Weihs, H.: The Israeli XBRL adoption experience. Account. Perspect. **14**(2), 117–133 (2015). https://doi.org/10.1111/1911-3838.12044

36. Janvrin, D.J., No, W.G.: XBRL implementation: a field investigation to identify research opportunities. J. Inf. Syst. **26**(1), 169–197 (2012). https://doi.org/10.2308/isys-10252

37. Bonsón, E., Cortijo, V., Escobar, T.: Towards the global adoption of XBRL using International Financial Reporting Standards (IFRS). Int. J. Account. Inf. Syst. **10**(1), 46–60 (2009). https://doi.org/10.1016/j.accinf.2008.10.002

38. Debreceny, R.S., Farewell, S.M., Piechocki, M., Felden, C., Gräning, A., D'eri, A.: Flex or break? Extensions in XBRL disclosures to the SEC. Account. Horiz. **25**(4), 631–657 (2011). https://doi.org/10.2308/acch-50068

39. Panizzolo, D.: Architettura di una tassonomia XBRL: il caso della nota integrativa al bilancio. In Zambon, S. (ed.): XBRL e informativa aziendale. Traiettorie, innovazioni e sfide, I, pp. 54–85, Milano, Franco Angeli (2010)

40. Sòstero, U.: La tassonomia XBRL italiana della nota integrativa: analisi delle fonti normative. In Zambon, S. (ed.): XBRL e informativa aziendale. Traiettorie, innovazioni e sfide, I, pp. 86–103, Milano, Franco Angeli (2010)

41. Valentinetti, D., Rea, M.A.: Adopting XBRL in Italy: early evidence of fit between Italian GAAP taxonomy and current reporting practices of non-listed companies. Int. J. Digit. Account. Res. **11**, 45–67 (2011). https://doi.org/10.4192/1577-8517-v11_3

42. Ramin, K.P., Prather, D.A.: Building an XBRL IFRS taxonomy. CPA J. **73**(5), 50 (2003)

43. Fradeani, A., Regoliosi, C., D'eri, A., Campanari, F.: Implementation of mandatory IFRS financial disclosures in a voluntary format: evidence from the Italian XBRL project. In: Reshaping Accounting and Management Control Systems, pp. 331–347. Springer (2017)

44. Valentinetti, D., Rea, M.A.: IFRS Taxonomy and financial reporting practices: the case of Italian listed companies. Int. J. Account. Inf. Syst. **13**(2), 163–180 (2012)

45. Linsley, P.M., Shrives, P.J.: Risk reporting: a study of risk disclosures in the annual reports of UK companies. Br. Account. Rev. **38**(4), 387–404 (2006)

46. Saemann, G.: An examination of comment letters filed in the US financial accounting standard-setting process by institutional interest groups. Abacus **35**(1), 1–28 (1999)
47. Larson, R.K.: An examination of comment letters to the IASC: special purpose entities. Res. Account. Regul. **20**, 27–46 (2008)
48. Quagli, A., Ramassa, P., D'Alauro, G.: The users' primacy principle in the European accounting directive: an analysis of the standard-setting process. Eur. J. Econ. Finance Adm. Sci. **72**, 55–75 (2015)
49. Krippendorff, K.: Content Analysis: An Introduction to Its Methodology. Sage, Thousand Oaks (2004)
50. Ingram, R.W., Frazier, K.B.: Narrative disclosures in annual reports. J. Bus. Res. **11**(1), 49–60 (1983)
51. Jones, M.J., Shoemaker, P.A.: Accounting narratives: a review of empirical studies of content and readability. J. Account. Lit. **13**, 142 (1994)
52. Smith, M., Taffler, R.J.: The chairman's statement-A content analysis of discretionary narrative disclosures. Account. Audit. Account. J. **13**(5), 624–647 (2000). https://doi.org/10.1108/0951 3570010353738
53. Pinsker, R., Wheeler, P.: Nonprofessional investors' perceptions of the efficiency and effectiveness of XBRL-enabled financial statement analysis and of firms providing XBRL-formatted information. Int. J. Disclos. Gov. **6**(3), 241–261 (2009). https://doi.org/10.1057/jdg.2009.6
54. Arnold, V., Bedard, J.C., Phillips, J.R., Sutton, S.G.: The impact of tagging qualitative financial information on investor decision making: Implications for XBRL. Int. J. Account. Inf. Syst. **13**(1), 2–20 (2012). https://doi.org/10.1016/j.accinf.2011.12.002
55. Henderson, C., Huerta, E., Glandon, T.: Standardizing the presentation of financial data: does XBRL's taxonomy affect the investment performance of nonprofessional investors? Int. J. Digit. Account. Res. **15**, 127–153 (2015). https://doi.org/10.4192/1577-8517-v15_5
56. Li, S., Nwaeze, E.T.: The association between extensions in XBRL disclosures and financial information environment. J. Inf. Syst. **29**(3), 73–99 (2015). https://doi.org/10.2308/isys-5100 5
57. Ly, K.: Extensible business reporting language for financial reporting (XBRL FR) and financial analysts' activity: early evidence. Acad. Account. Financ. Stud. J. **16**(2), 25–44 (2012)
58. Liu, C., O'Farrell, G.. The impact of XBRL on forecast accuracy across nations. Int. J. Serv. Stand. **8**(3), 247–263 (2013). https://doi.org/10.1504/IJSS.2013.057238
59. Liu, C., Yao, L.J., Sia, C.L., Wei, K.K.: The impact of early XBRL adoption on analysts' forecast accuracy-empirical evidence from China. Electron. Mark. **24**(1), 47–55 (2014). https://doi.org g/10.1108/IJAIM-03-2013-0023
60. Liu, C., Wang, T., Yao, L.J.: XBRL's impact on analyst forecast behavior: an empirical study. J. Account. Public Policy **33**(1), 69–82 (2014). https://doi.org/10.1016/j.jaccpub-pol.2013.10. 004
61. Dhole, S., Lobo, G.J., Mishra, S., Pal, A.M.: Effects of the SEC's XBRL mandate on financial reporting comparability. Int. J. Account. Inf. Syst. **19**, 29–44 (2015). https://doi.org/10.1016/j. accinf.2015.11.002
62. Garsva, G., Danenas, P.: Xbrl integration into intelligent system for credit risk evaluation. Transform. Bus. Econ. **10**(2), 88–103 (2011). https://doi.org/10.1108/02686900310500497
63. Pinsker, R.: XBRL awareness in auditing: a sleeping giant? Manag. Audit. J. **18**(9), 732–736 (2003). https://doi.org/10.1108/02686900310500497
64. La Rosa, F., Caserio, C.: Are auditors interested in XBRL? A qualitative survey of big auditing firms in Italy. In: Mancini, D., Vaassen, E.H.J., Dameri, R.P. (eds.) Accounting Information Systems for Decision Making, pp. 13–45. Springer, Berlin Heidelberg (2013)
65. Roncagliolo, E., Di Fabio, C., Avallone, F., Ramassa, P.: The effects of XBRL adoption: a literature review. In: Proceedings of the 11th European Conference on Information Systems Management (2017)
66. Quagli, A., Ramassa P.: L'efficacia delle tassonomie tra esigenze di standardizzazione e prassi aziendale. In: Zambon, S. (ed.) XBRL e informativa aziendale. Traiettorie, innovazioni e sfide, pp. 147–160, Milano, Franco Angeli (2011)

Information Security Policies in Organizations

How Convention Theory Can Serve as a Framework to Inform Information Security Research and HR Practice

Dominik Zellhofer ⓘ

Abstract The increased use of information technology throughout organizations led to a surge in concern for information security. Information security standards guide information security policy implementation, but the challenge of ensuring compliance is still a major issue, despite extensive information security research. The lack of versatility in theoretical approaches spurred calls for sociological approaches to contribute to the literature, but they were only partly addressed. The proposed framework of convention theory can serve as a fruitful approach by providing a holistic perspective and a strong theoretical foundation. The use of human resource information systems (HRIS) und electronic human resource management (e-HRM) extends the concern for information security to human resource (HR) practices and data privacy is no longer an issue solely for external stakeholders but for employees alike. At the same time, the role of HR practices in contributing to compliance with information security policies seems to be underestimated in existing literature. This paper introduces main concepts of a convention theory-based framework and illustrates implications for information security research and suggests that HR practices can contribute to ensuring information security in organizations.

Keywords Information security policy · HR practice · Convention theory

D. Zellhofer (✉)
Interdisciplinary Institute for Management & Organizational Behaviour,
WU Vienna (Vienna University of Economics and Business), Welthandelsplatz 1,
1020 Vienna, Austria
e-mail: dominik.zellhofer@wu.ac.at

© Springer International Publishing AG, part of Springer Nature 2019
F. Cabitza et al. (eds.), *Organizing for the Digital World*, Lecture Notes in Information
Systems and Organisation 28, https://doi.org/10.1007/978-3-319-90503-7_5

1 Introduction

In 2013, the New Yorker published an article titled "Steamrolled by Big Data" [1], depicting the triumph of this buzzword in the recent years. Indeed, there is a sense of gold fever regarding data in many sectors of the economy, fueled by the advances in information technology. As a consequence of the growing availability of big data, organizations rely heavily on large amounts of data in almost aspects of their business, from supply chain management to marketing. As data processing is based on modern information technology, with interfaces not only to customers but other stakeholders as well, organizations need to ensure data security from outside and inside threats. In 2014, a substantial security breach caused a leak of account information of 145 million eBay-users [2], drawing major media scrutiny. An international, IBM-sponsored study finds that the average cost of a data breach in 2016 was four million dollars, with the cost per incident having increased by 30% since 2013 [3]. Although hackers are frequently the culprits in such incidences as mentioned above, the threat does not exclusively stem from external factors. In fact, Stanton et al. [4] report that between 50 and 75% of all data security violations are caused by internal stakeholders. Despite of the obvious image of a disgruntled employee, non-compliance to security standards is often unintentional, a problem of awareness [5], the lack thereof leading to (non-malicious) non-compliance.

Attempts to minimize these inherent risks of information processing led to the development of standardized information safety procedures, reflected through information security standards like ISO27000, COBIT or ITIL, which in turn are implemented through organization policies. These policies target issues concerning the organizational environment and intra-organizational processes alike.

In the past, technology-focused research on information systems security was successful because information technology was largely an issue of a single function in the organizational hierarchy, whereas today organizations rely on information systems in every aspect of their business [6]. This trend also directly impacts HR practice, not only because of the need for proper training, e.g. concerning information security awareness [7]. HR departments increasingly rely on human resource information systems (HRIS) and electronic human resource management (e-HRM) [8]. Beadles et al. [9] found in their study that 80% of HR-directors reported that HRIS increased the usefulness of information and their ability to disseminate it, while 90% thought that HRIS added value to the organization. The intent of use of HRIS is not limited to improving efficiency and cutting costs of information processing. As Kovach et al. [10] note, it is not restricted to maintaining employee records anymore, but is used as decision support systems, communication systems, transaction processing systems and more. While there is no unique definition of e-HRM [11], it generally denotes the interface to other stakeholders in the organization, making the HR department internal HRIS accessible to employees while both HRIS and e-HRM are now often embedded in organization-wide information systems [8]. Besides efficiency and cost benefits of these systems, the privacy of employee and customer data alike must be guaranteed or organizations face a loss of legitimacy, not only in the legal context, but in the broader societal context. The obvious challenge therefore is to ensure acceptance and compliance of good security practices in organizations, guided through the implementation of security policies.

Zafar and Clark [12] note that the term "information security" has a plurality of definitions, depending on the perspective, seeing a progression from mere technological viewpoints to behavioral, managerial, philosophical, and organizational perspectives. In an attempt to provide a holistic view of information security, they derive a definition that includes the identification and assessment of risks and associated threats, training of personnel in security awareness and best practices, the implementation and monitoring of technologies to prevent security breaches, the implementation of policies and procedures to prevent misuse and loss in the event of a security breach, and lastly the incorporation of information security governance as part of corporate governance. Williams [13] gives a similar description, grouping tasks of information security in availability, confidentiality, integrity, authenticity and non-repudiation of information systems. In an attempt to provide a model of factors that contribute towards information security specifically in HRIS and e-HRM, Zafar [8] provides a similar account of significant aspects, including policies.

2 Information Security Policies

I focus on information security policies to depict the perspective of a convention theory-based framework as they show the conventional nature of coordination in a very material way, a document that describes "good" practices, guided by international industry standards and implemented with the intent to shape the organizational members' day-to-day practices. In general, a policy is simply a general rule to limit the discretion of subordinates in an organization [14]. Similarly, management information systems research defines policies as a control instrument to establish limits of acceptable behavior, guide and restrict decisions and serve as standards [15]. While the formulation of such documents, including the exact wording, is important, the generation and implementation process itself is also important, because it must aim to ensure acceptance within an organization. Knapp et al. [16] acknowledge that there is a plethora of frameworks and guidelines in literature concerning the formulation and implementation of security policies, but they did not find a framework illustrating the overall process of developing and managing information security policies within the organizational context. Their framework is based on the account of practitioners, thereby providing an overview that is based on actual practices in organizations. When comparing their framework with the list of what information security entails given above, it is clear that the process of applying information security policies entails all these aspects. I intentionally chose the word application over implementation, as the latter does not sufficiently convey the dynamics of policy use (see Fig. 1). Practitioners are aware of continuous tasks like awareness trainings, monitoring and policy enforcement, while also acknowledging influences of organization culture and institutional pressures of industry standards and legislation.

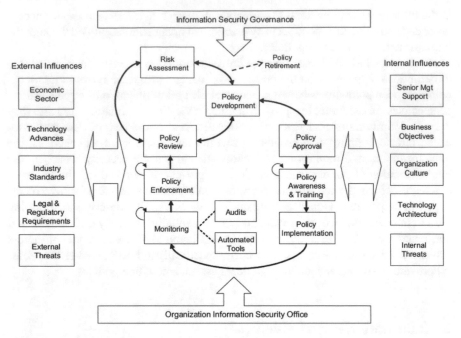

Fig. 1 Comprehensive information security policy process model [16]

Measures to increase information security awareness are considered an important step in achieving compliance [7]. These measures serve to make employees aware of their "security mission" [17] and therefore foster compliance with security policies. This hints at the need for (constant) dialogue and the insufficiency of just writing up a policy [18]. The focus on individual behavior is reflected in information security research, Warkentin and Willison [18] state that much of the focus within the behavioral security research community has been on information security policy non-compliance by employees. On the other hand, Orlikowski and Barley [19] argue that, while information technology research occasionally references organization studies, it is still underrepresented and call for a stronger focus on the institutional context. Interestingly, they find that the reverse is also true, organization studies often carelessly neglect how technologies shape organizations.

Clearly, the problem of information security is an inherently complex one, combining technical issues with social, psychological, and organizational aspects, therefore a holistic approach to tackle these problems requires interdisciplinary efforts [20]. Earlier calls for sociology to provide a strong theoretical foundation to enrich information security research were made but only partly addressed [21] and the framework of convention theory proposed in this paper is a sociological perspective that attempts to integrate the aforementioned aspects.

Institutions play an important role in the coordination of persons and objects but at the same time, the capabilities of the individuals to shape the situations he or she is in are extremely relevant too. Focusing the analysis on the level of the situation instead of the collective or the individual, convention theory also acknowledges that the materiality of the environment is a fundamental aspect of its framework, as coordination is not only necessary between human agents, but also with material objects, which in turn shape the view of the world of the actors. In the following, I will introduce essential concepts of the theoretical framework after briefly situating convention theory in the history of sociology.

3 Convention Theory—A Pragmatist Approach

In the first half of the twentieth century, collectivism seemed to be the only alternative to the individualism proposed by the economic model of man. Durkheim et al. [22] was the most prominent proponent of the "old social sciences" [23]. In the late 1960s, Pierre Bourdieu moved the focus to the structural, hence his description as "philosophy without subject" [24]. Some twenty years later, a new French sociology, a movement consisting of sociologists, economists, political philosophers, and historians combined the Durkheimian notion of collective practices with individual action, thereby shifting the focus on the genesis of institutions or conventions [23]. In this new interpretation of human action, "convention" does not only address traditions, rituals or customs in a Weberian [25] sense of the word, but as culturally established logics of coordination [26]. The notion that conventions are essential for coordination stresses the aspect of legitimacy, a concept that is also inherent to institutions, although institutionalism has a more stable view of legitimacy. This is important because information security research mainly focuses on practices aiming to ensure regularities, like checklists and protocols, which shows that it is implicitly assumed that the goals of information security are commonly agreed on [6]. This leads to a neglect of the essential role of legitimation of said goals [27] and therefore to an underestimation of the relevance of legitimizing information security governance practices.

3.1 Orders of Worth—Defining Qualities of People and Things

For coordination, it is necessary to agree on what is "good." This means that for coordination to be successful, people have to reduce the uncertainty about persons and objects by qualifying them, which means ranking them in regard to some kind of worth. Boltanski and Thévenot [28] initially identified the six most common *orders of worth*, but they argue there are many more left to discover. To understand how those orders of worth are relevant to coordination, one may consider the question how organizations maintain their legitimacy regarding relevant stakeholders. For the organization to maintain its legitimacy, it has to sustain the harmonious arrangement of things and persons in a state of general agreement [29]. To reach that agreement, one has to objectively qualify or classify things and people. This evaluation and qualification process is guided by orders of worth, which people refer to in disputes and which have to meet certain political and moral requirements [28, 30]. One example in the context of information security would be using the standard category of a Chief Security Officer (CSO) to convey responsibilities and power to a person and she would rank higher in terms of governing information security than the average employee. This would be a qualification along the *industrial worth*, where standardization is of value, because some kind of certification (along a standard), governing what a CSO is, would form that category. Important is that one has to refer to common orders of worth, because this negotiation happens in a public arena and referring to some very personal order of worth would not have legitimacy with other persons. Another example is the argument about how to apply technical equipment to produce a product or service in an organization. A security policy may change the use of a computer in another way than the employees traditionally used to, their argument would be based on the *domestic worth*, where tradition ranks high in importance. An overview of the initial six orders of worth and their attributes is given in Table 1. This requirement for justification in discourse and action with reference to more objective orders of evaluation is a clear distinction to traditional institutionalist approaches and requires actors to have specific competencies [29]. Once an agreement or compromise on orders of worth (there can be multiple orders at play at once) is reached, legitimate conventions that serve coordination based upon them can be established. Conventions "convene" qualified objects and human beings, they give a sense of what dimension of time and space is relevant.

Contrary to classic notion of institutions as being relatively stable, conventions are frequently put to a *reality test*. For example, established standards guide actions, they give security on what is good practice and thereby serve as a common logic of coordination. But these moments of "being at ease" with them are interrupted with moments of doubt, where the standard is unmasked as arbitrary, conformist, formulaic and inauthentic [32], where proof of legitimacy has to be given and the standard has to be justified. To be able to argue about the quality of things and people, one has to engage in discourse, but to be able to do so, information has to be put in a general form [33]. Convention theorists call this process *investment in form,* with the term "investment" hinting that this is a costly effort and depend on the capabilities of the actor. One may consider how programmers translate ideas into functions and methods, guided by the syntax of a programming language. A device does not know how to process an idea, but the compiler knows how to handle code. Note that there is a common understanding of what "good" code is, but there is also dispute about what good programming style is. It is important to keep in mind that when convention theorists talk about information transmission, they do not focus on the content but on the form of it, as Thévenot [34] notes: "*Information here refers to [...] coordination, with the understanding that coordination is always problematic.*" This notion reveals that different forms generate different "forms of the probable", which defines what can be proved and offered as evidence [30].

Table 1 Schematic summary of orders of worth [31] (adapted)

	Market	Industrial	Civic	Domestic	Inspired	Opinion
Mode of evaluation (worth)	Price, cost	Technical efficiency	Collective welfare	Esteem, reputation	Grace singularity creativeness	Renown, fame
Test	Market competitiveness	Competence, reliability, planning	Equality and solidarity	Trustworthiness	Passion, enthusiasm	Popularity, audience, recognition
Form of relevant proof	Monetary	Measurable: criteria, statistics	Formal, official	Oral, exemplary, personally warranted	Emotional involvement and expression	Semiotic
Qualified objects	Freely circulating market good or service	Infrastructure, project, technical object, method, plan	Rules and regulations, fundamental rights, welfare policies	Patrimony, locale, heritage	Emotionally invested body or item: the sublime	Sign, media
Qualified human beings	Customer, consumer, merchant, seller	Engineer, professional, expert	Equal citizens, solidarity unions	Authority	Creative being	Celebrity
Time formation	Short-term, flexibility	Long-term planned future	Perennial	Customary past	Eschatological, revolutionary, visionary moment	Vogue, trend
Space formation	Globalization	Cartesian space	Detachment	Local, proximal anchoring	Presence	Communication network

The concepts of orders of worth, tests, and investing in forms make it possible to understand the implementation and functioning of a firm or other conventional resources like standards, rules and policies, all oriented towards specific values or worth, e.g. in the case of standards usually towards efficiency [35].

3.2 Regimes of Engagement

The process of investing in forms hints at a second main concept of convention theory, the idea that these most legitimate orders of worth (also *regimes of coordination*) are fabricated on more basic *regimes of engagement* [30, 36]. As already mentioned, the evaluation and justification as described above happens in a public arena, but action or agency happens in another kind of engagement with the world. This engagement is associated with a different kind of confidence, and this confidence in turn is dependent on the power or capacity attributed to the agent and the support he or she recognizes in the environment [37]. Thévenot consciously avoids the terms action or practice, as these focus attention on the human agent, but neglects the person's dependence on the environment and the different conceptions of what is "good" (the French term *engagement* captures not only the very mechanical conception of engaging with something in the English sense of the term, but the notion of engagement with moral and political commitments as well [38]). Each regime of engagement implies a distinct cognitive format related to a different kind of access to the human environment of nature and artifacts [30]. Cognitive formats characterize the actor's access to reality and thereby how he coordinates his behavior within a certain apprehension frame [34]. The mechanisms previously described happen in the *regime of justification*, where confidence in politics and institutions are relevant. This regime demands the highest degree of legitimacy, the actor cannot rely on personal convenience as a way of qualification, but must rely on more common orders of worth as Boltanski and Thévenot [28] identified them. The format of information is also more conventional, e.g. reports are much more conventional than everyday language use [38]. On the other hand, the *regime of familiar engagement* describes an engagement with the world where the immediate material and human surroundings are deeply personal and the individual accommodated himself in them [37]. As already described, each engagement has its own format of information, and in this regime of engagement, information cannot easily be transferred by discourse, it is formatted in the language of the body. So the "good" which governs coordination of herself with her environment is a deeply personal good. An obvious example in the context of the topic at hand would be the employee's customization of his or her computer. A desktop wallpaper with pictures of family has no functional use, but it generates a kind of good that is hard to make obvious. It serves to making the work environment your own, just as the habit of suspending your coat on your chair, although it is against its original function and makes the chair less efficient to sit on. New information security policies might prevent the worker from changing desktop wallpaper, but in this case, he will have a hard time justifying this behavior and criticizing this new standard, because this kind of customization will mostly likely not rank high in common orders of worth which are at play in this situation. In contrast to the familiar engagement, the *regime of planned action* describes a more functional orientation with the environment, also to facilitate coordinated action with other actors. The good with which one grasps their environment is not entirely focused on the functional nature, but, as the name suggests, on successfully realizing a plan. The difference of this regime to the most public regime of justification is that the notion of what is good is loosely reliant on everyday narratives, on common knowledge, one is supposed to know what counts as "good working order" [38]. To illustrate, imagine the scenario of a shared workplace, where planned action is necessary to achieve a common goal of being productive. Conventions of how a workstation ought to be arranged to be suitable for coworkers may lead the worker to removing the very convenient post-it with handwritten passwords from the monitor.

The concept of regimes of engagement proves to be important when considering the process of applying information security policies in organizations: Establishing and maintaining legitimacy of said policies as a common mode of coordination is only one (nevertheless important) aspect. The coordination via planned action makes the functional aspect of a convention visible. The most intimate form of engagement with the world may hint at why employees' actual practices deviate from planned action based upon policy and could serve as a starting point when looking for potential sources of or reasons for dispute and non-compliance.

3.3 Organizations as Compromising Devices

While other theories often grant organizations a reality on their own, convention theory is not interested in a concept of organization as a mode of coordination on its own [26]. Thévenot [30] defines an organization as a compromising device. He criticizes the common notion of a stable and collective order. Aspects of this idea are rules, hierarchical prescriptions, rationalizing and bureaucratic methods, social structures, shared representations and common culture which are seen as constraints, which Thévenot defines as "over-socialized" representations of this idea. He argues for a notion of coordination more open to uncertainty, critical tensions and creative arrangements. As a result, this conception of organization explicitly appreciates informal and personal practices, which could be an important piece of the puzzle regarding non-compliance to formal policies, without necessarily interpreting it as a pathology of organizations.

Conceptualizing organizations as compromising devices appreciates the tension created in organizations by different orders of worth governing coordination. For example, an organization must deal with the tension brought on by the need to standardize processes to ensure survival on the economic market. Driven by the value of efficiency, this may undercut practices that are based on trust and tradition, values that characterize the domestic world, leading to dispute and critique.

4   Contributions for Research and Practice

I will briefly illustrate a selection of aspects of how a conventionalist approach can inform information security research and argue that this perspective shows the relevance of HR practices in this matter, which seems to be neglected in both research and practice.

Convention theory moves the focus to the dynamic process of how coordination is established. The introduced concepts have several implications for research: The concept of orders of worth suggests that research should pay attention to justification and evaluation as an ongoing process, as described by reality tests. As this is done in a public arena, the level of analysis cannot solely focus on the individual. At the same time, the capabilities of the actor (e.g. his ability to invest in forms and bring arguments to the dispute) and how he or she perceives the world (which is again dependent on hints of objects in the coordination situation) are relevant too, which means that a mere focus on the collective level underappreciates the complexity of the situation. This is reflected in the methodological stance of convention theory, which can be seen as a "complex pragmatic situationalism" [26, 39]. The reference to particular orders of worth shape the cognitive format, as do the different engagements with the world. As a consequence, the concept of rationality is altered and shifted towards a "situated rationality" [14, 35]. This makes seemingly paradox irrational behavior interpretable. Because of the strong emphasis on the influence of the particularities of the situation, qualitative research approaches are at an advantage, although there are examples of the successful application of quantitative or mixed methods [40]. By valuing the influence of materiality, the proposed framework is particularly potent for providing insights in technology-rich contexts and appreciating the implications of socio-technical systems [41, 42]. The concept of regimes of engagement extends the framework beyond evaluation and dispute to the application of conventions. It can show how standards are applied [32] and make tensions between the most public and most intimate engagement with the world visible, while also differentiating a mode of coordination that is concentrated on following a plan, thereby it is possible to integrate into the analysis the aspect of legitimacy, functional use, and the role of familiarity and personal aspects, without drawing on theoretically separated models for each engagement. The examples I provided throughout the text highlighted some of details needed to be considered when conducting research, but issues of high importance remain which cannot be discussed here in full length.

Although much of information security research is behavioral, there is a lack of literature that stresses the role of HR practices. Information technology seems to be relevant for HR when thinking about e-HRM or HRIS, but existing literature would suggest that there is no relationship vice versa. Recently, a literature review on information security management [43] called for a holistic approach in information security management, explicitly including human resource management. This call should go far beyond mere employee training in awareness and IT literacy. Policymaking should be approached in a holistic way, especially if it directly impacts the way employees conduct their work. With the spread of digital devices that are attached both to private and working life (e.g. smartphones), ambiguity of conventional use is likely. Convention theory can shed light on this matter via the concept of regimes of engagement. Flexible working time arrangements are inherently connected to this issue and HR practice can address the resulting tension (e.g. using devices in the way the planned action regime supposes in an inherently personal environment of your home) by searching for compromise between differing orders of worth. This could speed up the process of setting up an information security policy by facilitating the shift from a regime of justificatory action to the application in the planned action regime. IT specialists usually prefer solely technical solutions, putting much effort in restrictions of possible actions of employees, but the effectiveness of tools like information security awareness trainings hint at a social dimension of the problem. This is also pointed out by research on information security culture [44]. Informing employees via training is only part of the solution, the aspect of personal engagement with the functional environment, implicitly addressed by the term "user behavior" must be considered too. This notion is entailed in the concept of reality tests, which also underlines the revolving nature of accepting and disputing standards. HR practices like performance evaluations or appraisal interviews could be used to investigate this aspect on a regular basis, without relying on solely technical instruments (as for example "automated tools" suggest in Fig. 1). External audits are a standard practice for information security policies, but they often fail to detect workarounds in actual practice, institutionalists would denote a systematic disparity of official practice and actual routine as decoupling [45]. Lastly, e-HRM could be a promising way to foster security behavior by "formatting" learning routines with services like e-learning. With respect to gathering data with HRIS, convention theory may provide a new perspective on resistance against these instruments by employees. While these instruments provide value in terms of efficiency and standardization (industrial worth), trust and privacy are important values in the domestic worth, as well as tradition. When a company decides to introduce HRIS, the extended use of these instruments may be seen as a breach of trust, because the system does not qualify within the domestic order of worth. Therefore, legitimacy is an important issue and HR practitioners have to be aware that compromising between those orders may be more fruitful way of solving dispute than relying solely on arguments of efficiency.

4.1 Limitations and Future Research Agenda

Due to the scope of convention theory to cover a range of societal issues, grasping an understanding of the framework can seem daunting, which may stunt the spread to narrower fields like information security research or research on digitalization of HRM. The methodological standpoint can prove challenging when research traditions in some fields are purely quantitatively oriented and qualitative research is less common. Operationalization of constructs can seem daunting too considering the wide-ranging implications of the concepts. As Jagd [46] noted, the relevance of the framework for organizational processes has only been partly explored. The full potential of this framework can only be explored if future research applies it to a variety of topics, information security research is one promising direction that can add to a growing body of literature (for an overview of this research see [47]). The extension of the body of applied research may also strengthen the repertoire of implications for practitioners, and case-based formatting of research findings may help to make contributions visible for non-sociologists. The intent of this paper is not to provide a comprehensive account of convention theory and its application to the topic at hand, but should serve to foster discussion of the potential benefits for information security research and HR practice alike.

References

1. The New Yorker. http://www.newyorker.com/tech/elements/steamrolled-by-big-data
2. Heise Medien GmbH & Co.KG: https://www.heise.de/security/meldung/145-Millionen-Kund en-von-eBay-Hack-betroffen-2195974.html
3. Cost of Data Breach Study: Global Analysis. Ponemon Institute (2016)
4. Stanton, J.M., Stam, K.R., Mastrangelo, P., Jolton, J.: Analysis of end user security behaviors. Comput. Secur. 24, 124–133 (2005)
5. Bulgurcu, B., Cavusoglu, H., Benbasat, I.: Information security policy compliance: an empirical study of rationality-based beliefs and information security awareness. MIS Q. 34, 523–548 (2010)
6. McFadzean, E., Ezingeard, J.-N., Birchall, D.: Anchoring information security governance research: sociological groundings and future directions. J. Inf. Syst. Secur. 2, 3–48 (2006)
7. Bauer, S., Bernroider, E.W., Chudzikowski, K.: Prevention is better than cure! Designing infor- mation security awareness programs to overcome users' non-compliance with information security policies in banks. Comput. Secur. 68, 145–159 (2017)
8. Zafar, H.: Human resource information systems: information security concerns for organiza- tions. Human Resour. Manag. Rev. 23, 105–113 (2013)
9. Beadles, I., Aston, N., Lowery, C.M., Johns, K.: The impact of human resource information systems: an exploratory study in the public sector. Commun. IIMA 5, 6 (2005)
10. Kovach, K.A., Hughes, A.A., Fagan, P., Maggitti, P.G.: Administrative and strategic advantages of HRIS. Employ. Relat. Today 29, 43–48 (2002)
11. Strohmeier, S.: Research in e-HRM: review and implications. Human Resour. Manag. Rev. 17, 19–37 (2007)
12. Zafar, H., Clark, J.G.: Current state of information security research in IS. Commun. Assoc. Inf. Syst. 24, 572–596 (2009)
13. Williams, P.: Information security governance. Inf. Secur. Tech. Rep. 6, 60–70 (2001)
14. Simon, H.A.: Models of Man; Social and Rational. Wiley, New York (1957)
15. Davis, G., Olson, M.: Management Information Systems: Conceptual Foundations, Methods and Development. McGraw-Hill, New York (1985)
16. Knapp, K.J., Franklin Morris Jr, R., Marshall, T.E., Byrd, T.A.: Information security policy: an organizational-level process model. Comput. Secur. 28, 493–508 (2009)
17. Siponen, M.: A conceptual foundation for organizational information security awareness. Inf. Manag. Comput. Secur. 8, 31–41 (2000)
18. Warkentin, M., Willison, R.: Behavioral and policy issues in information systems security: the insider threat. Eur. J. Inf. Syst. 18, 101 (2009)
19. Orlikowski, W.J., Barley, S.R.: Technology and institutions: what can research on information technology and research on organizations learn from each other? MIS Q. 25, 145–165 (2001)
20. Siponen, M., Oinas-Kukkonen, H.: A review of information security issues and respective research contributions. SIGMIS Database 38, 60–80 (2007)

21. Dhillon, G., Backhouse, J.: Current directions in IS security research: towards socio-organizational perspectives. Inf. Syst. J. **11**, 127–153 (2001)
22. Durkheim, E., Solovay, S.A., Mueller, J.H., Catlin, S.G.E.G.: The Rules of Sociological Method, by Emile Durkheim (trans: Solovay, S.A., Mueller, J.H. and Ed: Catlin, G.E.G.). Free Press, New York (1982)
23. Wagner, P.: A History and Theory of the Social Sciences. Sage Publications Ltd., London (2001)
24. Bourdieu, P., Passeron, J.-C.: Sociology and philosophy in France since 1945: death and resurrection of a philosophy without subject. Soc. Res. 162–212 (1967)
25. Weber, M.: Wirtschaft und Gesellschaft: Grundriss der verstehenden Soziologie. Mohr, Tübingen (1922)
26. Diaz-Bone, R.: Die "Economie des conventions": Grundlagen und Entwicklungen der neuen französischen Wirtschaftssoziologie. Springer VS, Wiesbaden (2015)
27. Hirschheim, R., Klein, H.K.: Four paradigms of information systems development. Commun. ACM **32**, 1199–1216 (1989)
28. Boltanski, L., Thévenot, L.: On Justification: Economies of Worth. Princeton University Press, Princeton (2006)
29. Patriotta, G., Gond, J.-P., Schultz, F.: Maintaining legitimacy: controversies, orders of worth, and public justifications. J. Manag. Stud. **48**, 1804–1836 (2011)
30. Thévenot, L.: Organized complexity: conventions of coordination and the composition of economic arrangements. Eur. J. Soc. Theory **4**, 405–425 (2001)
31. Thévenot, L., Moody, M., Lafaye, C.: Forms of valuing nature: arguments and modes of justification in French and American environmental disputes. In: Rethinking Comparative Cultural Sociology: Repertoires of Evaluation in France and the United States, pp. 229–272 (2000)
32. Thévenot, L.: Postscript to the special issue: governing life by standards a view from engagements. Social Stud. Sci. **39**, 793–813 (2009)
33. Thévenot, L.: Rules and implements: investment in forms. Soc. Sci. Inf. **23**, 1–45 (1984)
34. Thévenot, L.: The plurality of cognitive formats and engagements moving between the familiar and the public. Eur. J. Soc. Theory **10**, 409–423 (2007)
35. Thévenot, L.: Conventions of co-ordination and the framing of uncertainty. In: Intersubjectivity in Economics: Agents and Structures, pp. 181–197. Routledge, London (2002)
36. Thévenot, L.: Die Person in ihrem vielfachen Engagiertsein. Trivium. Revue franco allemande de sciences humaines et sociales—Deutsch-französische Zeitschrift für Geistes-und Sozialwissenschaften (2010)
37. Thévenot, L.: Institutions and agency: differentiating regimes of engagement. In: Conference on Economy and Society
38. Thévenot, L.: Pragmatic regimes governing the engagement with the world. In: Knorr-Cetina, K., Schatzki, T., von Savigny, E. (eds.) The Practice Turn in Contemporary Theory, pp. 56–73. Routledge, London (2001)
39. Diaz-Bone, R.: The methodological standpoint of the "économie des conventions". Hist. Soc. Res./Historische Sozialforschung 43–63 (2011)
40. Richards, M., Zellweger, T., Gond, J.P.: Maintaining moral legitimacy through worlds and words: an explanation of firms' investment in sustainability certification. J. Manag. Stud. **54**, 676–710 (2017)
41. Latour, B.: Reassembling the Social: An Introduction to Actor-Network-Theory. Oxford University Press, Oxford (2005)
42. Orlikowski, W.J., Scott, S.V.: Sociomateriality: challenging the separation of technology, work and organization. Acad. Manag. Ann. **2**, 433–474 (2008)
43. Soomro, Z.A., Shah, M.H., Ahmed, J.: Information security management needs more holistic approach: a literature review. Int. J. Inf. Manag. **36**, 215–225 (2016)

44. Schlienger, T., Teufel, S.: Information Security Culture. In: Ghonaimy, M.A., El-Hadidi, M.T., Aslan, H.K. (eds.) Security in the Information Society: Visions and Perspectives, pp. 191–201. Springer, US, Boston, MA (2002)
45. Meyer, J.W., Rowan, B.: Institutionalized organizations: formal structure as myth and ceremony. Am. J. Sociol. **83**, 340–363 (1977)
46. Jagd, S.: Pragmatic sociology and competing orders of worth in organizations. Eur. J. Soc. Theory **14**, 343–359 (2011)
47. Knoll, L. (ed.): Organisationen und Konventionen. Die Soziologie der Konventionen in der Organisationsforschung. Springer VS, Wiesbaden (2015)

E²mC: Improving Rapid Mapping with Social Network Information

Jose Luis Fernandez-Marquez, Chiara Francalanci, Sharada Mohanty, Rosy Mondardini, Barbara Pernici and Gabriele Scalia

Abstract E²mC aims to demonstrate the technical and operational feasibility of the integration of social media analysis and crowdsourced information within both the Rapid Mapping and Early Warning Components of Copernicus Emergency Management Service (EMS). Copernicus is a European Commission programme developing information services based on satellite earth observation. A fundamental innovation with E²mC is to combine the automated analysis of social media information with crowdsourcing, with the general goal of improving the quality and dependability of the information provided to professional users within the Copernicus network. The automated analyses will focus on multimedia information (mainly pictures), which is most useful for rapid mapping purposes. A fundamental challenge to enable the effective use of multimedia information is geolocation. The paper presents a methodology to extract, integrate and geolocate information from social media and leverage the crowd to clean, validate and complement this information. Preliminary results from testing the methodology are presented based on the analysis of tweets on the earthquake that struck Central Italy in August 2016.

Keywords Emergency management systems · Information extraction
Social media · Crowdsourcing

1 Introduction

The availability of a number of information sources from social media makes it possible to use it as a basis for gathering information to support decision making and other activities. Social media have proven particularly valuable in collecting

J. L. Fernandez-Marquez · R. Mondardini
University of Geneva, Geneva, Switzerland

C. Francalanci (✉) · B. Pernici · G. Scalia
Politecnico di Milano – DEIB, Milano, Italy
e-mail: chiara.francalanci@polimi.it

S. Mohanty
EPFL, Lausanne, Switzerland

© Springer International Publishing AG, part of Springer Nature 2019   63
F. Cabitza et al. (eds.), *Organizing for the Digital World*, Lecture Notes in Information
Systems and Organisation 28, https://doi.org/10.1007/978-3-319-90503-7_6

information in emergency situations, such as in earthquakes, in particular in very destructive ones such as Haiti and Nepal, and in large floods and hurricanes, such as Hurricane Matthew and floods in the Philippines, in the different phases of such events [3]. Several social media platforms are used in crisis management, including text analytics, event detection, image and video analysis, geospatial analysis; on the other hand, also crowdsourcing initiatives are often started in crisis situations, for mapping purposes such as in Humanitarian OpenStreet Map projects (https://www.h otosm.org/) or to gather information with the support of networks of volunteers, such as in the case of the Haiti earthquake, where four different crowdsourcing initiatives were used providing the information needed to coordinate the emergency response, namely Open Street Map, CrisisCamp Haiti, Ushahidi, and GeoCommons [2, 3].

In this paper, we propose to combine information gathering from social media and crowdsourcing for supporting a specific task that needs to be performed in such events with stringent temporal constraints: Rapid Mapping. The production of updated maps helps rescue teams and field operators to understand how the area has been affected, the severity of damages, the grouping of persons in given areas, and they need to be produced within the first 24–72 h after the events. Such activity is currently supported by earth observation activities such as Copernicus, with Emergency Management Services (EMS) (http://emergency.copernicus.eu/mapping/), with tools to produce maps based on satellite data. The goal of this paper is to present how rapid mapping activities can be supported by images extracted from social media and with crowdsourcing, and to delineate a path for improving the quality of additional information to the available satellite data to prepare more timely and more precise maps. The goal of reducing mapping times significantly and improving their precision is being studied within the E^2mC (Evolution of Emergency Copernicus services) H2020 European Project (https://www.e2mc-project.eu/).

The paper is structured as follows. In Sect. 2, we briefly introduce the E^2mC goals and architecture. In Sect. 3, the E^2mC approach to image extraction and geolocation is illustrated, and in Sect. 4, we discuss how a process including crowdsourcing tasks can improve the quantity and quality of available information for rapid mapping.

2 E^2mC: Goals and Architecture

E^2mC aims at integrating social media analysis and crowdsourcing in a new *Copernicus Witness EMS (Emergency Management System) Service Component*, to improve the timeliness and accuracy of geo-spatial information provided during the crisis management cycle and, particularly, in the first hours immediately after the event. The focus of E^2mC is on rapid mapping. To this aim, the project aims to leverage social media analysis and crowdsourcing techniques. These techniques should be used in combination, by exploiting the synergies of both within a unified Social and Crowd platform. Personnel involved in crisis management currently uses social media as a source of information that is considered useful at the beginning of the response phase. Information is searched for manually and classified by manual inspection or by contacting the author of the information (for example, geotagging information is often gathered by writing to the social media users who have posted interesting pictures). This manual process allows employees to make a fast, although rough, assessment of the impact of the crisis, in particular when satellite images are not yet available. On the other hand, when official information emerges after some time from the start of the crisis, they use social media information only to confirm official data when their interpretation is not straightforward.

While crowdsourcing has been previously applied to mapping, the use of social media information (i.e., the information that is spontaneously published by social media users on general purpose social channels, such as Twitter) for mapping purposes is limited. In particular, to the best of our knowledge, multimedia information, that is pictures and videos, have not been previously collected, automatically processed and practically used to improve maps produced with satellite technologies in the context of emergency management.

While there exists a vast body of literature either on social media and emergency management, or on crowdsourcing and emergency management, there is a lack of experiences and technologies that allow the conjunct exploitation of social media and crowdsourcing in the context of emergency management in the early warning and rapid mapping phases. Technical research aimed to provide integrated Social and Crowd solutions has also been explicitly called for in the pivotal survey paper published in [6].

3 Automated Extraction and Geolocation of Social Media Content

Rapid mapping can significantly benefit from associating a location to the extracted multimedia, especially images. However, this association is often challenging. Most social media allow users to *geotag* the items that they post (that is, attaching a geographical location to the items in the form of metadata), but, in practice, only a small percentage of the content posted on social media is geotagged. For example, it is estimated that, on average, only the 0.5–2% of tweets are geotagged [2, 7], but could be lower than that in specific and particularly unfortunate emergency contexts [4]. Moreover, the location associated to a content, such as an image, does not necessarily coincide with the location of the post, leading to interpretation errors. Many social media, including Twitter, process images when uploaded by removing the associated location-related metadata and, therefore, a common solution is to infer the location of an image based on the location associated with the related post (*tweet*) [2].

Focusing on natively geotagged content would limit the number of images available for rapid mapping, potentially excluding the bulk of the useful multimedia content. Being able to increase the percentage of posts with geolocation information could be extremely helpful. Assigning a location to an item can be based on both implicit and explicit geographical references contained in the item. Indeed, "while explicit metadata about locations may be absent, many messages in social media do contain implicit references to names of places" [6].

In [5], authors discuss the feasibility of geolocating images shared on Twitter messages by extracting implicit geographical references from the text of the tweet, and highlight a correlation existing between text features and image features. A traditional pipeline setting has been employed, based on a *recognition* phase, where location names are recognized in the text, followed by a *disambiguation* (or *geocoding*) phase, where location names are geocoded according to the locations they refer to. Besides the challenges related to the usefulness of the extracted locations, like their precision, accuracy and credibility, the extraction phase is challenging and introduces errors (false positives and false negatives), due to ambiguities which exist between location names and other proper or common names. These are called *geo/non-geo* ambiguities, such as the Italian city called None, which coincides with a very common word in the English language. There are also ambiguities among location names themselves (*geo/geo* ambiguities, as in London, UK; London, ON, Canada; London, OH, USA; London, TX, USA; London, CA, USA) [7].

To overcome these problems, the idea of using implicit geographical references has been refined by taking into account the social network of a post to obtain an *additional context* potentially useful in overcoming ambiguities and, at the same time, privilege the extraction of locations related to the target event [10].

The algorithm selects a set of candidate locations for each tweet, identified as the *n*-grams which potentially refer to a location. In the current implementation, they are obtained using high-recall NER (Named-Entity Recognition) with multi-language capabilities [1, 9], but, in general, they could also include other kinds of candidates, such as *n*-grams matching predefined patterns. Then, the algorithm tries to disambiguate candidate locations by building a *local* context, that is searching for geographical correlations among candidate locations. Only the locations for which it is possible to find a correlation are disambiguated, while the others are considered ambiguous. This technique is traditionally used for longer and context-rich documents, like web pages, but the short and decontextualized nature of tweets tends to reduce its effectiveness. Working on a case study (the earthquake that struck central Italy in August 2016), we have found that less than 4% of tweets have locations that can be disambiguated by building a local context. We have extended the algorithm to connect tweets in a *behavioral social network*, that is a social network based on implicit interactions among messages rather than explicit relationships among users [2]. In particular, tweets are connected if they share a similar content or belong to the same conversation. The social network provides an additional context by connecting tweets with both implicit and explicit relationships, thus building a *global* context. The global context overcomes the limits of the local contexts, allowing the disambiguation of their location or, alternatively, the inference of a related location if no locations are explicitly mentioned in the tweet's text.

The idea of leveraging a behavioral social network is very recent, but has been used successfully in other research areas, such as topic identification [8].

Using the global context, the algorithm is able to disambiguate locations in more than 20% of tweets with a precision >90% in the Italian earthquake case study. As

presunta vittima a #Saletta estratta viva dalle macerie poco fa! Ci sono ancora persone da tirare fuori, avanti così! #terremoto

- Saletta, Ferrara: population 1469
- **Saletta, Amatrice**: population 33

- Global context

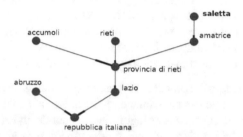

Fig. 1 Example of disambiguation of the location "Saletta" using the *global* context provided by other tweets in relationship

an example, let us consider the tweet in Fig. 1: the global context, below, is built using the neighbors of the tweet and allows not only the identification of "Saletta" as a location, but also the correct disambiguation of "Saletta" as a small town close to Amatrice, rather than one of the other more populated locations named "Saletta" that exist in Italy.

The algorithm is currently under development to further improve performance. Even if improving recognition, disambiguation and inference reduce geolocation errors, false positives/negatives cannot be totally avoided and represent an issue that can be successfully tackled with crowdsourcing (see Sect. 4).

Challenges are not only limited to the location extraction, but involve the extracted information itself: there exist a series of *imprecisions*, *uncertainties* and *ambiguities* in the information that can be extracted from Twitter, which evolves over time during an event. A content item (e.g., an image) can be re-posted at different points in time with a location information that can vary in *precision* (the granularity of the location) and *accuracy* (the likelihood that the data reflect the truth). Moreover, an item is not necessarily linked to a single user and, therefore, there could exist several versions of the same item which bring complementary or contradictory information. Also the correlation among the different items is not guaranteed: the image attached to a message could describe a different location with respect to the text, or could describe the right location, but be related to another previous event. When the same image is posted by several different users after an event with different descriptions, on one side, the different descriptions may allow increasing the precision and accuracy of geolocation information, on the other hand they can also create ambiguities that are difficult to be solved automatically when there is a conflict in the information provided by different authors. In Sect. 4, we discuss how crowdsourcing can help make decisions to solve the ambiguities in time-related information.

4   A Social and Crowd Methodology

This section describes a methodology combining social media analysis and crowd-sourcing for both Rapid Mapping and Early Warning components of the EMS. Additionally, this section describes the crowdsourcing contribution to overcome the limitations of automated analysis of social media content.

The Social and Crowd methodology is composed of the following processes:

1. **Data gathering** is the process of extracting relevant information for a given crisis event. Information can be obtained by the automatic analysis of social media, or by the crowd using browser plugins and/or mobile phone app.
2. **Automatic data validation and geolocalization** is an automatic process for establishing the relevance of the information gathered previously, and extract potential localization of the content as mentioned in Sect. 3.
3. **Crowdsourcing data validation and geolocalization** is a crowdsourcing process to validate the information extracted automatically for the social media analysis and solve disambiguations regarding potential locations.
4. **Information aggregation and visualization** merges the information coming from different sources and visualize it. Information gets ready to be used on the crisis management.

A more detailed information about the interaction between the different processes is presented in Fig. 2.

The combination of crowdsourcing with the automated analysis of social media information allows:

1. Reducing the amount of data gathered by the automated analysis of social media by filtering non-relevant data.
2. Increasing the data quality by contributing on the geolocalization process and solving disambiguation.
3. Increasing the relevant media information by allowing the crowd to inject media content in the system.

4.1   Reducing the Amount of Data

Automated analysis of social media information usually provide false positives, i.e., information not related for the crisis management. In this methodology we propose the use of crowdsourcing for the validation of the social information gathered from automatic analysis. Figure 3 shows an example of the crowdsourcing project where

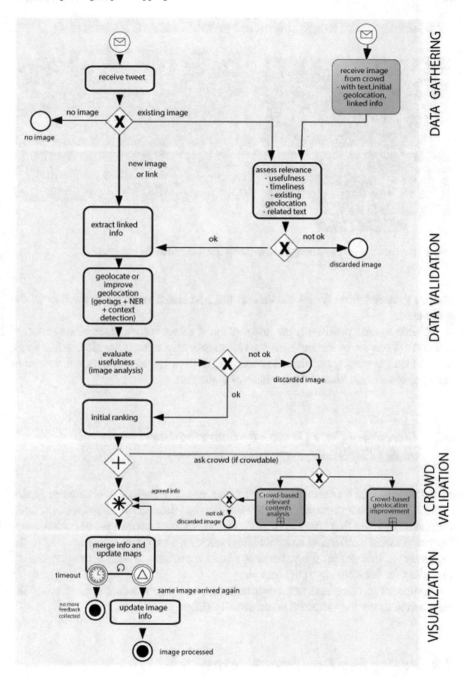

Fig. 2 S&C methodology

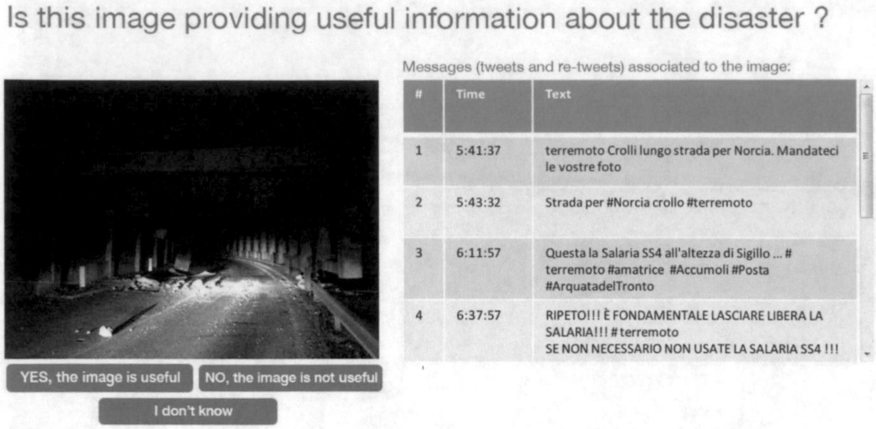

Is this image providing useful information about the disaster ?

Fig. 3   The crowd helps eliminating content that is not relevant to the emergency

images gathered from social media and the associated texts are presented to the volunteers.

Volunteers answer whether the information is relevant for a given crisis situation or is not. When an agreement between the answers from the crowd is reached (e.g., 8 out of ten answers agreed that the content is relevant), the information is moved to the aggregation and visualization phase or discarded.

4.2   Increasing Data Quality by Contributing on the Geolocalization Process

Many of the social media content such as images related with a crisis are not geolocalized. The automatic extraction of the location can produce different options, or an inaccurate location (e.g., region, or city). Figure 4 shows an example of crowdsourcing project where different candidate locations for a given image are provided to the volunteer. In this project the volunteers would contribute to reduce the uncertainty regarding the localization of the image.

Additionally, volunteers can contribute to add a more accurate location of the image than those one extracted automatically (Fig. 5).

4.3   Adding New Data from the Crowd

Automatic extraction of social media information related with a crisis is usually limited to the main social media platforms such as Twitter or Instagram, while many other channels remain unexplored. This unexplored channels would include blogs,

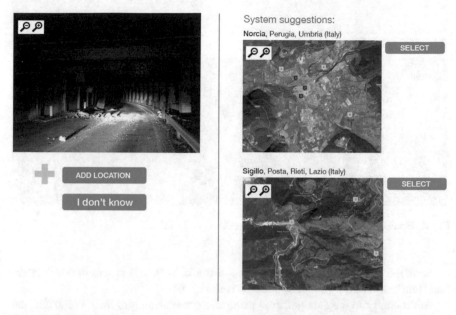

Fig. 4 The crowd helps geolocating content by selecting among possible locations proposed automatically by the geolocation algorithm

Fig. 5 The crowd geolocates content by proposing a location that is more precise than that proposed by the geolocation algorithm

online newspapers, or public email list. As already implemented by the GeoTag-X platform (https://geotagx.org/), a simple firefox plugin allows volunteers to quickly add information that they considering relevant for a crisis management. Just with one

Fig. 6 Firefox plugin (as developed by GeoTag-X)

click on the plugin, the link to the source of the information is sent to our database and transferred to the validation process (see Fig. 6).

Additionally to the data gathered using the browser plugin, local volunteers can contribute by submitting media content such a images and video relevant to the crisis. This media content can be submitted in two ways: (1) Simply tweeting it with a specific hashtag, or (2) using a specific mobile application. Using Twitter simplifies the process, but images metadata is automatically removed when the image is submitted. Moreover, the text related with the images is unstructured requiring text processing techniques to classify the media content. Using a mobile phone tools, such as Epicollect (http://www.epicollect.net/), allows sending the media content with metadata, attached position gathered from the mobile phone GPS and add a form attached with image where volunteers can help to provide extra information regarding the situation in that location. Figure 7 shows an example of Epicollect project for school assessment.

5 Conclusions

Images shared on social media can represent a fundamental aid to rapid mapping activities. Their relevance to mapping is dramatically increased by the availability of geolocation information. Unfortunately, this type of information is rarely available. Starting from the assumption that, at the current state of the art, algorithms can help geolocate multimedia content, but are not error free, a fundamental goal of the E^2mC project is to combine algorithms and crowdsourcing in a unified methodological approach. In turn, this approach will be supported by an integrated platform.

Fig. 7 Epicollect example

In this paper, we have presented the first step that the research team has taken to create a unified methodology that combined a software-based and a crowdsourcing approach to filter, disambiguate, classify, and geotag social media information for rapid mapping purposes. Our approach is innovative in that it is based on a novel geolocation algorithm that leverages the real-time, content-based connections among tweets. This algorithm can propose to the crowd a geolocation for a significant percentage of images. Working on the algorithm's output, the crowd can more easily validate and, if necessary, complement the algorithm's results. Even individuals who have no direct, personal knowledge of the location hit by the emergency can contribute to the improvement of the quality of the information that is then fed to the professionals performing the mapping tasks. In this paper, we have highlighted the questions to be forwarded to the crowd depending on the algorithm's output and we have organized the combined work of the algorithm and crowd in a unified information management process.

Acknowledgements This work has been partially funded by the European Commission H2020 project. E^{2}mC "Evolution of Emergency Copernicus services" under project No. 730082. This work expresses the opinions of the authors and not necessarily those of the European Commission. The European Commission is not liable for any use that may be made of the information contained in this work. The authors thank Paolo Ravanelli for his support in data management and software development.

References

1. Al-Rfou, R., Kulkarni, V., Perozzi, B., Skiena, S.: POLYGLOT-NER: massive multilingual named entity recognition. In: Proceedings of the 2015 SIAM International Conference on Data Mining, pp. 586–594 (2015)
2. Castillo, C.: Big Crisis Data: Social Media in Disasters and Time-Critical Situations. Cambridge University Press. New York, NY, USA (2016)
3. E^2mC Team: Critical review of crowdsourcing and social media use associated with Copernicus EMS service evolution challenges. Deliverable D1.1, public, Jan 2017
4. Francalanci, C., Pernici, B.: Data integration and quality requirements in emergency services. In: Lazovik, A., Schulte, S. (eds.) Advances in Service-Oriented and Cloud Computing. Communications in Computer and Information Science. Springer (2017)
5. Francalanci, C., Guglielmino, P., Montalcini, M., Scalia, G., Pernici, B.: IMEXT: a method and system to extract geolocated images from Tweets—analysis of a case study. In: IEEE RCIS'17, Brighton, UK, May 2017
6. Imran, M., Castillo, C., Diaz, F., Vieweg, S.: Processing social media messages in mass emergency: a survey. ACM Comput. Surv. (CSUR) **47**(4), 67 (2015)
7. Inkpen, D., Liu, J., Farzindar, A., Kazemi, F., Ghazi, D.: Detecting and disambiguating locations mentioned in Twitter messages. In: International Conference on Intelligent Text Processing and Computational Linguistics, pp. 321–332. Springer (2015)
8. Nugroho, R., Yang, J., Zhao, W., Paris, C., Nepal, S.: What and With Whom? Identifying Topics in Twitter Through Both Interactions and Text. IEEE TSC, in press (2017)
9. Sakaki, T., Okazaki, M., Matsuo, Y.: Tweet analysis for real-time event detection and earthquake reporting system development. IEEE TKDE **25**(4), 919–931 (2013)
10. Scalia, G.: Network-based content geolocation on social media for emergency management. Master's Thesis, Politecnico di Milano, April 2017

Potential Difficulties During Investigations Due to Solid State Drive (SSD) Technology

James Cox and Peter Bednar

Abstract This paper discusses potential complications for Forensic Investigations due to the spread of Solid State Disc (SSD) technologies and influence of socio-technical factors. The discussion is drawing upon a study based on interviews with an experienced Forensic Investigator from Hampshire Constabularies Hi-Tech Crime Unit (HTCU), located in the United Kingdom. The goal of this study was to identify examples of what experienced forensic investigators believe the biggest drawbacks with examining SSDs are. Background case studies have been made in assistance to identify specific characteristics and features that may impact forensic investigations. Key characteristics include that SSD features may pose a threat as potential evidence can be rendered inaccessible; possibly impacting the case or project negatively. The main themes discussed in this paper are related to: Hardware-based encryption, Garbage Collection (GC), the TRIM command, Controller technology, SSD Interfaces, and SSD User needs. Socio-technical influences were acknowledged during the interviews with the Investigator, showing uncertainty to alternative Forensic methods. These themes have been scrutinized to identify how they impact and limit Investigations.

Keywords Socio-technical · Solid state drives (SSDs) · Digital forensic investigations

J. Cox (✉) · P. Bednar
School of Computing, University of Portsmouth, Portsmouth, UK
e-mail: jamesalcox@googlemail.com

P. Bednar (✉)
Department of Informatics, Lund University, Lund, Sweden
e-mail: peter.bednar@port.ac.uk

© Springer International Publishing AG, part of Springer Nature 2019   75
F. Cabitza et al. (eds.), *Organizing for the Digital World*, Lecture Notes in Information
Systems and Organisation 28, https://doi.org/10.1007/978-3-319-90503-7_7

1 Introduction

It is unclear what potential threats Solid State Disc's (SSDs) technologies may cause to Digital Forensic Investigations due to them being a changing technology which commonly replace Hard Disk Drives (HDD). SSD technology is becoming more common within the technological world [12]. *"The adoption of flash-based SSDs in laptops and desktop computers continues at pace and continues to eat into traditional HDD applications"*. This means that conventional HDD technologies are becoming replaced, as SSD popularity is growing. SSDs have faster processing speeds, and less power consumption than HDDs [33, p. 18], suggesting that SSDs are superior alternatives in more and more use cases.

However, compared to HDD, the behavior and characteristics of SSDs may in practice make SSDs unexpectedly unpredictable, as implied by Gubanov and Afonin [7]. These authors suggest that (in comparison with HDDs) conducting investigations on SSDs have always been a challenge for Forensic Investigators, comparing investigations of SSDs to the Schrödinger's Cat theory, in that *"one will never know if the cat is alive before opening the box"*. In context of forensic investigations, this concerns the recovery of data from an SSD after a quick format has commenced, meaning that you do not know what you will find (the data may be there or not). This is just one of the many anomalies that surround SSDs.

Socio-technical factors is a complementary reason for why potential problems occur during investigations. Whitworth [34, p. 394] defines the term socio-technical systems (STS) as the combination of social and technical needs. To assist with his point, he uses an example of a pilot and a plane that are *"side-by-side systems with different needs, one mechanical (plane) and one human (pilot)"*. The author goes onto explain that *"Human Computer Interaction (HCI) suggests these systems should interact positively to succeed"*. Like the pilot, a Forensic Investigator will interact with their machine (the computer) and will have to do this successfully to complete investigations. *"As computing evolved, the problems it faced changed"* [34, p. 394]. SSDs may have an appearance of functionality like HDDs, but are a development in technology and a change from the conventional HDD application with changed technology [12]. This suggests that an evolution in Digital Forensic methods is needed by Investigators. Additionally, it is not known what socio-technical implications exist because of the changed technology. Investigators can be very experienced in HDD technologies and too busy to pay closer attention to all the revolutionary changes and implications of SSD technologies which replaces HDD in practice. Expectations, competence, skills, tools, resources and methods are all influencing the socio-technical practices of professional investigators.

The aim of this paper is to find examples of what potential difficulties occur (and why) during Investigations, while also looking at potential issues due to technical influences of SSDs, with an added socio-technical baring. This study is drawing upon interviews of an experienced expert forensic investigator. An additional exploration has been made into SSD technology to assist with this, as by understanding the influences that SSDs have, appropriate steps can be taken to restrict these effects on future investigations. To help accomplish the aim, this paper will briefly reflect on examples of how Forensic Tools made for data recovery on HDDs behave when being used for data recover on SSD instead, what the different technologies incorporated into SSDs are, what features (specifications) SSDs possess that cause potential impacts, what influence Operating Systems (OSs) have on SSD technology, and how these different factors can cause socio-technical influences that can limit examinations.

2 Background

There is very little previous research in this area, but some has considered comparisons between SSDs and HDDs features. "*SSDs are a game changer for Forensic Investigators*" [35], as SSDs store data "*in a manner which seems to randomly place sectors of any file in any physical sector*". Simply, this means that there is no simple system in which memory allocation is storing data, as it is random. Current Forensic Tools which our interviewed investigators are familiar with have all been tailored with the primary purpose to conduct investigations on HDDs, meaning that they may not be compatible with recovery processes for SSDs as the technology is different; for example, the data mapping. Investigators too may not be accustomed with investigating SSDs, causing socio-technical limitations to arise, as their knowledge of SSD technology can be limited.

Solid State Drives, as the name suggests, do not rely on any moving parts [8]. "*Data is saved to a pool of NAND flash*" and the "*NAND itself is made up of what are called floating gate transistors*". This is very different to the way HDDs magnetically write and store data. Sieber [24] shares her explanation of what happens when a HDD has been "*quick formatted*" and overwritten. She expresses that data "*is not physically deleted during formatting*", but the data is marked for overwrite. The drive then waits until the area on the HDD is required for reuse before the existing data is physically removed. Once overwritten, this is an irreversible step and the lost data cannot be restored. This is extremely different to an SSD: the memory allocation process for an SSD is organised in a '*grid*' format, referred to as a '*block*' [8]. This '*block*' is made up of individual rows called a '*page*'. Once data is deleted it is erased physically using background "*garbage collection*" processes rather than being marked for overwrite. Figure 1 shows the memory allocation process for an SSD.

Regarding HDDs, "*there are two different technologies for recording data*" [24]. Both of which have identical principles, that use magnetic fields to write data to a disk (platter), via a recording head (actuator). The most modern technology emerged post 2005 in which the recording layer was modified in a perpendicular orientation. This meant that the binary code was represented by an upwards and downwards magnetisation. An additional layer was added below the recording layer of the drive to assist with this capability. As a result, the HDD storage capacities where enhanced as more data could fit on the platter. Figures 2 show a representation of the newest HDD technology (Post 2005).

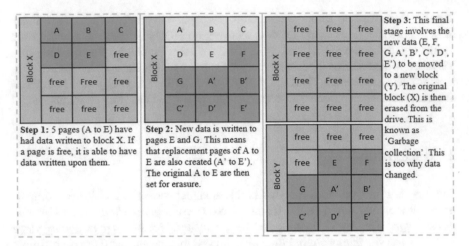

Fig. 1 Memory allocation process for an SSD

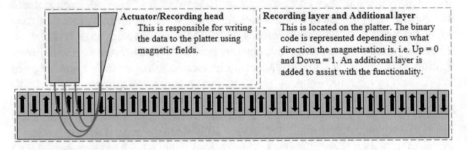

Fig. 2 HDD technology post 2005

To assist the research presented in this paper, a background study included an inquiry into the 25 of the most popular SSDs (in accordance to a selection of technology reviewing websites). The purpose of this was to help identify notable features that may implement a Forensic investigation and compliment explanations in the following sections. This research will therefore be referred to as the 'SSD support study' throughout the rest of this paper and the results of this research will be highlighted at relevant stages as support. The features considered in this SSD support study include, encryption; chipset (i.e. Controller, Interface, NAND); write/erase cycles; data transfer speeds (read/write); storage; SSD software, and special features (i.e. TRIM). The 'SSD support study' looked at the following SSDs:

- Samsung 850 EVO, 840/850 PRO
- Toshiba Q300
- SanDisk Extreme PRO
- Kingston KC400 SSDNow
- WD Blue SSD

- PNY CS2211
- OCZ ARC 100
- Kingston HyperX Savage
- Intel 600p
- Samsung SM961
- Toshiba OCZ VX500 SSD
- Patriot Hellfire M.2 NVMe
- Intel 520
- OCZ Vertex 450
- Transcend SSD 720
- AData XPG SX900
- Seagate 600
- SanDisk Extreme II
- Corsair Neutron GTX
- Crucial M500, MX200/300 and BX200.

Bednar and Katos [2] talk about '*garbage collection*' (GC) and how it uses '*House-keeping algorithms*' to "*manage erasure of data that is no longer valid, to prepare a cell for reuse*". Other utilities such as the TRIM command may play a role in this process by marking data blocks for erasure. TRIM is an Operating System (OS) based command and may not operate on SSDs without the OS being localized to the drive. However, this can still pose a threat to investigations as TRIM will be active on SSDs holding modern OSs from Windows 7 onwards [3]. Tian et al. [29, pp. 121–124] support this claim with an experiment, involving a primary SSD (holding the OS), a secondary SSD and a third USB SSD (both not holding the OS). This experiment entails SSDs retaining JPEG images until the capacities are filled, to which they were then quick-formatted and recovered, proving data can be retrieved from SSDs not holding post Windows 7 OS' [29]. SSD Housekeeping operations are all conducted from the SSD Controller. Telecomsys.com [28, p. 1] defines an SSD controller as "*the heart and brains of the system*". "*It implements in its hardware and firmware, the storage protocol commands, and other functions that provide for the reliable storage*" [28, p. 1]. Regarding the effect on an investigation, the Controller will implement GC algorithms with the assistance of TRIM or TRIM equivalent software, meaning, potential evidence may be erased. TRIM causes a lot of vital data to become unrecoverable for Investigators and they may not know of alternative processes to recover the data, showing clear socio-technical drawbacks.

It is important to understand the effect interfaces have on SSDs, as some entities, like TRIM, can influence SSDs and the data recovered from them, depending on their interfaces [3]. Although, this is just one example. The 'SSD support study' revealing that, one of the main impacts Interfaces have on investigations stems from the port compatibility. Such interfaces as ATA/IDE are older and usually incompatible with current SSD interface ports (without conversion). The SSD support study demonstrated that interfaces, particularly SATA (and M.2 less so), are far more common. This means that SATA ports can easily connect to Forensic equipment to be examined, as these are the most common '*standard*' interfaces.

While SATA dominates, other interfaces must not be ignored, as these are ones Investigators will have trouble with. The additional question, therefore, is how do (if at all) interfaces like PCIe and NVMe potentially influence the Forensic Investigation? (See Sect. 3.)

Another potential issue is related to the process the SSD Controller is responsible for. For example, the handling of *"wear levelling to even the access across the NAND and extend the life of the SSD in the face of flash wear out"* [28, p. 1]. *"SSDs have duty-cycles and lifespan limitations"* [27], meaning that SSDs have a capacity to the times that data can be written. *"Often listed in Total Bytes Written or Bytes Per Day, directly affect how many times the flash memory can be written to"* [27], therefore, eventually becoming un-writable and an SSD may fail. A disadvantage is evident, as data can possibly be unrecoverable. This was not the first technology to have this limitation: the *'old-fashioned'* audio and video cassette tapes *"get damaged after some time due to regular usage"* [14], much like that of an SSD. Cassette tapes are considered as *"electronic and digital evidence"* [6, p. 555], meaning, that this may have been a problem during examinations long before SSDs, but on another technology, all together. Perhaps this has always been a problem for Investigators and the emergence of SSDs have added to a growing problem. But considering that tapes are not commonly used anymore many investigators might not have any practical experience of related difficulties. Clearly, lack of experience and suitable tools do add a significant amount of uncertainty to the investigation.

Regarding SSD technology, *"standard flash lifetimes are up to 100,000 cycles per block before failure is possible"* [35]. Depending on the application of the SSD and type of NAND memory, cycles can vary. The 'SSD support study' presented that a majority of SSDs offered Multi-Level Cell (MLC) NAND, which only has capabilities of approximately *"3,000–15,000 write/erase cycles"* [10]. Single Level Cell (SLC) NAND has approximately *"100,000"* [10] cycles. This is the largest amount of write cycles but none of the popular SSDs in accordance to the study have this type of NAND. It is possible that some user needs will result in disk failures, as all write cycles will be used up at a much faster rate. In addition, Triple Level Cell (TLC) NAND flash has *"1,000–5,000 write/erase cycles"* [10]. Only a handful of SSDs looked at have TLC NAND, meaning some user needs for these SSDs may not be suitable in some situations (i.e. a business application [25]). Business systems require large amount of data being shifted to and from them over their lifetime [17, p. 6]. Intel Corp has conducted an experiment, that entails employees having their notebooks fitted with SSDs instead of HDDs [17, p. 6], and then monitored and recorded over a 3-year period. SSDs *"have a shorter lifespan than Hard Drives"* [5] because of them utilising their write cycles. While at the same time this is self-contradictory as modern SSDs for many home users normally would be expected to have a longer life span than their actual computer (home computers tend to have many more read cycles than write cycles under normal usage).

"Encryption or destroying sensitive information on hard drives was straightforward, locate the data and overwrite the bits" [36]. This, however, is not the case with SSDs due to *"wear-levelling algorithms"* changing their data structure; meaning another approach has taken place to encrypt SSDs. *"Hardware-based encryption"*

has been incorporated into SSDs, using such strategies as *"Advanced Encryption Standard (AES)"* encryption. This is unlike *"software-based encryption"* [36] such as BitLocker (Windows' encryption software), as the hardware-based encryption *"is handled by a dedicated cryptoprocessor on the drive"*. This author explains further that *"all user space data, including the operating system, is completely inaccessible until the user is authenticated"*. If an Investigator was trying to gain access to the data located in the user space, they cannot without authentication. *"Modern encrypted SSDs us a 128 or 256-bit AES algorithm along with two symmetric encryption keys"* [36], meaning, that two keys are required. One key is the user key (*"Authorization Key"*), and the other is the key located on the Controller chip (*"the 256-bit number generated randomly"*).

3   Analysis of Findings (The Interviews)

Only a minority of entities thought to affect Investigations on SSDs have already been identified. The aim of this paper is to show all the potential problems with investigating SSDs and recognize why these complications happen. To do this, a series of semi-structured interviews with a competent Forensic Investigator from the HTCU (High Tech Crime Unit) with years of experience has ensued, in which pre-made topic questions were focused on. Notable discussions believed to help identify what the potential implications to investigations are have been recorded. Examples of thought-provoking answers which stand out in our interviews have been selected and discussed in Sect. 4. While the interviews only draw upon the ideas of a single individual, arguably creating an element of significant limitations and bias, they nonetheless reflect the experiences of a highly skilled senior expert in the field, who has encountered many issues while investigating SSDs and HDDs for many years. Therefore, the findings from the interviews have a degree of validity and certainly are of significance for our research topic especially when related to other research and the reflections on the state of contemporary SSD technologies and their common use.

3.1   The Initial Verdict

In assistance from the interviews and background research, several key points that may be issues during investigations have been uncovered, including:

- TRIM marking data for erasure
- Controllers implementing Garbage collection and removing data
- Hardware-based encryption built into SSDs, encoding the data so its unreadable
- Interface incompatibility even if plug-in cards are present due to drivers not being present. The data can therefore not be accessed

- A user implication due to write/erase cycles being utilised until the drive fails. The data once again cannot be accessed
- Investigators not knowing of any alternative methods or tools to examine SSDs.

The Investigator expressed that "*the biggest limitation SSDs have during investigations are the effects of Garbage Collection*". The Investigator describes TRIM as a hindrance on investigations, as this is responsible for data marking, which is used to assist in the erasure of vast amounts of data that may hold potential evidence. After querying whether Controllers held a larger impact over TRIM, he proposed that this was not the case. TRIM is a common accordance on SSDs encountered by him, as he explains "*only the best and most modern SSDs hold Controller technology able to surpass the performance of TRIM*". He believes "*Controllers will be a huge factor in future investigations, due to technology advancing, taking on and outperforming TRIM processes*" The Forensic Investigator expressed that to, entirely remove this implication, "*GC would have to be disabled once the drive is powered on. Data remnants can then be recovered*". Furthermore, he presents that "*TRIM changes data as soon as power is presented to the drive*". Changing data was against practice, causing the investigation to be rendered redundant in a court of law. This was until a change was made to Association of Chief Police (ACPO) guidelines, that a "*competent Investigator will have to explain this change to the data*". The Investigator expressed an idea that "*TRIM and GC would have to be disabled once the drive is powered on. Data remnants can then be recovered*", and this (it is hoped) will then solve the issue.

The Investigator has highlighted that there are no current Forensic Tools (that he knows of), which are specifically tailored for a Solid-State Drives. He explains "*there are no different forensic processes that are used for SSDs in comparison to HDD procedures*". This itself is a clear warning sign that highlights a potential limitation during examinations. Additionally, he expresses that the Forensic Tools used by him at the HTCU include (Table 1).

Table 1 Forensic tools used by the investigator at the HTCU

Forensic tool	Company
EnCase v7 and v8	Guidance software
FTK imager	Access data
MacQuisition	Black bag technologies
Internet evidence finder (IEF)	Magnet forensics
NVU	NVU
Virtual forensic computing (VFC 3)	MD5
VMware workstation 10	VMware inc
Categorizer for ALL (C4ALL)	Royal canadian mounted police (Trevor Fairchild)
NetClean analyze	Griffeye

The Investigator explains that the *"non-SATA based SSD interfaces are a rarity"*. From his experience, *"when interfaces such as; PCIe are encountered, there is no issues with connecting them* via *a converter card into the write blocker"*. The only limitation he has encountered with this is that older interfaces, such as ATA, may have connectivity issues due to limited resources. SSD encryption was another topic raised to the Investigator. The Investigator states *"encryption can be an issue during investigation, but only if the suspect is not willing to part with their encryption key"*. Therefore, the Investigator is not able to decrypt data, making it unreadable, halting the examination until this key is obtained.

All points explained in this section will assist with an evaluation in the following section to help conclude with what the potential problems are during examinations.

4 Evaluation

To support an idea of the situation and assist with further technical discussions, the key issues in investigating SSDs have been identified. Short explanations have been used to show how the issues may be encountered by Investigators (Table 2).

4.1 Controllers Making TRIM Obsolete

TRIM can have a direct correlation to issues during examinations, as demonstrated during the interviews. TRIM and background GC should not be construed as being the same thing, stating *"TRIM is a hybrid technology intended to allow SSDs to work more efficiently"* [2]. The Investigator explained that TRIM was responsible for modifying evidence, as the hash, which is used to monitor data change, was altered because of data erasure from GC. As explored earlier TRIM may still indulge in OS (Windows 7 onwards) based SSDs, meaning TRIM is still something to be mindful of. Moreover, TRIM management software can be used to disable TRIM to enhance SSD performance [32]. Therefore, ensuring that data is not set for erasure. Considering all these factors, it can be suggested that it is rather *"hit and miss"* regarding whether data can be recovered, as one would not know if TRIM is active or not.

"Existing features of TRIM could be dealt with in the background by the onboard SSD controller" [2, p. 5]. The Investigator expressed a similar concern. A Controller chip is located on every SSD, as demonstrated by the 'SSD support study'. This means that the risk of data marking for erasure is now not limited to OS based SSDs (i.e. TRIM SSDs). Modern SSDs may not have a requirement for TRIM, as *"if your controller has good onboard garbage collection algorithms, you should be fine even without TRIM"* [9]. To justify this, most controllers have *"refresh"* [9] abilities specific for non-TRIM environments. Having said, all SSDs in the 'SSD support study' supported TRIM, insinuating that their own Controller algorithms are not yet

Table 2 Key issues with investigating SSDs

Key issues	Situations under which these may be encountered by investigators
Interfaces (i.e. SATA, M.2, PCI-E) having compatibility issues	SSDs as demonstrated by the 'SSD support study' come in a variety of interfaces; most commonly SATA. As explored previously, if an NVMe Interface SSD was to be encountered by an Investigator they may not be able to investigate it, due to incompatibility with the Forensic equipment
TRIM marking data for erasure	TRIM may have implemented its processes and marked data blocks for erasure. When the investigation has started and power is resumed to the drive, these actions would be picked up by the controller, subsequently implementing the garbage collection algorithms. This therefore results in data (potential evidence) being permanently erased. Controllers will develop and take control of this process entirely
Controllers implementing GC and taking over from TRIM	
Encryption/Hardware based encryption Securing data	The suspect in question may have prior to the seizure of evidence encrypted their drive, causing the Investigator to not have access to the data without the encryption key being present, resulting in potential evidence not being accessible or uncoverable
Disk failures (due to the utilisation of write cycles)	As previously explored, if an SSD was in an application that was demanding on its data (i.e. a business application that required the writing and erasure of data) write/erasure cycles can be used up, therefore, causing the failure of drives. If an SSD was seized and it has failed due to this, the potential evidence on the drive is inaccessible for the Investigator
Limited knowledge of SSD specific forensic tools	If an investigation was to transpire and the Investigator has no knowledge of SSD specific Forensic Tools, SSDs could be examined inappropriately, causing other limitations to arise. For instance, data change, which is against the ACPO guidelines. If the SSD was examined under the same conditions as a HDD, using HDD specific Tools, potential evidence may not even come to light. SSDs are themselves a different technology and it is unknown how they act under SSD specific tools

superior. However, the SandForce Controller feature technology called "*DuraWrite*" [4], which along with a certain amount of overprovisioning, has the capabilities to outperform TRIM. Over-provisioning is "*the inclusion of extra storage capacity in a solid-state drive*" [21]. This is essentially a percentage of a SSDs storage space dedicated to other programs to assist with performance. Depending on the Controller and the features it offers, some SSDs can outperform TRIM, as acknowledged by the Investigator. He explains that features are developing and older Controllers rely on TRIM to assist in data marking. When it comes to the actual investigation, it is difficult to know exactly what the Investigator is dealing with. Gubanov and Afonin [7] were not wrong to compare conducting investigations of SSDs to the Schrödinger's Cat theory.

At the point of obtaining the SSD for examination, TRIM (or an equivalent Controller feature) may have already been implemented. "*An SSD drive connected* via *a write blocking device will continue performing background garbage collection, possibly destroying the last remnants of deleted information from the disk*" [7]. The Investigators idea to disable GC would counter this problem, but as it stands, TRIM and Controller technology marking data blocks and implementing GC is a significant limitation for Investigators that will perpetuate as Controllers will evolve and begin to outperform TRIM. This, therefore, is a growing area of uncertainty that will no doubt continue to cause potential issues for investigations, and without adequate future training in this to understand the developed technology, socio-technical limitations will arise.

4.2 SSD Interface Incompatibility

Landsman [15, p. 4] shows a block diagram of a PCIe SSD that has 3 paths to 3 different interface Controllers. Path 1 leads to the SATA Controller, path 2 to the ACHI (PCIe) Controller, and path 3 to the NVMe Controller ("*accessed through the NVMe driver—installed on the system with the device*"). This is an example of an SSD that needs specific drivers to run as a specific interface. It can be suggested that this may be the case on other SSDs. As established previously, SATA can be implied as the standard Interface. If a PCIe SSD does not have a SATA driver, this will not work in a converter card, rendering data inaccessible and the drive cannot be found during examinations. This may not be the case with M.2 SSDs via PCIe and SATA interfaces as they all use the same "*AHCI driver built into the OS*" [16]. If the SSD is not detected by the system, the M.2 interface may need to be enabled in the system Basic Input Output System (BIOS), to be used. If a M.2 SSD was to be connected via a SATA plug-in card, the host system may not support the interface protocol and will not be found by the BIOS. This may vary depending on what system is used, as some systems may support the interface protocol via SATA ports (and vice versa), while others cannot. So, while SSDs may be connected with converters the assumption that they can therefore be accessed may not necessarily always be true.

SoInfected [26] explains that they have had an issue with their M.2 SSD. They expressed that the "*X99 Motherboards are not yet able to create RAID with M.2 drives*" and motherboards with such "*Z170 chipsets*" only currently have this capability. This again implies that interface incompatibility is only an issue with certain chipsets. Chipsets are "*the name given to the set of chips used on the motherboard*" [30]. The Investigator clarified that he personally has not had an issue with the SSDs not being detectable. This suggests that the chipset on his motherboard can support Redundant Array of Independent Disks (RAID) for the SSD interfaces he has encountered. RAID is essentially a technology that combines numerous drives in a single component [22]. If the situation of incompatibility were to arise during an investigation, a simple solution would be to use another motherboard that supports RAID for the SSDs interface being examined. Although, this new motherboard may not be accessible, causing socio-technical limitations during investigations as the Investigator will be caught in an impasse with the examination. Additionally, there is an issue with PCI based SSD's which use their own brand dependent interfaces (including hardware connectors on their SSD daughter cards) while access is dealt with via their own software. Such SSD's cannot be accessed without the specific hardware connectors *and* their management software (which can be operating system dependent). Such interfaces and software may not be overcome with software available from third parties. It would create difficulties when SSD's are investigated separately from the computer where they were installed.

4.3   *User Needs and Write Cycles*

The 'SSD support study' demonstrates most SSDs analysed have a write/erase cycle of "*3,000–15,000*" [10], due to them being MLC NAND. A suggestion can be made that these write cycles can eventually run out, causing the drive to fail [18]. Ngo [18] compares SSD write cycles *writing on a piece of paper*", suggesting that you can erase the writing so many times until the "*paper becomes worn out or even torn*". No more information can be written down onto the piece of paper, similarly to that of an SSD: if an investigation was to be conducted on a worn out SSD, it may have failed and no data can be recovered. As demonstrated earlier in this paper, some applications can themselves cause this limitation. A business application for example may require high volumes of data written, every day, over a long period of time, eventually maxing out the NAND write/erase cycles. While SSD write/erase cycles running out are a reality, this may not be a concern with regards to investigations. Bamburic [1] says, high demand users of an SSD would not come close to reaching its write/erase cycle limits. This author presents a test conducted on the "*HyperX 3K and the 840 Pro*" SSDs, explaining that they would not exceed their write/erase cycles limit until around "*2 petabytes*". This is equivalent to "*2,097,152 GB of data*". To add to this, he explains over a 10-year period, this would be "*574.4 GB*" of data each day.

SSD failure rates are an unlikely phenomenon, as shown from a test describe by Intel which states "*SSDs have a 90% lower failure rate than HDDs over a 3-year period*" [17, p. 6]. This, however, does not guarantee that SSDs are impervious to failures. SSDs failing because of write/erase cycles running out are simply less of a threat Investigators may face during investigations.

4.4   SSD Hardware-Based Encryption

AES-256 Bit encryption is supported by a large percentage of SSDs, in accordance to the 'SSD support study'. The Investigator stressed that this is a problem during investigations, especially if the suspect in question refuses to hand over their encryption key. Certain laws, such as the Regulation of Investigatory Powers Act 2000 (RIPA) and the Investigatory Powers Act 2016 [11, p. 193], "*gives the UK power to authorities to compel the disclosure of encryption keys or decryption of encrypted data by way of a section 49 notice*" [19]. The Investigatory Powers Act 2016 has adapted RIPA within its legislation with the same section 49 notice strategy [20]. If the suspect in question complies, this issue is thereby not a problem during investigations. The suspect, however, may not comply and refuse to give up the key or decrypt the data. "*Refusal to comply can result in a maximum sentence of two years imprisonment*" and the data cannot be examined. The person in question may see the threat of a 2-year sentence more appealing than that of a longer sentence if incriminating evidence if found against them. Additionally, the charge of refusing to part with an encryption key may be more appealing to the suspect, if they know the alternative charge is worse (i.e. Regarding indecent images of children, "*the indecent images offences have a statutory maximum of five years' imprisonment for possession of images and 10 years' imprisonment for the distribution*" [23]). This would be a limitation for investigations and a requirement for another approach to counter this situation is needed. Additionally, this can be a socio-technical drawback as an Investigator may be unclear about alternative Digital Forensic procedures, as outlined during the interviews. Also, this does not address the problem when a suspect is not available.

As it stands, current procedures for overcoming encryption on drives (like SSDs) are clearly not 100% fool-proof and can perhaps be a gamble for attempting to retain potential evidence [13]. After the interviews with the Investigator, the current procedure to overcome impacts of encryption is shown to be more of an incentive to the suspect. Simply, if the suspect complies and hands over the key, they will not face potential sentencing time for failing to comply. While in some cases this is effective, the suspect may refuse to comply and the impact of encryption is not erased. Obviously the suspect might not know or be able to comply. Even with the current procedure, it is not adequate as it does not always conquer the problem. There are also examples of when for example anti-theft protection systems can re-encrypt content after specified time so that even the owner cannot access it anymore. But overall, it can be argued that it may be the more effective in comparison to other potential procedures such as: live acquisition, manipulation of volatile memory (RAM), and brute forcing [13]. Encryption, not only on SSDs, but in general, is a potential problem during investigations and there are no fool-proof procedures to avoid it. Maybe there should not be a guaranteed procedure to overcome encryption, as investigations can be done both for legitimate as well as for illegitimate purposes.

4.5   *Standalone SSD Forensic Tools and Processes*

The Interviews uncovered several socio-technical implications during investigations. For example, the Investigator has expressed uncertainty in relation to alternative Forensic methods to tackle SSD technology. Consequently, this can be a problem as there are no strategies to counter most of the mentioned issues, such as TRIM and Controllers implementing GC etc., causing potential evidence to be removed. This is a clear limitation in practice, as it shows adapted procedures and Forensic Tools are not inherently adapted to SSDs and only appear to support interactions with SSDs on a superficial level. While Hampshire Constabulary may not use specifically tailored SSD Forensic Tools or procedures, and the Investigator does not know of any, it doesn't mean none exist (although we did not find any explicit and dedicated solutions either). Gubanov and Afonin [7] present a possible solution to the effects of TRIM and GC during investigations, involving entirely disconnecting the built-in Controller that handles the GC algorithms. Custom hardware is used to implant the flash NAND from the SSD into a *"FPGA-based device"*, to which data recovery is then performed on the NAND using specialist software. Bednar and Katos [2, p. 4] suggests similar ideas, one of which is *"to disassemble the SSD and read the memory chips independently of the built-in controller"*. The other is to *"disassemble the controller and to exchange it with one especially designed for forensic investigations"*. This clearly shows that there are at least some examples of other means (even if tentative) of conducting investigations on SSDs but they are not evident in practice, explicit in methods and guidance documents, nor are they known by Investigators. In a sense, this is clear socio-technical restriction, as the Investigator lacks the knowhow of how to overcome these technical drawbacks and there appear not to be any explicit support available for the investigator to overcome the problematic situation. Subsequently causing a bigger problem that potential evidence is lost and questions are left unanswered during investigations. This is explored further in the conclusion of this paper.

5   Conclusion

This paper has identified several potential problems during investigations due to Solid State Drive (SSD) technology becoming more and more common and widespread replacement of HDD's. While most of these issues can be theoretically countered, this may not be the case in current practice, therefore we are outlining some of these as existing problems during investigations. These problems are:

- The implementation of Garbage Collection by Controllers and the assistance of, for example the TRIM command, resulting in the permanent erasure of potential evidence.
- The chipset influence causing incompatibility with various SSD interfaces, meaning the drive is undetectable by the PC and the investigations cannot progress or even take place.
- The effects of drive failures because of the maximum write/erase cycles being fulfilled, causing the drive to not work and therefore an examination cannot take place.
- The impacts of drive encryption causing inaccessibility to the SSD data, again meaning the investigation cannot progress or take place.
- The socio-technical implications of not knowing of alternative Forensic Tools and procedures within industry to conduct investigations on SSDs.

From a socio-technical point of view, the interviews showed an unawareness amongst modern Forensic practices (including tools, methods and guidance), in the way that one is unprepared for developing technology. As previously presented, the interviewee (Investigator) expressed that they are currently unaware of alternative methods to perform investigations on SSDs, and the procedures do not differ from that conducted on HDDs. There was also no available support guidance or methods we could find which address any of these potential issues. Bednar and Katos [2] too express this point, explaining that changes to the ACPO guidelines while good for live forensics, is not suitable for an SSD application. TRIM has been identified as a key limitation during investigations due to its data marking capabilities, causing vast amounts of potential evidence being erased by GC. This itself has been recognized to breach ACPO as this changes data, therefore, being the cause of a secondary limitation. Current Forensic Tools and procedures cannot change this from happening when SSDs are investigated. Unfamiliarity about SSD technology is shown along with a doubt of how to investigate them correctly. This is to the case when asking the Investigator about Interface compatibility, in which he stated that "*converter cards to SATA can be used to examine drives with other Interfaces (i.e. PCI-E)*". A disregard was made towards whether different Interface drivers are required to perform these examinations, as uncovered earlier in this paper. Without the correct Interface driver, the drive may not be visible and the examination is therefore meaningless, as no data can be obtained. It was also clear that many contemporary technologies had not yet appeared in investigations. This suggests socio-technical limitations as this shows unclarity with the Investigator understanding (for example) of Interface protocols, which can lead to halts in investigations.

Many of the points highlighted (i.e. TRIM and the ongoing evolution of more and more sophisticated Controller technology) throughout the paper by Bednar and Katos [2] are still a problem in modern practice today (6 years later in 2017), as demonstrated by the interviews with the Investigator from the HTCU. During the interviews, the Investigator mentioned that "*there is currently a 6 month back log of work at the HTCU, and this number will rise*", implying that there is little time to familiarise themselves with new technology as work demands are forever increasing. An article by Travis [31] highlights police budget cuts within the UK, showing examples of cuts in staffing, such as "*specialist armed police*". The Investigator mentioned that due to these cuts, "*no new Instigators are being employed to assist with the extra work load, and new training opportunities are a rarity, due to the financial cost*". This could mean that as time moves on, Investigators will become more unprepared for developing technology, uncovering more socio-technical implications, difficulties and conflicts of interest. These implications hypothetically being that a new technology (not only the developing SSD) will be involved in an examination and the current Forensic procedure will become even less adequate. The technology can already result in many unexpected alterations to the data (and recovery process), entirely compromising examinations and existing procedures might even mistakenly be breaching existing policies (i.e. ACPO). The investigator may not know what to do or how to fix the issue, rendering the examinations and the Investigator competencies redundant. Whitworth [34, p. 394] implies that technology is always evolving. If this is the case, SSDs too will develop and will continue to grow as an area of uncertainty. This growing problem will therefore require further research to improve Digital Forensic practices to keep up with the evolution of potential problems for forensic investigations.

References

1. Bamburic, M.: Modern SSDs can last a lifetime. https://betanews.com/2014/12/05/modern-ss ds-can-last-a-lifetime/
2. Bednar, P., Katos, V.: SSD: New challenges for digital forensics. In: ItAIS, pp. 4–5. Research Gate, Rome (2011)
3. Belkasoft: Recovering evidence from SSD drives in 2014: Understanding TRIM, Garbage Collection and Exclusions. https://articles.forensicfocus.com/2014/09/23/recovering-evidenc e-from-ssd-drives-in-2014-understanding-trim-garbage-collection-and-exclusions/
4. Ben, M., O.: With An OWC SSD, There's No Need For TRIM. https://blog.macsales.com/21 641-with-an-owc-ssd-theres-no-need-for-trim
5. Bonheur, K.: SSD: advantages and disadvantages of solid-state drive | Version Daily. http:// www.versiondaily.com/ssd-advantages-disadvantages-solid-state-drive/
6. Dutelle, A.: Introduction to Crime Scene Investigation. Jones & Bartlett Learning (2016)
7. Gubanov, Y., Afonin, O.: Why SSD Drives Destroy Court Evidence, and What Can Be Done About It. Belkasoft Ltd. (2012)
8. Hruska, J.: How Do SSDs Work?—ExtremeTech. https://www.extremetech.com/extreme/210 492-extremetech-explains-how-do-ssds-work
9. Hutchinson, L.: Ask Ars: "My SSD does garbage collection, so I don't need TRIM right?". https://arstechnica.co.uk/gadgets/2015/04/ask-ars-my-ssd-does-garbage-collection-s o-i-dont-need-trim-right/
10. Hyde, S.: TLC vs MLC vs SLC, performance, benchmarks and reliability. http://shawnhyde.c om/post/2013/09/11/TLC-vs-MLC-vs-SLC-Performance-benchmarks-and-reliability
11. Investigatory Powers Act 2016. TSO (The Stationery Office) (2016)
12. Kaese, R.: StorageNewsletter 2016 trends and driving forces in HDD and SSD. https://www.s toragenewsletter.com/2015/12/24/2016-trends-and-driving-forces-in-hdd-and-ssd/

13. Kaplan, B.: RAM is Key. Carnegie Mellon University (2007)
14. Kumar, V.: Pros and Cons of Cassette Player. http://www.sooperarticles.com/shopping-article s/appliances-articles/pros-cons-cassette-player-1200547.html
15. Landsman, D.: AHCI and NVMe as Interfaces for SATA Express™ Devices—Overview (2017)
16. M.2 FAQ|Kingston. https://www.kingston.com/en/ssd/system-builder/m2_faq
17. Micheloni, R., Marelli, A., Eshghi, K.: Inside Solid State Drives (SSDs). Springer, Dordrecht (2012)
18. Ngo, D.: Want your SSD to last a long time? Then do this. https://www.cnet.com/uk/how-to/h ow-ssds-solid-state-drives-work-increase-lifespan/
19. Regulation of Investigatory Powers Act 2000. The Stationery Office Limited (2000)
20. Regulation of Investigatory Powers Act 2000/Part III—ORG Wiki, https://wiki.openrightsgro up.org/wiki/Regulation_of_Investigatory_Powers_Act_2000/Part_III
21. Rouse, M.: What is overprovisioning (SSD overprovisioning)?—Definition from WhatIs.com. http://searchsolidstatestorage.techtarget.com/definition/over-provisioning-SSD-overprovisio ning
22. Rouse, M.: What is RAID (redundant array of independent disks)?—Definition from WhatIs.com. http://searchstorage.techtarget.com/definition/RAID
23. Section six: Indecent images of children
24. Sieber, T.: Why It Is Impossible To Recover Data From An Overwritten Hard Drive [Technology Explained]. http://www.makeuseof.com/tag/impossible-recover-data-overwritten-hard-drive-t echnology-explained/
25. Solid State Drives for Business | Samsung Business-Copy, http://www.samsung.com/us/busin ess/products/computing/solid-state-drives/
26. Solnfected: M.2 SSD not showing up in BIOS—[Solved]—Motherboards. http://www.tomsh ardware.co.uk/answers/id-2950809/ssd-showing-bios.html
27. Stanek, W.: Windows Server 2016: Installing & Configuring. Stanek & Associates (2016)
28. The Importance of SSD Controller Technology to the Defense and Avionics Indus- tries. http://www.telecomsys.com/Libraries/Collateral_Documents/SSD_Controller_Whitepa per.sflb.ashx
29. Tian, J., Jing, J., Srivatsa, M.: International Conference on Security and Privacy in Communi- cation Networks. Springer International Publishing (2015)
30. Torres, G.: Everything You Need to Know About Chipsets—Hardware Secrets. http://www.h ardwaresecrets.com/everything-you-need-to-know-about-chipsets/
31. Travis, A.: Simple numbers tell story of police cuts under Theresa May | Alan Travis. https://www.theguardian.com/uk-news/2017/jun/05/theresa-may-police-cuts-margare t-thatcher-budgets
32. Trim Enabler 4: Enable Trim And Maximize Your Mac SSD Performance. https://cindori.org/ trimenabler/
33. Wang, G., Zomaya, A., Martinez Perez, G., Li, K.: Algorithms and Architectures for Parallel Processing. Springer International Publishing, Cham (2015)
34. Whitworth, B.: A Brief Introduction to Sociotechnical Systems. IGI Global, Auckland (2008)
35. Wiebe, J.: Forensic Insight into Solid State Drives. http://www.forensicmag.com/article/2013/ 05/forensic-insight-solid-state-drives
36. Wu, C.: Securing SSDs with AES Disk Encryption. http://electronicdesign.com/memory/secu ring-ssds-aes-disk-encryption

AIS and MCS for Port Community Systems: An Empirical Analysis from Italy

Assunta Di Vaio, Luisa Varriale and Federico Alvino

Abstract This study investigates the role of Accounting Information Systems (AIS) and Management Control Systems (MCS) in the information management within seaports when an information technology platform has been adopted, such as the Port Community Systems (PCSs). We conducted a literature review on PCSs and on how AIS and MCS could contribute to the platform in order to support the decision-making processes of port players, like forwarder and shipping agents. Starting from previous studies focused on Italian seaports, by using the case study methodology, we collected data through semi-structured interviews to managers of the selected seaport. Indeed, we have outlined the usefulness in adopting AIS and MCS for PCSs in the forwarder and shipping agents perspective.

Keywords Port community system · Accounting information systems · Management control systems

1 Introduction

Over the last 30 years the seaports aim to increase the efficiency and the effectiveness. For achieving this goal, the port reforms developed four different port models. More

---

Large parts of this chapter are freely taken from previous study by Di Vaio A., Varriale L. (2017), "AIS and reporting in the port community systems: An Italian case study in the landlord port model" in Corsi, K., Castellano, N.G., Lamboglia, R., Mancini, D. (Eds.) Reshaping Accounting and Management Control Systems New Opportunities from Business Information Systems, Springer series: Lecture Notes in Information Systems and Organisation (LNISO), 20, pp. 153–165.

A. Di Vaio (✉) · L. Varriale · F. Alvino
University of Naples "Parthenope", Naples, Italy
e-mail: susy.divaio@uniparthenope.it

L. Varriale
e-mail: luisa.varriale@uniparthenope.it

F. Alvino
e-mail: federico.alvino@uniparthenope.it

specifically, the most widespread organizational form is represented by the landlord port where there is a distinctive separation between public (e.g. PA) and private (e.g. concessionaires) [1–6]. Hence, the information on traffic flows, managed by concessionaires and other port players, would be readily available and easily accessible for PA by responding to the requirements of its the control, coordination and promotion activities. In this perspective, in order to be and keep to be competitive for seaports it is crucial to adopt PCS. At the same time, the use of AIS in the relationships among the port players, and more specifically between these last and PA, that are averaged provided by PCS, could support PA in the decision-making process to develop the seaport.

Drawing from these contributions in the literature, this study aims to analyse the role of AIS and MCS in the information management where we observe the adoption of an information technology platform in the relationships system, such as the PC, characterizing the PCs. A literature review on the PCSs and AIS in PCSs has been conducted. Adopting a case study methodology, some semi-structured interviews to forwarders and shipping agents have been conducted that use the PCS implemented in seaports of "Seaport System Authority of South Adriatic Sea", including Bari, Brindisi, Manfredonia, Barletta e Monopoli. Due to the recent establishment of the "System Authority", this study focuses the attention mainly on seaports of Bari, Brindisi e Manfredonia, also known as seaports of Levante.

The paper is structured as follows: Sects. 2 and 3 focus on the analysis of PCS in the seaports literature. The Sect. 4 evidences the role of AIS in the PCS. Sections 5 and 6 outline the methodology adopted and the description of the case study. Finally, in the last section some results of the interviews have been investigated and some final considerations have been provided.

2   Literature Review

In the last 30 years, for facing the new challenges derived from the numerous changes occurred in the world, such as the high competitiveness of markets and the increasing innovativeness of the supply and demand, the seaports need to adopt the international regulations regarding the organizational and managerial models and information technologies (IT) in the decision-making process. The seaports have to manage specific criticisms concerning "the evolution of the international trade and container throughput, the introduction of ultra-large container vessels, the deep changes of customers' demand, and the development of IT, addressing the same seaports to assume a strategic position as 'hub ports'" [7].

With concern of the increasing role of IT by the seaports, these organizations need more and more to adopt IT tools for supporting all their processes, in particular, the requirements related to containerized and passengers traffic. The technology makes seaport users able to manage data and information with real time about cargo and passenger flows, availability of port facilities, and also IT supports ships and terminals to collaborate by working together, thus they assume a collaborative orientation as parts of an integrated office infrastructure [8]. In this perspective, seaports adopt IT tools for effectively and efficiently carrying out customs control [9]. Thus, in the seaports which implement IT, all the actors involved, that is terminal operators, port administration, customs, truckers, freight forwarders, carriers, ship agents, and other organization, are electronically linked by the IT systems, make better information and data sharing within the port community [8].

The Port Community Systems (PCSs) have been introduced for facilitating the communication process and the development of the inter-organizational relationships among the actors in the port community.

There are different and interesting definitions of PCSs concept in the literature with focus on role, functions, or their network nature. For example, Srour and colleagues [10: 3] defined PCSs as "holistic, geographically bounded information hubs in global supply chains that primarily serve the interest of a heterogeneous collective of port related companies". This definition concerns as the heterogeneous companies mainly the terminal operators, carriers (ocean, road, and rail), freight forwarders, enforcement agencies (i.e. customs), port authorities, various lobby groups (including workers' unions, environmentalists, and other policy makers), and also other shareholders of maritime transportation [10, 11]. Moreover, another definition of PCSs conceives them as "networks which link up the port with all the companies that use it" [12]. On the contrary, the European Port Community Systems Association [13] has conceptualized PCS as an electronic platform that allows at connecting the multiple systems operated by numerous organizations that make up a seaport community explaining the integration of each organization to the port community system [12, 14].

PCS allows "an easy, fast and efficient information exchange", that is Electronic Data Interchange (EDI) [15: 1]; "the customs declarations; the electronic management of all information about the handling operations in import and export; the traceability of the traffic flows along supply chain; the reporting and statistics, and so forth" [15]. Besides, PCS stimulates both collaboration and integration, allowing both members of the community to immediately access to relevant data, to interact and control data improving the quality of the same data among the stakeholders, and also preventing the replication of the same [16]. Likewise, according to Carlan and colleagues [17: 1] PCS has been defined as "an electronic platform which connects the multiple communication systems of each of its members". In this definition, the focus is on the main tasks related to PCS which concerns the improvement of the port operations efficiency, and the increase of the competitiveness along the supply chain, that needs the cooperation between private and public stakeholders.

Hence, thanks to PCSs it is possible to have a fast and safe exchange of information between both private and public organizations in order to improve the competitiveness of seaports [17, 18]. From this perspective, all the organizations have to efficiently and effectively collaborate to create the critical prerequisites for optimizing all the logistic processes using a single data submission [9].

PCSs play a fundamental function by consisting in making the users to manage the service required and directly upload their information into the port's information system. In fact, PCSs can significantly reduce paperwork, and can improve data quality, also allowing at integrating data among different stakeholders, and supporting the port management for operations. In this direction, despite a crucial role recognized to PCSs for the competitive power of the port, numerous organizations still show strong resistances to adopt them [10, 14]. In the different way, the seaports tend to invest growing resources in infrastructure and also improve their operation systems, enclosing port community systems, which are "computer networks which link up the port with all the companies that use it, including hauliers, rail companies, shipping lines, feeder ports, shippers and customs officers" [14].

With reference to the architectures of the inter-organizational relationship systems for the information and data sharing in the port community, four different architectural types have been distinguished [10]: bilateral, private hub, central orchestration hub, and modular distributed plug and play architecture.

The bilateral architectural type of PCSs regards one-to-one connections where two partners are strongly linked sharing and integrating their data and information and services requests, mainly using easy communication channels and technological tools, such as phone and fax. On the other side, also adopting Electronic Data Interchange (EDI), the two partners can be easily integrated without the need of intermediaries. The private hub and central orchestration hub, respectively the second and third architectural types of PCSs, allow connecting to many partners by reducing linkages, in fact, only one connection point or more than one connection point are required. Indeed, "two different typologies of hubs perform: in the private hub only one party owns the same hub and all the connections (generally large), whereas in the central orchestration hubs the parties perform and are interconnected in a kind of network". More specifically, the private hub is composed by a one-to-many type, instead the central orchestration hubs consist of many-to-many. The forth and last architectural type of PCSs, "modular distributed plug & play architecture", concerns hubs in which parties are not permanently connected and mainly considering their plug and connect capabilities; indeed, they can connect and share information and data only when they need to interact to quickly conduct businesses and it is no possible to standardize the information and data sharing and communication process.

In summary, many ports tend to consider as main means of communication the EDI in all the architectural types of PCSs, and at the same time independently on their definition, because of the high costs for the initial investments and the historical evolution of dislocation [19]. As a consequence, small ports face more difficulties to implement EDI as outlined in some empirical studies in the literature [10, 15, 20–22].

PCS ha four different stages in designing and implementing of PCS [21]: project initiation, systems analysis and design, implementation and adoption, and maintenance and growth. In fact, the process begins with the correct and clear identification of the need for an information system, and then it continues analyzing the business setting and the goal to achieve, including the design of the architecture and the following selection of the communication language.

"As already evidenced, PCSs are generally based on EDI technology. EDI has been widely recognized as a system in which data and information about commercial or administrative transactions are transferred from computer to computer on the basis of an agreed standard [19]. Thanks to EDI technology, the information within an organization are managed by computers but for their transferring and sharing between organizations, papers, forms or printouts are not necessary, easily all the data transfer occurs between the organizations' databases" [22–24]. The benefits of EDI can be grouped in three main categories, that is [24: 74]: "direct benefits, such as paper savings, avoiding repetitive administrative procedures or reducing administrative personnel; indirect benefits, such as avoiding errors, faster payments/improved cash flow; and finally strategic benefits, such as increasing business relationships with companies using EDI or improving customer loyalty".

3 PCSs in the Seaport Systems

Most studies in the literature on PCSs evidence that still few seaports worldwide, although important seaports for their volume of traffic, have implemented this innovative system (e.g., UK, Germany, Spain, Belgium, France, China, USA, Netherlands, Singapore, South Korea) [7, 10, 17].

In the literature there is a systematic review of the main contributions during the years 1994–2015 regarding the adoption of PSCs by seaports outlining that the focus was primarily on the costs and benefits of the PCSs [17]. In addition, this systematic review evidenced the presence of many descriptive studies, for instance, Tijan and Sasa [25], or Donselaar and Kolkman [26], by using the case studies or benchmarking analysis methodology. Although only few studies aimed to identify the performance indicators, such as Duran and Cordova [27].

Furthermore, previous studies outline that the first ports that adopted the Port Community platforms (PCp) are located in Germany (Hamburg and Bremen), France (Le Havre), UK (Felixstowe), Singapore. In these seaports, the most investigated PCS platform is Portnet in Singapore because of its organizational model and specific features; indeed, this platform is characterized by high levels of development allowing a very strict connection between the representative port community system and the PSA's terminal operating system (CITOS) and custom declaration system (TradeXchange) of Singapore government [7].

Moreover, additional ports adopted the port community platforms, like the ports of Los Angeles and Long Beach (USA) which adopted eModal; the ports of Amsterdam and Rotterdam (Netherlands) which respectively implemented Portbase after Portnet; the port of Hong Kong (China), a public port (service port) that implemented the OnePort after Tradelink [7, 17].

These systems developed very slowly maybe because of the high costs for the investment [17], and also because other variables, like training and education, beyond the size of the ports, were not crucial in pushing to adopt the PCSs [7]. Forward [28] clearly showed these limitations in the study on Cyprus.

The adoption of PCSs has been significantly facilitated by advanced technical infrastructures in the seaports because the employees have better skills and are more comfortable to use the platforms, above all due to their growing experience and exclusive knowledge regarding PCSs. Differently, major studies have outlined the key role played by trust especially when the reliability of the system decreases [7]. Thus, the benefits of the system are recognized more important than the costs, above all the reliability of the same system.

4   MCS and AIS for Information Management by PCSs

Thanks to the new technology it is possible to provide information and data to the port players (carriers, shippers, transport operators, labour and government bodies, etc.) with real time concerning the status of cargo, paperwork, and availability of port facilities, thus, ships and terminals are able to work together by using an integrated system [8].

Appropriately, port players used paper-based methods, such as sending fax or handing in documents directly for the delivery of cargo. In addition, port stakeholders, especially port users, utilized via e-mail channel for sending documents through the internet channel. Whenever ports have to type again the information and data inn their information systems spending more time and with higher risk to make mistakes [7].

In this context, port users, adopting the technology can receive significant and important advantages in the port community above all concerning the integrated information technologies very relevant and useful for the Accounting Information Systems (AIS).

A large amount of internal and external information need to be managed by the port community, by making the decision-making process more complex [29]. By applying new accessible and integrated information technologies, useful for AIS, the information and data collecting and management can be significantly facilitated.

Hence, thanks to AIS in the PCSs, port stakeholders, especially PAs as the main regulatory institution, receive relevant benefits, such as a faster and clearer information and data management process, in terms both of easy quantitative information and significant qualitative knowledge. The port players can get important factors and knowledge with details about the accounting and financial areas, and as a consequence, the value of the ports. Briefly, thanks to the AIS the data and information "speak for themselves" among all the port stakeholders, supporting their decision-making process, also considering that the system is not able to easily integrate these features. Likewise, due to the characteristics of the landlord port model where PAs perform their activities through the concessionaires agreement to private operators, the reporting assumes a crucial role for the PAs. Thus, the fast sharing and managing information and data in the real time is really supported by IT and all the actors are also helped by the accounting activities and controlling function. Implementing an integrated information system, instead of using spreadsheets, gets firms to provide higher quality information being more rapid and efficient. The major theoretical and empirical contributions in the literature outline the positive effects of IT on the firms performance and its crucial role in supporting management accounting activities and to facilitating exchange of information among firms [30].

The PCSs, with a comparison to the AIS in the port community, provide a large function regarding the controlling and reporting activities of all the port actors in the port community contingent upon the infrastructural model of the platform. Hence, PCSs allow at improving "the coordination and collaboration for transferring goods and their information and data among all the involved stakeholders". In this perspective, combining AIS and PCS should create positive circumstances for improving the relationships between the Port Authority and all the stakeholders in the port community also getting more effective and efficient the different port organizational models, in short service port, tool port, landlord port, and private port models [8].

Otherwise, past studies on PCSs focused on the private and public partnerships between the port stakeholders [31], or they mostly investigated the collective work made by the port community or the adoption process [32].

In this context, port users received interesting and relevant advantages thanks to the technology adopted, especially considering the integrated information technologies useful for the Management Control Systems (MCS). Some scholars argue that MCS plays a crucial role in supporting the business strategy in order to achieve the competitive advantage and high standards of performance [33, 34]. In this direction, information and data management and sharing, regarding the processes within the inter-organizational relationships established between port users, require more attention in order to be effectively provided. Thus, these port users have to manage and share a lot of information, both internal and external, making more complex the decision-making process.

These port players can be significantly supported by IT in rapidly sharing and managing information and data in real time and also the accounting activities and controlling functions can be supported in preventing and reducing the negative effects on the environment of their activities.

According to this perspective, considering MCS we might create positive conditions for improving the relationships among the players in the port community, also making the different port organizational models more effective and efficient.

5 Methodology

Adopting the case study methodology, this paper investigates different Italian seaports which are under governed and managed by the same port authority (PA), that is PA of Levante that includes Bari, Brindisi e Manfredonia seaports. We chose this PA because it has been one of the first which implemented the PCS, called "Generalized Automatic exchange of port Information Area" (GAIA). The system was introduced since 2012, and it is mainly oriented to manage passengers, vehicles and goods in the port supply chain.

Starting from our previous study conducted on the same issue [35], this qualitative research considers the perspective of one specific port user, which has the functions of forwarder and shipping agency. We conducted three semi-structured interviews by phone, lasting 1 h each to managers of the port user selected. Besides, the case study has been developed also using other sources, that is documents and reports of the PA on the PCS implemented, indirect observations and archival data analysis. The case study approach allows us to deeply explore the complex issues with multifaceted vision.

5.1   GAIA Case Study Description

GAIA has been implemented thanks to the cooperation between several actors, that is the PA and other more partners, such as the PA of Igoumenitsa (a public administration specialised in the public services financed by EU allowing the joint between Occidental Greek and the Adriatic ports), the University of Bari, and the Diophantus Institute (Centre for the Information and Technology Research). GAIA has been financed by "Fondo Europeo di Sviluppo Regionale" (75%) and by National co-found of Italy and Greece.

The adoption of this digital platform allows to public and private organisations, in general port users, to be connected thanks to information technology in order to manage the operational processes (i.e. import process, export process, boarding passengers, and so forth). Several reasons can justify the introduction of this digital platform in these seaports. Firstly, the need to reduce the time and paper used in the information management process among more port players. The PCS management is entrusted to the Port Authority to guarantee the confidentiality of data that the private operators include in the system.

Secondly, GAIA provides also some significant innovative services, like the Wi-Fi free in the areas for passengers' stopping. Finally, it is integrated with other digital platforms used by public authorities, that are localized within seaports of Levante. Indeed, this digital platform permits to join other three digital platforms which make up a larger projects on the port digitalisation, named PIC INTERREG IIIA. This project includes the following three sub-project: ADRION (addressed to the information management and reporting about the processes in the ports); GIPSY (used for the tracking and tracing in real time of passengers and cars in the ports); STP (used for the security management and control). In addition, GAIA is also integrated with a system for the automatic identification, in fact it includes more functions. Indeed, joining three digital platforms in one promotes the development of digital services in new zones of these seaports. Furthermore, the platform permits to: integrate all passengers information; realise one "passengers and events hub" of information useful to ensure the security; exchange of data using the wireless; provide a "data hub" as "service oriented" that can guarantee, in real time, all information required by PA and other port players. GAIA is also repository of offline data useful to support the making decision processes by public authorities and other selected players.

This type of PCS has an intuitive interface, therefore, the training courses for workers were not difficult requiring very basic skills.

This digital platform is structured in more modules, the information included in these modules allows to users to make quickly decisions. The modules are: a. GATE, this service has been developed thanks one partnership between the PA of Levante and Selex Elsag S.p.A. It permits to check the passenger and vehicle accesses in the ports and the port facilities provided by terminals, and the passenger and ferry management; b. PASS, it is an access service to the ports used from port players, the service does not require papers; c. PRECLEARING, it is a support service useful for ensuring the custom check on the container flows; d. SHIPS, it is the tracking service of the ships which produces text message when the ships aren't on time, and more in general on the port procedures, it affords to publish the data related to the ships. These data are collected by other systems (e.g. AIS) that are collocated within ports publishing in real time the position of ships; e. ALERT, it is a security service that can be used only by police, harbour authority, custom police and so forth. This service allows at having the control of all vehicles that transit in ports; f. IRIS, it is a special service for the passengers passing through ports. Consequently, there are information points that provide information about the port cities and other services provided by ports. In some LCD or LED windows there is a lot of information about departures and arrivals of ships. This information is processed in real time by AIS platform for each ship; g. TRAVEL, it is a service for intermodality of transit passengers, specifically, it concerns the time schedules of ships, train, flight and public transport; h. METEO, that provides the information related to climate conditions. These last data are provided to GAIA from another platform located in Bari city; i. STATS, it is related to passengers and goods, and it receives data collected by GATE module and it produces statistics and reports related to the traffic within ports, l. DATA TRAFFIC, that is the compulsory communications obtained by all ports of the system to process the statistic data; m. WASTE, it is dedicated to the garbage management within ports; n. EVENTS, that allows to manage the events in the ports, for controlling the processes and creating the emergency plans; n. UIRNET: this module consents the link with the National Logistics platform; o. e-GAIA, that is the service for the communication on mobile phone; p. TIMETABLE, a service by the maritime authority related to the moorings plan to the quay; q. DATA WAREHOUSE, that is a service that processes the statistics data to support the making decision process of port authority; r. REA, it is the service for the data and administrative procedure management of port authority.

Thus, the adoption of PCS in these seaports has allowed at integrating the ports of Bari, Barletta and Monopoli, and recently also the ports of Brindisi and Manfredonia, as a consequence of Italian port reform by Legislative Decree no. 169/2016 entered into force on 15th September, 2016 addressed to the rationalisation processes in the public sector passing by no. 24 port authorities to no. 15 (Seaport System Authority) (SSA).

In summary, the main advantages derived by the GAIA adoption are: 1. the reduction of the time for the processes management; 2. the integration with IT mobile support; 3. the traceability of the traffic flows.

GAIA can afford and positively respond to all the innovative systems of communication between traders and port authority of Levante. It consents the exchange and display of data among the port players (e.g. ocean carriers, freight forwarders, terminal, customs, institutions of public control and road carriers). Thanks to this PCS, the brokers, the terminal concessionaires, the importers and the exporters can easily communicate.

Therefore, it is a information support for the public authorities, and, at the same time, GAIA represents one "centralized data" system.

In the perspective of forwarder and shipping agency, it would seem that all the benefits of the platform have improved the relationship between the port stakeholders and all the players involved in the main operating processes.

First, fast and easy communication between actors enhances the process management. However, the system should be improved to manage information between the port players and the customs for import processes.

6   Concluding Remarks

This research contributes to the existing literature on PCSs by studying the role of AIS and MCS for the PCSs in the port players, especially port users, perspective, specifically, adopting the forwarder and shipping agency perspective. The study has been conducted on a port system that includes more ports subordinated and managed by the PA which has coordination tasks and control of the information on traffics.

The descriptive analysis highlights that the adoption of GAIA promotes the adoption of more effective coordination mechanisms in the relationships among the port players and the information management on the traceability of passengers, vehicles and goods seems to meet the goals of PA and other users within seaport. The main benefits are identified in the reduction of papers and timing schedules in the management processes.

Regarding the main instruments of the AIS (e.g. reporting), it is possible to observe that the reports are produced by the system thanks the module STATS, by permitting the traceability of traffic flows. According to the analysis of documents and reports of PA it seems that the PA managers can access to the system providing the reports on the information flows. In add, it seems that the reports do not include financial and qualitative information on traffic flows, instead in the AIS the financial information is important to the decision-making process by top and middle management.

In summary, these results seem in line with previous studies on PCS, where scholars have verified that the PCS adopted by Italian authorities is still limited to the transfer of information among the port players, but not to strategic management of information to support the making decision processes by PA. Indeed, the role of AIS and MCS is still missing, at least in the perspective of port players investigated.

This research presents some limits, as the analysis conducted considering only one perspective that does not permit to clearly define the role of AIS and MCS.

Otherwise, these instruments, or control systems, are relevant for this issue, PCS adoption, especially concerning the case PA of Levante.

In the future development of this study, for deeply and clearly knowing the determinants which limit the benefits of AIS and MCS using PCS, we aim to extend the study to other organizations involved in the modules described in this research.

Acknowledgements The authors are grateful for the contributions of the managers interviewed. The authors would like to thank Mrs. Michela Maresca for supporting their study through some interviews conducted during her bachelor thesis. Any errors are entirely attributed to the authors. The research has been published thanks to the financial support received by Parthenope University, Naples, entitled "Bando di sostegno alla ricerca individuale per il triennio 2015–2017", Annualità 2015 and 2016.

References

1. Goss, R.: Economic policies and seaports: the diversity of port policies. Marit. Policy Manag. **17**(3), 221–234 (1990)
2. Baird, A.: Privatisation of trust ports in the United Kingdom: review and analysis of the first sales. Transp. Policy **2**(2), 35–143 (1995)
3. Liu, Z.: Owner and productive efficiency: the experience of British ports. In: McConville, J., Sheldrake, J. (eds.) Transport in Transition: Aspects of British and European Experience, pp. 163–182. Aldershot, Avebury (1995)
4. De Monie, G.: Privatisation of port structures, in ports for Europe: Europe's maritime future. In: Bekemans, L., Beckwith, S. (eds.) In a Changing Environment, pp. 267–298. European Interuniversity Press, Brussels (1996)
5. Baudelaire, J.: Some thoughts about port privatisation. In: Goulielmos, A.M. (ed.) Essays in Honour and in Memory of Late Professor Emeritus of Maritime Economics Dr. Basil Metaxas, pp. 255–260 (1997)
6. Di Vaio, A., Medda, F.R., Trujillo, L.: An analysis of the efficiency of Italian cruise terminals. Int. J. Transp. Econ. **38**(1), 29–46 (2011)
7. Keceli, Y., Choi, H.R., Cha, Y.S., Aydogdu, Y.V.: A study on adoption of port community systems according to organization size. In: Third 2008 International Conference on Convergence and Hybrid Information Technology, pp. 493–501 (2008)
8. World Bank: Port Reform Tool Kit—Module 2—The Evolution of Ports in a Competitive World, 2nd edn. (2007)
9. Long, A.: Port community systems. World Cust. J. **3**(1), 63–72 (2009)
10. Srour, F.J., van Oosterhout, M., van Baalen, P., Zuidwijk, R.: Port community system implementation: lessons learned from international scan. In: Transportation Research Board 87th Annual Meeting, Washington DC (2008)
11. Aydogdu, Y.V., Aksoy, S.A: Study on quantitative benefits of port community systems. Marit. Policy Manag. **42**(1), 1–10 (2015). https://doi.org/10.1080/03088839.2013.825053
12. Rodon, J., Ramis-Pujol, J.: Exploring the intricacies of integrating with a port community system. In: 19th Bled eConference eValues. Bled, Slovenia (2006)
13. EPCSA, European Port Community Systems Association: White Paper, The Role of Port Community Systems in the Development of the Single Window (2011)
14. Keceli, Y.: A proposed innovation strategy for Turkish port administration policy via information technology. Marit. Policy Manag. **38**(2), 151–167 (2011). https://doi.org/10.1080/030888 39.2011.556676
15. Srour, F.J., Ruoff, K.: Transportation XML: building a framework for the next paradigm of web services and federated databases. In: The TRB 83rd Annual Meeting Proceedings, Washington, D.C. (2004)

16. Hoffer, A., George, J.F., Valacich, J.S.: Modern Systems Analysis and Design. Pearson Education, Upper Saddle River, NJ (2005)
17. Carlan, V., Christa, S., Thierry, V.: Port Community Systems costs and benefits: from competition to collaboration within the supply chain. In: Paper Presented at WCTRS-SIG2 (11-12/5/2015), Antwerp, pp. 1–27 (2015)
18. Tsamboulas, D., Moraiti, P., Lekka, A.M.: Port perform implementation evaluation for port community system implementation. J. Transp. Res. Board 2273, 29–37 (2012)
19. Iacovou, C.L., Benbasat, I., Dexter, A.S.: Electronic data interchange and small organizations: adoption and impact of technology. MISQ Q. 19(4), 465–485 (1995)
20. Muller, G.: INTERMODAL Freight Transportation. Eno Foundation Inc., Washington, D.C. (1999)
21. Peterson, D.M.: Power to the BPEL: a technology for Web services. Bus. Commun. Rev. 33(6), 54 (2003)
22. van Heck, E., Ribbers, P.M.: The adoption and impact of EDI in Dutch SME's. In: Proceedings of the 32nd Hawaii International Conference on System Sciences, Hawaii (1999)
23. Vincent, S.: Making EDI Work in India, Article 4: Port Community Systems and EDI in the Future. Exim India (2003)
24. Jimenez, J., Martinez, Polo-Redondo, Y.: The influence of EDI adoption over its perceived benefits. Technovation 24(1), 73–79 (2004)
25. Tijan, E., Sasa, A.: Seaport cluster information systems—a foundation for Port Community Systems' architecture. In: 37th International Convention on Information and Communication Technology, Electronics and Microelectronics (MIPRO). IEEE (2014)
26. Donselaar, P.W.-V., Kolkman, J.: Societal costs and benefits of cooperation between port authorities. Marit. Policy Manag. 37(3), 271–284 (2010)
27. Duran, C., Cordova, F.: Conceptual analysis for the strategic and operational knowledge management of a port community. Inf. Econ. 16(2), 35–44 (2012)
28. Forward, K.: Recent Developments in Port Information Technology. Digital Ship Ltd., London (2003)
29. Fernandèz-Alles, M.D.L.L., Valle-Cabrera, R.: Reconciling institutional theory with organizational theories; how neoinstitutionalism resolves five paradoxes. J. Organ. Change Manag. 19(4), 503–517 (2006)
30. Rom, A., Rohde, C.: Management accounting and integrated information systems: a literature review. Int. J. Acc. Inf. Syst. 8(1), 40–68 (2007)
31. Bagchi, P.K., Paik, S.K.: The role of public-private partnership in port information systems development. Int. J. Public Sect. Manag. 14(6), 482–499 (2001)
32. Rodon, J., Ramis-Pujol J.: Exploring the intricacies of integrating with a port community system. In: BLED 2006 Proceedings, Paper no. 9, pp. 1–15 (2006). http://aisel.aisnet.org/bled 2006/9. Accessed 27 May 2015
33. Kaplan, R.S., Norton, D.P.: Using the balanced scorecard as a strategic management system (1996)
34. Langfield-Smith, K.: The management control systems and strategy: a critical review. Acc. Organ. Soc. 22(2), 207–232 (1997)
35. Di Vaio, A., Varriale, L.: AIS and Reporting in the Port Community Systems: An Italian Case Study in the Landlord Port Model. Reshaping Accounting and Management Control Systems, pp. 153–165. Springer, Cham (2017)

Securing National e-ID Infrastructures: Tor Networks as a Source of Threats

Paolo Spagnoletti⬤, Gianluigi Me⬤, Federica Ceci⬤ and Andrea Prencipe⬤

Abstract Securing national electronic identification (e-ID) systems requires an in depth understanding of the associated threats. The trade of identity related artefacts in the darknet facilitates illegal activities such as identity theft in both physical and virtual worlds. This paper reports the findings of an exploratory analysis of identity trading in the darknet. We capture the key features of three major markets of fake IDs in Tor networks, and apply attack-defense trees to show how the security of an e-ID infrastructure is affected by this phenomenon.

Keywords Identity theft · Tor · Attack tree · Identity management · Black market

1 Introduction

Electronic identification (e-ID) infrastructures are considered a key enabler for the development of e-services in both public and private sector. In the last decade, many European countries have started nation-wide initiatives to develop their own e-ID infrastructures [1]. Such infrastructures differ in terms of architectures, institutional actors involved, and on the range of services that can be accessed by citizens using digital identities. In some cases, e-ID can be seen as platforms enabling authenticated citizens to access online services provided both by public administrations and private companies. Such platforms are based on federated authentication and authorization architectures in which few certified companies act as Identity Providers (IdP) under the supervision of a governmental institution [2]. Identity Providers must guarantee the identification of citizens and securely manage their personal data while enabling access to Service Providers (SP) in the ecosystem, by the means of standardized protocols.

P. Spagnoletti (✉) · G. Me · A. Prencipe
LUISS University, Rome, Italy
e-mail: pspagnoletti@luiss.it

F. Ceci
G. d'Annunzio University, Pescara, Italy

© Springer International Publishing AG, part of Springer Nature 2019
F. Cabitza et al. (eds.), *Organizing for the Digital World*, Lecture Notes in Information
Systems and Organisation 28, https://doi.org/10.1007/978-3-319-90503-7_9

Alike e-payment systems, e-ID infrastructures can be considered as multi-sided platforms [3]. Depending on the policies defined by governmental sponsors, different strategies can be implemented at the level of provider, technology and users. For instance, in Italy a competitive strategy at the level of Identity Providers has been recently established by AGID, the Public Agency in charge of promoting digitalization. At the moment, the governmental sponsors have accredited five Identity Providers and they are requested to manage citizens' identities by opening the platform through APIs to any public and private e-service. Citizens can join the SPID (Digital Identity Public Service) at no charge and benefit of a Single-Sign-On service when accessing to e-services connected to the national e-ID infrastructure. The economic sustainability of the overall system relies on transaction fees payed by private companies to the Identity Provider that performs the authentication.

Despite the huge market potential of e-ID platforms, which coincides with the whole state population, governments are struggling in developing e-ID infrastructures and attracting a critical mass of users and service providers [4]. Possible challenges in the development of such infrastructures are related to privacy concerns, lack of inter-governmental coordination, lack of private-public sector cooperation, and tensions such as the trade-off between usability and security. Among those issues, security plays a crucial role by enabling the development of trusted e-service ecosystems. Security is a multidimensional property of systems, data and information [5]. When referred to an IT infrastructure in a business context, information security is often intended as the organizational goal of mitigating operational risks by protecting information from threats to confidentiality, integrity, availability and accountability [6]. However, today's pervasiveness of digital technologies in both work practices and citizens' private life, extends the scope of risk to safety and other human rights. Undesired e-payment transactions, data breaches of healthcare and financial information, sabotage of critical infrastructures (e.g. transportation, electricity, oil and gas, etc.) and unauthorized access to e-voting systems are only few examples of serious violations of rights such as ownership, privacy, safety and freedom [7]. Since e-ID infrastructures serve as a gateway to a vast array of services, their vulnerabilities can have a tremendous impact on organizations and society. In fact, systems integration and interoperability of services enable the propagation of security incidents well beyond the boundaries of a single service with potential effects on the performance of an entire ecosystem [8].

While previous studies have addressed the problem of e-ID security from a technical perspective, in this paper we focus on the risk that malicious users get unauthorized access to federated services by acting on behalf of another user. In order to access e-services, users are requested to demonstrate their identity in the enrolment phase and then to perform an authentication process every time they need to enter the system. The ways in which these activities are performed is defined by IdPs and SPs and regulated by contracts. Every time a successful authentication is performed, users can act by the means of a digital identity, a set of attributes that are exchanged with the SP. Therefore, authorization and authentication processes transfer the user agency to digital identity (e.g. password, scanned documents, e-card, etc.) whose theft and illegal exchange threatens the accountability and hence the security of the overall system. The risks of identity theft are today amplified by the availability of online markets in the Deep Web that allow users to exchange goods anonymously. Within such markets, digital identities can be exchanged like many other illegal goods thus potentially reaching every Internet user. The goal of this study is to explore the emerging risks of identity theft in the cyberspace and to discuss implications on the design and governance of e-ID infrastructures.

Although some empirical studies have emphasized the business potential of the Deep Web as an intelligence tool [9], it is commonly accepted that the presence of a cyberinfrastructure ensuring anonymity generates new threats for both businesses and citizens. The rise of black markets in the darknet is in fact transforming the ways in which criminals interact in trading illegal products and services [10–12]. These markets are also used to sell identity related goods either in the form of digital information or as physical artefacts such as for instance ID cards and driving licences. We argue that the trade of identity related artefacts in the darknet represents a new source of risk for trusted e-service environments. When federated e-ID infrastructures are in place, fake identities provide criminals with unprecedented capabilities of harvesting private data and acting on behalf of others. Our goal is to shed light on this phenomenon by showing how the illegal trade of identity related product and services on the darknet pave the way to new forms of attacks to e-ID infrastructures.

In this paper, we address this issue by exploring the market of identity documents in the darknet and identifying attack scenarios emerging in the new cybercrime ecosystem. We conduct a case study on the black market of Italian citizens' identities in Tor networks and discuss the implications for the development of secure e-ID infrastructures.

The paper is structured as follows. We first illustrate some key features of black markets in the dark net based on findings from previous studies. Then, we formulate our research question by focusing on the market of illegal identities in the darknet and on the potential risks for e-ID infrastructures. In the third section, we describe the research methodology and the data collection process. In the fourth section, the results of our empirical analysis are presented and the implications of emerging attack scenarios on the development of e-ID infrastructures is discussed.

2 Related Works

2.1 Black Markets in the Darknet

A darknet is an overlay network that can only be accessed with specific software, configurations, or authorization, often using non-standard communications protocols and ports. Contents of the darknet are not indexed by common search engines such as Google. Black markets existing within the dark net present unique features that make them extremely interesting. For our purposes, we find three particularly interesting features: anonymity of users, anonymity of payments, and resilience.

The first aspect relates to the choice of communities who use and manage black markets to keep their identities secret [13]. The main motivation for anonymity is the illegal nature of the activities carried out by vendors and buyers [14, 15]. However, in some cases, the use of anonymity is chosen to avoid stigma or limit liability, as in the case of purchasing of drugs or political manuals [16, 17]. The need for anonymity has important impact on the organizational choices of markets and communities that manage them: research has shown that criminals often design their organizations not to maximize efficiency but to be able to better hide their activities [18] and to limit the dissemination of potentially incriminating information [19]. From a technical viewpoint, the anonymity is guaranteed by protocols that establish end-to-end circuits in which data are tunnelled using public-key cryptography. In these networks, each node only knows its predecessor and successor. New generation anonymity systems, such as Onion Routing networks handle a variety of bidirectional TCP-based applications like web browsing, secure shell, and instant messages. The Tor package is a set of free software tools implementing the Onion Routing network design. Tor users can therefore browse the web, publish web sites and other services without revealing their identity and the location of the site. Anonymity is guaranteed also while accessing and performing transactions on e-marketplaces such as black markets. In these markets identities of vendors and customers are anonymous, no email or other identification are required for the registration to the website, except for their nicknames. To create a system of trust in an area susceptible to scams and overcome the risks of anonymity, buyers can leave feedback on sellers. Moreover, a marketplace can show the number of transactions that buyers and sellers have made under a given nickname.

With regard to the second aspect, the payments are performed by exchanging crypto-currencies like Bitcoin (BTC) by all major black markets. The BTC is a peer-to-peer currency based on the blockchain technology and indexed to the US dollar to avoid excessive inflation or deflation [20, 21]. Because of its decentralized control, it is often considered a threat or an alternative to the conventional central banking system [22]. Although the BTC is characterized by high volatility, it is used on a large scale as an alternative payment system (the market value of bitcoins exceeds 100 billion dollars). Supporters argue that it is the first truly global currency, it does not discriminate against its members on grounds of nationality or position, it is always running, without holidays, it is easy to achieve with very low rates of usage. On the other hand, critics argue that BTC is widely used to buy illegal items and to launder large sums of money [21]. BTC per se do no assure anonymity of transaction; anonymity and untraceability of payments can be obtained hiding IP addresses while making a transaction, or using "mixing" or "tumbling" services. "Mixing" services work by mixing transactions with a large number of other transactions from different sources. By doing this, it becomes difficult or impossible to link specific payments into the mixing service with specific payments coming out of the mixing service. To satisfy the increasing need for anonymity, recently, alternative forms of payments are accepted in black markets. An example is Monero (XMR) that, possessing significant algorithmic differences, assures higher level of privacy and anonymity then Bitcoin.

Finally, regarding resilience in networks, previous studies have emphasized that resilience is a dynamic process, associated to systems that exist and carry out their main tasks under the pressure of external shocks [23]. Sutcliffe and Vogus [24] analysed the existence of two critical conditions implicit in the concept of resilience: (i) "exposure to threats, stress or adversity" and (ii) "the achievement of positive adaptation despite the presence of stress or adversity" (p. 108). Bakker et al. [14] defined the resilience of a dark net as the ability of the network to remain operative in the middle of bumps or attacks ("robustness capacity") or to recover from unpleasant events, transforming over time ("rebound capacity"). Empirical evidence shows that the communities underlying black markets can quickly re-organize after major attacks. For example, SilkRoad, an e-commerce site founded in 2011 and whose products were classified as contraband by the majority of the world's jurisdictions, was closed October 3rd, 2013 by the FBI. On 6th November of the same year, SilkRoad 2.0 was reopening by the same managing team under the same alias Dread Pirate Roberts, although the FBI has arrested the person that was hidden behind that name. On November 6th, 2014 SilkRoad 2.0 was again closed by the FBI.

2.2 The Market of Identities in Cyberinfrastructures

Digital identity is the set of information and resources provided by a computer system to a particular user on the basis of a process of identification. Digital identity is assuming an increasingly important role, given the already widespread use (that will likely increase in the future) of digital identities by public administrations (e.g. SPID), private companies (e.g. Google and Facebook) and individual users (e.g. web reputation). In parallel, there is a new-born black market for digital identities that generates new security threats [25–27].

Previous studies on identity in the information society have emphasized the multiplicity of tensions, themes, application domains and disciplinary approaches related to this subject [28]. However, few studies so far have addressed the impact of illegal trade of identity related goods in the deep market on the security profiles of e-service infrastructures.

3 The Case of Italian Identity Trading in the Tor Network

3.1 Data Retrieving Methodology

A particular boost to the spread of empirical studies in this area is due to the possibility to access historical data about transactions, vendor profiles and feedbacks. Such amount of data allows researchers to test hypotheses and to implement simulation methods. Despite the potential advantages of applying longitudinal approaches to

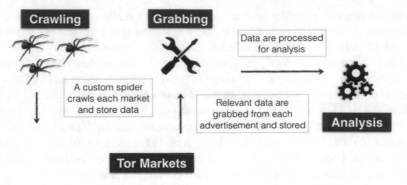

Fig. 1 Tor marketplaces data retrieval system

study evolutionary market dynamics, in this paper we focus on the structural characteristics of anonymous marketplaces in a single point in time.

In order to build the dataset, we crawled six marketplaces in December 2016, visiting each market in order to create a snapshot dataset ready for the analysis. The marketplaces we analyzed were AlphaBay, Dream Market, Hansa, Leo, Outlaw and Bloomfield. Each market adopts a different set of categories for products and services. Our attention was focused on those categories that are potentially related to identity theft activities such as "Counterfeit items/Fake IDs" and "Fraud/Personal information and scans" on AlphaBay, "Digital goods/Fraud" on Dream market and "Fraud Related/Documents and Data" on Hansa. Therefore, we collected items' pages concerning identity documents, and their related images.

For each marketplace, we designed and implemented a custom spider using the Scrapy[1] framework. Spiders are configured to use Tor to have the capability of reaching anonymous marketplaces. Figure 1 shows the logical workflow of our system for the collection, elaboration and analysis of anonymous marketplaces data.

Spiders request pages with different waiting times between each request. We also deny the possibility of sending concurrent request to marketplaces. Clearly, these precautions increase the crawling time for each market. Such settings are natively supported by Scrapy, and we resort on them for spiders' configuration.

We gathered data from a dataset of 36 GB in size, where the crawl of each market ranged from 1,682 to 18,831 pages/images, and crawling time took from several hours up to few days. Specifically, we crawl only listings' pages and items' pages. We scraped listing pages to collect items' pages URL, but we store only item's pages, together with items' images. Finally, to prevent undesired actions execution, such as adding items to cart or sending messages, each spider is designed to request only URL of interest.

From each item's page we extracted the information needed to fulfil the table fields reported in Table 1. To grab such information, we took advantage of the HTML structure of each page. A generic HTML page is enclosed in a main HTML tag

---

[1] Scrapy: A Fast and Powerful Scraping and Web Crawling Framework http://scrapy.org.

Table 1 Fields

Name	Vendor_name	Escrow
Description	Marketplace	Product_Type
Ships_to	Price	Ships_from

and divided in two sections identified by the tags head and body. Tags inside the body contain information we look for. The data we want to extract are enclosed in different tags at different level of the HTML structure. Each marketplace has a different structure for its pages, thus we implemented a customized parser for each marketplace. Therefore, every single parser identifies the nodes within the Document Object Model (DOM), through the Xpath selector.

The target of data grabbing is to reduce an offer to a tuple containing the relevant field for the purposes of the analysis, as shown in the Table 1.

The marketplace mechanism to place offers makes the overall raw dataset quality very low. In fact, every vendor can place his offer regardless of almost any control, leading to have empty or duplicated offers (in the raw dataset), mistakes in key-text fields, non-uniform metrics/currency. Moreover, offers can be misplaced in the different categories, leading to mismatching overall amounts of offers. Hence, for the abovementioned reasons, the data preparation phase assumes a crucial role in order to achieve reliable results.

Data scrubbing, also called data cleansing, is the process of correcting or removing data in a dataset that is incorrect, inaccurate, incomplete, improperly formatted, or duplicated. This step is important since the validity the data analysis process depends not only on the algorithms, but also on the quality of the data collected. In order to avoid biases in the dataset, it should be characterized by correctness, completeness, accuracy, consistency and uniformity. Residual dirty data can be detected by applying statistical data validation methods and also by parsing the texts or deleting duplicate values. In fact, missing data can lead to bad analysis results.

It is worth to mention that our dataset has some limitations. First, in our case all offers have been considered real and possible scams have been ignored. Second, the "ships from" value is considered reliable since the shipping of identity documents are basically invisible to customs as compared to the exchange of other illegal goods (e.g. drugs, weapons, etc.). Third, the classification of offers into categories is made by vendors which may apply subjective views in this process. It is possible to find offers related to the same kind of product classified under different categories. For instance, the crawler will not detect the offer of a fake ID card if it has been classified under the drug category. Finally, feedback has not been taken into account since it can be biased by vendor tactics such as exit scams. However, feedback could be used in future studies to estimate the revenues of a vendor.

Table 2 Categories with placed identity documents offers

Carded_Items	CVV_Cards	Fraud
Counterfeit_Items	Data	Fraud_Related
Counterfeits	Digital_Goods	Fraud_Software
IDs_Passports	Other_Dig_Products	Personal_Info

3.2   Data Analysis

The resulting dataset has been analysed per category and keyword. In particular, the only categories crawled and analysed were those in Table 2. The resulting dataset was the following collection of offers per marketplace: AlphaBay (9120 offers), Dream Market (18,506 offers), Hansa (13,068 offers), Leo (382 offers), Outlaw (1714 offers) and Bloomfield (111 offers).

   The overall resulting offers fields in Table 1 were matched against a set of keyword based on the location and good description (e.g. passport, identity, spid, driving, ita, etc.).

   Hence, we selected Alphabay, Dream and Hansa Market as the three most interesting marketplaces in terms of offers size. For each of these marketplaces we investigated every single offer in order to find data possibly enabling identity theft for the Italian Digital Identity Public Service (SPID). Hence, key offers were those containing Italian documents and their related prices.

   The collected data resulted in 58 offers matching these requirements, posing the pillars for the threat detection and evaluation via the attack tree model, further explained in next section.

3.3   Threat Detection via Attack Trees

As Bruce Schneier wrote in his introduction to the subject, "Attack trees provide a formal, methodical way of describing the security of systems, based on varying attacks. Basically, it is a model to represent attacks against a system in a tree structure, with the goal as the root node and different ways of achieving that goal as leaf nodes" [29]. Therefore, attack trees provide structure to the risk assessment process, facilitate interactions among stakeholders, and allow to catalogue the identified threats. Furthermore, some tools and techniques based on attack tree models enable advanced quantitative risk analysis with security metrics, e.g. expected time of attack or worst-case impact. Attack trees have been effectively adopted to understand the protection of critical infrastructures such as buildings, pipelines, electrical transmission lines and ATM [30].

   Attack trees work well as a building block for threat enumeration: in particular, whereas there are several ways to use attack trees to enumerate threats, we created a tree to detect threats from the scratch. Creating new trees for general use is challenging, even for security experts.

Even assuming that all feasible attacks (identified through pruning) have some non-zero probability, that is still only half of the risk equation. Hostile risk is generally accepted to be the combination of two factors:

$$\text{Attack Risk} = \text{Attack Probability} \times \text{Victim Impact}$$

In order to model threats to a single e-ID provider, we used SecurITree to model how the attacker can obtain a certified digital identity from a generic e-ID infrastructure. The resulting model needs to include the impact each attack scenario will have on the defender.

SecurITree[2] is a graphical Attack Tree modeling tool introduced by Amenaza Technologies. It is a Java application and runs on all major computing platforms. SecurITree allows to draw complex conclusions using capability-based modeling. SecurITree allows an analyst to describe possible attacks against a system in the form of a graphical, mathematical model. The capabilities of motivated attackers are compared with the resources required to perform specific attacks in the model through a process called "pruning". Attacks that are beyond the adversary's capability are removed from the model. The remaining attacks are considered highly likely.

4 Discussion

4.1 The Market of Italian Citizens' Identities

In this section, we describe the main findings of the research, with the aim to provide an overview of the offerings in the market of Italian citizens' identity.

Offerings in black markets are similar to the offerings of usual e-commerce websites present in the surface web such as eBay. An offering can include the following information: description of the product, price proposed and bids (if allowed), profile of the vendor with a classification of the vendor in terms of experience (no. of products sold) and level of trust, feedbacks on the products provided by previous buyers, cost and time for shipping.

The richness of such details varies across products, influenced by the marketing attitude of vendors and typology of products sold. In Fig. 2 we report a screenshot of a typical offer in the market.

Evaluations of vendors are highly considered since they represent a way to obtain credibility with buyers and therefore to increase sales. For instance, in the marketplace called AlphaBay, level and trust of vendors are calculated as follows: level is displayed on listing pages and on the user's profile page and it is influenced by the

---

[2]SecureITree, http://www.amenaza.com/documents.php.

Fig. 2 Screenshot of a typical offer

Table 3 Size and structure of the three markets

Market	N. offerings	N. vendors	CR10 (%)
Hansa	13,068	201	66,6
AlphaBay	9120	1213	14,5
Dream market	18,506	254	68,1

number of sales, the volume of sales (in $) and the percentage of positive feedback. Trust is independent from the vendor level. Trust increases over the amount of trust gained on the marketplace and the formula for how trust is calculated is not made public.

In our research in the black markets of digital identity, we found 42,901 offering from the relevant categories as listed in Table 2 in the 6 most important black markets, distributed as follows: 9120 offerings on AlphaBay; 18,506 offerings on Dream; 13,068 offerings on Hansa; 382 offerings on Leo; 1714 offerings on Outlaw; 111 offerings on Bloomfield.

We selected the three markets with the higher number of offering (AlphaBay, Dream, Hansa) and we reported number of vendors and distribution of offerings to calculate the CR10 (concentration ratio for the first 10 vendors). Results are reported in Table 3. Results shows that Hansa and Dream Market are more concentrated than Alphabay and each market has a different structure.

Table 4 Distribution of relevant offerings

Product_Category	AlphaBay	Dream market	Hansa	Tot.
Carded_Items	1	–	–	1
Counterfeit_Items	11	–	–	11
Counterfeits	–	–	3	3
CVV_Cards	4	–	–	4
Data	–	1	–	1
Digital_Goods	–		2	2
E-Books	1	1	–	2
Fraud	–	2	–	2
Fraud_Related	–	11	5	16
Fraud_Software	–	–	–	0
IDs_Passports	–	4	–	4
Other_Digital_Products	1	–	–	1
Other_Fraud	–	–	–	0
Personal_Information	9	–	–	9
Services	–	–	1	1
Social_Engineering	1	–		1
Tot.				58

Among all the offerings listed in the identified categories, we identified 58 offering of interest for the market of Italian citizens' identity. Offerings are distributed as follows: 28 in Alphabay: 19 in Dream Market and 11 in Hansa. Offerings are placed by 38 vendors, 4 of which ship directly from Italy. A detail of the distribution of the offering across marketplaces and categories can be found in Table 4.

From an analysis of the relevant offering, we identify three typologies of items that can be purchased to have access to fake identities:

1. Scan/PSD: offering that allows to buy scan of real documents or template to produce a fake ID (e.g. Adobe Photoshop)
2. Fake: offering that allows to buy fake ID
3. Guide/Manual/Info: offering related to guides or tutorials useful to realize fake ID.

The number of offerings related to the three categories is reported in Table 5.

4.2 Attack Scenarios for e-ID Infrastructures

In this section, the results of attack tree analysis from the perspective of a generic e-ID provider is presented. We identified 21 different generic attacks in the attack tree, mainly resumed in:

Table 5 Distribution of offerings among product typologies

	Scan/P-D	Fake	Guide/Manual	Tot:
Id_Card	11	4	6	19
Passport	21	–	6	21
Driving license	8	7	4	15
Codice fiscale	1	4	–	5
Other docs	5	–	2	6

- e-Id credentials physical theft;
- e-Id credentials purchase on Tor;
- e-Id credentials online purchase through criminal closed groups;
- e-Id credentials exfiltration through third parties attacks;
- valid registration through different authentication factors (smartphones, CNS, e-ID card, SSN etc.).

For every single main attack subtree, we checked the feasibility with respect to the items sold in Tor. In particular, the cost associated with a given attack scenario (which may involve several leaf level activities) can be calculated by examining the resource requirements of the scenario's leaf level activities. If the exploit consumes a resource, then the total requirement for that resource is the sum of the scenario's leaf nodes' resource metrics. If the resource can be reused (such as is the case with technical ability) then the resource cost is the maximum of the scenario's leaf nodes' resource metrics. This result can be achieved via the pruning technique, which represents a simple way for evaluating the feasibility of a given adversary performing an attack scenario. The technique compares the resources available to the adversary with the scenario's behavioral indicator costs. Those scenarios with resource requirements greater than the adversary's capabilities can be safely eliminated from consideration (since it is not possible for that adversary to provide them). The attacks that remain are feasible and, depending whether they are desirable to the threat agent, have some, non-zero level of probability.

The 21 attack scenarios, containing noticeability and technical ability needed to succeed, among which it is possible to identify those affected by the presence of a black market of identities in the dark web.

In particular, the Fig. 3 shows an online registration weakness due to the ease fake identity document retrieval in Tor. In fact, in order to achieve a successful registration to e-ID, in the examined case, we needed a (a) physical SSN, (b) a physical ID card and (c) a de-visu identification performed by an employee of the e-ID provider. Authentication factors in (a) and (b) can be retrieved in Tor marketplaces (e.g. Alphabay), for an average expense of EUR 500. Hence, all the burden of the identification and authentication is on employee responsibility, which should be trained and equipped to tackle the counterfeited documents. However, this situation is not frequent, because identification is carried out as an ancillary task: for the

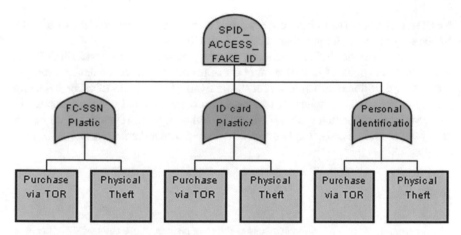

Fig. 3 Successful attack subtree

abovementioned reasons, the Fig. 3 represents a practical vulnerability to obtain a not legitimate e-ID.

Moreover, additional factors have an impact on the risk of attack:

- the cost, as above mentioned, is cheap and could not be considered an inhibitor or barrier to commit this crime;
- the technical ability needed is very low, related to the capability to purchase items on Tor marketplaces;
- time is not a relevant variable in this case;
- the noticeability is very low, in case of untrained and unequipped operator for identification, due to the impossibility to verify fake documents.

The exploitation of the abovementioned vulnerability represents a severe threat for all the services based on e-ID: in fact, it harms the reliability and trust of the whole e-ID systems, whose overall security is chained to the weakest provider. A secondary negative effect is represented by the overall situational facilitation enabling even occasional criminals to carry out the identity theft [31].

5   Conclusion

The paper presents a measurement study on identity theft in the form of exchange of identity credentials via Tor Hidden Services. With the final goal of investigating the impact of darknet activities on the surface web of digital services, we explore three black markets in search of identity-theft related offers. The phenomenon is then analysed in more detail in the Italian case, where the findings shows that fake passports and id-cards are the most common offers related to identity theft. Finally, we use attack trees to show how the security of national e-ID infrastructures is affected by the easy access to anonymous cyberinfrastructures.

Our study provides both methodological and practical contributions. First, from a methodological point of view, it shows how data collected from the darknet complement more traditional data sources for the analysis of new forms of crimes. Second, it stresses the need to implement technical and organizational countermeasures [5, 6], in order to enhance the link of the e-ID to the physical ID card, which can be easily counterfeited and cheaply purchased from darknet marketplaces.

References

1. Kubicek, H., Noack, T.: Different countries-different paths extended comparison of the introduction of eIDs in eight European countries. Identity Inf. Soc. 235–245 (2010)
2. D'Atri, A., Spagnoletti, P., Za, S.: Institutional trust and security, new boundaries for virtual enterprises. In: Proceedings of 2nd International Workshop on Interoperability Solutions to Trust, Security, Policies and QoS for Enhanced Enterprise Systems, IS-TSPQ2007, March 26th, Funchal (Madeira Island), Portugal (2007)
3. Ondrus, J., Gannamaneni, A., Lyytinen, K.: The impact of openness on the market potential of multi-sided platforms: a case study of mobile payment platforms. J. Inf. Technol. **30**, 260–275 (2015)
4. Melin, U., Axelsson, K., Söderström, F.: Managing the development of e-ID in a public e-service context: challenges and path dependencies from a life-cycle perspective. Transform. Gov. People Process Policy **10**, 72–98 (2016)
5. Åhlfeldt, R.M., Spagnoletti, P., Sindre, G.: Improving the information security model by using TFI. In: New Approaches for Security, Privacy and Trust in Complex Environments, pp. 73–84 (2007)
6. Baskerville, R., Spagnoletti, P., Kim, J.: Incident-centered information security: managing a strategic balance between prevention and response. Inf. Manag. **51**, 138–151 (2014)
7. Cavelty, M.D.: Cyber-security. In: Collins, A. (ed.) Contemporary Security Studies. pp. 362–377. Oxford University Press (2015)
8. Hanseth, O., Ciborra, C.: Risk, complexity and ICT. Edward Elgar Publishing Limited, Cheltenham, UK (2007)
9. Obreja, A.R., Hart, P., Bednar, P.: Potential benefits of the deep web for SMEs Andreea-Roxanna. In: Caporarello, L. (ed.) Digitally Supported Innovation. pp. 63–80. Springer International Publishing (2016)
10. Kraemer-Mbula, E., Tang, P., Rush, H.: The cybercrime ecosystem: online innovation in the shadows? Technol. Forecast. Soc. Change **80**, 541–555 (2013)
11. Soska, K., Christin, N.: Measuring the longitudinal evolution of the online anonymous marketplace ecosystem. In: 24th USENIX Security Symposium (USENIX Security 15), pp. 33–48 (2015)
12. Christin, N.: Traveling the silk road: a measurement analysis of a large anonymous online marketplace. In: Proceedings of 22nd International Conference on World Wide Web, pp. 213–224 (2013)
13. Bok, S.: Secrets: on the ethics of concealment and revelation. Vintage (1989)
14. Bakker, R.M., Raab, J., Milward, H.B.: A preliminary theory of dark network resilience. J. policy Anal. Manag. **31**, 33–62 (2012)
15. Brinton Milward, H., Raab, J.: Dark networks as organizational problems: elements of a theory 1. Int. Public Manag. J. **9**, 333–360 (2006)
16. Hollenbaugh, E.E., Everett, M.K.: The effects of anonymity on self-disclosure in blogs: an application of the online disinhibition effect. J. Comput. Commun. **18**, 283–302 (2013)

17. Hudson, B.A., Okhuysen, G.A.: Not with a ten-foot pole: core stigma, stigma transfer, and improbable persistence of men's bathhouses. Organ. Sci. **20**, 134–153 (2009)
18. Baker, W.E., Faulkner, R.R.: The social organization of conspiracy: illegal networks in the heavy electrical equipment industry. Am. Sociol. Rev. 837–860 (1993)
19. Stohl, C., Stohl, M.: Secret agencies: the communicative constitution of a clandestine organization. Organ. Stud. **32**, 1197–1215 (2011)
20. Nakamoto, S.: Bitcoin: A peer-to-peer electronic cash system (2008)
21. Ron, D., Shamir, A.: Quantitative analysis of the full bitcoin transaction graph. In: International Conference on Financial Cryptography and Data Security, pp. 6–24. Springer (2013)
22. Dierksmeier, C., Seele, P.: Crypto currencies and business ethics. J. Bus. Ethics. 1–14 (2016)
23. Batabyal, A.A.: Human actions, the survival of keystone species, and the resilience of ecological–economic systems. Resour. Policy. **28**, 153–157 (2002)
24. Sutcliffe, K.M., Vogus, T.J.: Organizing for resilience. In: Positive Organizational Scholarship: Foundations of a New Discipline, vol. 94, pp. 110 (2003)
25. Han, W., Cao, Y., Bertino, E., Yong, J.: Using automated individual white-list to protect web digital identities. Expert Syst. Appl. **39**, 11861–11869 (2012)
26. Maler, E., Reed, D.: The Venn of identity. IEEE Secur. Priv. **6**, 16–23 (2008)
27. Mont, M.C., Pearson, S., Bramhall, P.: Towards accountable management of identity and privacy: sticky policies and enforceable tracing services. In: Proceedings of 14th International Workshop on Database and Expert Systems Applications, 2003, pp. 377–382. IEEE (2003)
28. Halperin, R., Backhouse, J.: A roadmap for research on identity in the information society. Identity Inf. Soc. **1**, 14–15 (2008)
29. Schneier, B.: Attack Trees. Dr. Dobb's J. Softw. Tools **24**, 21–29 (1999)
30. Fraile, M., Ford, M., Gadyatskaya, O., Kumar, R.: Using attack-defense trees to analyze threats and countermeasures in an ATM : a case study. In: Horkoff, J., Jeusfeld, M., Persson, A. (eds.) The Practice of Enterprise Modeling, PoEM, pp. 326–334. Springer, Cham (2016)
31. Willison, R.: Understanding the offender/environment dynamic for computer crimes. Inf. Technol. People. **19**, 170–187 (2006)

A Giant with Feet of Clay: On the Validity of the Data that Feed Machine Learning in Medicine

Federico Cabitza, Davide Ciucci⦿ and Raffaele Rasoini

Abstract This paper considers the use of machine learning in medicine by focusing on the main problem that it has been aimed at solving or at least minimizing: uncertainty. However, we point out how uncertainty is so ingrained in medicine that it biases also the representation of clinical phenomena, that is the very input of this class of computational models, thus undermining the clinical significance of their output. Recognizing this can motivate researchers to pursue different ways to assess the value of these decision aids, as well as alternative techniques that do not "sweep uncertainty under the rug" within an objectivist fiction (which doctors can come up by trusting).

Keywords Decision support systems · Machine learning · Uncertainty

1 Motivations and Background

It is a truism to say that uncertainty permeates contemporary medicine—not much differently than it has always been—as it has also been confirmed by extensive studies in the field of sociology and medicine itself (e.g., [20, 49]). We cope with some form of uncertainty when we cannot pinpoint a phenomenon exactly or when we cannot

An extended version of this paper can be found on the arXiv platform at the following address: https://arxiv.org/abs/1706.06838.

F. Cabitza · D. Ciucci (✉)
Università degli Studi di Milano-Bicocca, Milan, Italy
e-mail: ciucci@disco.unimib.it

F. Cabitza
IRCCS Istituto Ortopedico Galeazzi, Milan, Italy
e-mail: federico.cabitza@unimib.it

R. Rasoini
IRCCS Don Gnocchi Foundation, Milan, Italy
e-mail: raffaele.rasoini@tiscali.it

measure it precisely (i.e., approximation, inaccuracy); when we do not possess a complete account of a case (incompleteness, inadequacy); when we cannot predict what it will come next (unpredictability for randomness or excessive complexity); when our observations seem to contradict each other (inconsistency, ambiguity); and, more generally, when we are not confident of what we know. In clinical practice, all of these phenomena occur on a daily basis, several times. Medical doctors can be uncertain on almost every aspect of their practice: on how to classify patients' conditions (diagnostic uncertainty); why and how patients develop diseases (etiological u., pathophysiological u.); what treatment will be more appropriate for them (therapeutic u.); whether they will recover with or without a specific treatment (prognostic u.), and so on. In this picture, technology has often been proposed—and seen—as a solution. In the words by Reiser [44, p. 18]: *From the beginning of their introduction in the mid-nineteenth century, automated machines that generated results in objective formats [...] were thought capable of purging from health care the distortions of subjective human opinion [and] to produce facts free of personal bias, and thus to reduce the uncertainty associated with human choice.*

Clearly, also computing technology has been proposed to address all of the above areas of uncertainty—to either control or minimize it: the first computational support, what was then called a rule-based expert system, was introduced more than 40 years ago to propose a "quantification scheme which attempts to model the inexact reasoning processes of medical experts" [48].

After the introduction of many and different computational systems, a new class of applications has recently emerged in the health care debate: the *decision support systems* embedding predictive models that have been developed by means of *machine learning* methods and techniques. These systems, which for the sake of brevity we will call ML-DSS, have recently raised a strong interest among the medical practitioners of almost every corner of the world in virtue of their high accuracy at an unprecedented extent [19, 23]. This is reflected by the stance of commentators that have recently shared their thoughts from some of the most impacted journals of the medical community (e.g. [32, 38]). These voices do not clearly indulge in techno-optimistic claims and do not refrain from offering some words of caution [11]; however, the recent successes of ML-DSS in medical imaging pose the issue of how these systems and their improved versions will impact in the near future those medical professions whose tasks are mostly based on pattern recognition, like radiologists, pathologists and dermatologists and how it will impact health care in general [32, 38]. In regard to this, two elements should be object of further scholarly interest and research, which are bound together by a feedback loop making their mutual influence subtle but yet hard to pinpoint. First: how ML-DSS can bias human interpretation and decision, or *automation bias*. Second: how human interpretation and classification can bias the ML-DSS performance, or *information bias*. While the former case is still neglected but some first studies are shedding light on it [39], in this paper we will focus on the latter case, which is almost completely ignored, especially by the computer scientists and designers of ML models. Nevertheless information bias, which we will define in the next section, regards the quality[1] of both the training and input data of ML-DSS, and hence has got the potential to undermine the reliability of the output of ML-DSS. Our point is that a renovated awareness of the irreducible nature of the uncertainty of medical phenomena, even in regard to their plain representation into medical data, can help put in the right perspective the current potential of ML-DSS and motivate the exploration of alternative ways to conceive them and validate their indications.

2 Information Bias, the Open Secret of Medical Records

Before considering information bias from a medical perspective, let us recall what a ML predictive model is. A predictive model, no exception those developed with a machine learning approach,[2] are *functionally relational* models that bind input data to one category out of a set of predefined ones (most of the times encompassing only two options, like positive/negative). This category is the output (or prediction) of the model. To this aim, the model is progressively fine-tuned on the basis of what ML experts call *experience* [37, p. 2], that is input data that have been already classified in terms of a specific category. In the case of medical classification (for both diagnostic or prognostic aims) the above "experience" is a set of cases that have been already classified "correctly" *according to some gold standard method*. In so doing, the machine can learn the model, that is the hidden relationship between the cases (as long as they are represented in terms of the same attributes and characteristics), and hence their correct interpretation. Grounding on this model, the ML-DSS can "predict" the right category or label when fed with new cases, as long as these are sufficiently similar to those ones with which it has been trained.

The point we address here is: how much valid and reliable is the above "experience" on which ML-DSS learn their predictive model? Here it comes the concept of information bias [2], and the related one of information variability, which both undermine the extent we can be certain of the available data, and hence of the predictions ML models can infer from them. Information bias is a collective name for all the human biases that distort the data on which a decision maker (or a computational decision support) rely on, and that account for the validity of data, that is the extent these represent what they are supposed to represent accurately.

This kind of bias[3] can take various forms including, most manuals concur, measurement error, misclassification and miscoding. However, this bias should *not* be only associated with errors and mistakes by the physicians due to either negligence,

---

[1]This is a vague term: here we mean data quality mainly in terms of accuracy and validity.

[2]In what follows we introduce the concept of ML predictive model with reference to supervised discriminative (or classification) models, by far the most frequently used in medicine.

[3]While biases are, strictly speaking, mental prejudices, idiosyncratic perceptions and cognitive behaviors producing an either impairing and distorting effect, here we rather intend the effect (by metonymy), that is the "error" in the data recorded and the decisions taken caused by the bias itself.

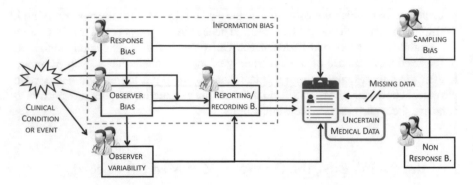

Fig. 1 The main biases affecting the validity and reliability of medical data. Sampling and non-response biases are indicated to account for the lack of information that, if present, could reduce uncertainty of representation

incompetence or inexperience. In medicine, information bias can be due to both patients and physicians in different but intertwined ways (see Fig. 1). Patient can (often unaware) contribute in terms of *response bias*, that occurs whenever what the patient says or reports is inaccurate, incomplete or both. This bias occurs when patients either exaggerate or understate their conditions (for many reasons and often in good faith), or whenever they intentionally suppress some information (e.g., like in case of sexually transmitted diseases or drug history for the related social stigma) or distort it or when their recall is limited or flawed, or simply because they do not understand what physicians ask them or they aim to respond how (they believe) physicians expect them to (cf. the particular kind of response bias known as "social desirability bias"). A large extent of response bias can be related to the inability of the observer to get confidence of the respondent. As an example, a recent study [47] focused on the degree of concordance agreement between patients and cardiologists in regard to the presence of angina pectoris and its frequency. The study showed that when patients reported monthly angina symptoms, cardiologists agreed only 17% of time, while among patients with angina symptoms reported daily/weekly, approximately one quarter of them were noted as having no angina by their physicians. Besides the above mentioned condescending bias, it is well known that patients can exhibit behaviors (cf. Hawthorne effect), or even levels of some physiological parameter (usually blood pressure in what is also known as 'white-coat effect') when they are under examination in a clinical setting that they would not exhibit in other settings.

Physicians introduce *observer bias* in their data due to both perceptual, cognitive and behavioral traits, weaknesses or just "bad habits"; this bias also occurs whenever they favor one type of response or measurement over others (cf. confirmation bias). Those who observe a clinical condition are often those who report it in the medical record. In this case observer bias can blur with is denoted as either recording, reporting, or coding bias. In particular, this latter distorting factor can be traced back to many causes, from the least common and most poorly studied, like digit preference and conflictual coding, to the most pervasive ones, like the intrinsic inadequacies of any classification schema. Conflictual coding can affect the accuracy and complete-ness of medical data when proper reporting clashes with the personal interests of those who are supposed to document a clinical condition (like in the case of blood pressure recordings within a quality and outcome assessment framework of incentives [13]). Digit preference occurs when measurements are more frequently recorded ending with 0 or 5, or as results of arbitrary rounding off. In [27] the authors observed a much larger occurrence of these two digits in renal cell carcinoma measurement and concluded that this recording behavior could affect the determination of tumour stage, "with resulting consequences in regard to prognosis and patient management". Moreover, coding variability that leads to a lack of reliability can happen even when instructions on how to proper code are well known: a study [3] compared consistency of coding supposedly clean and high-quality data-source like clinical research form from observational studies among three professional coders, each using the same terminology and with the same instructions. All three coders agreed on the same core concept 33% of the time; two of the three coders selected the same core concept 44% of the time; and, no agreement among all three was found 23% of the time. Moreover, no significant level of agreement beyond that due to chance was found among the experts. On the other hand, the shortcomings of classifying taxonomies and measurement scales would deserve a study of its own. In a famous work, Star and Bowker [6, p. 69] hinted at some of these inadequacies, which include: temporal rigidity; a one-size-fits-all nature in regard to meaning and implications; and, as also discussed in [52], the reflection of disciplinary interests, agendas and priorities.

Last, but not least, information bias in medicine can also be traced back to some sort of *intrinsic ambiguity* of the medical conditions being documented, due to either their instability over time, or to variability across subjects and across observers. A noteworthy example of this sort of ambiguity can be found in a recent study by Dharmarajan and colleagues [16]. This study focused on elderly people diagnosed (at hospital admission) with one of the following conditions: pneumonia, chronic obstructive pulmonary disease, or heart failure. These are three common conditions of the elderly that are responsible for breathlessness and other warning symptoms usually requiring hospital admission. The authors showed that patients regularly received, during hospital stay, concurrent treatment for two or more of the above cardiopulmonary conditions and not only for the main diagnosis identified at hospi-tal admission. This exemplifies the fact that in real-world clinical practice, patients' clinical pictures are often blurry and not capable of being associated with clear-cut labels as expressed instead in textbooks and clinical practice guidelines. Indeed, even common clinical syndromes have disease presentations that often fall in-between traditional diagnostic categories. The common and relevant overlap of medical treat-ments as in the case mentioned above highlights the intrinsic ambiguity of clinical phenomena and the downstream uncertainty that medical doctors face in choosing what they deem a single right therapeutic strategy for a specific disorder.

This latter sort of variability, as well as the biases mentioned above cannot be addressed by improving the accuracy of any measurement tool, or by any other contrivance conceived from the engineering standpoint. Moreover, the extent these biases are expressed in a clinical setting varies a lot: although they look as abstract and general categories, biases are always exhibited by someone in particular, they are highly situated, and depend on personal skills, like clinical perspicuity, life-long acquired competencies, and contingent workloads. Since the impact of personal biases are difficult (if impossible) to prevent, medical organizations try to minimize them with redundancy of effort, like relying on double checking and on second (or multiple) opinion. However, multiple opinions are both a resource to fight biases (by averaging multiple observations and measures), and, paradoxically enough, a source of low reliability and further uncertainty ('Quot capita, tot sententiae'). Indeed, when more than one physician are supposed to determine the presence of a sign, make a diagnosis, or assess the severity of a condition, *observer variability* is introduced to account for the discrepancies in their decisions and for any difference in considering the same conditions. Observer variability has to do with the reliability of the judgment of so called medical "raters", and with the agreement that these latter ones reach independently of each other when they either measure, classify or interpret the *same* phenomenon (e.g. an electrocardiogram, a radiography, a pathological sample, etc.) to make a decision, mainly a diagnosis.

In medicine, not only multiple raters could classify the same phenomenon in different ways, but also the same doctor can disagree with herself, examining the same case after a certain amount of time, or in different environment conditions (e.g., with respect to workload, interruption rate, work shift).

To account for the extent the majority decision (in case of multiple raters) or the category chosen more frequently can be considered reliable, and hence "true", the so called *inter-rater agreement* (or reliability, IRR) is measured.

3   Between Gold Standards and Ghost Standards

A "gold standard" (or with a less evocative but more correct expression "criterion standard") is a reference method to ascertain medical truth in regard to the accuracy of any diagnostic test. By 'reference' here we mean the 'best one' under reasonable conditions, that is the method that 'by definition' is capable to pose the so called "ground truth" for any practical aim, including the development of a ML-DSS. However, the degree of truth that a gold standard usually reaches is far from resembling an accurate, unambiguous and unique representation of medical facts that computer scientists long for their "ground-truthing", i.e., the process of gathering objective data to train a ML model. In fact, even in regard to those tests that are usually considered the most reliable and definitive gold standards, like post-mortem, histological and genetic examinations, whenever there is a human factor, variability, and hence uncertainty, can emerge [7, 55, 56] as if the observers were called to observe and account for phantom phenomena. In all of these cases, IRR scores can give an idea of the extent the data that doctors collect, which glitter in medical datasets, are golden or alloyed.

Medical researchers use several techniques to measure IRR: the most frequently used is the Cohen's Kappa, although this is applicable only to categorical values assigned by two raters. Recently also the Krippendorf' Alpha has found some application, probably for its known advantages on the kappa, like the capability to address any number of raters (not just two), values of any level of measurement (i.e., categorical, ordinal, interval, etc.), and datasets with missing values, which are very common in medical records.

All these metrics are intended to assess the degree of agreement *beyond chance* (that is considering the fact that raters can agree not only because they believe the same thing, but also by chance). As such, there is a lot of controversy on their validity (lacking any model of how chance affects the rater decisions, let alone of the different ways to *misinterpret* a phenomenon) and, above all, regarding how to interpret their scores [34].

To give an example of the above concepts, we consider an ambit where ML-DSS have recently reached levels of diagnostic accuracy (at least) on a par with human doctors. A convolutional neural network was recently trained and then evaluated in regard to the detection of diabetic retinopathy (which is cause of 1 case of blindness out of 10) in a wide dataset of retinal fundus photographs [23]. In this study, the authors reported high levels of both sensitivity and specificity for their ML-DSS according to the gold standard that they decided to adopt, i.e. the majority decision of a panel of board-certified ophthalmologists analyzing the same retinal fundus photographs. As a matter of fact, some authors reported that the adoption of this gold standard can be considered controversial [59], since this may compare unfavorably with other gold standards used in previous studies on diabetic retinopathy (i.e. standardized centralized assessment of images or optical coherence tomography). In fact, the prevalence of diabetic retinopathy may vary significantly whether this condition is evaluated through monocular fundus photographs or, rather, through optical coherence tomography [58]. This could turn out to be relevant since diagnostic accuracy metrics are dependent on the prevalence of diseases according to the Bayes' theorem. Thus, two questions are at stake here. On the one hand, whether similar successful results would have been obtained if a different gold standard (e.g., optical coherence tomography) had been used. On the other hand, even if we assume eye fundus photographs as an indisputable, unique and reliable gold standard for the diagnosis of diabetic retinopathy, IRR among ophthalmic care providers has been shown to be very low (i.e., kappa between 0.27 and 0.34 for different diagnostic analyses); and still inadequate, even if higher, among retina specialists (kappa between 0.58 and 0.63) [46].

4 Garbage In, Gospel Out

The question of the quality of medical record and of the data extracted from there is still understudied [9]. The assumption that medical data could support secondary uses has been challenged since almost 25 years ago, and also strongly so, e.g., by Reiser [45], who described several cases of erroneous, missing and ambiguous data, and by Burnum [8], who provocatively wrote that "all medical record information should be regarded as suspect; much of it is fiction" (p. 484)", and that the introduction of health information technology had not led to improvements in the quality of medical data recorded therein, but rather to the recording of a greater quantity of "bad data".[4] In those same years, van der Lei was among the first ones to warn against the reuse of clinical data for other goals other than care and proposed what since then is known as the first law of informatics: '[d]ata shall be used only for the purpose for which they were collected' [54]. These claims are reflected in some recent research articles in higly impacted medical journals that warn about the risks and challenges related to the use of routinely collected data (e.g. from electronic health records) for clinical decision making [1, 28].

In light of the phenomena of both low quality and uncertainty that are intrinsic to the production of medical data, what are the main implications for the machines that are fed with this information? As widely known, many factors can contribute in downsizing the performance of a ML-DSS. Just to mention a few that we observed in the hospital domain: the fact that medical data seldom meet the common assumptions that training data should ideally possess: their attributes are seldom independent and identically distributed (IDD); their distribution is not uniform or normal; missing data do not occur randomly (in fact they often indicate an either good or just better health condition that relieves practitioners from the need to record it with continuous effort); data can be strongly unbalanced with respect to the number of healthy and positive cases, or to the real incidence of a pathological condition; they are not temporally stable (for instance, computer interpretations of electrocardiograms recorded just one minute apart were found significantly different in 4 of 10 cases in [50]); they can fall short of representing the target population (*sampling bias*) or to make explicit any potential confounding variable (especially those related to "external" medical interventions [41]).

In this view, misclassified cases by information bias could be seen as just another issue to cope with. However, our point is that to consider misclassification a defect of data collection is a conceptual error as long as it is considered a *mis*-classification: as we saw above, it is just a classification where independent observers disagree and classify the same phenomenon differently, to the best of their competence, perspicacity and perceptual acuity.

This variability if often neglected even by doctors, and few studies indulge in reporting low IRR scores. No wonder then that the related uncertainty is dispelled as closely as possible to the "source", as also the official guidelines for medical coding and reporting (International Classification of Diseases, Ninth Revision, Clinical Modification, ICD9-CM) ratify in an explicit way: *"If the diagnosis documented at the time of discharge is qualified as 'probable', 'suspected', 'likely', 'questionable', 'possible', or 'still to be ruled out', or other similar terms indicating uncertainty, code the condition as if it existed or was established"* [43, p. 90]. Alternatively uncertainty is sublimated in the (statistically significant) consensus of a sufficiently wide group of experts [51].

---

[4]Moreover, Burnum traced back this lie of the land to "standards of care and a reimbursement system [that is] blind to biologic diversity".

Adopting different gold standards could affect ML-DSS significantly. We illustrate this by mentioning the case of Carpal Tunnel Syndrome (CTS): this is a kind of functional hand impairment that is frequently observed due to the compression of the median nerve at the wrist. This syndrome is commonly diagnosed and often referred to surgical treatment through either the sole physical examination by *orthopedic surgeons* or by a nerve conduction examination (electromyography) by *neurologists* [4]. In the last years, alternative diagnostic methods have been proposed to improve diagnostic accuracy for CTS, like the ultrasonography of the median nerve of the arm. These tests which have shown different results in accuracy metrics when compared to the previous standards mentioned above (i.e. physical examination or electromyography) [4]. These diagnostic divergences, if neglected in the training of a ML classifier aimed at the diagnosis of CTS [36], may result in the ossification into the model of an arbitrarily partial version of the ground truth (that is whether patient X is really affected by CTS or this syndrome can be ruled out) and hence to unpredictable downstream *clinical* consequences. For instance, it has been observed that a number of patients diagnosed with CTS who had undergone surgery did not receive any relevant benefit from the invasive treatment, and that this could be explained in terms of wrong upstream diagnoses [21]. A ML-DSS that has learned the *uncertain* (i.e., right for a standard, wrong for another) mapping between the patient's features and one single diagnosis will propose its advice within a dangerous "close-world assumption" (that is: all the relevant features have been considered and the mapping between the input and the desired output is acquired as accurate and reliable), which is never challenged *by design*.

On the other hand, in the open world of hospital wards physicians are used to observer variability and less-than-perfect gold standards whenever they consult the medical data that are produced by their colleagues and even by themselves. Conversely, designers of computational systems usually do not consider the case that the input of their system can be inherently and irremediably biased and inaccurate (to some extent), they assume it true. The primary concern of ML-DSS designers are the completeness, timeliness and consistency [9] of the datasets that they feed into the machines. There is little (if any) recognition that medical data could not be any better than "dirty" data with which to think to optimize a ML model adequately would be highly optimistic if not over-ambitious. Contrarian thinking would then suggest to look with some caution at the high accuracy rates that are often reported in the specialist literature (e.g. in [19]) even assuming that model overfitting has been duly avoided.

This is hardly considered when medical data are taken from the context where they have been natively produced to support coordination, knowledge sharing, sense making and decision making and they are transformed into data sets to feed in some computational systems. Neglecting the gap between the primary use of medical data (i.e., care) and any secondary use (e.g., ML-DSS training) could mislead those who have to design trustworthy decision support systems, and also probably jeopardize the actual improvement of the ML-DSS performance on new and real data other than the training data.

This points to the difference between *research data*, which are usually used for ML-DSS training and optimization; and *real-world* data, which are produced in real-life clinical situations. While research data are not made up on purpose to get high accuracy, they are nevertheless selected, cleansed, and *engineered* to an extent that is completely unrealistic or unfeasible to replicate in actual clinical settings. This is not only a matter of generalizability and interpretability of the model. It is also a matter of different ways to evaluate ML-DSS. The most common one can be considered *essentialist* [12], in that it focuses on accuracy and other performance measures (like F1-scores and AUC-ROC) that are appraised in a laboratory setting (i.e., *in laboratorio*). An alternative and still neglected approach, which is the *consequentialist* one, focuses on the actual clincal outcomes (consequences) produced in situated practice (i.e., *in labore*), that is in the original context of work of the physicians involved and in their actual relationship with patients, when decisions must be converted into real-life choices that must align with the patients' attitudes, preferences, fears and hopes, as well as with the economic feasibility of the available options.

5   Embracing Uncertainty, Also in Computation

As hinted above, there are many types of uncertainty in medicine, which affect medical records in different ways. For a certain attribute (i.e., variable) that is pertinent for a certain case, users could ignore what value is applicable, let alone true; or what single value is true among a finite set of values that are known to be equally applicable. Users could be uncertain between two values from the above set, or among many. Moreover, they could prefer some options with respect to others. If single users are certain about a value, they could nevertheless disagree among each other (and even with themselves over time). Ultimately, they could be uncertain among different values at various levels of confidence with respect to each other (e.g., in a dichotomous domain, which is the simplest, doctor A is *fairly* certain that the condition is pathological, doctor B is *strongly* certain).

As shown by Svensson et al. in [51], the performance of ML-DSS is negatively impacted and deeply undermined when fed with medical datasets that are intrinsically uncertain. Their idea is to employ conventional statistical tests to reduce the variability of the data produced by different observers by choosing the values that have been proposed by a statistically significant majority of the observers. However effective, this could be also seen as a way to discard the richness of a multi-value representation that accounts for a manifold phenomenon, which competent and skillful observers can describe each in her own, and partially sound yet specifically irreproachable, way.

Thus, if we take the "dirtiness" and "manifoldness" (seen as sides of the same coin) of medical data as a given factor of medicine, one could wonder: how can ML techniques take these constraints seriously, and even exploit them to get a richer picture of the phenomena of interest; and hence build models that could really support human experts in their daily, and uncertain, practice?

First of all, let us remark once more that there exist different kinds of uncertainty, as exemplified above. Indeed, if we look at the different classifications and taxonomies of uncertainty [40], we find a long list of terms, such as: Absence, Ambiguity, Approximation, Belief, Conflict, Confusion, Fuzziness, Imprecision, Inaccuracy, Incompleteness, Inconsistency, Incorrectness, Irrelevance, Likelihood, Non-specificity, Probability, Randomness, . . . Each form has its own tools to represent and manage it, to name a few: probability theory, fuzzy sets, possibility theory, evidence theory, rough sets. By large, the predominant role is played by probability theory, and machine learning is not an exception in this attitude. However, there exist solutions (in some case preliminary attempts) to incorporate other tools in machine learning (see e.g., [5, 15, 30]). There are several reasons why these approaches are not well established in ML, as widely discussed in [31] for the fuzzy set case: sometimes the new tools are naïves; there is not a connection among different communities; there is a problem of credibility for many young, or at least not as well established as probability theory, disciplines. However, if we want to deal with all the different forms of uncertainty, it is needed and possible to directly manage them. Indeed, it is our belief that the above discussed flaws in data can be addressed in machine learning by making use of the appropriate tools. In the following we give some hints on how this can be done, making reference to the biases previously discussed.

At first, let us consider the problem of representing a rater reliability. It is always assumed that ratings are exact, though they may be classified as "deterministic" or "random", where random means that "the rater is uncertain about the response category" [24]. More than a question of randomness, this description points to a form of epistemic uncertainty which can be handled by not assuming exactness and introducing graduality on the judgment scale of a rater. For instance, we could have three levels of certainty (i.e., low/fair/good) on the assigned score and/or the rater can express her uncertainty by selecting more than one score with its own level of certainty. This kind of uncertainty can be applied also to the input data and we can represent the fact that a patient has *low* headache and *high* nausea, whereas in a dichotomic situation we were forced to say *no* headache and *yes* nausea. This situation can be handled with Possibility Theory and, in particular, with its simplified form of certainty-based model [42], which is more interpretable and simple from a computational standpoint. Of course, machine learning tools have to be modified to comply with this model, though some steps in this direction already exists [25, 29]. Worth mentioning is also the fuzzication of the Arden syntax aimed "at simplifying programmes which process indeterminate data by means of fuzzy logic" [57].

As another problem, let us consider a numerical information, such as the one obtained by some measurement. Of course, any point value brings an imprecision, due to the instrument itself or to an average among repeated measures, etc. Thus, we can consider to represent the information in form of an interval and directly work with it. To this scope, interval arithmetics and fuzzy arithmetics [35] give the formal instruments to operate with this kind of representation.

Finally, it is well known that data often come with missing values. A standard approach in ML is to impute them in order to get a complete dataset. Of course, in this way, we loose the original information and some errors or at least imprecisions are introduced. On the contrary, we should not get rid of the missing values and moreover take into account that a missing value can have several meanings, such as ignorance, non existence, etc. Rough set theory includes rule induction methods that comply with missing values and also with different meanings of it. In particular, we point the attention to the works by J. Gryzmala-Busse and his MLEM algorithm [22]. We also notice that some attempts to directly deal with missing values exist also in other ML approaches, such as fuzzy clustering [26].

6 Conclusions

Fox [20] in her relevant work on the sociology of medical knowledge once wrote that uncertainty has become the hallmark of the entire field of medicine. For this reason, confronting uncertainty has been the first and foremost driver for the introduction of computational Decision Support Systems in medicine and their increasingly wide adoption in clinical settings. We could just speculate on why medicine has turned to technology to "make sense of health data" (to cite a position paper on Nature published a couple of years ago [18]). Quite subtly, Katz [33] has argued that the traditional mechanisms that physicians use to adopt to cope with uncertainty (e.g., terminological standards, standard care protocols, guidelines based on statistical studies) can slowly push them towards disregarding or even opposing uncertainty.

Irrespective of the root causes of this situation, the digitization of medicine has contributed to shifting the idea of uncertainty, from being a natural and irreducible element of medical practice [49] in the interpretation of subtle and sometimes contradictory clues in the existential and complex context of idiosyncratic patients, into the domain of those rational problems that can be modeled to pursue an engineering solution, or even a computational one.

In this paper we have briefly explored the blurring boundaries between what computer scientists and medical doctors pursue in medical data: data accuracy and completeness the former ones; trustworthiness and meaningfulness the latter ones [9]. We have also shed light on information bias and observer variability, which separate us from getting an absolute true, universal and reliable *representation* of a physical (let alone psychological or mental) phenomenon. In particular for the ML designers, we have pointed out that information bias does not regard only the labelling of data set, i.e., the information on which a ML-DSS is trained to predict other labels accurately; but it also (and above all) affects the whole input data, in both training and prediction, especially in regard to nominal and ordinal variables.

In light of these different viewpoints, we outline a couple of recommendations along the general framework by Domingos, who conceives ML problems as a combination of *representation*, *optimization* and *evaluation* [17]. From the representation perspective, computer scientists should not settle for "polished data" but rather "get to the source" of medical data: the multiple, possibly divergent opinions of experts. This means to be wary of researches where the gold standard is not reported or it is a dataset annotated by a single, or just a couple of physicians. Moreover, if the adopted gold standard is based on a consensus reconciliation of divergent opinions, the authors of those researches should also be aware that they proceed considering all of these divergences plain mistakes. If they are less than certain this is fair, they should offer a word of caution on the potential arbitrariness of the clearly-cut classification they have used in their study. In the study design phase authors could also ask the competent observers the degree of self-perceived confidence with which they share their ideas and produce their data. This ordinal scale could be used to weight the multiple values of a single representation, so that the ML algorithms can leverage again the knowledge of the domain experts to build a coherently *fuzzy* representation. Furthermore they could annotate the representativeness of each value in terms of a three-way partitioning (e.g, belonging to the majority opinion, belonging to the minority, belonging to neither with statistical significance [10]). In any case, ML researchers should always report how they did collect their ground truth, relying on what gold standard.

In regard to optimization, further research should be devoted in transferring techniques and methods from the rough set theory [53] domain into the ML arena.

In regard to evaluation, the ball could be passed to the medical practitioners again. They should develop a wariness of any essentialist evaluations of ML-DSS performance that are carried out *in laboratorio*, on *research data* and are expressed as *accuracy metrics*. Rather, they should demand to the ML-DSS designers (and their advocates) *evidence-based* validations of their systems, that are focused on *health outcomes* and adopt them only once some further information has been given about, e.g. the trade-off between the internal (i.e., bias) and external (i.e., variance) validity of the model (regarding also the extent the ML-DSS could fit multimorbid cases, instead of being excessively specialized for one disease); and between its prediction power and its interpretability [14], that is its *scrutability* by doctors and lay users to understand why the ML-DSS has suggested them a certain decision over possible others and make the "hybrid" agency of man-and-machine more accountable towards the colleagues, the patients and their dears. Even more than that, ML-DSS should be object of a *value-based* assessment, where researchers invest time and effort on the evaluation of their systems in the mid- long-term after their deployment in real settings and their appraisal is conducted in terms of user and patient satisfaction, in terms of effect size on clinical outcomes, and eventually in terms of cost reduction or better service provision. All these elements should not be overlooked or given for granted, especially in light of the perils of automation bias (such as deskilling, technology overreliance and overdependence) not least the surreptitious increase of trust by doctors in numbers and the "objective facts" (cf. McNamara fallacy) that the reckless application of *machine learning* in response to an excessive *human yearning* for certainty could bring in, especially in fields where this is likely to turn out to be only a dream of ignorance.

References

1. Ahmad, F.S., Chan, C., Rosenman, M.B., Post, W.S., Fort, D.G., Greenland, P., Liu, K.J., Kho, A., Allen, N.B.: Validity of cardiovascular data from electronic sources: the multi-ethnic study of atherosclerosis and HealthLNK. Circulation 117 (2017)
2. Althubaiti, A.: Information bias in health research: definition, pitfalls, and adjustment methods. J. Multidiscip. Healthc. **9**, 211 (2016)
3. Andrews, J.E., Richesson, R.L., Krischer, J.: Variation of SNOMED CT coding of clinical research concepts among coding experts. J. Am. Med. Inf. Assoc. **14**(4), 497–506 (2007)
4. Bachmann, L.M., Jüni, P., Reichenbach, S., Ziswiler, H.R., Kessels, A.G., Vögelin, E.: Consequences of different diagnostic gold standards in test accuracy research: Carpal tunnel syndrome as an example. Int. J. Epidemiol. **34**(4), 953–955 (2005)
5. Bello, R., Falcon, R.: Rough Sets in Machine Learning: a review, pp. 87–118. Springer International Publishing, Cham (2017)
6. Bowker, G.C., Star, S.L.: Sorting Things Out: classification and its consequences. MIT press (2000)
7. Braun, R., Gutkowicz-Krusin, D., Rabinovitz, H., Cognetta, A., Hofmann-Wellenhof, R., Ahlgrimm-Siess, V., Polsky, D., Oliviero, M., Kolm, I., Googe, P., et al.: Agreement of dermatopathologists in the evaluation of clinically difficult melanocytic lesions: how golden is the gold standard ? Dermatology **224**(1), 51–58 (2012)
8. Burnum, J.F.: The misinformation era: the fall of the medical record. Ann. Int. Med. **110**(6), 482–484 (1989)
9. Cabitza, F., Batini, C.: Information quality in healthcare. In: Data and Information Quality, Chap. 13, pp. 421–438. Springer (2016)
10. Cabitza, F., Ciucci, D., Locoro, A.: Exploiting collective knowledge with three-way decision theory: cases from the questionnaire-based research. Int. J. Approx. Reason. **83**, 356–370 (2017)
11. Cabitza, F., Rasoini, R., Gensini, G.F.: Unintended consequences of machine learning in medicine. Jama **318**(6), 517–518 (2017)
12. Cappelletti, P.: Appropriateness of diagnostics tests. Int. J. Lab. Hematol. **38**(S1), 91–99 (2016)
13. Carey, I., Nightingale, C., DeWilde, S., Harris, T., Whincup, P., Cook, D.: Blood pressure recording bias during a period when the quality and outcomes framework was introduced. J. Hum. Hypertens. **23**(11), 764 (2009)
14. Caruana, R., Lou, Y., Gehrke, J., Koch, P., Sturm, M., Elhadad, N.: Intelligible models for healthcare: Predicting pneumonia risk and hospital 30-day readmission. In: Proceedings of the 21th ACM SIGKDD International Conference on Knowledge Discovery and Data Mining. pp. 1721–1730. ACM (2015)
15. Denœux, T., Kanjanatarakul, O.: Evidential Clustering: a review, pp. 24–35 (2016)
16. Dharmarajan, K., Strait, K.M., Tinetti, M.E., Lagu, T., Lindenauer, P.K., Lynn, J., Krukas, M.R., Ernst, F.R., Li, S.X., Krumholz, H.M.: Treatment for multiple acute cardiopulmonary conditions in older adults hospitalized with pneumonia, chronic obstructive pulmonary disease, or heart failure. J. Am. Geriatr. Soc. **64**(8), 1574–1582 (2016)
17. Domingos, P.: A few useful things to know about machine learning. Commun. ACM **55**(10), 78–87 (2012)
18. Elliott, J.H., Grimshaw, J., Altman, R., Bero, L., Goodman, S.N., Henry, D., Macleod, M., Tovey, D., Tugwell, P., White, H., et al.: Informatics: make sense of health data. Nature **527**, 31–32 (2015)
19. Esteva, A., Kuprel, B., Novoa, R.A., Ko, J., Swetter, S.M., Blau, H.M., Thrun, S.: Dermatologist-level classification of skin cancer with deep neural networks. Nature **542**(7639), 115–118 (2017)
20. Fox, R.C.: Medical uncertainty revisited. Handb. Soc. Stud. Health Med. 409–425 (2000)
21. Graham, B.: The diagnosis and treatment of carpal tunnel syndrome: surgery whether open or closed works, but only if the diagnosis is right. BMJ. Br. Med. J. **332**(7556), 1463 (2006)

22. Grzymala-Busse, J.W., Grzymala-Busse, W.J.: Handling missing attribute values. In: Maimon, O., Rokach, L. (eds.) Data Mining and Knowledge Discovery Handbook, pp. 33–51. Springer, US, Boston, MA (2010)
23. Gulshan, V., Peng, L., Coram, M., Stumpe, M.C., Wu, D., Narayanaswamy, A., Venugopalan, S., Widner, K., Madams, T., Cuadros, J., et al.: Development and validation of a deep learning algorithm for detection of diabetic retinopathy in retinal fundus photographs. Jama **316**(22), 2402–2410 (2016)
24. Gwet, K.: Handbook of inter-rater reliability. STATAXIS Publishing Company (2001)
25. Haouari, B., Amor, N.B., Elouedi, Z., Mellouli, K.: Naïve possibilistic network classifiers. Fuzzy Sets Syst. **160**(22), 3224–3238 (2009)
26. Hathaway, R.J., Bezdek, J.C.: Fuzzy c-means clustering of incomplete data. IEEE Trans. Syst. Man Cybernet. **31**(5), 735–744 (2001)
27. Hayes, S.: Terminal digit preference occurs in pathology reporting irrespective of patient management implication. J. Clin. Pathol. **61**(9), 1071–1072 (2008)
28. Hemkens, L.G., Contopoulos-Ioannidis, D.G., Ioannidis, J.P.: Agreement of treatment effects for mortality from routinely collected data and subsequent randomized trials: meta-epidemiological survey. BMJ **352**, i493 (2016)
29. Hüllermeier, E.: Possibilistic instance-based learning. Artif. Intell. **148**(1–2), 335–383 (2003)
30. Hüllermeier, E.: Fuzzy sets in machine learning and data mining. Appl. Soft Comput. **11**(2), 1493–1505 (2011)
31. Hüllermeier, E.: Does machine learning need fuzzy logic? Fuzzy Sets Syst. **281**, 292–299 (2015)
32. Jha, S., Topol, E.J.: Adapting to artificial intelligence: radiologists and pathologists as information specialists. JAMA **316**(22), 2353–2354 (2016)
33. Katz, J.: The silent world of doctor and patient. JHU Press (2002)
34. Krippendorff, K.: Content analysis: an introduction to its methodology. Sage (2012)
35. Lodwick, W.A.: Fundamentals of interval analysis and linkages to fuzzy set theory, pp. 55–79. Wiley (2008)
36. Maravalle, M., Ricca, F., Simeone, B., Spinelli, V.: Carpal tunnel syndrome automatic classification: electromyography vs. ultrasound imaging. TOP **23**(1), 100–123 (2015)
37. Mitchell, T.M.: Machine learning, Burr Ridge, IL: McGraw Hill **45**(37), 870–877 (1997)
38. Obermeyer, Z., Emanuel, E.J.: Predicting the future big data, machine learning, and clinical medicine. New Engl. J. Med. **375**(13), 1216 (2016)
39. Parasuraman, R., Manzey, D.H.: Complacency and bias in human use of automation: an attentional integration. Hum. Factors J. Hum. Factors Ergon. Soc. **52**(3), 381–410 (2010)
40. Parsons, S.: Qualitative Approaches for Reasoning Under Uncertainty. The MIT Press, Cambridge, Massachussets (2001)
41. Paxton, C., Niculescu-Mizil, A., Saria, S.: Developing predictive models using electronic medical records: challenges and pitfalls. In: AMIA Annual Symposium Proceedings. vol. 2013, p. 1109. American Medical Informatics Association (2013)
42. Pivert, O., Prade, H.: A certainty-based model for uncertain databases. IEEE Trans. Fuzzy Syst. **23**(4), 1181–1196 (2015)
43. Prevention, C., et al.: For disease control, ICD-9-CM official guidelines for coding and reporting. Technical Report Centers for Medicare & Medicaid Services, Atlanta, GA, USA (2011)
44. Reiser, S.J., Anbar, M.: The Machine at the Bedside: strategies for using technology in patient care. Cambridge University Press (1984)
45. Reiser, S.J.: The clinical record in medicine Part 2: Reforming content and purpose. Ann. Intern. Med. **114**(11), 980–985 (1991)
46. Ruamviboonsuk, P., Teerasuwanajak, K., Tiensuwan, M., Yuttitham, K., for Diabetic Retinopathy Study Group, T.S., et al.: Interobserver agreement in the interpretation of single-field digital fundus images for diabetic retinopathy screening. Ophthalmology **113**(5), 826–832 (2006)
47. Shafiq, A., Arnold, S.V., Gosch, K., Kureshi, F., Breeding, T., Jones, P.G., Beltrame, J., Spertus, J.A.: Patient and physician discordance in reporting symptoms of angina among stable coronary artery disease patients: Insights from the angina prevalence and provider evaluation of angina relief (appear) study. Am. Heart J. **175**, 94–100 (2016)

48. Shortliffe, E.H., Buchanan, B.G.: A model of inexact reasoning in medicine. Math. Biosci. **23**(3–4), 351–379 (1975)
49. Simpkin, A.L., Schwartzstein, R.M.: Tolerating uncertainty the next medical revolution? New Engl. J. Med. **375**(18), 1713–1715 (2016)
50. Spodick, D.H., Bishop, R.L.: Computer treason: intraobserver variability of an electrocardio-graphic computer system. Am. J. Cardiol. **80**(1), 102–103 (1997)
51. Svensson, C.M., Hubler, R., Figge, M.T.: Automated classification of circulating tumor cells and the impact of interobsever variability on classifier training and performance. J. Immunol. Res. **2015** (2015)
52. Timmermans, S., Berg, M.: The Gold Standard: the challenge of evidence-based medicine and standardization in health care. Temple University Press (2010)
53. Tsumoto, S.: Medical diagnosis: rough set view. In: Thriving Rough Sets, pp. 139–156. Springer (2017)
54. van der Lei, J., et al.: Use and abuse of computer-stored medical records. Methods Archive **30**, 79–80 (1991)
55. Van Driest, S.L., Wells, Q.S., Stallings, S., Bush, W.S., Gordon, A., Nickerson, D.A., Kim, J.H., Crosslin, D.R., Jarvik, G.P., Carrell, D.S., et al.: Association of arrhythmia-related genetic variants with phenotypes documented in electronic medical records. Jama **315**(1), 47–57 (2016)
56. Veress, B., Gadaleanu, V., Nennesmo, I., Wikström, B.: The reliability of autopsy diagnostics: inter-observer variation between pathologists, a preliminary report. Int. J. Qual Health Care **5**(4), 333–337 (1993)
57. Vetterlein, T., Mandl, H., Adlassnig, K.P.: Fuzzy arden syntax: a fuzzy programming language for medicine. Artif. Intell. Med. **49**(1), 1–10 (2010)
58. Wang, Y.T., Tadarati, M., Wolfson, Y., Bressler, S.B., Bressler, N.M.: Comparison of prevalence of diabetic macular edema based on monocular fundus photography vs optical coherence tomography. JAMA Ophthalmol. **134**(2), 222–228 (2016)
59. Wong, T.Y., Bressler, N.M.: Artificial intelligence with deep learning technology looks into diabetic retinopathy screening. JAMA **316**(22), 2366–2367 (2016)

Towards the Development of an Agile Marketing Capability

Ludovica Moi⬤, Francesca Cabiddu⬤ and Moreno Frau⬤

Abstract This study aims to explore the key theoretical foundations for the development of an Agile Marketing Capability (AMC) framework, through the performance of an in-depth literature review on IT and dynamic marketing capabilities. Our framework enables us to (1) advance the understanding of how IT and dynamic marketing capabilities evolve into agile marketing capabilities (2) unpack the distinctive and ongoing processes and features through which the Agile Marketing capabilities are accomplished (3) define the key propositions for a new marketing capability: the Agile Marketing Capability. This work may represent a useful framework for managers and decision makers to better understand the competitive advantages which could derive from the employment of agile marketing capabilities in order to improve their skills in challenging the continuous changes in market and customers' needs.

Keywords IT capabilities · Dynamic marketing capabilities · Agile marketing capability

1 Introduction

Marketing scholars and practitioners recognize marketing capabilities as crucial drivers in the process by which firms develop their competitive advantages and achieve higher levels of performance e.g. [4, 7, 8]. Indeed, firms have to reconfigure their marketing activities towards more agile approaches as primary condition to survive [1, 20]. Dynamic marketing capabilities constitute important drivers for a sustainable competitive advantage, specifically for firms which perform in technological and turbulent sectors. Managers who employ dynamic marketing capabilities are able to effectively and continuously respond to market changes, in order to develop new strategies, get market knowledge, and promptly reconfigure their business [4]. Additionally, the literature also suggests that IT capabilities are increasingly impor-

L. Moi (✉) · F. Cabiddu · M. Frau
Università degli Studi di Cagliari, 74, 09123 Cagliari, Italy
e-mail: ludovica.moi@unica.it

© Springer International Publishing AG, part of Springer Nature 2019
F. Cabitza et al. (eds.), *Organizing for the Digital World*, Lecture Notes in Information Systems and Organisation 28, https://doi.org/10.1007/978-3-319-90503-7_11

tant means to these ends. A firm active in product development must be able to gather technical and market information effectively and disseminate it throughout the organization. These IT capabilities facilitate internal communication and cross-functional integration [36]. Better IT is associated with greater strategic flexibility and, ultimately, with better performance and greater organizational success. A key characteristic of a strategic flexibility is agility.

Agile marketing is a new trend in marketing domain, particularly for smaller firms which need to develop more agile marketing capabilities to design strategic responses and be more competitive. Agility is a business-wide capability that embraces organizational structures, information systems, logistics processes, and, in particular, mindsets. It concerns the ability of an enterprise to quickly adapt to market changes, in a productive and cost-effective manner. These processes require many specific capabilities that enable the firm to carry out activities necessary to move its products or services through the value chain. The process of development and creation of new capabilities within a sector may be the result of a procedure of innovation, and may follow a procedure where a company develops a new capability, which is then imitated or adopted by another company in the same sector and so on [23].

Despite the growing importance of this topic, particularly for its managerial implications, there is still a lack of attention by scholars towards this field of study. The state of art requires to further investigate how firms develop their dynamic capabilities with reference to the specific business area of marketing [11], which actually represents a critical and relevant area for firms to develop capabilities able to fit customers' needs and preferences [29]. Thus, agile marketing represents a new way through which firms try to fill these objectives, but currently it constitutes a field of research which needs to be deeply explored, both from a theoretical and managerial point of view [17].

For these reasons, the purpose of this article is to provide more insights about the interaction between dynamic marketing capabilities and IT capabilities. With this object in mind, we took a stepwise approach to the agile capability-generating process Specifically, our aim is to perform an in-depth literature review on the new trends in the study of capabilities in the marketing domain, in order to define an agile marketing capability, and set the basis for the future development of research towards this really innovative topic. Indeed, we will try to answer to the research question: what are the key constructs for the development of the agile marketing capability?

The findings of this study provide the main constructs that enable firm to develop the agile marketing capability which contributes to extend the previous literature about the agile marketing literature [17]. The current work is structured as follows: in Sect. 2, we provide the literature review on IT and dynamic marketing capabilities; in Sect. 3, we perform the literature review on agile marketing, and then develop a theoretical model that explains the key dimensions for an agile marketing capability. The article ends with the discussions and conclusions that highlight the contributions of agile marketing capability to current literature on dynamic capabilities.

2   Dynamic Marketing Capabilities and IT: A Literature Review

2.1   Dynamic Marketing Capabilities

According to the marketing literature [11] it is growing the need of developing marketing capabilities as necessary condition to get a competitive advantage in foreign markets, be more market-oriented [8], survive in contexts of high competitive rivalry [39], and improve competitive resources to co-create customer value [9]. Dynamic marketing capabilities originate from the resource-based view [3], according to which firm's competitive advantage derives from firm's resources and capabilities, and the dynamic capabilities theory [13, 43], according to which firms performing in dynamic environments can develop dynamic capabilities to reconfigure continuously their internal and external resources, skills and competencies to cope with changing environments, and implement new strategies in response to new market conditions in order to gain economic advantages [43]. Broadly speaking, dynamic marketing capabilities are defined as "capabilities that use market knowledge to adapt organizational resources and capabilities" [4, p. 13]. The key theoretical patterns concerning dynamic marketing capabilities may be synthetized in terms of features, functions, components and types.

In terms of *features* [4], the literature highlights: **market knowledge** [34], which refers to the capacity to strategically absorb market knowledge towards customers, competitors, environmental trends, partners etc. in order to trigger organizational adaptation processes [28], the implementation of new strategies, and also foster innovation [7]; **cross-functional marketing capabilities**, which imply that dynamic marketing capabilities shape the performance of transversal departments and people within and outside organizations [7, 49]; **stakeholder portfolio** [14], since firms develop specific dynamic marketing capabilities according to the nature of their stakeholders portfolio, such as allied, cooperative, neutral and entrepreneur stakeholders, customers, employees, suppliers and other non-economic actors, who determine the development of different types of capabilities related to marketing activities, and influence the way in which firms develop new ideas, methods, knowledge and skills [51].

In terms of *components*, dynamic marketing capabilities own the **absorptive capability**, or the capacity to absorb market knowledge, and **knowledge management**, since after absorbing knowledge firms have to design proper mechanisms to integrate it throughout the organization, and transform it into organizational routines [4].

In terms of *functions*, dynamic marketing capabilities are conceived as cross-functional processes which renew the organizational resource base of firms. Accordingly, they aim to the **renewal of resources/capabilities** [4, 14] and CRM or management of **customer value**, both supported by the service-dominant logic [26].

In terms of *types*, throughout literature, there are several types of dynamic marketing capabilities stressed by the scholars, for instance, **new product development**

[4, 14], proactive **market orientation** [4, 14], **R&D expenditure** [34, 49], **brand equity** [14], the **Information Systems (IS) capability for agility** [42] etc.

2.2 IT Capabilities

A capability represents a peculiar ability owned by an organization or a person to achieve a specific aim [44], and derive from the combination of different resources, as people, processes and technology, that are managed by companies to cope with particular market conditions [13]. According to the literature [21], IT capabilities insert in the context of the resource-based view and dynamic capabilities theories [32], and are conceived as competitive resources owned by companies, which serve to develop high-quality IT products and services. Additionally, IT capabilities are the combination of multiple elements as internal and external human resources, software applications, etc., aimed at producing IT-enabled outputs which will represent the inputs for creating final goods or services. Following the same scheme of dynamic marketing capabilities, also the key theoretical patterns concerning IT capabilities can be synthetized in terms of features, functions, components and types.

In terms of *features*, IT capabilities are characterized by **flexibility** for the successful performance and competitiveness of firms. IT capabilities should be flexible in the international relationships, to better exploit external resources to enhance competitive performance [31]. Flexible IT capabilities enable firms to own proper external resources in order to promptly react to market changes, cope with turbulent environments, adjust efficiently their offerings, and achieve scalability of information systems [40]. Furthermore, the concept of **coordination** makes IT capability an organizational capability which serves as key driver to the sharing of information across different functions and departments [5], to pursue first-to-market initiatives, and improve their market-linking by facilitating the sharing of market knowledge and intraorganizational communication flows [36]. This mechanism allows enterprises to improve operational stability, reduce errors, increase inventory, enhance customer order cycle times etc. [18]. IT capabilities are also characterized by the feature of organizational **agility** [25], which implies higher investments in IT. Agility is a broad concept, which means that firms develop proper speed up in decision making, quickly responses to changing conditions and business environments, and particularly innovation. Accordingly, there are two corresponding categories of agility: market capitalizing agility, which refers to monitor and quickly respond to market changes in order to promptly satisfy customers needs; operational adjustment agility, which refers to the firm's ability to adapt its internal business processes to new market or demand conditions [25]. The concept of agility relates also to the concept of ambidexterity [24], which means that IT capabilities play a mediating role or dual capacity of both exploring and exploiting IT resources and practices to enhance firms' agility, and facilitate their ability to perform in dynamic environments. Moreover, agility is defined in terms of IT-enabled operational agility [41], or ability to quickly capture business opportunity quickly, be cost-efficiently and manage uncertainly, for instance by aligning and integrating processes and organizational units, creating networks to facilitate financial flows, enhancing continual adjustments on IT requirements etc.

In terms of *types*, the development of IT capabilities is an issue of **skills and competencies**. To be proper antecedents of firms' competitive performance and to create "uniqueness", groups and personnel should develop and own learning experience, skills, competencies, knowledge etc. on IT field [5], and align these IT skills and competencies with firm's business units [2]. IT skills are both externally and internally-focused capabilities [38], since externally they represent resources and accumulated knowledge which help firms to timely cope with market changes, customer and suppliers needs etc., whereas internally, they represent resources and accumulated knowledge to provide adequate and cost-efficiently offerings. This approach is also a mechanism of capability building [50], or "firm's ability to mobilize and deploy IT resources effectively to perform strategic IT planning, develop IS, leverage and use IS, and manage IT function and IT assets" (p. 329).

In terms of *functions*, IT capabilities are important drivers of **outsourcing** relationships [15]. Accordingly, IT capabilities enable firms to improve outsourcing relationships with the aim of better exploiting resources and capabilities, and improving the quality of the relationships among organizations. Moreover, outsourcing allows to develop superior market knowledge and its value [15], and also to deploy capabilities at both the client (in-sourcing) and the supplier (outsourcing) perspectives [52]. The development of IT capabilities is also highly important for driving **innovation**. Particularly, IT is a key enabler of predevelopment stage in new product development process [33], by enhancing communication and collaboration with several external and internal stakeholders to develop NPD projects, more efficient team collaboration and a higher number of prototypes generated during the predevelopment stage. Particularly, in turbulent and high competitive environments, firms need to timely access to relevant information, to share information across business partners, and to transfer this knowledge to business units in order to facilitate the development of innovative ideas. Indeed, due to the fact that IT capabilities provide enterprises the ability to be flexible and agile in responding to market changes, IT capabilities facilitate the ability of firms to be innovative, and capture new market trends and demand's needs in order to quickly adapt their offerings and business to new market conditions and requirements [25].

In terms of *components*, IT capabilities, by facilitating the flow of information and knowledge, enhance the **absorptive capability** of firms to use and assess external market knowledge to improve their business performance [15]. Indeed, from an international marketing perspective, the adoption of IT systems and the development of IT capabilities provide firms with the proper organizational and human resources to monitor market and demand changes, and in turn to improve their internal business processes [27].

3   Agile Marketing

Agile marketing is a new approach that has recently grown in marketing domain as a way through which firms are able to develop more appropriate marketing capabilities to implement strategic responses and be more competitive [19], by leveraging on organizational structures, information systems, logistics processes to quickly and cost-efficiently adapt to market changes. Following again the same scheme adopted for dynamic marketing capabilities and IT capabilities, we synthetize the key theoretical patterns concerning agile marketing in terms of features, functions, components and types. In this way, we will manage to discuss the similarities between IT capabilities, dynamic marketing capabilities and agile marketing, in order to develop the main propositions for defining an Agile Marketing Capability.

In terms of *features*, when considering agile marketing it is strongly important to deal with **omnichannel coordination**. Currently, firms cope with the big challenge of creating multiple channels to better communication with their customers in order to foster the "journey experience" that they demand. Accordingly, an omnichannel coordination allows to implement more effective marketing programs aimed at increasing profitability, customer experience and customer satisfaction [46, 53]. Omnichannel coordination leverages on both coordination capabilities and cross-functional capabilities. Coordination capabilities enable to achieve customer centricity by adopting multichannel marketing across different departments and units, and internal coordination [45]. Thus, the use of information systems aims to integrate customer information and data across channels, in order to create superior multichannel shopping experiences, and support decision-making and organizational ability to manage customer information, collect data and respond to customer feedback [22]. Cross-functional capabilities lead to develop cross-functional teams, new marketing roles related to digital marketing, networked organization, in order to inspire all levels of the company with the brand purpose and strengthen commitment, pride, motivation, collaboration, and customer experience [10].

In terms of *functions*, agile marketing is strictly related to **e-marketing**, or the adoption of information and communication technologies (ICT) for marketing purposes [1]. E-marketing leads firms to embody proper IT skills, such as managers' attitude or entrepreneurial orientation towards an e-business or eVision [35], online marketing mix or Web 2.0 applications [20, 45] as key enablers of business activities. Additionally, e-marketing enables to implement user-centered business models, to exploit the potential benefits from the use of technologies as marketing tools to access to new customers' targets [20], achieve higher customer value and be more market-oriented [35]. Furthermore, e-marketing enhances the improvement of firms' flexibility by transforming traditional marketing focus on control with an open and more collaborative approach that is appropriate to perform in current business environments [16]. The growing importance of digital technologies has affected the dynamics of corporate competition, globalization, lifestyles, customer relationships, and has radically changed how the process of buying, selling, exchange products and services take place [20]. Managers strongly benefit from the exploitation of ICTs to get quickly and more effective insights of their businesses, and to increase their level of flexibility and agility in developing marketing practices. Consequently, e-marketing enhances the absorptive capacity of firms, since it facilitates collaborative working both within business organizations and also between organizations, to get closer both to suppliers and customers [48].

In terms of *components*, agile marketing lies on **lean and agile practices**, which comes from the manufacturing sector and represent practices aimed at reducing waste and unnecessary production steps [12]. These practices in marketing field enable to achieve flexibility in terms of systematic and continuous improvement process in order to eliminate waste and inefficient processes, speed up production cycles and increase the expertise of people with the support of technology [30]. Actually, the context of turbulence and unpredictability in which firms perform, require them to constantly be ready for changes and to adapt their strategy. This core competency called "agility", defined as "the strategic mix of standardization and flexibility, targeted at those organizational pressure points where they're not only needed today, but will most likely be needed tomorrow" [6], enables firms to manage dynamic environmental scenarios. Agility management is linked to strategic innovation management [47], as well as other initiatives as create change; realize partnerships; find solutions; transfer capabilities; foster continuity [47]. Agile practices provide organizations with the proper flexibility to adopt a selected subset of principles and practices on the basis of their culture, values, types of system [37], with the aim of accommodating change during the development lifecycle, improving quality, increasing the return on investment, reducing development periods, improving customer satisfaction and team morale, reducing waste, increasing predictability etc.

In terms of *types*, agile marketing leverages on the development of **digital capabilities**. Nowadays, there is a proliferation of new tools of communication facilitated by technology advancement that digital marketers should take into account within their organization, such as digital marketing. Digital capabilities are defined as IT skills, or more specifically as those "processes, structures and skills adopted for planning and implemented digital marketing" [10]. Specifically, digital capabilities enable to: review current digital marketing approach and identify areas for improvement; identify a benchmark to cope with competitors in the same industry or sector; define good practices from more advanced adopters; to set targets and develop strategies for improving capabilities and creating a roadmap for future improvement.

3.1 Agile Marketing Capability

Working from the literature review presented above, we define Agile marketing capability as the organizational capacity of being flexible and agile in absorbing and manage market knowledge in order to implement marketing initiatives aligned to changing market conditions. The key drivers are the exploitation of IT tools and strong digital capabilities.

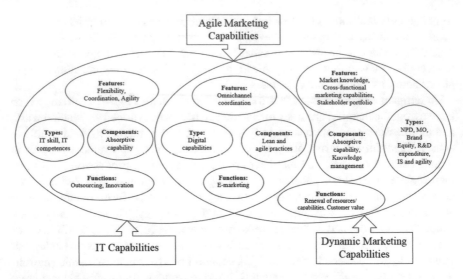

Fig. 1 Theoretical framework graphic representation

Starting from this definition we develop a theoretical model (Fig. 1), explaining the main features of an agile marketing capability. The model includes a series of propositions that explain the condition under which the agile marketing capability could be developed.

As previously described, flexibility and agility enable firms to quickly react to market changes [40] and implement the proper business adjustments [25]. Additionally, together with higher level of coordination both internally among departments, and externally with market [5, 36], firms are able to pursue marketing programs which foster customers' "journey experience" [46, 53]. Thus, we suggest the following general proposition:

Proposition 1 *Higher (lower) levels of flexibility and agility, together with coordination, in marketing field, will be associated with higher (lower) levels of agile marketing capabilities.*

The activity of outsourcing allows firms to exploit external resources to achieve superior performance and customer value [15]. Consequently, it strongly relates to innovation in providing new products and services which better respond to new market conditions [25], facilitated by the use of IT tools for marketing purposes [1]. This leads to the following proposition:

Proposition 2 *Higher (lower) levels of outsourcing and innovation for marketing activities, will be associated with higher (lower) levels of agile marketing capabilities.*

The development of absorptive capacity of market knowledge, and the management of this knowledge throughout the organization [4], enable firms to reduce waste and unnecessary steps [12] for implementing proper marketing activities which respond to changing environmental scenarios.

Proposition 3 *Higher (lower) levels of absorptive capacity and knowledge management, will be associated with higher (lower) levels of agile marketing capabilities.*

New marketing trends require firms to develop strong IT skills and competencies as well as digital capabilities in order to be proactive and timely cope with market changes, customer and suppliers needs etc. [50].

Proposition 4 *Higher (lower) levels of IT skills and competencies, and digital capabilities, will be associated with higher (lower) levels of agile marketing capabilities.*

4 Discussions and Conclusions

The concept of "agile", traditionally related to the field of software development, has recently shifted and growing towards the development of agile marketing [46]. The core reference of the agile philosophy is contained in the Agile Marketing Manifesto, which highlights how, differently from traditional marketing approaches, the presence of agile elements in marketing strategies enables to overcome traditional practical problems such as long product development cycles, wasted of time and resources etc., in order to provide iterative and incremental responses, putting customer feedbacks at the centre. Firm's agility in marketing field is an attitude of proactiveness in the marketplace, aimed at reconfiguring marketing activities at short notice to better respond to market feedbacks. Despite the importance of this field of research, prior literature lacks of the clear definition of proper capabilities related to agile marketing, which are particularly necessary from a practical perspective due to the features of current business environments in which firms perform, characterized by turbulence, dynamism and high competitive rivalry. Additionally, the literature does not shed light on how capabilities of agile marketing originate, and what are the key features that characterize them.

Our paper make the following contribution. First, we advance the understanding of how IT and dynamic marketing capabilities evolve into agile marketing capabilities. Second, we unpack the distinctive and ongoing processes and features through which the Agile Marketing capabilities is accomplished. Third, we define the key theoretical foundations of the agile marketing and develop the key propositions for a new marketing capability: the Agile Marketing Capability.

From a managerial perspective, the topic of agile marketing is particularly useful since managers strongly need to develop agile marketing capabilities in order to own the proper skills to get a competitive advantage and quickly adapt to ongoing changes in market and customers' needs.

With our research, we try to set the basis for future research towards this innovative topic, which could be interesting to deepen from a theoretical perspective and to explore through empirical case studies.

References

1. Alford, P., Page, S.J.: Marketing technology for adoption by small business. Serv. Ind. J. **35**(11–12), 655–669 (2015)
2. Aral, S., Weill, P.: IT assets, organizational capabilities, and firm performance: how resource allocations and organizational differences explain performance variation. Organ. Sci. **18**(5), 763–780 (2007)
3. Barney, J.: Firm resources and sustained competitive advantage. J. Manag. **17**(1), 99–120 (1991)
4. Barrales-Molina, V., Martínez-López, F.J., Gázquez-Abad, J.C.: Dynamic marketing capabilities: toward an integrative framework. Int. J. Manag. Rev. **16**(4), 397–416 (2014)
5. Bhatt, G.D., Grover, V.: Types of information technology capabilities and their role in competitive advantage: an empirical study. J. Manag. Inf. Syst. **22**(2), 253–277 (2005)
6. Browning, R., Duffy, J., Linde, K.: How to build an agile foundation for change (2008)
7. Bruni, D.S., Verona, G.: Dynamic marketing capabilities in science-based firms: an exploratory investigation of the pharmaceutical industry. Br. J. Manag. **20**(s1), S101–S117 (2009)
8. Cacciolatti, L., Lee, S.H.: Revisiting the relationship between marketing capabilities and firm performance: the moderating role of market orientation, marketing strategy and organisational power. J. Bus. Res. **69**(12), 5597–5610 (2016)
9. Ceric, A., D'Alessandro, S., Soutar, G., Johnson, L.: Using blueprinting and benchmarking to identify marketing resources that help co-create customer value. J. Bus. Res. **69**(12), 5653–5661 (2016)
10. Chaffey, D.: Applying organisational capability models to assess the maturity of digital-marketing governance. J. Mark. Manag. **26**(3–4), 187–196 (2010)
11. Davcik, N.S., Sharma, P.: Marketing resources, performance, and competitive advantage: a review and future research directions. J. Bus. Res. **69**(12), 5547–5552 (2016)
12. Dewell, R.: The dawn of Lean marketing. J. Digit. Asset Manag. **3**(1), 23–28 (2007)
13. Eisenhardt, K.M., Martin, J.A.: Dynamic capabilities: what are they? Strateg. Manag. J. 1105–1121 (2000)
14. Evers, N., Andersson, S., Hannibal, M.: Stakeholders and marketing capabilities in international new ventures: evidence from Ireland, Sweden and Denmark. J. Int. Mark. **20**(4), 46–71 (2012)
15. Han, K., Kauffman, R.J., Nault, B.R.: Research note—returns to information technology outsourcing. Inf. Syst. Res. **22**(4), 824–840 (2011)
16. Harris, L., Rae, A.: Social networks: the future of marketing for small business. J. Bus. Strategy **30**(5), 24–31 (2009)
17. Hoogveld, M., Koster, J.M.: Implementing omnichannel strategies the success factor of agile processes. Adv. Manag. Appl. Econ. **6**(2), 25 (2016)
18. Iyer, K.N.: Demand chain collaboration and operational performance: role of IT analytic capability and environmental uncertainty. J. Bus. Ind. Mark. **26**(2), 81–91 (2011)
19. Izvercianu, M., Serban, M., Sabina, P., Larisa, I.: An Agile approach for designing marketing activities. In: European Conference on Knowledge Management. Academic Conferences International Limited (2015)
20. Kim, H.D., Lee, I., Lee, C.K.: Building Web 2.0 enterprises: a study of small and medium enterprises in the United States. Int. Small Bus. J. **31**(2), 156–174 (2013)
21. Kishore, R., Swinarski, M.E., Jackson, E., Rao, H.R.: A quality-distinction model of IT capabilities: conceptualization and two-stage empirical validation using CMMi processes. IEEE Trans. Eng. Manag. **59**(3), 457–469 (2012)
22. Kotler, P., Rackham, N., Krishnaswamy, S.: Ending the war between sales and marketing. Harv. Bus. Rev. **84**(7/8), 68 (2006)
23. Lampel, J., Shamsie, J.: Capabilities in motion: new organizational forms and the reshaping of the Hollywood movie industry. J. Manag. Stud. **40**(8), 2189–2210 (2003)
24. Lee, O.K., Sambamurthy, V., Lim, K.H., Wei, K.K.: How does IT ambidexterity impact organizational agility? Inf. Syst. Res. **26**(2), 398–417 (2015)

25. Lu, Y., Ramamurthy, K.: Understanding the link between information technology capability and organizational agility: an empirical examination. MIS Q. 931–954 (2011)
26. Lusch, R.F., Vargo, S.L.: Service-dominant logic: reactions, reflections and refinements. Mark. Theory **6**(3), 281–288 (2006)
27. Matthyssens, P., Kirca, A.H., Pace, S., Bryan Jean, R.-J., Sinkovics, R.R., Kim, D.: Information technology and organizational performance within international business to business relationships: a review and an integrated conceptual framework. Int. Mark. Rev. **25**(5), 563–583 (2008)
28. Morgan, N.A.: Marketing and business performance. J. Acad. Mark. Sci. **40**(1), 102–119 (2012)
29. Peteraf, M.A., Bergen, M.E.: Scanning dynamic competitive landscapes: a market-based and resource-based framework. Strateg. Manag. J. **24**(10), 1027–1104 (2003)
30. Piercy, N.C., Rich, N.: Strategic marketing and operations relationships: the case of the lean enterprise. J. Strateg. Mark. **12**(3), 145–161 (2004)
31. Rai, A., Tang, X.: Leveraging IT capabilities and competitive process capabilities for the management of interorganizational relationship portfolios. Inf. Syst. Res. **21**(3), 516–542 (2010)
32. Ray, G., Barney, J.B., Muhanna, W.A.: Capabilities, business processes, and competitive advantage: choosing the dependent variable in empirical tests of the resource-based view. Strateg. Manag. J. **25**(1), 23–37 (2004)
33. Reid, M., Hultink, E.J., Marion, T., Barczak, G.: The impact of the frequency of usage of IT artifacts on predevelopment performance in the NPD process. Inf. Manag. **53**(4), 422–434 (2016)
34. Sharma, P., Davcik, N.S., Pillai, K.G.: Product innovation as a mediator in the impact of R&D expenditure and brand equity on marketing performance. J. Bus. Res. **69**(12), 5662–5669 (2016)
35. Simmons, G., Armstrong, G.A., Durkin, M.G.: An exploration of small business website optimization: enablers, influencers and an assessment approach. Int. Small Bus. J. **29**(5), 534–561 (2011)
36. Song, M., Nason, R.W., Di Benedetto, C.A.: Distinctive marketing and information technology capabilities and strategic types: a cross-national investigation. J. Int. Mark. **16**(1), 4–38 (2008)
37. Soundararajan, S.: Assessing Agile Methods: Investigating Adequacy, Capability, and Effectiveness: An Objectives, Principles, Strategies Approach (2013)
38. Stoel, M.D., Muhanna, W A.: IT capabilities and firm performance: a contingency analysis of the role of industry and IT capability type. Inf. Manag. **46**(3), 181–189 (2009)
39. Takata, H.: Effects of industry forces, market orientation, and marketing capabilities on business performance: an empirical analysis of Japanese manufacturers from 2009 to 2011. J. Bus. Res. **69**(12), 5611–5619 (2016)
40. Tallon, P.P.: Inside the adaptive enterprise: an information technology capabilities perspective on business process agility. Inf. Technol. Manag. **9**(1), 21–36 (2008)
41. Tan, F.T.C., Tan, B., Wang, W., Sedera, D.: IT-enabled operational agility: an interdependencies perspective. Inf. Manag. **54**(3), 292–303 (2017)
42. Tarafdar, M., Qrunfleh, S.: Agile supply chain strategy and supply chain performance: complementary roles of supply chain practices and information systems capability for agility. Int. J. Prod. Res. **55**(4), 925–938 (2017)
43. Teece, D.J., Pisano, G., Shuen, A.: Dynamic capabilities and strategic management. Strateg. Manag. J. 509–533 (1997)
44. Ulrich, W., Rosen, M.: The business capability map: the Rosetta Stone "of business/IT alignment". Enterp. Archit. **14** (2014)
45. Valos, M.J., Ewing, M.T., Powell, I.H.: Practitioner prognostications on the future of online marketing. J. Mark. Manag. **26**(3–4), 361–376 (2010)
46. van den Driest, F., Weed, K.: The ultimate marketing machine. Harv. Bus. Rev. **92**, 54–63 (2014)
47. Vassileva, B.: Innovation management and agile strategies for change. In: Managing Innovation and Diversity in Knowledge Society Through Turbulent Time on Proceedings of the MakeLearn and TIIM Joint International Conference, pp. 401–409. ToKnowPress (2016)

48. Wagner, C.: Breaking the knowledge acquisition bottleneck through conversational knowledge management. In: Knowledge Management on Proceeding Concepts, Methodologies, Tools, and Applications, pp. 1262–1276. IGI Global (2008)
49. Wang, E.T., Hu, H., Hu, P.J.H.: Examining the role of information technology in cultivating firms' dynamic marketing capabilities. Inf. Manag. **50**(6), 336–343 (2013)
50. Wang, N., Liang, H., Zhong, W., Xue, Y., Xiao, J.: Resource structuring or capability building? An empirical study of the business value of information technology. J. Manag. Inf. Syst. **29**(2), 325–367 (2012)
51. Wang, H.M.D., Sengupta, S.: Stakeholder relationships, brand equity, firm performance: a resource-based perspective. J. Bus. Res. **69**(12), 5561–5568 (2016)
52. Weigelt, C.: Leveraging supplier capabilities: the role of locus of capability deployment. Strateg. Manag. J. **34**(1), 1–21 (2013)
53. Weinberg, B.D., Parise, S., Guinan, P.J.: Multichannel marketing: mindset and program development. Bus. Horiz. **50**(5), 385–394 (2007)

Stepping on the Cracks—Transcending the Certainties of Big Data Analytics

Peter M. Bednar and Christine Welch

Abstract Every aspect of modern life is dominated by decision-making and the availability of data. We constantly access, process and evaluate data as we navigate complex and uncertain problem spaces. Communication and Information Technologies (ICTs) have developed to a point where it is possible for very large data sets, measured in Exabyte, to be stored across many servers and gathered by many different people and organizations, for multiple purposes. At the same time, research into Artificial Intelligence has progressed to a point where human decision-making can be supported, or even replaced, by intelligent agents and robotics. We recognize that many routine jobs that were once carried out by people can now be done faster and more flexibly using robotics, and software robotics has now moved beyond the factory and into administrative processes. The possibilities for such systems are enormous and can deliver many benefits to business, governments and ordinary citizens. However, there is also a downside to be considered. Is there still a role for human experience and intuition? How can we ensure that the benefits of analytics and AI continue to outweigh threats? How should we approach management of BI and AI on an on-going basis? This paper advocates an open systems approach in which B&AI may be incorporated with tools that support complex methods of inquiry.

Keywords Decision support · Big data analytics · Business intelligence
AI · Open systems · Dempster-Shafer theory · Complexity

P. M. Bednar
School of Computing, University of Portsmouth, Portsmouth, UK
e-mail: peter.bednar@port.ac.uk

P. M. Bednar
Department of Informatics, Lund University, Lund, Sweden

C. Welch (✉)
Operations & Systems Management Group, Portsmouth Business School,
University of Portsmouth, Portsmouth, UK
e-mail: christine.welch@port.ac.uk

© Springer International Publishing AG, part of Springer Nature 2019
F. Cabitza et al. (eds.), *Organizing for the Digital World*, Lecture Notes in Information
Systems and Organisation 28, https://doi.org/10.1007/978-3-319-90503-7_12

1 Introduction

Analytics, and particularly Big Data analytics (BDA), have caused a lot of excitement within business and IS research and practice over the past few years. There have been many instances of companies achieving improved results through better understandings of their customers and markets as a result of investments in Big Data. Indeed, there is some evidence that business confidence in the form of stock market values tends to rise when announcements are made that a Big Data investment is to be made [1]. The development of the BDA phenomenon has been traced through three phases [2] (see Fig. 1).

The first phase is described as 'data centric', growing out of more traditional data collection and structuring in company and other databases. As volumes of data grew, analytical techniques were embraced based in statistical modelling. Reference was made to data 'warehouses'. Data mining techniques were developed to surface patterns, in association with on-line analytical processing (OLAP). During this phase, so-called executive information systems were made available with ad hoc querying, graphical reporting, score cards and dashboards to support the domain of Business Intelligence. The authors [2] identify the second phase in the emergence of Big Data systems with Web-based data gathering. User search and interaction data could be mapped using server logs, cookies, etc. Web-based analytical tools began to emerge that could track individual user activities and purchasing habits. The emergence of social media, virtual worlds and other Web-based activities increased opportunities to gather a wealth of data about user views and desires. As the second phase of development progressed, potential arose for those who wished to market products, services and ideas to engage in one-to-one conversation with individuals in the target market, using the power of Web tools.

Phase three [2] was heralded by the expansion in ownership of mobile devices and the plethora of downloadable applications that ensued. These include games, utilities, information services and educational or recreation apps, all of which generate valuable data about the choices, habits and desires of individuals who use them. At the same time, the emergence of the Internet of Things has led to a growth in sensor-based content. Every individual leaves an electronic trail of signals from sensor devices such as cameras, Radio-frequency identification (RFID) tags, travel card readers and bar codes. This development will continue apace with everything from cars to domestic appliances becoming connected and generating data. Although Chen et al. [2] are careful to distinguish Business Intelligence from the field of Artificial

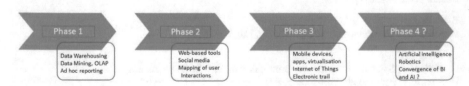

Fig. 1 Phases in the development of big data analytics

Intelligence (AI), it seems inescapable that we are at the dawn of a new convergence of technologies as the potential of AI and Big Data analytics are brought together in new applications.

Artificial Intelligence research has progressed over the past twenty or so years to go beyond the limited scope of domain-specific, knowledge-based systems to produce intelligent agents capable of independent learning. The field of robotics was embraced by industry some time ago, and we are now familiar with the idea of robots on the production line that can work faster and more flexibly than human operatives. Now, AI applications and robotics are moving further into the zone of information and knowledge work. Intelligent software is now being introduced to manage whole business processes, delivering improved efficiency, error reduction and cost savings. Robots can interact with computer systems, and, unlike previous generations of automated systems based on algorithms, can adapt to changing circumstances. Applications have been seen in many areas with repetitive tasks, such as accounting, payroll and customer service. Examples where robotics have made an impact include Finnish Government back-office services, the London Borough of Enfield's system to process citizen requests, and process automation in banks in the Nordic region [3]. SEB bank in Sweden has introduced a pilot use of a customer service robot (named Amelia) [4]. Using semantics of language, Amelia learns to solve business process queries. It can read and assimilate existing text rapidly, and can also observe human-customer interactions in order to learn by experience, with capability to operate in 20 languages.

Clearly, robotic applications such as this may be linked to data analytics in order to expand their potential for learning and to generate new capabilities. Bradbury [5] reports on a number of applications of an intelligent agent developed by IBM: 'Watson'. Some of these deployments have been very successful, e.g. in the field of oil and gas exploration. Others, however, have been less successful. A problem arises because robots are very good at work that human beings already carry out very efficiently, but may be less effective where qualities that are exclusively human are involved. An example can be found in attempts to use Watson in the field of medical research. Governance protocols, based in medical ethics, are kept under constant review. So far, it appears that Watson is unable to deliver results within the tight time-frame before further revision of governance protocols renders its knowledge outdated.

Advocates of agents such as 'Amelia' are quick to suggest that their introduction will free up human agents from repetitive work so that they can deal with the more complex or unusual problems requiring experience and discretion. A paradox arises here—how will human agents build their capability to deal with such problems if not through experience in dealing, day-in, day-out, with the ordinary and 'normal' aspects of the work?

It is important that we do not get carried away by the potential of technological developments so that we fail to see the difficulties and challenges they may pose for us. In the next section of the paper, we consider some of the philosophical underpinnings that influence our view of automated systems as support for decision makers.

We will go on to discuss some of the complexities and challenges we perceive to arise, before attempting to draw some conclusions.

2 Epistemic Uncertainty

A 'decision' may be designed to close a perceived, instrumental gap between an experienced state and goals desired by the decision-maker. Action to close this gap involves drawing on existing 'knowledge', but does not produce any new 'knowledge' (where the decision-taker is an intelligent agent, the knowledge may be newly-learned but not novel to the context of use). This description reminds us of 'zero order learning' in work by Bateson [6], and also of 'single-loop learning' as described by Argyris and Schon [7]. However, many, if not most, business decisions are not instrumental but *epistemic* in nature. Popper [8, 9] took the view that human beings are adaptive by nature, and that knowledge development must be seen as an emergent consequence of human activities. People can use trial-and-error in striving to solve adaptive problems, drawing on their previous knowledge and experiences. Popper set out a framework for knowledge production that he regarded as basic to human experience. This begins with problem perception, moving to conjecture, design of a range of tentative solutions, testing of these solutions against experience, and evaluation that attempts to refute each tentative solution. Those found not to be viable are discarded along the way. Some solution(s) survive testing and evaluation better than others but there may remain a range of viable alternatives. Following further efforts at evaluation through reflection, new 'knowledge' emerges. Furthermore, Popper's framework does not end with evaluation. Any chosen solution invariably suggests new problems, which trigger further episodes of conjecture. As human beings, we have no alternative but to think. Conjecture leads to perception of new epistemic problems that are 'better', i.e. more sophisticated or more interesting than the old ones.

Choice of a solution could be random, e.g. faced with two alternative opportunities, I could flip a coin to decide between them. However, the term 'evaluation' suggests that people have some sense that one choice might serve their purposes better than others. Decision support systems must therefore include not only potential for generating solutions, but solutions that meet some particular set of criteria. Design of such systems must therefore take into account both *praxeology* [10]—the notion that humans engage in purposeful behaviour; and *axiology* [11]—consideration of ethical or aesthetic dimensions. The former leads us to consider in any particular context what it is possible and practical to do, and how compatible this would be with our other actions. The latter leads us to consider how compatible a particular choice would be without our values and beliefs. Hart [11, p. 29] suggests that the:
'problems and issues axiology investigates have been with us from the moment man began to reflect upon conditions of his life, the structure of reality, the order of nature and man's place in it. In all probability the quest for values, for things and events

which are conducive to survival and the enhancement of life, engendered the quest for knowledge of reality'.

Of course, human beings do not think in algorithms of binary choices—reflection upon usefulness of a potential solution may well elicit the response 'It depends' or 'Let us keep our options open', and may also result in disagreement among people engaged in collaborative decision-taking. For this reason, it is desirable to have decision-support systems that will provide for para consistent logic [12], i.e. maintaining several possible alternatives in the decision frame far into a process of discussion, without rushing to premature exclusion or forced consensus. An example of such support might be creation of Diversity Networks [13].

Human actors live, and experience an open and unbounded world. Within the limitations of human senses and physiology, we receive continual sensory data which we must interpret. Human beings are social and tend to interact with one another, using the vehicle of language and individual and collective sense-making of context. Thus, when we consider our need to close epistemic, rather than instrumental gaps through decision-taking, we must assume an open world [14]. As we perceive gaps and conjecture about possible means to close them, based on our sense-making about experience and data available, it is always possible that our understandings are flawed, that aspects of the problem space are changing or that information is missing, and that we will not arrive at a complete range of viable alternative solutions, or indeed any. Similarly, while we are engaging in conjecture, the world around us may change so that the conjectures we engage in cease to be valid, in terms of praxeology and/or axiology.

Taking an open systems approach also recognizes that creativity is needed in design of solutions—it is often unusual or outré ideas that lead to innovation and progress. It may be more logical to privilege, rather than exclude, solutions that appear out of the ordinary. Decision support tools based in Dempster-Shafer Theory [15, 16] may be helpful in such circumstances, where people are collaborating in design and discussion of candidate solutions. Such tools may be used to combine new observations with prior weights attributed to candidate solutions, in order to develop new weights, e.g. to update beliefs about relative probabilities of solution(s) being viable, given new information. DST assigns non-negative weights to each combination of possibilities. DST can apportion weight to a combination of alternative solutions—not just x or y independently, but (x or y) as a combination—in excess of the sum of the individual weights. This allows for the inclusion of information with unquantified uncertainty. Here, DST can model the range of confidence reflecting a state of knowledge. In DST, the probability assigned to a hypothesis need not be calculated, as in the case of classic probability theory. Probability could be a person's view on the validity of the respective hypothesis. In DST, hypotheses that are originally considered to be unlikely or counter-intuitive may nevertheless yield high levels of belief through combination. In some types of decision-support, this would be considered undesirable. However, it is ideas that were originally considered to be radical, controversial, or outside the norm that frequently provide a creative spark for new ventures and innovation in organizations.

Furthermore, the values we espouse and apply in selecting viable alternatives are likely to be unique to us as individuals, and yet more or less similar to those of other members of our social groups or organizational contexts. These values may also change over time as we reflect upon our experiences and the results from our previous choices. Thus, an open, systemic approach to decision-taking is needed. Human decision-making cannot be seen as a purely intellectual exercise, since our rational choices will always be tempered by emotions, whether overtly or unknowingly. Our value judgements can be seen to be based in what Vickers [17] referred to as our Appreciative Systems—those influences derived from experiences and beliefs that shape our unique world views.

An open systems approach to decision-taking will recognise that human actors are biased in many ways, and will recognise and engage with differences of perception of problem spaces. NB in using the term 'bias' we recognize that this may be conscious (attempting to manipulate the ideas and values of others) or unconscious—reflecting values of which we are ourselves unaware to some extent [18, 19]. For all these reasons, when we approach epistemic problems there will be benefit in an approach that supports playfulness, experiment, trial-and-error. Ciborra [20, p. 24] refers to the use of practical intelligence, which he describes as: *'the intelligence of the octopus – flexible, polymorphic, ambiguous, oblique, twisted, circular'*. Human beings, in their conjectures, can engage both reason and imagination; both cognitive and affective thinking.

Professional practice is suggested to be value-driven. Etzioni [21] considered how authority to take decisions is derived in organizations. Those in administrative roles derive their authority from formal structures, often arranged in hierarchical levels. In contrast, those in professional roles derive their authority from their own knowledge and skill. Tensions can arise where administrators attempt to take control over the actions of professionals, without a deep understanding of their practice. Professional groups maintain a collective view of the norms and values appropriate to their practice, and expect to be overseen by their peers. The outcomes that organizational stakeholders aspire to achieve can only be supported if structures and cultures are appropriate to deliver authority of the right kind to those who need to act to achieve these objectives. Noordegraaf [22] points out that conflicts have arisen in recent years, as a managerialist agenda (especially in public sector organizations) has sought to gain increased control over the domain of professional practice, while professionals have argued for greater autonomy and new ways to deal with the risks they inevitably incur. She argues that, if organizations are to achieve sustainability in their desired outcomes, there is a need to attain new forms of *organized professionalism*, strengthening viability and legitimacy of professional standards and practice in relation to changing 21st century business challenges.

Human systems are inherently complex. When we pursue purposeful activity, we must embrace this complexity and the uncertainties encompassed by it. Early phases of data analytics were undoubtedly designed in efforts to reduce these uncertainties so that business options became clear and outcomes predictable. The field of analytics itself is highly complex and as it moves into its third phase and convergence between Business Intelligence and Artificial Intelligence applications takes place, it may be

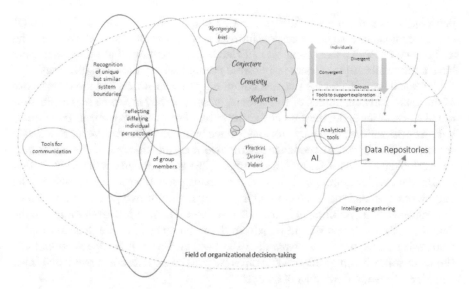

Fig. 2 'Complexifying' a field of organizational decision-taking

that the potential of these clever systems will continue to outstrip the possibility for human agencies to conceive optimal uses for them. An open systems approach would suggest that, rather than seeking to reduce uncertainties, future B&AI tools should offer opportunities to 'complexify' decision taking processes, by supporting conjecture, creativity and reflection (see Fig. 2). It will be interesting to see what scope can be found to combine the power of AI and data analytics with complex methods of inquiry, such as those discussed in this section.

3 Difficulties

As mentioned above, many difficulties arise along a path towards harnessing the potential of B&AI systems. The first of these lies in the possibility to gather and analyse huge volumes of data relating to citizens, with the potential to identify and profile any particular individual's ideas, choices and preferences. Clearly, these analytics open up the possibility to manipulate aspects of daily life. This can be beneficial to an individual. If, for instance, she sees only advertising that is actually of interest to her instead of a plethora of material in which relevant advertisements become buried, this could be perceived as helpful. However, it is more problematic when, as we have seen, it can be used to influence democratic processes or potentially implement forms of social control. Chavalarias [23] discusses these and other challenges to civil society, drawing upon second-order cybernetics. He quotes Von Foerster (1972) as saying that for a society to be healthy 'education is neither a right nor a *privilege: it is a necessity.*' Citizens must be empowered to exercise vigilance. Of course, companies also bear a responsibility for ethical practices. In considering the darker side of Big Data, Davenport and Harris [24] point out that senior managers have a responsibility to pioneer responsible practice within their organizations.

A second issue is that the size and complexity of data stores, and the complexity of the analytical capabilities of BI systems, mean that they are to be seen as institutional repositories under the direction and control of senior management. Individuals within organizations, who may previously have built and utilised more localised data services and tools, could experience disempowerment and their particular needs may be overlooked [25]. McAfee and Brynjolffson [26] have pointed out that exploitation of Big Data will require a radical review of management practice and, indeed, the culture of organizational decision-making. They highlight two potential difficulties in companies with ambition to become data-driven. The first is *over-reliance* on the data. Use of data-driven BI will transform the initial question for a decision-maker from 'what do we think?' to 'what do we know?' However, it is suggested that this should be followed up by questions such as 'where did the data come from' and 'how confident are we in the results of analysis?'

Furthermore, analytics may give reliable answers to queries, but experienced professionals from particular domains will still be indispensable in deciding what problems need to be tackled, and/or which require attention most urgently. These are value judgements. The second problem highlighted is the obverse of the first. Research has suggested that some senior managers believe their organisations to be data-driven, when in fact decision-makers are falling back on their own experience-based intuition as they have always done. *Cultural change*, organisational flexibility and leadership are needed to make such a transition.

Liedtke [27] suggests that analytics team members require a broad experience. He suggests that required domains of knowledge might include those shown in Fig. 3.

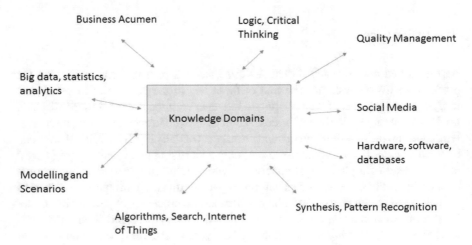

Fig. 3 Domains of necessary knowledge for an analytics team, from Liedtke [27]

Chen et al. [2], in their discussion of education for future developments in analytics, advocate that programs should expose candidates to a wide range of *knowledge domains*, including not only those of analysis but also accounting, marketing, operations management, finance and logistics. They go on to suggest (p. 1183) '*BI&A professionals need to know not only how to turn raw data and information (through analytics) into meaningful and actionable knowledge for an organization, but also how to properly interact with and communicate this knowledge to the business and domain experts of the organization*'. They also advocate experiential learning, incorporating opportunities for experimentation and trial-and-error, which they consider to be a requirement of Business Intelligence and Analytics practice.

A further issue is that there may be an illusion that experience and intuition are redundant, and hence will no longer require support or encouragement. Business relies upon creativity and vision in order to generate innovative and disruptive ideas that will yield future success. Data is by its nature historic. Although analytics can provide projections, they cannot look into the future to consider products, processes and technologies not yet invented or potential interactions between them. Harris [28] points out that *intuition* has not ceased to play an important role in business decision-making. It is intuition, based upon experience that is pivotal in shaping how an organisation can best harness analytics. Continuing research and experience is needed to ensure that such insights remain fresh and relevant. She cites an example in which a team of analysts was asked to set up a system to predict which buildings were most at risk of fire. The team began by introducing data on, e.g. complaints received, failure to pay taxes, rodent infestations, etc. but, on joining a buildings inspector on his rounds, were astonished to learn that he considered the state of brickwork to be the key to fire risk indicating how much the occupier cared about the building.

Of course, intuition can lead to bias in decision-making —something which AI and Big Data systems are suggested to overcome. Baer et al. [29] discuss how *debiasing* may be undertaken in organisations, pointing out a number of types of bias that could become problematic. These include *stability bias*—continuing to do what has previously met with success without recognizing that a new strategy might be even more beneficial; *action bias*—where those employed to engage in continuous improvement feel driven to generate change whether it is needed or not; and the impact of *group dynamics* in stifling debate and new ideas. However, they go on to point out that, while analytical tools can be efficient at eliminating bias in high-frequencies decisions, such as credit control, it is entirely possible for BI analytical systems to introduce *further* bias—the underlying data may be unreliable or a poorly-designed, algorithmic model may lock in bias-prone assumptions. An active and open-minded approach is needed towards design so that analytics does not become a 'black box with baked-in biases'. A further type of bias that may be encountered in data-driven decision-making could be '*survivor bias*' decisions may be based on the data that is available, ignoring that which is missing and so generating misleading advice [30].

The role of human experience cannot be over-emphasised. Langefors demonstrated through his Infological Equation [31, 32] that information I is the interpretation i that a person makes of a message D based on his/her pre-knowledge or receiving structure S during a specific amount of time t. Understanding of communicated messages (underpinning praxeological and axiological responses) is therefore crucially dependent upon reflection over prior experience. We have mentioned a paradox in that companies introducing robotics advertise that their staff are then free to undertake more interesting, problem-solving work—but where, in future, will they acquire the necessary experience and knowledge to enable them to do so? Furthermore, although robots can and do learn by experience [4, 5], this experience is by necessity bounded. A human being's intuition and creativity may bring into the decision space breadth of experiences gained from, e.g. military service, motherhood or kayaking on the Amazon, as well as direct experience of the business domain. Such experiences for robots, and the creative reasoning needed to relate them to diverse and open problem spaces, are still confined to the realm of science fiction.

4 Conclusions

Nobody can deny the Business and Artificial Intelligence resources and tools can be beneficial to both business organizations and the wider society. We need to ensure, however, that we give due consideration to their compatibility with the purposeful human systems and societies they are designed to serve. We advocate an open systems approach to design of decision-support, so that individuals and groups can create and critique boundaries around particular decision-spaces for themselves (see Fig. 4). In recent times, advocates of Big Data systems have suggested that it can deliver contextual solutions to problems of particular organizations. While *fine-grained* advice can undoubtedly be generated by systems based in phases two and three of Business Intelligence services described above, *contextual relevance* requires interaction with

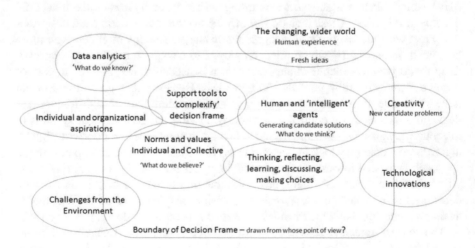

Fig. 4 Framing a decision space: a complex, open systems approach incorporating B&AI

and among unique understandings of engaged actors. Data-driven solutions must therefore be evaluated by such actors, using their contextually-dependent knowledge and intuition. We must give due consideration to design of tools, techniques and educational programs that will empower human agents to do this effectively.

Human experience, intuition and creativity will always be needed to harness the benefits of on-going developments in technologies. Support for collaborative inquiry into such complex problem spaces will therefore be needed. Business and society depends upon our ability to achieve a sociotechnical balance between systems that can deliver a rigorous and reliable source of advice, and systems that can support individuals to use it in relevant and meaningful actions. We look forward to future generations of B&AI tools that can combine the power of data analytics, intelligent agents and tools and techniques to promote complex, open systems inquiry.

References

1. Zhang, T., Wang, W.Y.C., Pauleen, D.J.: Big data investments in knowledge and non-knowledge intensive firms: what the market tells us. J. Knowl. Manag. **21**(3), 623–639 (2017)
2. Chen, H., Chiang, R.H.L., Storey, V.C.: Business intelligence and analytics: from big data to big impact. MIS Q. **36**(4), 1165–1188 (2016)
3. Haaramo, E.: Robotic automation takes off in the Nordics. Computer Weekly, 19 April 2017. http://www.computerweekly.com/news/450417014. Accessed 31 May 2017
4. Flinders, K.: Interview: how Swedish bank prepared robot for customer services. Computer Weekly, 28 October 2016. http://www.computerweekly.com/news/450401647. Accessed 31 May 2017
5. Bradbury, D.: Chatbots are boring. What's next? Learn to Use Machine Learning. The Register on-line, 29 March 2017, pp. 1–4. https://www.theregister.co.uk/2017/03/29/learn_to_use_ma chine_learning/. Accessed 17 April 2017
6. Bateson, G.: Steps to an Ecology of Mind. University of Chicago Press, Chicago (1972)
7. Argyris, M., Schön, D.: Theory in Practice: Increasing Professional Effectiveness. Jossey-Bass (1974)
8. Popper, K.R.: Objective Knowledge. Oxford University Press, London (1972)
9. Popper, K.R.: Knowledge and the Body-Mind Problem. In: Notturno, M.A. (ed.). Routledge, London (1994)
10. Von Mises, L.: Human Action: A Treatise on Economics. Scholars Edition 2008. Ludwig von Mises Institute (1949)
11. Hart, S.: Axiology-theory of values. Philos. Phenomenol. Res. **32**(1), 29–41 (1971)
12. Bednar, P.M., Anderson, D., Welch, C.: Knowledge creation and sharing—complex methods of inquiry and inconsistent theory. In: Proceedings of 6th European Conference on Knowledge Management, 8–9 September 2005. University of Limerick (2005)
13. Bednar, P., Welch, C., Katos, V.: Innovation management through the use of diversity networks. Int. J. Knowl. Learn. **4**(4), 357–369 (2008)
14. Dempster, A.P.: Upper and lower probabilities induced by a multivalued mapping. Ann. Math. Stat. **38**(2), 325–339 (1967)
15. Shafer, G.: A Mathematical Theory of Evidence. Princeton University Press (1976)
16. Katos, V., Bednar, P., Welch, C.: Dealing with epistemic uncertainty in the SST framework. In: Adam F. et al. (eds.) Creativity and Innovation in Decision Making and Decision Support, vol. 2. Decision Support Press, London (2006)
17. Vickers, G.: The Art of Judgment: A Study in Policy Making. Chapman & Hall, London (1965)

18. Guba, E.G.: Toward a Methodology of Naturalistic Inquiry in Educational Evaluation. CSE Monograph Series in Evaluation, vol. 8 (1978)
19. Banks, R.R., Ford, R.T.: (How) Does unconscious bias matter: law, politics, and racial inequality? Emory LJ **58**, 1053 (2008)
20. Ciborra, C.: Encountering information systems as a phenomenon. In: Avgerou, C., Ciborra, C., Land, F. (eds.) The Social Study of Information and Communication Technology. Oxford University Press (2004)
21. Etzioni, A.: Authority structure and organizational effectiveness. Adm. Sci. Q. **4**(1), 43–67 (1959)
22. Noordegraaf, M.: Risky business: how professionals and professional fields (must) deal with organizational issues. Organ. Stud. **32**(10), 1349–1371 (2011)
23. Chavalarias, D.: The unlikely encounter between von Foerster and Snowden: when second-order cybernetics sheds light on societal impacts of Big Data. Big Data Soc. **3**(1), 1–11 (2016)
24. Davenport, T.H., Harris, J.G.: The dark side of customer analytics. Harvard Business Review, May 2007
25. Bednar, P.M., Welch, C., Imrie, P.: Supporting business decision-making—one professional at a time. In: Proceedings of IFIP WG.8.3 Open Conference: DSS2.0—Supporting Decision-making with New Technologies, 2–5 June 2014. Université Pierre et Marie Curie, Paris, France (2014)
26. McAfee, A., Brynjolfsson, E.: Big Data: the management revolution. Harvard Business Review, October 2012
27. Liedtke, C.A.: Quality, analytics, and Big Data. Strategic Improvement Systems (SIS) Research Report (2016). http://strategicimprovementsystems.com/. Accessed 31 May 2017
28. Harris, J.G.: Does intuition matter in a Big Data World? Accenture, February 2017. https://www.accenture.com/us-en/insight-does-institution-matter-in-the-big-data-world. Accessed 31 May 2017
29. Baer, T., Heiligtag, S., Samandari, H.: The business logic in debiasing. McKinsey & Company, May 2017. www.mckinsey.com/business-functions/ris/the-business-logic-in-debiasing?cid=other-alt-mip-mck-oth-1705&hlkid=ff62c0e1e7e44. Accessed 31 May 2017
30. Shermer, M.: How the survivor bias distorts reality. Scientific American, May 2014. https://www.scientificamerican.com/article/how-the-survivor-bias-distorts-reality/. Accessed 31 May 2017
31. Langefors, B.: Infological models and information user views. Inf. Syst. **5**(1), 17–32 (1980)
32. Kettinger, W.J., Yuan, L.: The infological equation extended: towards conceptual clarity in the relationship between data, information and knowledge. Eur. J. Inf. Syst. **19**(4), 409–421 (2010)

Apulian Mobility Insight: A Data Management Framework for Analyzing QoS in Smart Mobility

Antonella Longo and Marco Zappatore

Abstract Modern urban infrastructures will depend heavily on local transportation services in the near future in order to reduce the number of circulating private vehicles and reduce air and noise pollution. Moreover, requirements and expectations from policy makers, commuters and service operators are increasing the pressure on how local transportation services need to be managed properly. Transportation services should be redesigned by aiming at sustainability and systemic approaches for improving both the offered and perceived Quality of Service (QoS). In this research work, we have considered several QoS flavors, each depending on a specific perspective (i.e., service providers, service customers, additional stakeholders) in order to define a modelling approach suitable to a systemic analysis of QoS for smart mobility and transportation scenarios. The designed architecture has been implemented as a framework for the Apulian Mobility Insight (i.e., the platform dedicated to QoS analyses). A technical and methodological validation has been performed with the help of the Apulia administrative Region, in Southern Italy.

Keywords Smart mobility · Service lifecycle model · Quality of service
Quality of experience · Smart cities

1 Main Challenges for the Quality of Service in Smart Mobility System

Several cities are nowadays showcasing smart solutions and applications for improving quality of life for their citizens as well as for increasing the effectiveness of their service offerings. The sector of urban mobility plays a relevant role in such a sce-

A. Longo (✉) · M. Zappatore (✉)
Department of Engineering for Innovation, WPO, University of Salento,
via per Monteroni, 73100 Lecce, Italy
e-mail: antonella.longo@unisalento.it

M. Zappatore
e-mail: marcosalvatore.zappatore@unisalento.it

© Springer International Publishing AG, part of Springer Nature 2019   161
F. Cabitza et al. (eds.), *Organizing for the Digital World*, Lecture Notes in Information
Systems and Organisation 28, https://doi.org/10.1007/978-3-319-90503-7_13

nario, since reliable and efficient transportation services can show how smart a city actually is [1–3]. However, in order to achieve such efficiency, several challenges have to be dealt with. First, in the majority of urban contexts, pre-existing transportation systems and infrastructures show structural inadequacies to the new mobility requirements and expectations from passengers. Second, current national and international regulations demand for greener vehicles and more effective route planning, but these requirements are usually in contrast with aged vehicles (both on rails and on tires) and difficulties in optimizing vehicle routes. Third, citizens are acquiring progressively a true environmental awareness, thus becoming capable of evaluating the environmental sustainability of transportation service offerings. Fourth, policy makers and service providers must be capable of attracting external investors in order to become more competitive.

From being a critical issue, however, urban mobility can lead to improvements and transformations in modern cities, since its management involves multiple entities (see Fig. 1). On the one hand, we have the citizens (depicted in yellow in Fig. 1), whose categories represents at the same time both the service consumers (as they need to move for personal needs, work, leisure and recreation) and the ones who live where the transportation services are provided (i.e., they suffer from transportation-related pollution). Service customers can be supported by advocacy groups and labor unions (also in yellow in Fig. 1). On the other hand, we have service providers, which are normally private companies that aim at efficient transportation of goods and products (depicted in green in Fig. 1). In addition to those entities, we should consider also public institutions and policy makers (in blue in Fig. 1) as they have a two-fold role management role in transportation services, being the ones who have to control citizens' satisfaction and, at the same time, the transportation providers' commitments.

The scenario sketched so far introduces us to the field of customer satisfaction and perceived service quality. Public and private investments in this sector are commonly addressed to improve these two factors and several studies have been dedicated to assess how effective these interventions can be. In Northern Europe [4], three Euro-

Fig. 1 The involved stakeholders in public transportation eco-system

pean cities (i.e., Helsinki, Stockholm and Oslo) have been monitored for assessing the potential biases between the customer's subjective journey experience and the objective conditions of the provided service. Similarly, in the U.S., a study about the relationships between the service reliability perspectives of both passengers and transit agencies has recently proposed several transportation service improvement strategies adopting an iterative, feedback-based mechanism [5].

The regulatory background in the EU and in Italy will be addressed in the next Section but it is worth to anticipate that, from a normative perspective, the EU has already adopted proper legislations and policies regulating mobility and passenger rights [6–8]. Moreover, the EU has introduced the concept of enforcement delegation, since specific agents have been assigned the task of monitoring EU regulations in each Member State. The proper compliance with the law is a way to guarantee a certain level of service quality to passengers and commuters.

As for the service providers' perspective, the current trend involves the publication and adoption of specific documents, named Chart of Mobility Services, assessing and regulating the respective service offerings. This trend is present also in Italy, where the charts of mobility services have been defined "Carte dei Servizi di Mobilità" (henceforth, CdSM). CdSMs include most aspects identifying a service (e.g., users, functions, offerings, modes of access, offered and perceived quality levels, etc.) and represent the reference for assessing the compliance against passengers' rights and transportation service norms.

In our vision, each CdSM is a contract between service customers (i.e., passengers) and transportation service providers: the providers declare the QoS and the passenger should ascertain it. Moreover, when public transportation systems are involved, local Public Administrations (PAs) sign specific contracts with providers. Even if some metrics related to the Quality of delivered Service (QoS) and Quality of Experience (QoE) are included within these CdSMs, there are no effective attempts to coordinate PAs, providers and consumers.

The role of QoE is relevant as well, since the QoE measures the customer experience with respect to a service and, therefore, it can ensure the value of the facility for the users. Since QoE represents the QoS from the user's viewpoint, QoE is an extension of QoS. In smart cities, the overall QoE demand involves the identification of technological, social and economic requirements within a regulatory framework. In terms of technology, equipment providers, content and service providers and network providers are expected to handle much higher traffic levels, offering improved quality. The social context also matters, since application/service/network usage will not be only influenced by the perceived QoE but also by the user's context and its relation with the other actors in the business chain. From an economical perspective, the main difficulty hereby for providers is the definition of service/price offers based on QoE differentiation and the potential acceptance by the subscribers [9]. In this scenario CdSM can be a very effective tool to enhance the relationship between passengers (customers) and providers if service provisioning contracts are monitored in light of the CdSM using appropriate IT tools for gathering and analyzing pertinent information. Whereas CdSM promises to be an effective supporting tool for both transportation service providers and service consumers, the current scenario is less than desirable. Very often, transportation service providers define their own CdSM based on their own requirements and service offerings, resulting in a wordy commercial document, very hard to be implemented through IT tools which should support the enforcement of CdSMs. Moreover, they are tailored by individual providers to their own situations and no set of standards or a formal approach has been defined to compare or to integrate them. Consequently at local, regional, national and European levels, the comparison and integration of CdSMs present an additional level of complexity. As a result, if the train and bus services are offered on the same route, it is hard to compare them. As described, in the EU and member states the scenario is quite complex for both rail-based and road-based services. In this paper we present a unified vision and a framework for analyzing Quality of Service. We have developed a computing system solution that is currently populated with 2 million instances of trips carried out by three transportation companies in the Apulia Region in Italy. It took over a year for us to investigate and understand the complexities involved and to get the buy-in of the local assessment agencies before we could embark on the design and implementation of the web-based tool. The Apulia region assessor office is currently using our computerized solution and populating it with data. This approach can be considered as a promising opportunity for working toward a Unified CdSM (CUdSM, which is the Italian for "Carta Unica dei Servizi di Mobilità"), capable of providing trustworthy indicators assessing service quality from the point of view of both service providers and service recipients. The research aims, therefore, are:

1. modeling the relationship of stakeholders in the transportation ecosystem, according to the service lifecycle management paradigm. We formalize relationships by service contracts between two contracting parties;
2. identifying quality factors for QoS assessment and categorizing quality indicators by developing a reference taxonomy;
3. providing data management supporting tools able to analyze these relationship;

The proposed model has been also validated in a pilot scenario located in the Apulia administrative region (Southern Italy), where we have involved service providers, associations of service customers and local authorities.

The paper is structured as detailed in the following: Sect. 2 offers a glimpse on the regulations for transportation services in Europe and Italy. The designed model and the accompanying taxonomy of indicators are described in Sects. 3 and 4 respectively. The analysis of the proposed tool and its validation are presented in Sect. 5. Conclusions as well as future research developments are sketched in Sect. 6.

2   Regulatory Background in Europe and in Italy

From 2004 onward, the EU proposed a set of regulations [6–8, 10] about passengers' rights and obligations for all transportation services (i.e., railways, roadways, airways and waterways) even on long-distance routes. The European legislators have considered the majority of typical issues a passenger could face, ranging from overbooking to cancellations, accidents, rerouting, obstacles for people with reduced mobility and so on.

Similarly, the Italian legislation has several norms regulating public service provisioning, (i.e. equality, impartiality and continuity, etc.). In 1995, the concept of Carta dei Servizi di Mobilità (the aforementioned CdSM) was defined as a general template for all the sectors of public transportation service provisioning, and in 1998 another law stated that public services must be provisioned "by promoting quality improvement, by guaranteeing citizens and users, by ensuring users' participation in the procedures of definition and evaluation of quality standards". In time the CdSM role has acquired even more centrality and in 2013 some guidelines about the minimal elements and principles to be put in public service contracts and in charts of local public services have been published. This document is particularly interesting because for the first time Consumers Associations (also known as Customer's Advocacy Groups) have been formally involved in the definition of services and service levels.

Transportation services should be managed by considering the corresponding QoS and, therefore, a proper QoS lifecycle must be referred to. The European Union, in 2002, proposed the UNI EN 13816:2002 [11]. This document assesses the QoS lifecycle for transportation services for both the service customers' and service providers' perspective, in order to: (1) define QoS metrics, (2) define QoS level objectives and (3) establish QoS indicators and measurement policies. However, according to the schematization proposed in Fig. 2, if we examine the public transportation services, several gaps can be highlighted. Several research works have also identified these gaps [12, 13] and several criteria and techniques are defined in [11] for assessing the overall quality of transportation services. However, the European norm mentioned above, only establishes rules to set objectives and evaluate results and this the reason why we consider pivotal to define a reference model for a Unified CdSM (in Italian, CUdSM) applicable on a European scale, as a fundamental complement to other governance tools in these sector [14, 15].

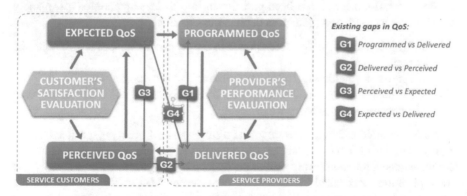

Fig. 2 The service quality lifecycle according to [11]

On a regional basis, the Apulia region (Southern Italy), which has been selected as a pilot site for testing the generalized model of CdSM, is promoting actions to improve transportation service quality as well as the definition of a regional CdSM, thanks to an agreement between the University of Salento and the Regional Agency for Mobility. The definition and adoption of CdSMs fosters the integration of transportation services, the improvement of passengers' security and access to information and brings about new efficiency standards. Similarly, CdSMs promote the adoption of novel technologies, such as the installation of sensors on vehicles and infrastructures as well as the direct engagement of passengers via the development and adoption of mobile apps.

3 Service Lifecycle Model

We have modeled rail and road transportation service scenario according to a 4-stakeholder perspective: Service Providers (SPs), Service Customers/Consumers (SCs), Guaranteeing Authority (GA), Additional Supporting Entities (ASEs). The stakeholders are enlisted below:

- SP (e.g., private companies, authorized companies, etc.): it delivers passengers with the transportation service,
- SC (e.g., citizens, passengers, etc.): it uses the transportation service in compliance with the service contract with the quality and rules declared by the provider,
- GA (e.g., the local public administration): it governs the transportation service contracts with providers and must guarantee public transportation service to passengers. Its aim is to reduce and minimize the gap between the quality promised by the provider companies and the quality perceived by passengers.
- ASE: it can enrich the above mentioned actors, such as, for instance, non-profit associations, labor unions, associations of citizens, advocacy groups, etc.

In order to properly match the stakeholders with the considered service scenario, the transportation service has been partitioned into three sequential steps, namely Service Lifecycle Phases (SLPs), as depicted in Fig. 3:

(1) SLP_1: pre-journey, which corresponds to the preparatory aspects preceding the journey;
(2) SLP_2: journey, which is the event of passengers' transportation;
(3) SLP_3: post-journey, which refers to the activities carried out when the physical transportation has ended.

Each stakeholders has a different role and can have a different perspective on each SLP phase. For instance, the preparatory activities in the pre-journey phase include, simultaneously, the monitoring actions performed by the guaranteeing authority, the route planning, performed by the service provider, and the action of ticket buying performed by the customer. The passenger can buy ticket for a planned train or bus only after the GA and SP have performed their activities. The Guaranteeing

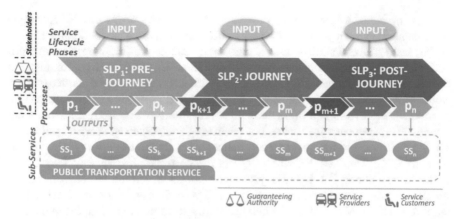

Fig. 3 The transportation service lifecycle

Authority supervises the planned trips and schedules according to obligations signed in the contract. This approach allows to achieve a structured and systematic view of the whole public transportation service from end to end, seen as a collection of sub-services $\{ss_i\}$, as depicted in Fig. 3. These sub-services can be modeled as the output of n different business processes p_i involving all the stakeholders, producing outputs on their own and referring to a given service lifecycle phase $SLPj$. Each process belonging to a given phase can receive several inputs and produces multiple outputs.

In the proposed modelling approach, the relationships amongst stakeholders are managed by revolving to a chain of service contracts and agreements. More specifically, the GA sign with each SP a multi-year contract to deliver (rail or/and road) transportation services, as detailed in the SP's service offering. On its turn, each SP sells the service to ASE or directly to SCs. Then, SCs can buy the ticket in order to benefit from the specific service levels declared by the SP in its CdSM. In addition, the GA monitors the delivered QoS and the perceived QoS, according to what is stated in SP's contracts (where service level agreements have been defined including service level related to delivered and perceived QoS).

4 Taxonomy of Quality, Indicators and Metrics

By recalling the model discussed in Sect. 3, the local GA is in charge of evaluating and ascertaining QoS and operational process performance of authorized SPs so that SCs can benefit from effective transportation services. This Section details how QoS is measured, according to our vision. The measurements for both the delivered QoS and the perceived QoS have been defined by referring to [11], by considering a set of *quality areas*. For each quality area, we have defined a taxonomy of *quality level indicators*, in order to make the Unified CdSM an effective governance tool for the whole ecosystem. Applying a top down approach, a series of *Quality Factors (QF)* were defined for each phase of the service lifecycle, as also described in [6, 11].

For each QF, metrics are defined in terms of indicators, for achieving a meaningful and explicit categorization. Interpersonal and inter-organizational communication also needs to be accounted for, since it directly impacts the perceived service quality. Some of the indicators include: ease of identification of service personnel, service personnel's behaviors and dress code (if a dress uniform is used). Indicators are quantitative parameters measuring both delivered and perceived service quality. As for the delivered service quality, each indicator I is defined as a set: *I{QF, SLP, tt, n, d, N, D, G, Tht, Thv, R}*, where: *QF* is the corresponding quality factor, *SLP* is the corresponding Service Lifecycle Phase during which the indicator has to be monitored, *tt* is the transportation type (i.e., rail or road), *n* and *d* are the name and the short description, *N* and *D* are the numerical quantities that represent the numerator and denominator of the algebraic formulation, *G* is the time granularity of samples used in the calculation, *Tht* is the threshold type (i.e., upper/lower threshold), *Thv* is the threshold value, *R* is the reference period.

Threshold values are the minimum targets defined by each GA. In the model, indicators are an integral part of Service Level Agreements (SLAs) in the contract between GA and SP and they are explicitly declared by SP in their service contracts. Once each indicator has been specified, it is possible to compare and publish service offering by adopting a unified and shared semantics, thus paving the way for the dissemination of open data on the quality of the mobility service.

Indicators under each QF have been identified according to the analysis of several Italian CdSMs and the Italian guidelines about the delivery of public service, defined by the Consumer Associations and the Association of Italian Cities.

The quality factors and the number of indicators (*nI*) involved in each factor are as follows:

- QF1, journey security (*nI = 3*);
- QF2, passenger personal and patrimonial security (*nI = 5*);
- QF3, service regularity and timeliness (*nI = 15*);
- QF4, vehicle cleanliness (*nI = 6*);
- QF5, passenger comfort and additional services (*nI = 8*);
- QF6, services for passengers with reduced mobility (*nI = 6*);
- QF7, information to passengers (*nI = 8*);
- QF8, communications and relationships between operators and passengers (*nI = 5*);
- QF9, environmental awareness (*nI = 4*).

The indicators adopted for the perceived QoS have been defined on the bases of the three methodologies proposed in [11] and by also referring to the European reports on passengers' satisfaction for road [16] and rail [17] transportation services. We have also considered the SERVQUAL method [12, 18], which is widely adopted worldwide. However, the implementation of SERVQUAL features has been performed partially since the method is: (1) inherently complex, also because of its size and scope; (2) mainly referred to service delivery aspects (as it does not address in the same way how the service is perceived); (3) mainly oriented towards passengers' expectations rather that to their behaviors (which we want to capture, instead); (4) poor in typical aspects the passengers typically evaluate when using public transport perceived QoS.

We have referred to a model rooted on five macro-dimensions that describe passengers' perceptions and expectations about mobility services:

1. tangible aspects (i.e., infrastructures, personnel, equipment and vehicles);
2. reliability (i.e., providing timely and trustworthy services);
3. answering capability (i.e., help and support to customers);
4. reassuring capability (i.e., relation between the staff from the service providing company and the customers);
5. empathy (i.e., availability of careful and personalized assistance to passengers).

From these elements, nearly 20 indicators about perceived quality have been identified; these indicators complement the ones defined for the delivered quality.

By collecting data referring to both QoE KPIs (Key Performance Indicators) and QoS KPIs, proper improvement and correction strategies can be defined by the GA, such as: (1) prioritizing a specific service management strategy matching both passengers' perception and providers' needs; (2) introducing new service quality indicators; (3) adopting comparative service perception and service delivery evaluation scales; (4) developing predictive models for passengers' expectations; (5) increasing cost-benefit analysis of transportation services, etc.

5 Apulia Mobility Insight: A Tool to Validate the Model

The proposed Unified CdSM model has been applied to the transportation services in the Apulia Region in Southern Italy for the years 2013–2015 as a validating pilot scenario. This action, started in 2013, has involved several stakeholders: the transportation service providing companies authorized by the regional administration; the passengers, the regional agency for the mobility (in Italian, "Agenzia Regionale per la Mobilità", A.Re.M.) the Innovation Engineering Dept. from University of Salento, the labor unions, and the consumers advocacy group. As a result, the Apulian Regional CUdSM represents a shared agreement between authorized companies and service consumers, guaranteed by the Apulia Region with respect to the quality and the modality of local transportation service delivery. It has been defined as a unified reference model, pertaining to both rail-based and road-based transportation services.

In order to instantiate CUdSM model, at first we performed an analysis of the seven transportation contracts and agreements enacted by Apulia Region with local providers and corresponding CdSMs. Several specifications and requirements from the available regulations were identified and the roles of the involved stakeholders were highlighted and rigorously formalized, thus achieving the first CUdSM draft. It has been shared and revised with the local customer's advocacy groups, labor unions, passengers and students. According to our model, the Apulia Region is in charge of managing the provided transportation service and monitoring its quality; the transportation service companies are responsible for the delivery of the transportation service to passengers; the citizens play the role of active and aware passengers for the transportation services. After this phase, we involved three local transportation service companies operating both on rail and road areas in the regional territory, which voluntarily contributed to validate the model by providing monitoring data about the indicators and public visibility to the collected data. This pilot phase has contributed to highlight several operational aspects necessary to implement an effective management of the CUdSM. A significant contribution has been represented by the identification of threshold values for the indicators, thanks to the efforts spent by the regional administrative authority and data provided by transportation providers. The involved stakeholders allowed us to define 62 threshold values both for rail and roads referring to the KPIs specified in Sect. 4. Some threshold values have not been defined since they have not been required by the current contracts nor did the transportation companies involved in the pilot had adequate tools to measure them. The model can be improved further by leveraging novel pilot experiences, possibly in different EU areas. For a complete overview of the proposed indicators, interested reader can refer to the institutional Website of Apulia Region, where the final deliverable of this research activity has been published [19]. As for the proposed technical architecture, we have designed and developed a traditional Data Warehouse (DWH)—based tool, because even if the system process big volume of data, the current purpose of the system is not to real time process data of perceived and delivered quality, in order to make fast analysis and to arrive at a decision or action within a short and very specific time line. Therefore it exploits a widely-accepted three-layer logical architecture requiring a series of ETL pipelines to process the data. The first layer gathers data from the available operational sources, which are provided by the transportation companies. During this step, a dedicated ETL pipeline manages data heterogeneity (e.g., CSV files, Excel files, etc.) by populating a staging area. The second layer represents the reconciled relational DB. The third layer is the DWH layer. A second dedicated ETL pipeline that manages data duplication (e.g., multiple records about the same route for the same company) feeds the star schemas (defined according to the DFM model) with data coming from the staging area. Finally, several OLAP cubes are created from the available star schemas in order to allow reporting and dash boarding. The delivered outputs offer relevant insights even if they do not provide real-time Business Intelligence (BI) capabilities. Very interestingly, the normalization showed several mismatches in data provided and helped in the definition of a shared format that will be required by the Region for following analyses. For instance, after the ETL pipelines, nearly 5000 runs having duplicated record have been found in the main company records (i.e., nearly 9% of the total). The proper identification of duplicated records is crucial for service providers in order to achieve better efficiency and better control on company assets. Specific attention has been paid to punctuality indicators because they are connected with contractual

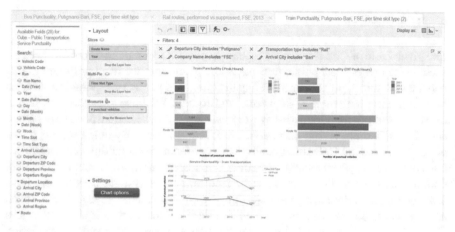

Fig. 4 The OLAP interface

economics. Specific dashboards were developed in order to support the Regional Department in monitoring and evaluation of the service and the contract. Figure 4 shows the OLAP interface for data related to years 2011–2014, for the analysis of punctuality on rail routes. The depicted bar charts in Fig. 4 represent train punctuality for a given transportation provider along a given route during peak hours (left bar chart) and off-peak hours (right bar chart) whilst the line chart represents the overall train punctuality trends. During this pilot activity, the achieved results have been very promising: the guaranteeing authority, represented by the Apulia region, can benefit from them in order to (1) manage the local transportation services, by verifying the compliance with the requirements and (2) manage the relationship between transportation service providing companies and passengers, by trying to constantly reduce the gap between the provided service quality and the delivered service quality [20]. At the end of the pilot, several results have been achieved. First, the central role of the guaranteeing authority has emerged as the principal stakeholder involved in the entire transportation service lifecycle and capable of monitoring processes and services. Moreover, the pilot experience has allowed to determine the involved stakeholders' active role, since they are institutionally recognized and they participate in the phases of monitoring tool definition, control and validation. Second, the definition of the reference model for the CUdSM is no longer a fragmented process, strictly related to one specific service providing company, but it is based on a common framework allowing the comparison between monitoring results and a rigorous evaluation of the service offering and covers transportation system service in its entirety from planning to post-delivery processes.

6 Conclusions

The pivotal role of QoS is nowadays specially clear in the domain of public services, such as the one of local public transportation. Therefore, we have proposed in this paper a systemic approach for modeling the quality of public transportation services by considering the whole system from end to end. We have grounded the model on two assumptions. First, we have represented the public transportation system according to a multi-stakeholder service lifecycle approach. By doing so, it is possible to determine the QoS sustainability when different expectations and constraints have to be faced systematically. Moreover, this fosters an improvement in the global collaboration across the entire local transportation eco-system. Second, we have asserted that the relationships amongst the different stakeholders can be conceived as contracts to be enforced. In this scenario, the Unified Chart of Mobility Services (Unified CdSM) is represented as a contract between passengers and transportation providers, chained with the contract signed between transportation providers and the public entity for the territory accountable of the transportation service. The model has been implemented and validated in a pilot project in the Apulia Region in the South of Italy. Most importantly, the unified CdSM reference model defined during the pilot experience represents a valuable tool for Smart Cities. Amongst the factors characterizing smart cities, the following are worth noting and we are striving to achieve them through the implementation of our tool for the Apulia region: (1) continuous participation of citizens in QoE evaluation campaigns thanks to Web-based and mobile-based applications; (2) real-time monitoring of transportation-related data thanks to vehicle-on-board sensors and infrastructure sensors; (3) real-time monitoring of vehicle routes, commuters' flow, and passengers' opinions; (4) availability of massive monitoring data for possible publication as open data in order to improve citizenships' awareness on transportation services. More specifically, mobile-based applications could benefit significantly from extensive data collection campaigns performed according to the Mobile Crowdsensing paradigms, in which the sensors embedded or pluggable into electronic personal devices such as smartphones and tablets are leveraged for as pervasive sensor data sources. We have already examined and discussed the effectiveness of this approach in several scenarios that dealt with noise and electromagnetic pollution monitoring [20–22].

We are also planning to deploy the model in other scenarios and further develop our tools to incorporate real-time monitoring data coming from sensors. The ambitious aim of this research is to study the multi-perspective approach to the smart cities context and its organization and social impact.

Acknowledgements The modelling design and the pilot site development phases of this research work have been partially funded by HSPI S.p.A. and HeSPlora.

References

1. Bharti, A.K., Dwivedi, S.K.: Integration of public transportation through national e-governance service delivery framework. J. Comput. Sci. Issues. **10**, 189–192 (2013)
2. Bharti, A.K., Dwivedi, S.K.: A BPR approach for e-governance in public transportation. Int. J. Strateg. Inf. Technol. Appl. **5**, 12 (2014)
3. Jones, S.L. (ed.): Urban public transportation systems. In: 3rd International Conference on Urban Public Transportation Systems, Paris, France (2013)
4. Hietanen, S.: "Mobility as a service"—the new transport model? ITS Transp. Manag. Suppl. **12**, 1–3 (2014)
5. Bouton, S., Knupfer, S.M., Mihov, I., Swartz, S.: Urban mobility at a tipping point. http://www.mckinsey.com/insights/sustainability/urban_mobility_at_a_tipping_point
6. International Rail Transport Committee (CIT): Regulation (EC) No. 1371/2007 of the European Parliament and of the Council on Rail Passengers' Rights and Obligations (2007)
7. European Union: Regulation (EU) No. 181/2011, Bus and Coach Passengers' Rights (2011)
8. European Union: Regulation (EU) No. 1177/2010, Rights of Passengers when Travelling by Sea and Inland Waterways (2010)
9. Ballesteros, L.G.M., Alvarez, O., Markendahl, J.: Quality of experience (QoE) in the smart cities context: an initial analysis. In: 2015 IEEE 1st International Smart Cities Conference ISC2 2015. (2015)
10. European Union: Regulation (EC) No 261/2004, Common Rules on Compensation and Assistance to Passengers in the Event of Denial Boarding and of Cancellation or Long Delay of Flights (2004)
11. European Union: Regulation UNI EN 13816:2002: Transportation. Logistics and Services. Public Passenger Transport. Service Quality Definition. Targeting and Measurement (2002)
12. Zeithaml, V.A., Parasuraman, A., Berry, L.L.: Delivering Quality Service – Balancing Customer Perceptions and Expectations. The Free Press, New York, NY, USA (1990)
13. Anderson, R.: Measuring and valuing convenience—a review of global practices and challenges from the public transport sector, London, UK (2013)
14. European Commission, F.: Public Service Contracts, Incentives and Monitoring—SPUTNIC (Strategies for Public Transport in Cities) Project, (2008)
15. Fellesson, M., Friman, M.: Perceived satisfaction with public transport service in nine European cities. J. Transp. Res. Forum. **47**, 99–103 (2012)
16. European Commission, Directorate-General Mobility and Transport, D.-G. for C.: Europeans' Satisfaction with Urban Transport—Flash Eurobarometer 382b (2014)
17. European Commission, Directorate-General Mobility and Transport, D.-G. for C.: Europeans' Satisfaction with Rail Services. Flash Eurobarometer 382a (2014)
18. Randheer, K., Al-motawa, A.A, Prince Vijay, J.: Measuring commuters' perception on service quality using SERVQUAL in public transportation. Int. J. Mark. Stud. 3, 21–34 (2011)
19. Apulia Region: Mobilità—Regione Puglia (in Italian). http://mobilita.regione.puglia.it/index.php/trasparenza/itemlist/category/132
20. Zappatore, M., Longo, A., Bochicchio, M.A.: Using mobile crowd sensing for noise monitoring in smart cities. In: 2016 International Multidisciplinary Conference on Computer and Energy Science, SpliTech 2016. pp. 1–6 (2016)
21. Longo, A., Zappatore, M., Bochicchio, M.A.: Towards massive open online laboratories: an experience about electromagnetic crowdsensing. In: Proceedings of 2015 12th International Conference on Remote Engineering and Virtual Instrumentation (REV2015). pp. 43–51 (2015)
22. Longo, A., Zappatore, M., Bochicchio, M.: Crowd-sourced data collection for urban monitoring via mobile sensors. ACM Trans. Internet Technol. **18**, 1–21 (2017)

Ethic Values for Sharing Communities

Stefano Poponi⊙, Enrico Maria Mosconi⊙, Alessandro Ruggieri⊙
and Michelangelo Arezzo di Trifiletti

Abstract The essence of sharing platforms and their role in the social context is related not only to technology, but especially to the way it is being used today. Ethics, social responsibility and sustainability have become part of this process of development and they stimulate the entrepreneurial mainspring of new market models, that are in evolution. In crowdfunding the "return investment expectancy" plays a key role also in the selection process of innovative ideas, where credibility becomes an essential asset for the business, as well as the need to demonstrate transparency, integrity and responsible governance as priorities. Recently, these platforms are adopting voluntary certification systems, the B Corp certification, to reconcile the need to conduct business under the ethics aspect and raise awareness of stakeholders to adopt guiding values for business, consumption, or the use of services. Our goal is to investigate the role of "ethics", conducted by the "B Corp" Standard Certification System, on sharing platforms. In particular we analyze how the Kickstarter Platform manages the ethical values of B Corp certification. The areas we analyze are: the community, governance, workers, the environment and customers. The closing chapter highlights the theoretical implications and limits of the analysis.

Keywords Crowdfunding · Ethic · B Corporation

S. Poponi (✉)
Università degli Studi Niccolò Cusano, Rome, Italy
e-mail: stefano.poponi@unicusano.it

E. M. Mosconi · A. Ruggieri
Università degli Studi della Tuscia, Viterbo, Italy
e-mail: enrico.mosconi@unitus.it

A. Ruggieri
e-mail: ruggieri@unitus.it

M. Arezzo di Trifiletti
Embassy of the United States of America, Rome, Italy
e-mail: michaelarezzo@gmail.com

© Springer International Publishing AG, part of Springer Nature 2019
F. Cabitza et al. (eds.), *Organizing for the Digital World*, Lecture Notes in Information
Systems and Organisation 28, https://doi.org/10.1007/978-3-319-90503-7_14

1 Introduction

The enhancement of information offered by sharing economy platforms of information and the new shape that digital economy is undertaking have pointed out the importance of how to use technologies, highlighting how the current socio-economic structure is influenced not so much by the availability of a given technology in the strict sense, but rather how the technology is used. In literature the concept of sharing economy is widely debated, although the definitions are progressively evolving due also to the success of the open-source movement, which has contributed to opening the sharing of new digital contents [1], or to the various areas of application [2, 3]. This term is associated with a heterogeneity of domains, from the sharing of product ownership, lending, renting products for the benefit of acquiring values with temporary access rights, or sharing transactions in peer to peer [4]. For Frenken et al. [5] this represents the way consumers give each other temporary access to unused physical activity ("inactive capacity"), even with money. This sharing works in social relationships and contributes to consolidating cultural practices [6], at the same time it generates a rise in well-being [1], but faces a number of criticalities from the point of view of Ethics and how this can be exercised or delivered within sharing platforms.

The transformation capacity and the influence that these platforms have on lifestyles, awareness and choices of consumers/users of products/services, puts us in front of ethical considerations, especially in terms of the influence that these tools have on people's behavior. This relationship is accentuated in crowdfunding platforms where the ethical problem has several implications regarding the type of projects funded, the appropriate amount of funding, the relationship between control needs and a balanced expenditure on the resources received, compliance with what was promised by the funded subject [1, 7], fraudulent campaigns, lack of privacy, misuse of funds raised [8], but also with respect to the impact that sharing has on sustainability [9, 10].

By operating in Crowdfunding, businesses can outsource a project to an indefinite number of potential collaborators by performing "open calls" [11–14], trying to overcome the structural limits that pass through traditional funding channels of innovation and allowing the building of a global line of conversation among entrepreneurs and their investors [15, 16]. In this way, collective intelligence is formed by having the knowledge of collaborating individuals meet, each contributing to the achievement of a project [17, 18].

Recently these cooperation procedures are considering some voluntary certification systems in order to regain the necessity to do business with the ethical (and environmental) aspect. The system of B Corp certification is spreading to an international level, according to an approach bottom up, especially for sensitize enterprises which pursue the adoption of strong ethical values to guide their business. These values valorize the ethical and environmental sensibility of enterprises and consumers, through a direct involvement of all the actors (workers, community, environment) that gravitate around it, realizing a model of alternative governance. On the basis of these considerations this paper aims at describing and discussing the potentialities offered by the B Corp certifications within the crowdfunding platforms. In particular, objective of this work is to understand—starting from the Kirkstarter platform analysis—how the platform succeeds in conveying a positive ethical mediated value of B Corp certifications.

The paper in Sect. 2 will give some brief considerations regarding the research methodology used to support this analysis, Sect. 3 will focus on the operation of the Kickstarter platform, Sect. 4 will outline the requirements of the certification application, the last section will describe and discuss the potential offered by this application in transferring the positive values. Implications and some final reflections will conclude the paper.

2 Methodology

This work has the purpose of describing and discussing the ethical factor proposed by B Corp certifications within Crowdfunding platforms. In particular, this paper wants to answer the question: *how is it possible to transmit ethical factors of the B Corp certifications within the Kickstarter platform?* To answer this question, the paper proposes a critical review of the potential offered by the B Corp certifications and the operation of crowdfunding platforms, focusing on the Kickstarter platform.

The paper adopts a methodological approach to qualitative research based on the study protocol of a descriptive case defined by Yin [19]. It represents an exploratory study based on a documentary analysis [20, 21]. For this study, the documents and information released by the B Corp certification system and related links have been taken into account, including the documentation published by Kickstarter PBC. The official annual reports and the direct exploration of the offered services have allowed us to identify the formal referenced properties that have consequently led to the identification of the role of the "ethical" factor in the platform.

This platform has been selected for its internationally recognized importance, in contrast to the number of community and business volume generated, compared to the funded projects, representing the benchmark for companies using the crowd to fund innovative projects.

The official annual reports and the direct exploration of the offered services have allowed us to identify the formal referenced properties. Previous studies and personal experiences complete our analysis [15, 16, 22–24].

The results will represent the starting point for deeper investigations, which will allow to better define the association between the functioning of the crowd and the ethical factor.

3   Crowdfunding: A Perspective Review

In the early 2000s, the evolution of social networks and the resulting affirmation of the Crowdfunding platforms [25], such as IndieGoGo "(2008), Kickstarter" (2009) and the Italian "Kapipal", allowed the community to Participate in collective initiatives and finance innovative ideas, seeking to gain value from online communities [26]. In literature, many authors identify the factors that affect the positive success of a project, such as the quality, the description, and in particular the social network of the creator [27].

Through these platforms, original channels of technological innovation promotion have been activated, pushing to overcome the structural boundaries that go through traditional channels of innovation financing, creating a new model that uses viral web [15] and generating obvious changes in the expectations of "lenders" and above all in the type of financing offered to businesses, significantly differentiating their inter-vention according to the type of reward received in return. These tools envisage four major types of reward (i) Lending-based Crowdfunding, representing the evolution of microcredit, (ii) Donation-based Crowdfunding, contributing to donor financing, usually of small amounts, without generating any cash return or any other form of tan-gible remuneration, (iii) Reward-based Crowdfunding, which is the most widespread instrument, and which associates funding with a reward or material premium, (iv) Equity Crowdfunding, which involves participation in the company [27–30].

These forms of funding are the result of the various form of participation offered by the Platforms [31]. In literature, it has been discussed the factors that can lead to the success of projects within crowdfunding platforms, such as the quality of the project proposal [27], the way it is described [32] and detail on the importance of social networking [30, 33, 34]. Furthermore Agrawal et al. [33] and Kuppuswamy and Bayus [35] confirm the importance of social structure, in particular, they emphasize the role of family or friends or followers in project financing, especially in the first phase of the campaign. This importance varies according to the different types of crowdfunding where reward-based crowdfunding seems to take priority over other forms of funding.

The ethical dimension, and the relationship with new technologies is represented as a complex and sometimes confused scenario because of the constant and rapid evolution that this concept is assuming [36], as well as its communicative dimension and its conceptualization in social-life context [37].

Participation in the Crowdfunding process makes ethics an essential element. In the dimension of communication (see for example Habermas [37]), the success of crowdfunding projects revolves around the concept of ethics and credibility. In literature, the dynamics linking the ethical aspect to the functioning of platforms and their ability to positively influence the structure of the proposed innovative projects and the involvement of the Community, as well as the ascendant that this factor may have on projects to be financially supported, has still been poorly developed.

According to the general principles of Floridi [38] on moral ethics and ethical aspects of computer ethics, we maintain that "ethics" is an essential input for the participation in the process of crowdfunding along with the key success factors mentioned above. The need to demonstrate transparency, integrity and responsible governance priorities in delivering not only service, but also data and information management as well as internal structure, takes up a priority and an equal level role, simultaneously for all stakeholders [39]. In crowdfunding, "investment return expectancy" plays a key role also in the selection process of successful design ideas, reflecting even more markedly since the early stages of design, the importance of respecting "ethical" values. The passage of the Kickstarter platform into a profit-making organization that pursues social well-being has led to an integrated approach to its "work-flow", also in terms of how the impact of expectations is measured over the individual investment project.

In this sense, instruments for internal evaluation in terms of parameters such as widening the audience and increasing the threshold of work opportunities, inclusive actions, pursuit of dynamic environmental objectives, contained in a very high level of transparency structure, have strengthen Kickstarter's ability to compete and penetrate competitively all players involved.

3.1 Kickstarter

Kickstarter is one of the most important crowdfunding companies in the world. From 2009 to 2015, there have been an exponential growth of total amount of successful projects (except for 2016 when there was a slight decrease of 5.84% compared to the previous year), when approximately 10 million people backed up Kickstarter projects, for a total value of $3,097,795,580 and a total of 126,414 funded projects [40].

The platform focuses on two types of users, creators and bakers (supporters). In the first case it provides a special section for the insertion of design proposals and a set of tools to foster the correct use of the platform and the formalization of the enterprise idea. The projects are grouped into 15 categories (Arts, Comics, Crafts, Dance, Design, Fashion, Film and Video, Food, Games, Music, Photography, Publishing, Technology and Theater), which can trace project drivers inside connecting areas transversally, according to the thematic goals, classified on the basis of "collections" or "radars". Kickstarter defines a project as something ending with a clear start and end, trying to push creators to make it simple to understand the goal and its purpose, specifying that donations to charitable causes, charities, or overheads are not funded. Defining Projects Kickstarter supports creators through a variety of tools, represented by platform guidelines, and a Help section where creators' roles and responsibilities are outlined. Specifically, the Platform defines the principles for community participation, provide a creator handbook to support planning and provide suggestions for developing the proposal, such as the directions for communication with the baker. Next to these tools, Kickstarter identifies a support system consisting of a Faq section, a campus, and a newsletter service. With Faq, the system wants to transfer basic platform knowledge to users, bakers or creators. The community represents the core of the platform, allows an indirect dialogue with users, by searching for answers already provided in the past, present in the database of the platform, or directly by giving new questions to the community or support team. In this area, it is offered access to profiles of the Kickstarter community team, that is to say all those who have been part of the funding or of the creation of projects. Alongside these forms of awareness, there is a thematic newsletter that allows you to be up-to-date on new projects, novelties and promoted events. In this first phase, the creators will contribute by adding the description of the project, identifying the goal and the purpose, the amount of funding required, and the duration of the campaign. The description of the project follows a communicative approach to transfer trust and credibility to the proposed idea, and uses emotion [36, 38, 41], in a virtual environment where sharing and exchange of information is done through video, photo or textual media, and where creators can talk with their supporters.

Kuppuswam and Bayus [35] define Kickstarter community as "sympathetic to an entrepreneur's plea for help" [....] And "an undefined crowd" where all citizens can be funders and supporters of a project without any geographical restriction. Conversely, presenting projects can be made by individuals resident in 21 states (initially projects could only be submitted by residents in the United States).

In the second case, the platform has a large community of members involved in financing creative ideas [35], which are organized by categories. The approach recalls the "all-or-nothing" form of reward based financing. Information presented to a possible funder recalls the project's purpose and objectives, highlighting the funding status (and possibly exceeding the limit set by the creator) and the remaining time available for the project campaign. The platform operates in a logic of transparency, in fact it can show the number of supporters for each form of pledge: a pledge without a reward or a pledge with a different level of reward. Finally, to help potential sponsors discover projects, Kickstarter activates a search function that allows cross searches across categories, collections, areas or i.e. to intervene on projects according to the amount financed/supported or the proximity of the deadline.

The passage of the Kickstarter platform into a profit-making organization that pursues social well-being has led to an integrated approach to its "work-flow" also in terms of how the impact of expectations is measured on individual investment projects. In this sense, tools for internal evaluation in terms of parameters such as widening the audience and increasing the threshold of work opportunities, inclusive actions, pursuit of dynamic environmental objectives contained in a very high level of transparency mechanism, reinforce Kickstarter's ability to compete and penetrate all players involved.

Kickstarter introduced its mission to the principles of Benefit corporation, publishing its first impact report in 2014 [42]. The platform is committed to pursuing a profit-driven path, but at the same time leads to a positive value of its actions, giving rise to creative projects that reflect the values of society and support a more creative and equitable world that employs the arts, and combats inequality.

4 B Corp Certification

According to B Lab, the Benefit Corporation is a new form of doing business, built on the simple principle that businesses should impact and serve more than just shareholders—they have an equal responsibility to the community and to the planet. These standards are intended to encourage the application of new business models, innovative for the approach they propose, to reconcile business performance (economically and financially) with respect for social, ethical and environmental responsibility values [43–44].

The new concept leads towards self-regulation model, in order to allow companies to govern themselves with transparency and re-positively impact on social and environmental well-being. This approach finds its formalization voluntarily in the B Corp certification management system, issued by B Lab [45, 46], a non-profit organization founded in 2006 with the goal of pursuing the diffusion of this type of certification through the establishment of a global business community interested in pursuing social and environmental goals. To encourage the development of a regulatory environment, suitable for legal recognition of enterprises pursuing benefit, B Corp has developed an innovative assessment standard. In order to obtain certification, companies must pass a B-Impact assessment, i.e. an assessment of the impact generated by the pursuit of the purposes for obtaining the certification. By compiling a questionnaire, tailored to the business size, the type of industry, and location, the business will receive a score that varies from a minimum of 80 points (requirement for obtaining the certification) and a maximum of 200 points. An Assessment Review with the staff of the B Impact Assessment will follow the self-assessment in order to guide the company in a position to improve itself and make appropriate adjustments to achieve a B Impact Score. The company will have to make its assessment credible, making available all the documents supporting the statements made and finally obtain a certification as a result of an audit.

To support and consolidate the impact of social responsibility initiatives, with the same control used by other companies to assess the company's financial risk and their return (i.e. Morningstar ratings), B Lab has set up the Global Impact Investing Rating System (GIIRS), A network-based organization that provides a comprehensive picture of sustainability [46] used to accelerate the impact of the investment. This system bases its work on the application of a set of principles underlying the B Corp Certification, fostering its application and addressing six key features: "Comprehensive", which allows the identification of the social model in which the business operates, "Easy to use", "transparent" in the awarding, "dynamic", which provides for an evaluation update every two years, "independently governed", adaptable to different business and "Comparable", which enables to pursue a benchmarking of companies in the same sector. The GIIRS maintains a general impact assessment framework to employ a standardized methodology, distinguished in five distinct areas of impact, tested on the basis of 120 social and environmental questions: (i) Governments, (ii) Workers; (iii) Community; (iv) Environment and (v) Customers.

In these areas, the "Impact Business Models" and Metrics are defined to provide a comparison based on an impact assessment of the company's characteristics, size, sectorial affiliation and geographical area of reference.

5 Discussion and Implication

B Corp Certification uses, as we have briefly mentioned in the previous paragraph, five major areas for assessing the actions of a company that wishes to be certified according to the proposed standard.

These areas are represented by Governance, Worker, Community, Environment, and they investigate how the Kickstarter platform leads to the ethical principles of certification. Table 1 associates each area of B Corp with Kickstarter initiatives that meet these principles.

The general picture revealed by these factors highlights the need for the platform to transmit its ethical values and, more generally, to pursue a broader possible dissemination of positive results, its commitment to society, and the effort for all platform users, from creators to bakers to public figures to feel part of a system, a community that contributes to culturally enriching society with its own ideas and innovations. It is the communication of the concept of the ethical value of the platform to the whole community that contributes to increasing its value in terms of credibility, security and confidence in the services offered. Credibility thus becomes a substantial element of crowd capital platforms that increase value in terms of the growth of investors (bakers) and/or donations. Creators are tempted to question themselves, to present their own innovative ideas, or simply bring their own testimonial by using appropriate channels/ discussion tools (e.g. TCI, Kickstarter-tips). Maximizing the impact of positive influence lies in the ability to convey these messages. In this sense, the community acts as a catalyst for ideas. Several authors [26, 27, 35, 47] argue that crowdfunding communities are anchored by a wider range of social or ideological values, and therefore the understanding of these values can link the community to a specific project, favoring funding (as a result of promotion and reward campaigns).

Ethical influence in projects is transmitted through review processes where recommendations or suggestions are provided on aspects such as environmentally conscious decisions or actions that will allow to intervene and prevent unfair practices. Projects that are able to interpret B Corp's principles are considered positively by Kickstarter, while others that do not show alignment are subject to a penalty, which results in requests for revision, suspension, and/or blocking of projects.

The working environment shows, at least as far as it is possible to analyze from documentary analysis, a diversified inclusion system (see for example Mingers [48]), aimed at overcoming diversity barriers (e.g. gender respect). The centrality of the cultural aspect and the ability to increase the knowledge of the worker are at the center of the company's policies and implemented through professional conversion programs (which loop the workers into the organizational system), but above all, it acts as a driving force towards the pursuit of innovative goals. The improvement of

Table 1 Ethics between B Corp and Kickstarter (*Source* Our elaboration)

Area	B Corp certification principles	Kickstarter: transfer of ethics values
Governance	The system of indicators clearly identifies the mission and the traceability (monitoring) of environmental and social performance, the responsibility, control and stakeholder engagement A Code of Conduct and Behavior, transparent financing, communication with customers and workers	Communication of the company's mission, Benefit Corporation values and principles. Quantification of the donation, scope, and publication of the data (benefit statement annually) Independent assessments on performance, and statistical data (job, pledge, fund and community) Policy for social welfare of the worker and work environment
Worker	The fairness of performance The ability of the organization to maintain the level of staff training, ensuring a level of transferability of skills/knowledge by identifying the degree of worker involvement Decision-making process. ("sustainable" working conditions and respect for the main values of working life) Trust in the company	Evidence of job positions and companies created Measure of the economic impact of creators and their community Incentives for cultural growth Social welfare through space green point NonMonetary acknowledgments Demographic data of workers
Community	Supplier integration and customer satisfaction (monitoring) Codes of conduct Promoting social well-being (inclusion policies and participation), including community services and charitable donations Access to basic services	Community engagement and their emotional involvement (Periodic discussion topics) Suggestions and recommendation for projects Sharing experiences from creators Control of unfair scientific project and ethical conduct Failures transparent Promoting of a free public event Support to the community through donations of 5% of its post-tax profit towards arts
Environment	Extending company policies to the environment performance Input factor: reduction of impacts and consumption (i.e. Energy, water and raw materials) Output factor: emissions and waste (e.g. as well as transport and distribution) Policies and actions to reduce environmental impact (design to solve an environmental issue, renewable resources, waste reduction, environmental culture)	Support of the development of environment projects Incentives to use sustainable means Awareness of local food and drink consumption Efficient lighting tool Guide to the creators toward environmentally conscious decisions Shareholders' votes for company engagement

(continued)

Table 1 (continued)

Area	B Corp certification principles	Kickstarter: transfer of ethics values
Customers	The impact that the policies/actions of the companies have on customers In particular, this section analyzes the assessment of the relationships that the company has with its community, measuring relationships with suppliers, diversity and involvement in the local community Promotion of public benefit (services or design of goods)	Programming the spreading/stabilization of Excellence Tools for the compatibility and interchange verification with creators • Interaction and dissemination • Tools for the success of the project proposal

social welfare and the push towards social programs in leisure time, thanks to the annual education scholarship, drives the worker to personal growth, motivating people, and indirectly acts on the viral community by strengthening the ethical principles pursued by the platform.

The customer concept, proposed by the certification, merges with the different users of the platform: bakers, creators, and the community (in general). The platform works in the utmost care of the use of tools to accompany the creative idea to the success of the project proposal, according to action programs that increase the impact of the activities (dissemination of excellence) or for interactive listening and dissemination of the excellence of creative projects.

The article suggests implications for the application and study of ethical value to crowdfunding platforms and more generally for the interpretation of community functioning. The paper examines the ways in which ethical values are conveyed by the B Corp certification in the functioning of crowdfunding platforms, but much has to be done about the influence that this factor may have on individual stakeholders. The evidence of this first exploratory study prospects the direct implications on community crowdfunding, users and political decision-makers, as well as on researchers.

5.1   Implications

An implication for platforms is to have a reference model that governs relationships, and the conditioning that can be triggered by individual actors. Our discussion highlights the great capacity of platforms to deliver messages and guide community choices. Having a strong certification tool in this case could support the adoption of shared practices, which tend to standardize and increase the maximum level of interoperability

The role of the community, the transfer of values, and the influence it may have on the choice of the various projects to be supported, clearly appears to be one of the critical factors in the discussion presented. In particular, the implications for the community also reflect the appearance of the social relations of the creators [1, 6], which has an appreciable impact on the success of fundraising campaigns.

The study represents a first reference point for orienting future studies so that the necessary conditions of transparency and ethical respect can be created to guide management to a rational use of platforms. In the case of policy makers, the paper may be a reflection point for addressing the definition of public policies and regulating ethical factors and may help avoid incentivizing certain situations considered to be at high risk, rather favoring the formation of forms of participation from the bottom.

Future studies should clarify the role of ethics and influence, as well as the level of conditioning that can be exercised on individual subjects participating in crowdfunding actions (including platforms). This would extend the perspective of analysis and consider factors that could have an effect on generating positive ethical performance.

6 Conclusion

The paper contributes to enrich literature on the use of crowdfunding and the application of the concept of ethics in sharing activities.

Motivated by research seeking to understand how crowdfunding platforms, in particular Kickstarter, are able to convey the ethical values of B Corp certification, this study offers a first reflection on the application of these concepts but at the same time provides the basis for a deep analysis of the ethical factor, and the prospects for applying B Corp certification. In particular, the work analyzes the different behaviors of Kickstarter regarding the ethical factors in community, governance, workers, customers and the environment.

In accordance with Wilburn and Wilburn [46] we believe that B Corp certification can contribute to a reasonable development of social benefit, including ethical factors, and profit.

The exploratory nature of the work and the documentary analysis carried out can represent the main limitations of this work, but may propose different implications and reflections to conduct studies on the subject. The ethics factor can be specifically tailored, through the analysis of specific case studies, or through the application of analytical models that consider our findings.

References

1. Frenken, K., Schor, J.: Putting the sharing economy into perspective. Environ. Innov. Soc. Transit. **23**, 3–10 (2017). https://doi.org/10.1016/j.eist.2017.01.003
2. Chemmanur, T.J., Yan, A.: A theory of corporate spin-offs. J. Financ. Econ. **72**, 259–290 (2004). https://doi.org/10.1016/j.jfineco.2003.05.002
3. Allen, D., Berg, C.: The sharing economy: how over-regulation could destroy an economic revolution. Inst. Public Aff. **5**, 24–28 (2014). https://doi.org/10.1177/1536504214567860.WINTER

4. Cho, M.J., Woo, C.R., Choi, H.R., Hong, S.G., Lee, K.B., Park, S.J.: Business model for the sharing economy between enterprises. Adv. Econ. Law Polit. Sci. Bus. 181–189 (2014)
5. Frenken, K., Meelen, T., Arets, M., van de Glind, P.: Smarter regulation for the sharing economy (2015)
6. Belk, R.: Sharing. J. Consum. Res. **36**, 715–734 (2010). https://doi.org/10.1086/612649
7. Frenken, K.: Sustainability perspectives on the sharing economy. Environ. Innov. Soc. Transit. 1–2 (2017). https://doi.org/10.1016/j.eist.2017.04.004
8. Snyder, J., Mathers, A., Crooks, V.A.: Fund my treatment!: a call for ethics-focused social science research into the use of crowdfunding for medical care. Soc. Sci. Med. (2016)
9. Botsman, R., Rogers, R.: What's Mine Is Yours—How Collaborative Consumption Is Changing the Way We Live (2010)
10. Schor, J., Wengronowitz, R.: The new sharing economy: enacting the eco-habitus (2017)
11. Perera, I., Perera, P.A.: Developments and leanings of crowdsourcing industry: implications of China and India. Ind. Commer. Train. **4**, 92–99 (2009)
12. Peng, X., Ali Babar, M., Ebert, C.: Collaborative software development platforms for crowdsourcing. IEEE Softw. **31**, 30–31 (2014)
13. Petrič, G., Petrovčič, A.: Individual and collective empowerment in online communities: the mediating role of communicative interaction in Web forums. Inf. Soc. **30**, 184–199 (2014)
14. Chung, C.J., Barnett, G.A., Park, H.W.: Inferring international dotcom Web communities by link and content analysis. Qual. Quant. 1117–1133 (2014)
15. Ruggieri, A., Mosconi, E.M., Poponi, S., Silvestri, C.: Digital innovation in the job market: an explorative study on cloud working platforms. In: Lecture Notes in Information Systems and Organisation, pp. 273–284. Springer (2016)
16. Ruggieri, A., Mosconi, E.M., Poponi, S., Silvestri, C.: Crowdfunding for innovative start up: a case study. In: Agrifoglio, R., Caporarello, L., Magni, M., Za, S. (eds.) Re-shaping Organizations through Digital and Social Innovation. Proceedings of the 12th Annual Conference of ITAIS, pp. 231–242. LUISS University Press—Pola Srl (2016)
17. Sørensen, I.E.: Crowdsourcing and outsourcing: the impact of online funding and distribution on the documentary film industry in the UK. Media Cult. Soc. 726–743 (2012)
18. Simula, H., Ahola, T.: A network perspective on idea and innovation crowdsourcing in industrial firms. Ind. Mark. Manag. **43**, 400–408 (2014). https://doi.org/10.1016/j.indmarman.2013.12.008
19. Yin, R.K.: Case Study Research: Design and Methods. Sage Publicaitons, Thousand Oaks, CA (2009)
20. Silverman, D.: Qualitative Research: Theory, Method and Practice. Sage Publications Ltd (2008)
21. Silverman, D.: Interpreting Qualitative Data: A Guide to the Principles of Qualitative Research. Sage Publications Ltd (2011)
22. Ruggieri, A., Mosconi, E.M., Braccini, A.M., Poponi, S.: Strategies and policies to avoid digital divide: the Italian case in the European landscape. In: From Information to Smart Society Environment, Politics and Economics, pp. 221–230. Springer (2013)
23. Poponi, S., Braccini, A.M., Ruggieri, A.: Key success factors positively affecting organizational performance of academic spin-offs. Int. J. Innov. Technol. Manag. 1750026 (2017). https://doi.org/10.1142/S0219877017500262
24. Mosconi, E.M., Silvestri, C., Poponi, S., Braccini, A.M.: Public policy innovation in distance and on-line learning: reflections on the Italian case. In: Organizational Change and Information Systems—Working and Living Together in New Ways, pp. 381–389. Springer, Berlin (2013)
25. Howell, J.M., Shea, C.M., Higgins, C.: Champions of product innovations: defining, developing, and validating a measure of champion behavior. J. Bus. Ventur. **20**, 641–661 (2005). https://doi.org/10.1016/j.jbusvent.2004.06.001
26. Gleasure, R., Feller, J.: A rift in the ground: theorizing the evolution of anchor values in crowdfunding communities through the oculus rift case study. J. Assoc. Inf. Syst. **17**, 708–736 (2016)

27. Mollick, E.: The dynamics of crowdfunding: an exploratory study. J. Bus. Ventur. **29**, 1–16 (2014). https://doi.org/10.1016/j.jbusvent.2013.06.005
28. Hörisch, J.: Crowdfunding for environmental ventures: an empirical analysis of the influence of environmental orientation on the success of crowdfunding initiatives. J. Clean. Prod. (2015). https://doi.org/10.1016/j.jclepro.2015.05.046
29. Kraus, S., Richter, C., Brem, A., Cheng, C., Chang, M.: Journal of innovation empirical paper campaigns. Suma Negocios. **1**, 13–23 (2016). https://doi.org/10.1016/j.jik.2016.01.010
30. Hossain, M.: Crowdfunding: Motives, Definitions, Typology and Ethical Challenges (2017). https://doi.org/10.1515/erj-2015-0045
31. Certomà, C., Corsini, F., Rizzi, F.: Crowdsourcing urban sustainability. Data, people and technologies in participatory governance. Futures **74**, 93–106 (2015). https://doi.org/10.1016/j.futures.2014.11.006
32. Allison, T.H., Davis, B.C., Short, J.C., Webb, J.W.: Crowdfunding in a prosocial microlending environment: examining the role of intrinsic versus extrinsic cues. Entrep. Theory Pract. **39**(1), 53–73 (2015)
33. Agrawal, A., Catalini, C., Goldfarb, A.: The geography of crowdfunding. SSRN Electron. J. (2010). https://doi.org/10.2139/ssrn.1692661
34. Cordova, A., Dolci, J., Gianfrate, G.: The determinants of crowdfunding success: evidence from technology projects. Procedia Soc. Behav. Sci. **181**, 115–124 (2015). https://doi.org/10.1016/j.sbspro.2015.04.872
35. Kuppuswamy, V., Bayus, B.L.: Crowdfunding creative ideas: the dynamics of project backers in Kickstarter. In: UNC Kenan-Flagler Research Paper No. 2013–15. Available at SSRN (2015). https://ssrn.com/abstract=2234765 or http://dx.doi.org/10.2139/ssrn.2234765
36. Floridi, L.: The Ethics of Information, p. 380. Oxford University Press (2013)
37. Habermas, J.: The Theory of Communicative Action, vol. 1. Reason and the Rationalization of Society. Beacon Press, Boston (1984)
38. Floridi, L.: Information ethics: on the philosophical foundations of computer ethics. Ethics Inf. Technol. **1**, 33–52 (1999)
39. Freeman, R.: The politics of stakeholder theory: some future directions. Bus. Ethics Q. **4**, 409–421 (1994)
40. Kickstarter Stats. https://www.kickstarter.com/help/stats
41. Gomez-Diago, G.: The role of shared emotions in the construction of the cyberculture: from cultural industries to cultural actions. The case of crowdfunding. In: Emotions, Technology, and Social Media, p. 49 (2016)
42. Kickstarter PBCIB Corporation. https://www.bcorporation.net/community/kickstarter-pbc
43. Schaltegger, S., Wagner, M.: Sustainable entrepreneurship and sustainability innovation: categories and interactions. Bus. Strateg. Environ. **20**, 222–237 (2011). https://doi.org/10.1002/bse.682
44. Kurki, S., Wilenius, M.: Organisations and the sixth wave: are ethics transforming our economies in the coming decades? Futures **71**, 146–158 (2015). https://doi.org/10.1016/j.futures.2014.09.001
45. Clark, J.W.H., Vranka, L.: The need and rationale for the benefit corporation: why it is the legal form that best addresses the needs of social entrepreneurs, investors, and, ultimately, the public. White Paper (2013)
46. Wilburn, K., Wilburn, R.: The double bottom line: profit and social benefit. Bus. Horiz. **57**, 11–20 (2014). http://dx.doi.org/10.1016/j.bushor.2013.10.001
47. Burtch, G., Ghose, A., Wattal, S.: The hidden cost of accommodating crowdfunder privacy preferences: a randomized field experiment. Manag. Sci. **61**, 949–962 (2015). https://doi.org/10.1287/mnsc.2014.2069
48. Mingers, J., Walsham, G.: Towards ethical information systems: the contribution of discourse ethics. MIS Q. **34**, 833–854 (2010)

Drift of a Corporate Social Media: The Design and Outcomes of a Longitudinal Study

Carla Simone, Angela Locoro and Federico Cabitza

Abstract The paper reports on two different adoption experiences of an in-house Enterprise Social Media (ESM), at the local and global level in a big company. It compares the deployment strategies and their impact on the users appropriation of the ESM in the two settings. Our observations let emerge how the local level design strategy aimed to link the initiative to concrete aspects of working practices and to their expected evolution. This met the companies goals, improved users work effectiveness, and led to a quite successful appropriation. The same success was not achieved at the global level, where a quite different strategy drove the initiative on a slippery slope towards a drift from success. The paper distills lessons that can shed light on how an ESM should be introduced within large organizations by taking care of different local conditions, consolidated practices and legacy technologies.

Keywords Enterprise social media · Longitudinal study · Adoption strategies
Socio-technical co-evolution

1 Motivations and Background

The paper reports on a longitudinal study about the introduction of an *Enterprise Social Media* (ESM) in a multinational corporation.[1] In this case study, we focus on a phenomenon that is often overlooked: when these tools are moved from a local

---

[1]The name of the company as well as the name of the ESM will be left voluntarily anonymous due to a non disclosure agreement between the authors of the present study and the company top management.

C. Simone · A. Locoro (✉) · F. Cabitza
Università degli Studi di Milano Bicocca, Milan, Italy
e-mail: angela.locoro@disco.unimib.it

F. Cabitza
e-mail: cabitza@disco.unimib.it

C. Simone
University of Siegen, Siegen, Germany
e-mail: simone@disco.unimib.it

© Springer International Publishing AG, part of Springer Nature 2019   189
F. Cabitza et al. (eds.), *Organizing for the Digital World*, Lecture Notes in Information
Systems and Organisation 28, https://doi.org/10.1007/978-3-319-90503-7_15

dimension to be deployed at a large scale corporate level, the dynamics of participation and care [12] that had been effective "in the small" [5] are poorly understood,
right when their scaling up has to be accurately planned and assisted instead. Indeed,
the adoption and user satisfaction do not follow the mere validation at the level of
functional and non-functional requirements [16], but also regard the integration of
a new technical element into an existing social milieu (when not directly into an
already existing socio-technical milieu) [1, 10]. Then the research question regards
how the strategy adopted by the management has an impact on the appropriation of
the technology by the prospective users and how the appropriation is related to the
technology design approach.

   This longitudinal study covers a period of three years, from 2013 to 2015, and
can be divided into two main phases, along the trajectory of the introduction of
the ESM in the company. In the first phase, the ESM was introduced in the ICT
department that was in charge of its development and that counted more than 300
permanents. Accordingly, this tool was initially aimed at stimulating the active participation of the ICT employees to the creative realignment of their work practices,
in front of a decision at the company's level toward the massive adoption of cloud
technologies and the related services for office productivity. The initial stage of our
study was focused on observing the strategy adopted by the ICT department in this
double faceted process (testing a technology and solving internal problems), and
on evaluating the technology in this circumscribed setting for identifying additional
improvements. In the second stage, the ESM was proposed to the whole company:
the study then focused on understanding the motivations behind the low acceptance
of the ESM at the global level, which disregarded the almost positive outcomes of
the first phase. The study then allowed us to compare the two experiences in terms
of different strategy, contextual conditions and outcomes.

   In reporting a sort of failure story, or, better yet, of *drift story*, we will distill some
lessons that can be learnt from the exploration and analysis of this real complex
setting and regard practical aspects that question the traditional approaches of IT
product delivery (i.e., stop caring about it once the technology is operative) as well
as research issues that should explore new and bolder solutions when in real complex
settings things scale up in a fast and demanding fashion, and the care that has been
taken locally is no more applied, if not applicable.

2   Framing the Object of Study

The explicit and more direct aim of an ESM is to support and improve the quality of the social interactions within an organizational context in the idea that this
would positively impact the business performance [18, 19, 30]. As noted in [14],
ESM users usually use it to achieve three concrete individual-level purposes: connecting with co-workers; advancing individuals' careers within the company; and
campaigning for projects. Complementarily, Richter and Riemer [26] focus on the

use value of (participating in a) ESM, which they trace back to the opportunistic value of increasing the number of acquaintances (i.e., the social network) to potentially turn to in case of need (cf. the notion of social capital by Putnam and Lin). These motivations affect what functionalities ESM afford, whether mainly communication-oriented [18], innovation-oriented [4], or collaboration-oriented [9]. In particular ESM can be seen as the enabling tool supporting initiatives of company building and brand identity [23], the continuous training of the employees, the increase of the corporate "social capital" [21], which is also declined in terms of the pragmatic need to find the available experts [6] and tap in existing expertise [2], knowledge sharing [20], and idea generation and circulation [32].

The complexity of any organizational setting requires that the introduction of an ESM is carefully planned [17] and even more carefully evaluated over time, to conceive and enact the necessary adjustments for its evolution and effective use. In fact, the adoption and success of an ESM, differently from any application that is used in a corporate domain (whose use is not optional but rather mandatory), highly depends on the motives driving the employees to use it. In [29], the authors claim that "despite the huge potential returns, few managers adequately invest in developing these kinds of networks and deliberately designing them to foster measurable business results [...] But experience in real-world companies suggests that these entities can and should be actively managed, albeit not with conventional forms of management". Therefore, for the interrelation and intersection of personal and institutional interests, the assessment of the impact of the introduction of ESM in terms of positive or negative outcomes, return of investment and other measurable business performance indicators has proven to be a difficult task [15, 19]. Benefits are reported anecdotally in terms of social capital development [31], business processes improvement, and faster decision making [28].

To overcome this fragmented scenario, a fruitful conceptual framework can be derived from the literature about the sustainability of (technological) initiatives that can be articulated in different levels of appropriation by the involved stakeholders [3, 27]: from an understanding of the goals and the involved technical features, to the ability to use these latter in an appropriate way in relation to the current context, up to the ability to adapt and create new solutions to face additional or unexpected needs. This framework offers a tangible way to position the considered initiatives and to compare them, if not to link performance criteria to the actors that play possibly different roles.

3 The Research Methodology

The study started when the first phase was almost concluded and the goal was to evaluate its effectiveness. During the initial part of the study that took four months we collected the data through documentation review and semi-structured interviews [35] with selected users involved with the ESM either as promoters or as target users, followed by a closed-ended questionnaire.

A total of 12 interviews were carried out, each lasting an average of one hour and a half. We digitally recorded the interviews with the consent of the interviewees, took extensive notes during them, and integrated the notes with full transcription from the recordings when necessary (and for relevant passages for later in-depth analysis). During the data collection, we focused on a number of topics, which can be considered our analytical coding scheme. These themes mainly encompassed the story of the introduction of the ESM, and especially how it was related with the infrastructures surrounding it: the organizational context; the existing technologies to support communication, collaborative tasks and the management of the most innovative projects; the key players and the change management initiatives that were conceived during the ESM implementation.

To get a more diffused feedback on the value of the ESM and to base its evolution on the needs expressed by the ICT community, the management decided to administer a closed-ended questionnaire that we participatory and iteratively designed with key representatives of both the middle management of the business unit and the internal relationship office.

After the introduction of the EMS at the whole company level, we co-designed with the Internal Communication Office of the company an online questionnaire by which to collect the opinions of the ESM users about the perceived value of the ESM and its perceived strengths and weaknesses. The survey was chosen as the most feasible means to reach as many employees as possible, also those located in different places and in different countries. We also analyzed the free-text comments by adopting techniques inspired by content analysis. In this light, we adopted an approach that may be called a "crowd-sourced qualitative research" [8]. While the detailed analysis of the two survey results is available in a previous work [11], in what follows we draw a narrative account of this investigation to highlight the features characterizing its two phases.

4   The Local Stage Strategy: A Continuous Care

The process under investigation started in 2010, together with the need of the company to improve its performances by designing and deploying a new private cloud computing infrastructure, which required a change in the governing policies and management of the several and heterogeneous applications used in the company worldwide.

The ICT dept was at the frontline of this change process, as it was the functional unit where innovation was perceived as mandatory, both by the local and the corporate top management. Indeed, the strategic choices of the company forced the ICT dept to start a reflection on its human resources. The members of this business unit had different professional backgrounds and professional trajectories: some of them were young or used to change work environment periodically, others were working for the company or in the same unit for a long time and may be those less keen to innovate their sedimented work practices and own skills and competences that the company could simply not afford to lose, but rather would like to preserve and value for an overall continuous benefit. One of the central issues became how to make this happen.

The recognition that introducing a new technology, i.e., an ESM in the specific case, always entails particular care and risk, convinced the ICT management of the company not to start with the technological side, but rather with the more human and social capital-oriented side of the innovation strategy.

With these initial considerations in mind, the CIO launched a project which: (i) should not construct a complex structure absorbing too many energies with the risk to drain the process itself; (ii) should produce results that could be monitored and verified in short time, in a step-by-step manner. The evaluation criteria should be related to the concrete impacts of the initiative on the ICT dept as well as on its client business units, and the project should focus on the human resources as target and means for the long-term sustainability of the project and of its results. This program had very clear objectives and entailed a clear trajectory to achieve those objectives.

The interviews showed that at the beginning of the project the main aim was to evaluate whether its initial objectives could be reasonably reached in a sustainable way. To this aim, the ICT management applied a continuous strategy of *care* [13] to make the unfolding of this innovation project successful.

Checking the feasibility—The exploratory nature of the initial steps led the management to challenge the ICT employees with a series of initiatives to test their reaction. First, a kick-off meeting identified about twenty people (hereafter called the team) interested in playing a leading role in the project: they owned quite different competences but, more importantly, felt highly committed to its aims. Then the team organized a series of meetings that were focused on the improvement of the business processes within the ICT dept. During these meetings, the attendees produced a number of ideas among which a subset was then selected with the supervision of the management: this was a necessary precondition for their actual feasibility. Soon afterwards, on the basis of those ideas, a number of workshops, one for each idea, started and could be organized without any constraints or direction from the outside, apart from the request to identify a unique spokesperson for each workshop. This involved altogether seventeen people. In this initial steps, the technology mainly supported the external visibility of the work performed within the workshops: a Skype-like Web application flanked the face-to-face seminars to illustrate the progress of the work, and a blog supported the asynchronous discussions about the work going on. These tools allowed the ICT employees not directly involved in the workshops to keep peripheral awareness of what was going on, and nevertheless they also triggered their curiosity. About after one year since the project kicked-off, the workshops that survived an intermediate evaluation passed a second test: that of the achieved results versus the expected ones; of their concrete impacts on the overall company and of their level of innovation; of the quality and feasibility of the roll-out plan; and of the prospective feasibility and maintainability of these results in the long run. The evaluation was organized as a contest in which all participants were rewarded with different kinds of incentives: however, the most valuable reward was perceived as the visibility acquired at the department level, not only during the workshops, but also during the awarding ceremony, organized as an event open to the whole company.

Towards sustainability—The project so far was perceived as successful by all the people involved: however, to make the process sustainable in the long term, the role of the team should change from that of stimulating the participation in the project of the ICT employees to that of coordinating more autonomous activities and playing as consultants in case of need. As the ICT employees became used to think of workshops as a way to interact and collaborate, the generation of new ideas was left to their initiative and a single workshop was kept open to all of the ICT employees wishing to propose new ideas in order to improve the organization and the work practices of their department. This stage was considered mature enough for the introduction of the ESM that the top management had commissioned to the ICT dept in the meantime to offer the standard functionality of an ESM with a focus on the privacy and security requirements typical of an enterprise setting. Specifically, the ESM allowed users to create, or alternatively join, virtual "working rooms" intended as collaborative spaces where interested people could meet virtually and informally (cf. [22]) to organize common projects, discuss specific topics, and address circumscribed issues with selected participants. In order to combine users autonomy with the need to monitor their activities, three main roles were agreed upon: the first was played by a member of the workshop and consisted in being accountable for the local objectives and activities; the second was played by a member of the team and consisted in cooperating with the former in monitoring the activities of the workshops in relation to the overall goals of the project, and in supporting the usage of the ESM and its evolution; finally, the third was played by a member of the ICT management and consisted in checking the coherence and applicability of the incremental outcomes, against the ongoing transformations at corporate level. This last and more structured step of the project lasted almost one year, and involved about 850 people in Italy and abroad. At the end of this step, an evaluation event was held with similar criteria and rewards of the previous one.

Evaluating the effectiveness: a diffused creativity toward innovation—The strategies adopted to govern and conduct the project and the deployment of the ESM laid the ground for a number of concrete ideas and themes of discussion that had been generated in a bottom-up fashion. We summarize these themes in terms of the actions that our interviewees reported as a concrete way to testify the positive combination of the strategy and the technology that was adopted. These actions were taken within different workshops that, while maintaining their autonomy, interacted and exchanged their results in the unfolding of the project. The first action was devoted to reduce the outsourcing costs and to farm in again some activities by carefully surveying the competences that were normally procured in outsourcing, or that had become outdated as they were no more mobilized within any current or prospective activity; anf by organizing a personalized learning programs accordingly. A similar action was undertaken toward a more international audience with the aim to strengthen the sense of belonging to the IT community of experts spread all over the world, and to make the learning programs more homogeneous across the distributed divisions.

From an initial participation of a few tens of people, requests to be enrolled in these programs grew by a factor of six in the following period.

Additional actions promoted the positive attitude to share work experiences, once again in a bottom-up fashion and on a voluntary basis. In this regard, the ESM played a central role, as it offered to the people interested in a specific theme the opportunity to open a dedicated working room. The management of this kind of working room (which were unusual for the ICT community) raised the interest of the leaders of the other workshops, and became the main topic of a meeting that involved all of the workshops leaders.

The projects generated an innovation in the IT production processes that is testified by different actions that produced specific tools and methods that are currently adopted in the production processes of the applications developed within the ICT department, and in the relationships with its client business units: these tools were described also in the documentation we had access to, though we were not allowed to report their contents in detail.

4.1 The Findings from the "Local" Questionnaire

The questionnaire involving the ICT employees was conceived as a tool to collect feedback and preferences on the prospective services to convey through the ESM platform to the frontline end-users. It was advertised through the ESM itself and left open for two weeks to the anonymous compilation of the ICT employees. The main outcomes of the questionnaire can be summarized as follows:

- more than one respondent out of two (57%) declared her willingness to be directly involved in sessions and workshops of participatory design for the evolution of the ESM, thus indicating a strong commitment to this initiative;
- the 85% of the respondents stated to have looked for some specific skill or competence at least sometimes in the last year, and almost one third of the sample (31%) said to do that "often" to solve some technical (89%) or organizational problem (49%), or to compose the best ad-hoc teams to involve in specific projects;
- the most frequently cited ways ti find a specific competence-or skill-related requirement were: (1) peer-to-peer word of mouth (69%): this indicates the importance of weak ties and interactions at arm's length in the company; (2) relying on the supervisor referral (68%), that is asking advice to the closest superior roles in the hierarchical structure: an option chosen by the 68% of the respondents; and also (3) of course reliance on personal memories of past work interactions with colleagues and professional consultants (58%); a few IT employees (5%) used the ESM to to this aim although a specific functionality was not afforded;
- the majority of the respondents would prefer an advanced search functionality of real people rather than a specific virtual space where to ask technical question and receive advice, like in modern knowledge markets (84%) or community question answering systems (72%). Then the ESM is seen more as a trigger or facilitator of

professional interactions that develop in the real world, rather than a virtual venue where to electronically confine de-contextualized problems and solutions;

- two third of the respondents showed a clear availability to share the whole electronic documentation regarding their work activities and the network of people that had been built in those activities, and even the subjects, headers and keywords of their written conversations (i.e., message threads and e-mail exchanges) gone on in those activities, provided that any private message could be discarded and kept confidential; however, the respondents seemed to be more wary to give the prospective system access to data directly related to their professional profile and progress;
- half of the respondents believe that the ESM could become the main tool to support collaborative activities and team work in the ICT department.

To sum up the outcomes of the adoption of the EMS in the ICT department, its management considered the project as a success since the people reacted with a level of participation that was higher than it was initially expected. The process required a relevant investment in terms of care, but the return of this investment was eventually considered as satisfactory: the activities of the project produced new tools and methods and contributed to a change of attitude toward an active collaboration that still persists after the conclusion of the project. One problematic aspect that this experience sheds light on regards the need to continuously motivate people to avoid that they turn back to their (more passive) old habits. The IT management was aware that maintaining the effects of the project requires a continuous investment, a continuous care until the ICT community becomes a self-maintaining community of practice [34]. At the same time, the data collected through the questionnaire indicate that the ICT employees not only have used the ESM to a great extent, but they are also interested in its evolution toward a more comprehensive support of their communication and collaboration, especially for what concerns the expertise finding activities.

5   Going Company Wide: A Top-Down Strategy

Following on from the perceived success of the ICT experience, the corporate top management decided to open the ESM to all of the departments and employees.

At the beginning of 2015, after observing a low participation from the ESM logs, the company involved us in this new phase of the project to collect feedback from the shop floor and try to understand through an online questionnaire why the ESM seemed to lag in reaching full and widespread adoption. The lowest redemption with respect to the previous initiative and in proportion to the number of people contacted (the whole company vs. only one department) gave to us the immediate sensation of a change with the respect to the initial enthusiasm and interest shown during the local phase. The results obtained just confirmed this sensation. The self perceived familiarity with the EMS was low after approximately three months since the system go-live. This fact probably explains a generally limited appraisal of the tool. More specifically, the respondents expressed a general and clear disagreement with the typical functions of an ESM (in sum, sharing information, improving collaboration and problem solving, and strengthening the social bounds within the company) and confirmed its limited capability to support expertise finding. They also expressed a low use value of the tool to improve their business goals since they declared a lack of knowledge and understanding of what could be done with the ESM in concrete terms. In particular, many comments addressed the redundancy and overlap of some of the functionalities of the ESM with respect to other applications already available to the company employees and its rigidity in how the contents had to be structured in the virtual working rooms in comparison with the more diffused Social Media (e.g., Facebook and the like). One of the main reported concerns regarded how the ESM could be "inserted" in the existing practices of the many communities within the company, which were not only functionally but also culturally various. On the more positive side, the survey showed a general awareness that most of the issues were but "sins of youth", and an appreciation of the opportunity offered by the tool for continuous learning through specific initiatives as well as for organizing informal meetings and small talks among colleagues, although this could sometimes go against the ESM aim to improve organizational practices. Also the organization of webinars on specific topics was explicitly mentioned as a desirable benefit of having at disposal a virtual and multi-channel communication tool. The survey showed also that some respondents associated the suppression of a couple of working rooms by the top management supposed to "infringe the ESM nctiquette" with the risk of being controlled, even censored, and with the malicious intent of conditioning and limiting the self-regulated participation in the EMS based activities, for example the time of the day when to perform some activities (e.g., English training), and the topics to be treated (e.g., leasure topics or only professional ones).

6 Comparing the Two Experiences

In the path of scaling the ESM adoption to the whole company, the responsibility of the initiative moved from the ICT department to the Human Resources Department, more specifically to the staff in charge of the Internal Communication (hereafter called staff): this choice, which sounds reasonable to many respects, had significant consequences on the success of the initiative.

The outcomes of the two studies show that the in-house development of the ESM did not directly involve the end users in the definition of requirements and functionalities. In the first case, since the attention was focused on the improvement of the current local work practices, the team monitored the usage of the ESM and collected some technical and usability-related problems that were solved to make the experimentation possible. The situation got worse when the ESM scaled up to the whole company. The application was mainly deployed as such, without any further consideration: for instance, the heterogeneous use and expertise of ICT tools by people of the disparate departments of the company. Some of them used the institutional Information System and common productivity tools on a regular basis to perform their administrative tasks; some others used sophisticated applications and knowledge management technologies to support their production activities. This motivated the different opinions that we collected about the ESM value in the second survey involving the whole company and, consequently, its low adoption, which contrasted the more positive value of the ESM as it was perceived by the ICT employees.

On the one hand, the staff was misled by the apparent simplicity and versatility of the ESM technology, whose functionalities could be nowadays easily appropriated also thanks to the wide adoption of Social Networking technology by the masses. Consequently, the staff expected a similar smooth acceptance of the ESM, made confident also by the success of the ICT department experience. On the other hand, the staff underestimated the different conditions in which the technology had been proposed and adopted in the ICT department. Here the ESM was not simply announced, deployed and then adopted; rather, its high level appropriation was the result of a much more complex process during which the ICT team did a big effort to create a common background and a shared understanding of the role of the new tool in the everyday practices and, more importantly, the technology was instrumental to a clear and self-contained goal to make people live the innovation process that was going on in a more conscious and fruitful way. In other words, the ICT community was encouraged and stimulated to secure the development of the initiative even before that the supportive technology had been introduced. This more virtuous approach was sufficient to avoid the functional drawbacks of the ESM that were contrasted by the ICT users perception of being part of a broader process and, sooner or later, of being able to (positively) influence the enhancement of the ESM, as it is testified by the positive attitude to be part of its development team in the future.

The different organizational culture of the ICT and Internal Communication departments, made this opportunity to be almost completely lost at the company level: when our collaboration with the company was over, it was not clear how the negative results collected with our help could influence the future actions of the staff to get a more significant adoption of the ESM in the company. On the contrary, the ICT department decided that their adoption of the ESM should continue in any case as they had the internal resources and competences to do so. However, a limitation of our study is that, when the ESM became corporate wide, we could not do interviews in other departments as we did in the ICT one, but we had to rely only on the qualitative study of the comments that we had collected through the global questionnaire.

7 Lessons Learnt

The overall study presented in the paper let us distill some lessons that have intertwined implications from the conceptual and practical perspective.

Often technological innovation is motivated by strategic management goals that have to be conveyed to the shop floor. In this case, the care paid by the management is a necessary element for the success of (complex) software applications in organizations [12] and of the new work practices around them, especially if it starts before the technology introduction to create the most favorable contextual conditions for its adoption.

The second lesson is that the organizational and technological culture of the promoters of a technology, as well as the culture of the setting in which the technology has to be deployed, play a fundamental role in avoiding the risk of failure. This means that the adoption of a technology at a global level has to be seen as the outcome of a constellation of local adoptions that take care of the local work practices. This is especially true in a mindset-changing scenario like the one evoked by the adoption of an ESM that has to be integrated in a possibly contrasting organizational culture.

Third, the kind of care "from the above", which we argued [7] is effective in a paternalistic relationship between the top management and the shop floor, should be overturned into a more dynamic and creative relationship to reach a high level technology appropriation: in the case of ESM a more individually motivated but transversal and contextual participation is required to let things (contents produced and consumed by simple, not-hierarchically arranged ESM "users") amalgamate, connect and flow "spontaneously" and "extemporaneously". In the same vein in [29] the authors claim that co-evolution is the suitable strategy to make the appropriation required by open technologies (as ESM are) possible: co-evolution can be based on the transformation of technologies that users are familiar with, and/or on a strict involvement of the users in the technology design. To meet this goal, the idea of *product*, and its deployment, must give way to the idea of *project* [33], and its local and participatory co-production.

The last lesson is that more effort is needed by both the companies and the researchers to understand how to apply the co-evolution approach in complex settings beyond the above mentioned local adoptions. Many contextual factors may interfere: we might refer to the research about the role of (not only technological) infrastructures in system design (e.g., [24, 25]). Irrespective of how these factors are called and defined, we need more cases and longitudinal studies to uncover and compare the (partially) positive solutions and the recurrent mistakes; as well as to uncover how a technology should be constructed to make its appropriation easier and more resilient to the unpredictable contextual changes occurring during its adoption.

8   Conclusions

The longitudinal study reported in this work belongs to the growing area of research convening the introduction of ESM, an apparently consolidated software application, that is still problematic. The result confirm previous studies claiming that the successful adoption of ESM is not specifically depending on the validity of their technical functionalities; but rather on the fit between the technical and the social dimensions of the overall socio-technical system.

Unlike the majority of the studies reported in the literature, the focus was on how the different strategies that led to the adoption of the EMS first in one department and then in the overall organization influenced the level of appropriation of the EMS by he stakeholders involved in these two situations. This perspective highlighted the different role of the management in the two phases as well as the need to critically reconsider the way in which the technology, and specifically an EMS, is traditionally designed.

The reflection on the results of the longitudinal study distilled a set of lessons learnt that that should be taken seriously by both the management and the technology designers to reduce the risk of failure by avoiding to underestimate the potential problems and by grafting more convivial and knowledge sharing practices (referred to as *network communities* in [9]) into already established communities with their consolidated work practices. To make the graft successful, both kinds of community should be put in the condition to co-evolve and become a hybrid organism that can thrive and yield innovative fruit and outcomes.

References

1. Ackerman, M.S.: The intellectual challenge of CSCW: the gap between social requirements and technical feasibility. Int. J. Hum. Comput. Int. **15**(2–3), 179–203 (2000)
2. Ackerman, M.S., Dachtera, J., Pipek, V., Wulf, V.: Sharing knowledge and expertise: the CSCW view of knowledge management. Comput. Support. Coop. Work (CSCW) **22**(4–6), 531–573 (2013)
3. Altman, D.G.: Sustaining interventions in community systems: on the relationship between researchers and communities. Health Psychol. **14**(6), 526–536 (1995)
4. Backhouse, J.: Social media: impacting the enterprise. In: European and Mediterranean Conference on Information Systems, pp. 1–9 (2009)
5. Bandini, S., et al.: WWW in the small towards sustainable adaptivity. World Wide Web **10**(4), 471–501 (2007)
6. Brzozowski, M.J.: WaterCooler: exploring an organization through enterprise social media. In: Proceedings of the 2009 international ACM SIGGROUP Conference on Supporting group work (GROUP09), pp. 219–228. ACM, Sannible Island, FL, USA (2009)
7. Cabitza, F., Locoro, A.: From care for design to becoming matters: new perspectives for the development of socio-technical systems. In: Caporarello, L., Cesaroni, F., Giesecke, R., Missikoff, M. (eds.) Digitally Supported Innovation. Lecture Notes in Information Systems and Organisation, vol. 18. Springer, Cham (2016). http://dx.doi.org/10.1007/978-3-319-40265-9_8
8. Cabitza, F., Locoro, A.: Questionnaires in the design and evaluation of community-oriented technologies. Int. J. Web Based **1**, 4–35 (2017) Inderscience. http://dx.doi.org/10.1504/IJWBC.2017.10001595
9. Cabitza, F., Simone, C.: Affording mechanisms: an integrated view of coordination and knowledge management. Comput. Support. Coop. Work (CSCW) **21**(2–3), 227–260 (2012)
10. Cabitza, F., Simone, C.: Building socially embedded technologies: implications about design. In: Designing socially embedded technologies in the real-world, pp. 217–270. Springer (2015)
11. Cabitza F., Locoro A., Simone C.: You cannot grow viscum on soil: the 'good' corporate social media also fail. In: De Angeli A., Bannon L., Marti P., Bordin S. (eds.) COOP 2016: Proceedings of the 12th International Conference on the Design of Cooperative Systems, Springer, Trento, Italy, 23–27 May 2016

12. Ciborra, C.: De profundis? Deconstructing the concept of strategic alignment. SJIS **9**(1), (1997)
13. Ciborra, C.: Introduction: what does groupware mean for the organizations hosting it? In: Groupware and Teamwork: Invisible AID or Technical Hindrance, Wiley, New York, NY, USA (1997)
14. Di Micco, J., Millen D.R., Geyer W., Dugan C., Brownholtz B., Muller, M.J.: Motivations for social networking at work. In: Proceedings of the 2008 ACM Conference on Computer Supported Cooperative Work (CSCW'08), pp. 711–720. ACM Press, San Diego, CA, USA (2008)
15. Holtzblatt, L., Drury, J.L., Weiss, D., Damianos, L.E., Cuomo, D.: Evaluating the uses and benefits of an enterprise social media platform. J. Soc. Media Organ. **1**(1), (2013)
16. Kai, R., et al.: Eliciting the anatomy of technology appropriation processes: a case study in enterprise social media. In: ECIS (2012)
17. Kaplan, A.M., Haenlein, M.: Users of the world, unite! the challenges and opportunities of social media. Bus. Horiz. **53**(1), 59–68 (2010)
18. Leonardi, P.M., Huysman, M., Steinfield, C.: Enterprise social media: definition, history, and prospects for the study of social technologies in organizations. J. Comput. Med. Commun. **19**(1), 1–19 (2013)
19. Megan, M., et al.: Social software for business performance the missing link in social software: measurable business performance improvements. Deloitte Cent. Edge (2011)
20. Moradi, E., Saba, A., Azimi, S., Emami, R.: The relationship between organizational culture and knowledge management. Int. J. Innov. Ideas **12**(3), (2012)
21. Nahapiet, J., Ghoshal, S.: Social capital, intellectual capital, and the organizational advantage. Acad. Manag. Rev. **23**(2), 242–266 (1998)
22. Orr, J.E.: Narratives at work: story telling as cooperative diagnostic activity. In: CSCW'86, pp. 62–72. ACM (1986)
23. Peruta, A., et al.: Organisational approaches to brand identity on social media: comparing brand websites and facebook pages. JDSM **2**(1), 91–102 (2014)
24. Pipek, V., Volker Wulf, V.: Infrastructuring: toward an integrated perspective on the design and use of information technology. JAIS **10**(5), 447–473 (2009)
25. Pollock, N., Williams, R.: E-infrastructures: how do we know and understand them? strategic ethnography and the biography of artefacts. Comput. Supported Coop. Work **19**(6), 521–556 (2010)
26. Richter, A., Kai R.: Corporate social networking sites—modes of use and appropriation through co-evolution. In: Proceedings of the 20th Australasian Conference on Information Systems. Melbourne, AUS (2009)
27. Scheirer, M.A.: Is sustainability possible? a review and commentary on empirical studies of program sustainability. Am. J. Eval. **26**(3), 320–347 (2005)
28. Schmidt, R., Selmin N.: BPM and social software. In: BPM, pp. 649–658. Springer (2009)
29. Sena, J., Sena, M.: Corporate social networking. Issues Inf. Syst. **9**(2), 227–231 (2008)
30. Steinfield, C., DiMicco, J.M., Ellison, N.B., Lampe, C.: Bowling online: social networking and social capital within the organization. In: Proceedings of the Fourth International Conference on Communities and technologies, pp. 245–254. ACM (2009)
31. Steinfield, C., Scupola, A., Lopez-Nicolas, C.: Social capital, ICT use and company performance: findings from the medicon valley biotech cluster. Technol. Forecast. Soc. Change **77**(7), 1156–1166 (2010)
32. Tierney, M.L., Drury, J.: Continuously improving innovation management through enterprise social media. J. Soc. Media Organ. **1**(1), (2013)
33. Varanini, F., Ginevri, W.: (eds.) Projects and Complexity. CRC Press (2012)
34. Wenger, E.: Communities of practice and social learning systems. Organization **7**(2), 225–246 (2000)
35. Yin, R.K.: Case Study Research: design and methods, Vol. 5. Sage (2009)

Changing Institutionalized Practices When Implementing a Mandated Technology

Lapo Mola, Renata Kaminska and Andrea Carugati

Abstract In knowledge intensive organizations—such as Information Technology (IT) companies or consultancy firms—knowledge sharing processes and collaboration represent key success factors for competing in a dynamic business environment. In small firms knowledge sharing and collaboration are facilitated by the physical proximity of the R&D or business development specialists. In large organizations, characterized by distributed settings, to speed up innovation and time-to-market, managers need to find ways to enable knowledge sharing and collaboration among individuals and teams located in different geographical areas. Managers have a choice of different strategies and IT tools to support employee collaboration. Through the institutional theory lens, the objective of this research is to better understand the challenges of selecting and using collaborative IT tools in a geographically distributed setting. To this end, we have collected data via a case study of a large IT organization that introduced a centralized mandated IT tool aimed at enabling collaboration among employees working in a distributed setting and belonging to different departments and functions. Our preliminary findings show that institutionalized practices, organizational silos as well as lack of time and incentives compromised the effective use of the mandated IT tool.

Keywords Institutional theory · Mandated technology · Institutionalized practices

L. Mola (✉) · R. Kaminska
Skema Business School, University Cote d'Azur (GREDEG), Lille, France
e-mail: lapo.mola@skema.edu

A. Carugati (✉)
Århus Business School, Århus University, Århus, Denmark
e-mail: anddrea@asb.dk

© Springer International Publishing AG, part of Springer Nature 2019
F. Cabitza et al. (eds.), *Organizing for the Digital World*, Lecture Notes in Information Systems and Organisation 28, https://doi.org/10.1007/978-3-319-90503-7_16

1   Theoretical Background

1.1   The Options in Information System Selection

A large proportion of studies on diffusion argues that organizations adopt new practices and resources, such as information technologies, for three main reasons: they
adopt a certain IT to achieve or defend a competitive advantage; they adopt a certain
IT because of the "influence" of external entities; they adopt a certain IT because it
is imposed by an external authority.

In the first case—*adoption as a choice*—the adoption called competitive isomorphism is a rational process whereby companies monitor their environment for
technologies and practices that allow them to improve their internal processes. Companies adopt the technologies and work practices that others use because of "a system
rationality that emphasizes market competition, niche change and fitness measures"
[4, pp. 149–150].

In the second case—*adoption resulting from persuasion* by external entities—organizations adopt new practices and new technologies because external
entities—such as consultancy companies or accreditation/certification bodies—per-
suade them to do so. These external entities have a stake in the technologies that
companies use and in the managerial practices that they adopt, but they do not have
any formal power to affect the choices of organizations [11].

Finally, adoption can be the result of an *imposition* by external entities. In this
case organizations adopt new practices and new technologies because external agents
force them to do so [2]. These agents have a stake in the technologies and in the administrative practices that organizations adopt and they have enough power to enforce
self-serving practices upon a group of organizations [18]. One set of entities includes
government bodies, standard-setting organizations, regulators, industry associations,
unions and any other organization that has formal power over organizations in a group
through the rule of law or through a set of contracts [12].

1.2   Institutionalization of Information Systems

According to Powell and DiMaggio [16, p. 8], institutions '*are social structures that
have attained a high degree of resilience*'. *This resilience is based on and sustained
by: cultural-cognitive, normative, and regulative elements that, together with associated activities and resources, provide stability and meaning to social life. Institutions
are transmitted by various types of carriers, including symbolic systems, relational
systems, routines, and artefacts. Institutions operate at different levels of jurisdic-
tion, from the world system to localised interpersonal relationships. Institutions by
definition connote stability but are subject to change processes, both incremental
and discontinuous*' [16, p. 8].

Institutional theory proposes that the regulative, normative and cognitive elements of institutions can be seen on the basis of compliance and legitimacy and in the mechanisms, logic and indicators that operate in the social structure, as per Table 1.

Institutional theory highlights the mechanism of isomorphism: '*a constraining process that forces one unit in a population to resemble other units that face the same set of environmental conditions*' [4, p. 149]. In this theory, similar actors (organizations and individuals) in the same environment tend to pursue similar courses of action. Isomorphism derives from three underlying types of pressure in the institutional environment: mimetic, normative and coercive.

Mimetic pressure arises from similar interpretations of the organizational field, such that actors mimic other successful actors that they consider as similar to themselves [4]. For example, the decision to implement a specific Information System (IS) or a specific business process often depends more on what other similar organisations are doing than on the objective needs of innovation processes [1, 14].

Normative pressures induce isomorphism through shared respect for unwritten codes of conduct or traditions. Over time, normative pressures permeate business organisation and dictate what should be done and how to approach problems. For example, when a firm realizes that most of its competitors are adopting a specific protocol and procedure, it will tend to adopt similar protocols and procedures to achieve legitimacy among its customers and business partners [21].

Coercive pressures emerge from legislation and technological changes that compel the organisation to adapt [19]. For example, when the European Union introduced the requirement of milk traceability and other norms, all actors operating in the milk supply chain were forced to begin declaring their procedures. A collective respect for these norms results in isomorphism [2].

It should be noted that isomorphic pressures can act both as a brake and as an accelerator of change, depending on the market's particular situation and the momentum that a particular initiative is having. Further, isomorphic pressures act on multiple levels [17]. Organisational fields, defined as '*organisations that, in the aggregate, constitute a recognised area of institutional life*' [4, p. 148], can develop professional codes of conduct, perhaps regardless of legislation, though [17] finds reciprocal interactions across levels, such that the societal level connects to the individual level through the organisational field level, and vice versa.

Table 1 Representation of regulative, normative and cognitive institutional elements, from [17]

	Regulative	Normative	Cognitive
Basis of compliance	Expedience	Social obligation	Taken for granted
Mechanisms	Coercive	Normative	Mimetic
Logic	Instrumentality	Appropriateness	Orthodoxy
Indicators	Rules, laws, sanctions	Certification, accreditation	Prevalence, isomorphism
Basis of legitimacy	Legally sanctioned	Morally governed	Culturally supported, conceptually correct

Therefore, it is sensible that Currie [3] encourages IS researchers to conduct multilevel analyses to enrich understanding, an approach also seen in [6]. Through institutional change and the diffusion of practices, top-down processes allow higher-level structures to shape the structure and action of lower levels, something seen as desirable in innovation processes, but that can also work in the opposite direction and frustrate initiatives.

Institutional theory, with its ability to highlight both change and resistance at multiple interconnected levels, is a powerful tool for understanding organizational change involving new ITs [13, 23]. In the present contribution, we use the institutional theory lens to explore the challenges involved in implementing a specific information technology from both decision-maker and user perspectives.

2 Methodology

2.1 Research Approach

This empirical study takes a socio-technical perspective, in which reality is constructed by the interaction of actors (human and non-human) in generating meaning. We adopted an interpretive case study approach [22], collecting and analyzing data following the basic principles of grounded theory methodology, such as constant comparison and theoretical sampling [8–10]. The combination of case studies and grounded theory methods is an appropriate way of exploring socio-technical problems in IS [7] and an effective approach when exploring phenomena in their own organizational and human contexts [15, 20]. This method allowed us to explore the substantive area of study, to explain the phenomena under observation in a manner that was informed, but not hijacked, by the literature or by the a priori adoption of a theoretical lens (as suggested by [5, 15]).

2.2 Data Collection

We collected our data on the implementation of the mandated collaborative IT tool at *Alpha Ltd. (a pseudonym),* a large European IT company that processes, manufactures and distributes IT products and services worldwide. The case organization provided access to documents, technology and key people, thus facilitating the longitudinal study, which consisted, until then, of three phases, as follows:

The first phase (2015) involved analyzing the processes and procedures used at Alpha in developing new products and services and examining the collaboration practices among team members located in different geographic areas. In order to understand the general context, we conducted 5 semi-structured interviews with 2 project managers, 1 manager of the Knowledge management center (KM center) in Europe, 2 developers—users of existing collaborative tools. With this background, we analyzed the content of the Alpha intranet and internal documents (for example institutional presentations of Alpha, internal communication about collaboration needs and objectives, etc.). Then, we conducted a 3-month field observation.

The second phase (2016) involved studying the nature and role of the different collaborative tools in Alpha. Semi-structured interviews were conducted with the KM manager (1), project manager (1) and with the developer-key users (3). We supplemented the interviews with analysis of internal documents. We also analyzed the features of the different tools and procedures used for developing the main services, searching for clues in the technology. This phase provided a more complete understanding of the technology and the challenges presented. The accounts suggested tensions between opposing forces regarding change.

During the third phase (2017–present) we aimed to investigate the different perspectives on the role and efficiency of collaborative tools. A key objective was to gather direct evidence from the different types of actors involved (developers, middle managers, sale force), as this is necessary to better understand the role and relevance of emerging constructs. We conducted 15 interviews with the Alpha KM manager (1), project managers (2), developer key users (3), and pilot users of the mandated collaborative IT tool (8). We also observed pilot users of the new platform to manage and record data related to their daily activities (Table 2).

Table 2 Data collection synthesis

Type of data	# of data	Detail	Theoretical goal
Interviews	25	2 managers of KM center, 5 project managers, 8 key users, 10 pilot users	Understand the differ views of the project and of the collaborative tool
Internal documents	15	10 PowerPoint presentations (on average 60 slides each, illustrating the main phases of the projects) 5 project reports	Understand the official view of the project
Direct observation	120 h	Two of the authors' MSc students working at Alpha were coached on the different tools used and on the new one	Understand the use of the available collaborative tools

3 Contextual Background—Case Description

3.1 Alpha Ltd.

Founded in the late '80s, Alpha Ltd. is a global IT enterprise, a leader in its domain. The exponential growth of Alpha Ltd. resulted in a multinational with a headcount of over 15.000 employees spread over all five continents. Initially specialized in one sector, Alpha Ltd. now provides technology solutions for a wide range of institutional customers in different domains and sectors. Alpha Ltd. has become very much a large IT company and with this status it has become vital to be as efficient as possible. Competitors are continuously evolving and Alpha Ltd. has understood that they must do the same. This is why the company is constantly searching all parts of the organization's solutions to increase their productivity and efficiency.

   Their overall goal is to find solutions that empower their business and help their customers enhance and improve results on a daily basis. To date, Alpha Ltd. has a large product and service portfolio but innovation remains one of the most important challenges. Every single product is meant to serve a certain need from one of the company's specific segments. Today Alpha Ltd. has two core businesses—Distribution and IT Solutions. They deliver powerful customer synergies by sharing a common technology platform and communications infrastructure. Alpha Ltd. is present in 190 markets representing 118 nationalities worldwide. Consequently, despite the existing IT tools, sharing knowledge and collaborating has become challenging because Alpha's employees are culturally diverse and geographically dispersed.

3.2 Collaboration Tools at Alpha Ltd.

Throughout the world Alpha Ltd. local and global teams develop many creative ideas and innovative products. In such a complex and distributed setting one of the main challenges that Alpha managers face is how to enhance knowledge sharing and collaboration to increase efficiency and innovation in the global team. To better serve the needs of these geographically dispersed employees and teams, a wide range of tools has been introduced throughout the company over the years. These include:

- SharePoint 2010-based tool for sharing approved information and documents with the wider audience
- SharePoint collaboration tool for document management and content sharing with a limited audience
- Internal Q&A forum related to Alpha's products, services and tools
- Mango Apps, a social platform that connects employees and allows them to create groups to discuss projects, topics of shared interest or coordinate teams
- Internal social network where employees can share their area of competencies
- Online meeting and video conferencing tool

Fig. 1 The four goals of
collaboration at Alpha Ltd

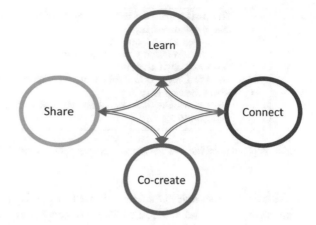

Fig. 1 The four goals of collaboration at Alpha Ltd

- Jabber, a chat tool
- Outlook, a classic corporate emailing tool
- Instant messaging tool for groups
- Co-creation tool mostly used by developers to share and exchange ideas
- Cloud platform that helps to securely store and share files
- Internal ideation platform to promote innovation inside the company
- Video and rich-media sharing tool
- Project mock-up sharing tool used by developers and designers
- Lotus Notes, the previous version of outlook, still used for posting offers (ex: buying or selling, help...)

The IT tools in use at Alpha have been introduced to support and integrate the four main aspects of the organization's view of collaboration: learning from peers; connection across sites and functions; co-creation of services and products; sharing ideas and expertise (Fig. 1).

3.3 Data Analysis and Results

3.3.1 Mandating a New Collaborative Tool

The official internal documents at Alpha witness the managerial team's increasing emphasis on the need to collaborate. In an internal newsletter, the Alpha CEO set the direction where Alpha should head: *"We have no alternative but to work together more effectively than we did in the past. Success in areas such as merchandising, mobile, payments and many others requires us to bring our talents and our expertise together, to collaborate and to compromise. Working together is one of our values and has to be an everyday reality to ensure our future success."*

> - **The ambition - A friction free business.**
> - **Discover anything**
>   - o Discover the answers and the information that you need, whenever and wherever you are
> - **Connect with anyone**
>   - o Find, connect and follow anyone, across the Alpha business
> - **Work in any way**
>   - o Choose the tools and channels that work best for you and your group.

Fig. 2 Alpha official internal communication presentation PROJECT-REF2.5

This official message has been reinforced by the Alpha Chief Operations Manager who recounted in the subsequent internal newsletter: "*In a global, dynamic and evolving working environment, how we interact, collaborate and share knowledge across geographies and teams must continuously evolve. An effective workplace **connects people** and makes **collaboration simple**, bringing together the true potential in our workplace – **your expertise and diversity**".*

These statements are also summarized in the guidelines for the upcoming Alpha project (Fig. 2).

Alpha's need to change the institutionalized practices is reflected in an official internal presentation of a new project: "*This is the change that's going to shape the next phase of our growth. Not following conventions but breaking them, not holding onto our past but learning from it. It's a change that's going to enable us to shape the future of our industry....*" (PROJECT-REF2.5). Pressure to change comes from the necessity to rapidly cater to customer needs in a highly competitive environment. As Alpha HR, Communication and Branding manager stated in another official communication: "*Alpha must become more collaborative and agile to truly support the customer in a VUCA [VUCA sands for: volatility, uncertainty, complexity and ambiguity] world. Alpha Future of Work is a key transformational programme to drive Alpha through that change*".

In the face of an increasing need for knowledge sharing and collaboration Alpha management promotes Alpha Group, the new centralized IT tool for collaboration. This tool is similar to the social networks that employees use at home. It offers the possibility to discuss and chat back and forth, post pictures, videos and other content. Alpha Group which was introduced to align employee interaction practices with the vision of the company which, to quote one of the project leader: "*is to really focus on the collaboration side in order to undo things socially that you could do differently or that you did differently often before*." Alpha Group has been linked to some other previously used IT tools with the aim of better meeting employees' needs. The management hopes that Alpha Group will effectively integrate all the tools and become the main collaborative tool used throughout the organization.

3.3.2 Barriers to Change Institutionalized Practices

If the top management view that emerges from the official documents and from the interviews conducted with middle management seems to be clear and shared, the reality of Alpha Group use appears more complex at employee level. As one of the employees recounted: *"the more Alpha is global, the more challenges it faces such as diversity in the culture of the country, resistance, usability differences and others"* (Alpha Key User 1).

A major barrier to the use of Alpha Group is the existence of organizational silos at Alpha, not only among the different business units but also among the different hierarchical levels and organizational functions. Our interviewees most frequently mentioned lack of interactions between IT developers and the sales and marketing staff. These two groups of employees seem to have conflicting goals and motivations. Firstly, IT developers are technology "geeks" who tend not to use the mandated tools (Alpha Group) because they have always developed their own IT solutions for their specific needs. Secondly, the rest of the organization (from marketing, finance or sales force mostly) also have communication and collaborative needs but are unable to develop their own tools or do not take time to develop them. These two groups seem to have different interests and tend not to interact easily with one another. As one of the employees confirmed: *"Our operations will say there are two different mentalities and often the developers will do something because they think everybody else is too slow, so they will do it in their own corner"* (Project Manager 2). Indeed, if the existing IT tool does not meet the developers' expectations, they do not wait for the official solution but resolve the problem by creating a solution themselves. This poses several challenges. First, by developing new tools, the developers contribute to the multiplication of the already large number of IT tools at Alpha. Second and most importantly, by developing their own tools, developers may bypass the official security enforcement processes. In other words, when developers come up with an IT solution that suits the specific needs of their team, they do not go through the entire security validation as would an Alpha approved tool. Furthermore, by multiplying collaborative tools used inside the organization, it becomes very difficult to keep track of information whereabouts. Hence, to enhance knowledge sharing and collaboration, the challenge is to implement an IT tool that satisfies the needs and expectations of the two different groups of employees mentioned above.

Our interviewees also mentioned insufficient liaison functions to facilitate knowledge sharing. Pilot user 1 has a cross-function role within the organization. Yet, she clearly stated that she does not have the time to truly work with each division or team to meet their needs. In sum, the multiplicity of existing collaboration IT tools and the fact that one group of employees, namely, the IT engineers have, over the years, developed their own tools tailored to their teams' needs, has reinforced the organizational silos between IT engineers and the rest of the organization. This had two main consequences. First, it resulted in frequent misalignment between customer needs and the IT solutions developed by the Alpha IT engineers. Second, it gave rise to the emergence of sub-cultures within IT development and sales and marketing staff resulting in misunderstandings and conflicts.

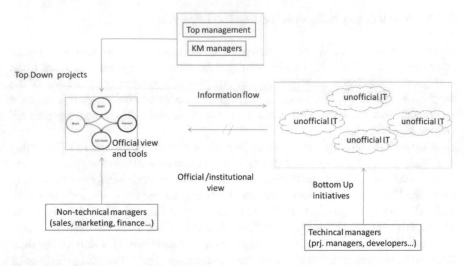

Fig. 3 The official versus the actual organization

Lack of time emerges as an important barrier on several levels. When analyzing data from the interviews, we also found that in some cases it was not unwillingness to use the technology that became a barrier to knowledge sharing and collaboration but rather the fact that employees did not have the necessary time to learn how to use the mandated tools. Also, no "*real*" incentives were offered by management to enhance the use of Alpha Group. As one Pilot user 2 recounted: "*We spend a large amount of time learning the tools. And we have a large number of sites. But in the end what counts is our objectives*". Furthermore, our interviewees reported that because of the time pressure everyone experiences, the tools are not completely suited to their needs: *The guys would need a lot more time to spend with the different team members in order to understand their activities and offer them a better adapted solution for them*" (Pilot user 1).

Figure 3 shows the existence of the different sub-organizations within the formal organization.

4 Discussion and Limitations

The first round of data analysis points to the existence of different external and internal pressures as well as different internal logics at Alpha. Alpha chose to introduce the new IT system (Alpha Group) to increase internal efficiency and because of mimetic pressure resulting from the persuasion of external entities such as experts and software vendors [4, 11]. The choice of the IT solution appears not to be in line with the existing and institutionalized practices. This misalignment creates tension between the top-down IT strategy pursued by the organizational decision-makers and the institutionalized practices of the users, some of whom continue to use the unofficial tools developed by the technical staff for the specific needs of their teams.

Contrary to previous research [2, 14], at the moment of data collection and analysis, the mandated IT artefact did not help to overcome the distance between the different sub-cultures (technical and non-technical) at Alpha. Instead, imposing rather than discussing the IS choice deepened the existing distance between them. The technical staff continued to use their unofficial IT tools and the non-technical staff followed the official path.

In line with institutional theory, our data show the difficulty of changing institutional practices at Alpha Ltd. It seems that the introduction of the centralized IT tool conflicted with the institutionalized practices of a substantial number of users and with the cultures and professional code of conduct already in place [17].

The main limitation of our study is the fact that our data was collected during the initial stage of the IT implementation project. To better understand the challenges involved in efficient adoption of the centralized collaborative IT tool, the authors are running a second round of data collection that will provide additional insights to the mechanisms that facilitate the evolution of institutionalized practices.

References

1. Ang, S., Commings, L.: Strategic response to institutional influences on information systems outsourcing. Organ. Sci. **8**, 235–256 (1997)
2. Carugati, A., Fernández, W., Mola, L., Rossignoli, C.: My choice, your problem? Mandating IT use in large organisational networks. Inf. Syst. J. (2018)
3. Currie, W.L.: Contextualising the IT artifact: towards a wider research agenda for IS using institutional theory. Inf. Technol. People **22**, 63–77 (2009)
4. DiMaggio, P., Powell, W.W.: The iron cage revisited: collective rationality and institutional isomorphism in organizational fields. Am. Sociol. Rev. **48**(2), 147–160 (1983)
5. Eisenhardt, K.M.: Building theories from case study research. Acad. Manag. Rev. **14**, 532–550 (1989)
6. Faik, I., Walsham, G.: Modernisation through ICTs: towards a network ontology of technological change. Inf. Syst. J. (2012)
7. Fernandez, W.D., Lehmann, H.: Case studies and grounded theory method in information systems research: issues and use. J. Inf. Technol. Case Appl. Res. **13**, 4–15 (2011)
8. Glaser, B.G.: Theoretical Sensitivity: Advances in the Methodology of Grounded Theory. Sociology Press, Mill Valley, CA (1978)
9. Glaser, B.G.: Doing Grounded Theory: Issues and Discussions. Sociology Press, Mill Valley, CA (1998)
10. Glaser, B.G., Strauss, A.L.: The Discovery of Grounded Theory: Strategies for Qualitative Research. Aldine Pub. Co., New York (1967)
11. Greenwood, R., Suddaby, R., Hinings, C.R.: Theorizing change: the role of professional associations in the transformation of institutionalized fields. Acad. Manag. J. **45**(1), 58–80 (2002)
12. Mezias, S.J., Glynn, M.A.: The three faces of corporate renewal: institution, revolution, and evolution. Strateg. Manag. J. **14**, 77–101 (1993)
13. Mignerat, M., Rivard, S.: Positioning the institutional perspective in information systems research. J. Infor. Technol. **24**(4), 369–391 (2009)
14. Mola, L., Carugati, A.: Escaping "localisms" in it sourcing: tracing changes in institutional logics in an Italian firm. Eur. J. Inf. Syst. **21**, 388–403 (2012)

15. Orlikowski, W.J.: CASE tools as organizational change: investigating incremental and radical changes in systems development. MIS Q. **17**, 309–340 (1993)
16. Powell, W.W., DiMaggio, P.J.: The New Institutionalism in Organizational Analysis. University of Chicago Press, Chicago, USA (1991)
17. Scott, W.R.: Institutions and Organizations: Ideas and Interests. SAGE Publications Inc., Thousands Oaks (2008)
18. Smith, S., Winchester, D., Bunker, D., Jamieson, R.: Circuits of power: a study of mandated compliance to an information systems security de jure standard in a government organization. MIS Q. **34**(3), 463–486 (2010)
19. Tushman, M.L., Anderson, P.: Managing strategic innovation and change: a collection of readings. Oxford University Press, New York (1997)
20. Van de Ven, A.H., Poole, M.S.: Methods for studying innovation processes. In: Van de Ven, A.H., Angle, H.L., Poole, M.S. (eds.) Research on the Management of Innovation: The Minnesota Studies. Harper & Row, New York (1989)
21. Vitharana, P., Dharwadkar, R.: Information systems outsourcing: linking transaction cost and institutional theories. Commun. Assoc. Inf. Syst. **20** (2007)
22. Walsham, G.: The emergence of interpretivism in information systems research. Inf. Syst. Res. **6**, 376–394 (1995)
23. Weerakkody, V., Dwivedi, Y. K., Irani, Z.: The diffusion and use of institutional theory: a cross-disciplinary longitudinal literature survey. J. Infor. Technol. **24**(4), 354–368 (2009)

Understanding the Contribution and Challenges of Using Soft Systems Methodology to Facilitate Cultural Change: A Case Study in the Public Sector

Sharon A. Cox and Sandi Kirkham

Abstract Collaboration between professional agencies in the public sector is essential to provide seamless, high quality services to citizens. Inter-agency working is often hindered by a prevalent silo culture, reinforced by resource-focused funding mechanisms. Checkland's Soft Systems Methodology (SSM) aims to facilitate organizational improvement or change through an organizational learning approach. In this study, SSM was used to help facilitate a move towards partnership working in the public sector. Interview data was collected from senior members of 16 professional agencies, four months after completing the SSM activity to reflect on the experience. The interviews were then repeated 12 months later in order to facilitate reflection on the use, role and impact of SSM beyond any immediate effect. From the interviews, we identified contributions of change that were attributed to the use of SSM and challenges of using SSM to facilitate cultural change. The challenges are explored in four themes: the process of stakeholder selection; the power of stakeholders; the ensuing power structure within the problem situation; the role of SSM and systemic change. These themes are discussed as contributing factors that practitioners of SSM need to be aware of to ensure the sanctity of SSM during periods of cultural change.

Keywords Soft systems methodology · Case study · Cultural change · Public sector

1 Introduction

The Soft Systems Methodology (SSM) is one of the most well-known of a group of alternative information system methodologies which have been designed to account

S. Kirkham (✉)
Staffordshire University, College Road, Stoke-on-Trent ST4 2DE, UK
e-mail: Sandi.kirkham@staffs.ac.uk

S. A. Cox
Birmingham City University, Curzon Street, Birmingham B4 7XG, UK
e-mail: Sharon.cox@bcu.ac.uk

© Springer International Publishing AG, part of Springer Nature 2019
F. Cabitza et al. (eds.), *Organizing for the Digital World*, Lecture Notes in Information Systems and Organisation 28, https://doi.org/10.1007/978-3-319-90503-7_17

215

for and integrate the human and social factors of organizations while information systems are being designed [3, 5, 36, 37]. The contribution of SSM to structural, process, or attitudinal change has been claimed by Checkland and Scholes [5] to be one of its most powerful characteristics. SSM offers a systemic framework which can be used to explore problem situations and result in some kind of change or improvement. Documented examples of the application of SSM exist (for example, [13, 14, 18, 31]) however there has been little attempt to evaluate the effectiveness of SSM in the process of change (for example, [6]). There is also a need for research focusing on the 'outcomes and successes of change in public organizations' [19].

The case study reported here is part of a wider research project that aims to examine the effectiveness of SSM to contribute to systemic change processes within public sector environments in the UK. SSM was applied in a local metropolitan borough council (MBC) to progress the design and implementation of an information management and technology (IM&T) strategy during a period of significant organizational change. Interviews with stakeholders were conducted four months after the SSM activity and repeated 12 months later. From these interviews we identified contributions of change attributed to the use of SSM and challenges of using SSM to facilitate cultural change. The challenges are categorized into contextual factors influencing the SSM activity and factors inhibiting organizational change. The challenges are further explored in four themes: the process of stakeholder selection; the power of stakeholders; the ensuing power structure within the problem situation; the role of SSM and systemic change. We discuss these themes and raise awareness of the contextual factors that practitioners of SSM need to be aware of when applying SSM in powerful organizational cultures.

The following section briefly explores previous literature on SSM and the role of partnership working in the public sector. The case study that provides the context for this research is then introduced and the research process is described. The findings from analysis of interview data are presented in Sects. 5 and 6, and discussed in Sect. 7. The paper concludes by discussing the relevance of the findings to SSM practitioners and reviews the limitations and future direction of the research.

2   Background

2.1   Soft Systems Methodology

SSM was initially developed to provide a structured methodology which could be used to carry out organizational analysis within what were seen as problematic environments. Two broad approaches to SSM have been developed. Checkland's interpretation advocates SSM as an organizational learning process with the aim of achieving organizational improvement or change. This approach accords considerable significance to the sociology, politics and culture of a situation during the process of organizational analysis as these factors are considered to play an important role in the process of change [5]. The second approach, associated with Wilson [36], is more specifically focused on the field of information systems development. Wilson's interpretation likewise places a strong emphasis on socio-cultural analysis, but the ultimate aim of using this approach is to produce information systems requirements sensitized to an organizational context. The systemic interpretation of social and cultural factors is deemed to be important in interpreting that context, but they are not accorded the strong causal status to be found in Checkland's work. The process of SSM involves the collection of each stakeholder's worldview, which is then used to create a systems model (a human activity system). Checkland's SSM comprises the following stages: (i) unstructured problem situation, (ii) problem situation expressed, (iii) root definitions of relevant systems, (iv) conceptual models, (v) comparison of conceptual models with expression of problem situation, (vi) identify feasible, desirable changes, (vii) action to improve problem situation. Although Checkland's approach is examined and utilized in what follows, consensus modelling from Wilson's approach has also been used to help move towards an agreed system of change.

2.2 Partnership in the Public Sector

The pressure for local authorities and health service environments to collaborate and join together in partnership was initially driven by funding arrangements. "Partnership is no longer simply an option; it is a requirement" [8]. There is however, no generally agreed definition of partnership; the term could apply to either the form or type of organization, or to a way of working. The ambiguity over structures versus process is compounded by confusion regarding the aims of partnerships. Knight and Harland [17] draw the distinction in problem focus between strategic issues and logistical or operational problems.

Open government requires transparency and participation within a culture of open communication and sharing of knowledge, which requires a fundamental cultural change [24]. The paradigm shift towards partnership working in the public sector is problematic. Partnership breaks down bureaucratic certainties and addresses realities which are complex and fragmented [33]. Integrated information systems are needed to facilitate collaborative working in the public sector [26] and support ambitions of open government. Lee and Kwak [20] outline five stages of open government maturity from the initial provision of a static public web page, through increased data transparency, open participation and open collaboration, to attain ubiquitous engagement demonstrated by seamless integration of public services accessible across mobile and computing platforms. A key challenge of moving from the initial conditions of stage one is the hierarchical culture of government and agency silos [20]. The "main barriers to data exchange are cultural rather than technical or legislative" [33]; trust is a prerequisite for both a successful partnership and an underpinning strategy of data and information exchange.

3   Case Study: The Unstructured Problem Situation

This case study is situated in a metropolitan borough council (MBC) in the UK with a population of approximately 316,720, comprising of a diverse ethnic mix. A Civic Partnership was formed made up of the major agencies of voluntary organizations, health, local authorities, police authorities, Chamber of Commerce, and local industries, in order to address the challenge of social deprivation in the area. The environment of the MBC was characterized by a myriad of different projects and initiatives as a consequence of separate and independent funding streams. The founding of the Partnership was influenced by the realization that larger projects could not be delivered solely by one agency. There was a desire to bring about change on a Borough-wide level and to underpin this change with joined-up services, creating new institutional forms based on inter-agency models of working.

A Partnership Information group was established, representing all the major service providers within the borough to define an Information Management and Technology (IM&T) strategy to support data exchange between professional agencies and to provide seamless delivery of services to citizens. The creation of an integrated information and communication strategy for the MBC was complicated by the idiosyncratic information requirements and data protocols of the various agencies and service providers. The NHS in the UK, for example, has been subject to significant change [15]. This presented a particular challenge to the creation of an integrated IM&T strategy because of incompatible legacy systems and issues of data protection relating to patient data and to the transference of information across agencies (between, for example, the health and police authorities). The motives for sharing data and information, and the use to which that information could be put, was not consistent across the Partnership.

The response to these issues was to attain agreement on a number of streams and principles for the strategy. An overall vision of what the IM&T strategy would mean to all the agencies and stakeholders was lacking and the formulation of the strategy stalled. This appeared to be because the agencies of the Partnership had become absorbed with their own localized information management issues and were not addressing how they could be resolved holistically, or at the level of the Partnership as a whole. A member of the Partnership was aware of SSM and believed it could be applied to this problem situation because it was an approach that enables problems to be explored at a systemic level.

4   Methodology

SSM is usually practised in either Mode One or Mode Two. In Mode One all the stages are generally followed sequentially [4]. In Mode Two users of the methodology tailor the use of the methodology to each situation, using the principles of the methodology as a sense-making device. In this case Mode Two was used to represent a practical

Table 1 Overview of research approach

SSM application	Phase 0: The unstructured problem situation (Checkland stage 1)	
	Phase 1: Expressing the problem situation (Checkland stages 2, 3 and 4): • Initial meeting to identify stakeholders • Individual meetings with 16 stakeholders to introduce SSM and derive worldviews • Formation of root definitions of relevant systems • Development of a conceptual model from each stakeholder interview	Phase 2: SSM modelling workshop (Checkland stages 4, 5 and 6; Wilson consensus modelling): • Group discussion of conceptual models • Development of consensus models • Agreement on action to be taken
Data collection and analysis	Phase 3: Post SSM application evaluation (4 months later): • Individual semi-structured interviews with stakeholders • Transcription and coding of interviews	Phase 4: Post SSM application evaluation (12 months later): • Individual semi-structured interviews with stakeholders • Transcription and coding of interviews
	Phase 5: Analysis of findings	

example of interpretive systems which can be applied to client-led design [28]. The problems are expressed through the model building, but the principles of systems thinking as supported by SSM are used to navigate a more flexible mode of enquiry. Table 1 presents an overview of the approach taken.

The application of SSM in the MBC (phases 1–2) was concentrated over two months due to institutional circumstances. A sense of urgency had arisen from previously unsuccessful attempts to move the IM&T strategy forward, resulting in a desire to focus the application into a contracted timescale, thus endowing it with tangible momentum.

Semi-structured assessment interviews were conducted to evaluate the impact of SSM in the change process, as perceived by the stakeholders within 4 months and then again 12 months following the commencement of the study. The longitudinal view was intended to facilitate an assessment of the impact of SSM beyond any immediate, tangible effect, in an attempt to surface deeper impacts, such as changes to organizational culture and modus operandi. Sixteen stakeholders took part in the SSM application and the first assessment interviews; as a result of changing roles and staff turnover, twelve stakeholders took part in the second set of assessment interviews. The impact of personnel turnover must be acknowledged during consideration of longitudinal data. Furthermore, any analysis of a longitudinal view of the impact of SSM must take into account the likely influence of other organizational events and changes in the problem situation (which may or may not have been prompted by SSM).

4.1   Participants' Engagement with SSM

The facilitator had been approached by a member of the Partnership who was familiar with SSM, and was invited to an initial meeting with senior members of the Partnership to discuss the approach and how it could be applied. Written materials explaining the approach were widely circulated, and time was allocated to explain the approach in more detail during one-to-one meetings with stakeholders, prior to the collection of worldviews. Following each worldview interview, a conceptual model was constructed and both facilitator and stakeholder worked through the model to ensure stakeholder ownership and deepen understanding. This process helped participants to understand the approach in more depth, particularly the systemic aspects of SSM, which enabled them to actively engage with the consensus workshops. Throughout the application, the facilitator collected observer's notes relating to both how the participants engaged with SSM and the degree to which the approach became embedded as a modus operandi for the organisation. These observations are briefly reported in the conclusion.

4.2   Phase 1: Expressing the Problem Situation

A number of initial visits were made to the MBC to discuss the application of SSM and to gather some information about the organization, the IM&T strategy work to date and the problem situation. The client organization required the modelling work to be completed within a 15 day period. This urgency was driven by the need to address a problem which had already been stagnating for some time. It also meant that assimilation of the methodology by the stakeholders and the preparation of the models had to be done in a very focussed and intense way.

The application of SSM to the problem situation began by identifying 16 stakeholders in the development of the IM&T strategy for the MBC, including senior representatives from the council, local health authority, education services, police and voluntary sectors. Initial meetings between the facilitator and each stakeholder were arranged. Written material about SSM was circulated to each stakeholder in advance of the meeting and discussed in detail during the initial meeting. The main purpose of the meeting was to gain the stakeholder's worldview and this was elicited through the question: What is your view of a borough-wide IM&T strategy?

Three themes emerged from these initial meetings, which provided preliminary insight into the reasons behind the deadlock on the IM&T strategy: the need for seamless joined up services; different views regarding the overarching Partnership strategy; and the relative importance of the technical agenda. Following each meeting, A CATWOE (customer/actor/transformation process/worldview/owner/environmental constraints) sequence and a conceptual model were drawn up for each of the stakeholders, based on their worldview.

4.3   Phase 2: Soft Systems Modelling

When the modelling of the worldviews had been completed, a workshop was held to debate the resulting models with stakeholders, facilitated by one of the authors. The aim of the workshop was to attempt to reach an accommodation of worldviews and construct one or more conceptual models which would help to drive the strategy forward. Two key themes emerged from the process of examining and debating the conceptual models:

- A need to reconcile a funding/budget driven culture within the Partnership with the need for a cohesive strategic agenda. This was identified as a Partnership issue.
- The requirement for a supporting infrastructure of information and knowledge management across the Partnership. This was identified as an information strategy issue.

In response to this, stakeholders initially agreed that a hierarchy of three systems needed to be considered: the need to create change within the Partnership; the adequacy of mechanisms for information management; and the technical infrastructure required to deliver any IM&T strategy. CATWOEs and conceptual models were developed, which were used to produce a business case for the appointment of a new post of Executive Director to lead the IM&T strategy. The stakeholders perceived this to be a considerable step forward and at this point, the SSM application process formally ended.

4.4   Data Collection and Analysis

Semi-structured interviews with stakeholders were held four months after the SSM workshop. The purpose of the interviews was to obtain each individual's view of the effectiveness of the application with regard to achieving an IM&T strategy for the Partnership and to reflect on the role of SSM in the change process. The interviews were repeated 12 months after the SSM application to obtain a longitudinal view of the effectiveness of the application and its role with regard to the achievement of an IM&T strategy. The interview data were analysed qualitatively using template analysis [7] and a basic form of grounded theory (open coding) [29]. King [16] positions this approach between content analysis [34], where codes are determined a priori and are statistically analysed, and the grounded theory approach of Glaser and Strauss [11] in which codes are not pre-determined. Template analysis therefore occupies a middle ground and enables researchers to adopt a flexible and less prescribed approach to analysis, reflecting the "differing philosophical orientations of researchers" [16]. It was recognized that this flexibility needed to accommodate the recognition of both

Table 2 Contributions and challenges of using SSM

Post SSM application evaluation (4 months)	Post SSM application evaluation (12 months)
Contribution of SSM activity to organizational change process: • Created organizational insight • Gave confidence to act • Empowered stakeholders • Created clarity and legitimacy • Defined agreed direction for action • Established a business case	Contribution of SSM activity to organizational change process: • Created organizational insight • Facilitated move towards partnership culture • Contribution of SSM difficult to quantify
Contextual factors inhibiting organizational change process: • Persistent silo culture • Espoused partnership culture • Tenacious political culture • Organizational history • Strategic events • Different priorities • Lack of momentum	Contextual factors inhibiting organizational change process: • Persistent silo culture • Espoused partnership culture • Tenacious political culture • Strategic events • Different priorities • Lack of momentum. o Lack of ownership o Lack of resources o Changes in personnel. o Lack of alignment of strategy and processes
Factors influencing participation in SSM activity: • Timing of SSM intervention • Lack of understanding of SSM • Potential intimidation • Unequal status and power • Hidden agenda • Facilitator intervention • Neutrality of facilitation	

a priori codes and codes which are not pre-determined; essentially this is a social constructionist view of analysis which was considered appropriate to an evaluation of SSM.

Themes yielded by the raw data of the interview transcripts were separated between those that were directly related to the application of SSM and those relating to the wider context in which the study took place. They are shown in Table 2 and discussed in the following sections. Factors influencing the SSM application were not discussed in the second interviews due to the time span since the workshop.

5   Phase 3: Post SSM Application Evaluation (4 Months)

5.1   Contributions of SSM Activity to Organizational Change Process

The interviews revealed that the use of SSM had led to tangible outcomes regarding organizational activity and appeared to have influenced to some degree the way that stakeholders thought and behaved. These areas are clearly interconnected (since, for example, a change of behaviour may lead to an organizational event taking place). It was also clear that the stakeholders could be divided into two groups:

(A)   those who were at the centre of and strategically connected to the Partnership, 'insiders' who perceived that the analysis had had some impact on the problem situation,

(B)   and 'outsiders' who were on the periphery of Partnership activity and who were largely of the opinion that no real change had occurred as a result of using SSM.

Analysis of the interview transcripts does not indicate that the application of SSM produced any substantial impact on this divide; indeed, it may even have exacerbated it. The following contributions of SSM emerged from the interview data.

Created Organizational Insight: The bureaucracy of the public sector had led to meetings where the *"agenda is fairly rigid"*. This has led to *"some very simplistic thinking"* about the Partnership. SSM provided a creative space to explore the *"quite major differences between partners"* and *"identify the complexity"* of the situation.

Gave Confidence to Act: In relation to the IM&T strategy, *"a piece of learning went on which... gave people confidence to shift from...thinking about solutions without ever doing anything about it to being willing to share those ideas...take risks...and then act on them* [the ideas]."

Empowered Stakeholders: Stakeholder 7 believed that the SSM application *"brought people together to get a view of where they were, of where they wanted to go."* This was reflected by Stakeholder 3, *"I've certainly seen a change...before, we were being very analytical and systematic and breaking it down and were actually going completely down the wrong path."*

Created Clarity and Legitimacy: SSM *"helped crystallize things at a critical moment."* The process provided *"an independent view...which underlined a particular perspective that in effect was there before the work was done which gave it legitimacy."*

Defined Agreed Direction for Action: Stakeholders suggested that SSM *"made us think and...we have taken a different approach...looking at what we've actually got in terms of the various initiatives...the common goal."* The common purpose of the Partnership was strengthened and the action needed to take the IM&T strategy forward was agreed.

Established a Business Case: As a direct result of SSM modelling work, the Partnership had a more robust profile, which added credibility to the IM&T strategy.

A business case was produced and used to justify an advertisement for an executive post to lead the IM&T strategy.

5.2 Contextual Factors Inhibiting Organizational Change Process

The interviews identified a number of factors which were not caused by or connected to SSM, but which were considered to be influential in some way in the process of change and in the context in which SSM was applied. There were seven sub-categories, all of which could be said to be directly connected to organizational factors which were beyond the control of the SSM analysis.

Persistent Silo Culture: Several stakeholders commented that "*some people are still in their silos*", however, Stakeholder 9 suggested that there has been recognition that "*We're all trying to reach something that's very similar...there's quite a lot of common ground.*" Yet, there was also a lack of communication and co-ordination as "*people beaver away not realising that down the corridors, somebody else is beavering away on something probably very, very similar.*"

Espoused Partnership Culture: The belief in a culture of Partnership was often declared by stakeholders but the competition for resources remained. Stakeholder 12 referred to the mistrustful ethos rooted in a resource-led culture where "*you don't want to tell people what you're actually planning or thinking in case they run off and get the money.*"

Tenacious Political Culture: One of the ways that political imperatives were manifested was in the reaction of some staff to the creation of the post of Executive Lead of the IM&T strategy. This role would carry status and power and there appeared to be some "*jockeying for position*" amongst staff who were interested in applying for it.

Organizational History: The MBC had a history of being unable to move forward and implement the strategies it had formulated. Stakeholder 12 gave an example of "*a strategy document that was produced five years ago*" of which "*not one of the actions had been implemented.*"

Strategic Events: There was substantial strategic change taking place across the MBC. For example, the introduction of Primary Care Trusts had been "*a terrific distraction*" for the Health Authority, constraining their participation in the SSM process. "*Some of these people may not have jobs, so they are retreating back a bit to protect what they can.*"

Different Priorities: Those who felt themselves to be on the periphery of the Partnership articulated a focus on the survival of their own organizations. For example, Stakeholder 3 indicated that local priorities were more compelling, in terms of commitment: "*can't give* (the IM&T strategy) *the time, because our organization has a separate agenda... the inter-collaboration things are not given the time to do it, nor do you get thanks for it.*"

Lack of Momentum: Once the SSM models had been produced and the facilitator had left the organization, the momentum for the IM&T strategy appeared to be lost. Stakeholder 15 explained, *"Whilst it was quite important on the day, people moved quite quickly away from it."* In contrast Stakeholder 12 believed that the SSM application had exerted a positive impact as *"the logjam that was there which prevented any real change and real things happening, seems to have been swept aside."*

5.3 Factors Influencing the SSM Application

The interviews also identified seven factors that appear to have inhibited open and candid participation in the SSM analysis, such as the presence of powerful managers and Chief Executives in the stakeholder group. The contribution of such senior personnel was, however, disputed; one stakeholder mentioned that the presence of such people gave the SSM work importance.

Timing of SSM Application: The SSM application occurred in parallel with wider discussion on how to move the stalled IM&T strategy forward and the SSM workshop may have served to *"unblock"* this situation. The precise timing of the SSM analysis emerged as being significant as there was *"a lot going on about shared services in* [the MBC]*"* forming *"a momentum of change."*

Understanding of SSM: Differences in the level of understanding of SSM were reported. Not all participants understood the holistic nature of the methodology, for example, regarding the language of SSM as *"inhibiting"* and that *"there wasn't enough common ground such that we all agreed... I'd much rather just go back down to the requirements sort of model"* (Stakeholder 1). Other stakeholders found the process a *"utilitarian way of working... that is very flexible"* (Stakeholder 6).

Potential Intimidation: No one claimed that they themselves were inhibited by the status of hierarchically powerful managers and their presence in the SSM process, but reference was made *"to the unequal power in the debate."* This was acknowledged by one of the Chief Executives as *"It's to do with how vocal people are...We're confident and it does make it difficult for other people to participate."*

Unequal Status and Power: The unequal influence of powerful agents in the process was underscored by references to the importance of status in the organization: *"Someone in this borough has got quite a high-paid job...and their job title altered recently, simply because their title... was perceived as low status."* However, Stakeholder 6 felt although they were *"probably the least senior person"* in the SSM workshop, they felt treated on their *"ideas, thoughts and abilities and not any perceived status."*

Hidden Agenda: References was made to senior staff being *"major distorters"*, for example, Stakeholder 15 thought that the political culture of *"jockeying"* to lead the IMT&T strategy had influenced the intervention of some stakeholders during the SSM analysis stage, *"some people have got their eyes on the job...and* (were) *also wanting to influence the person specification and the job description."*

Facilitator Intervention: Stakeholders regarded the facilitator and her interventions as fulfilling a number of roles: as *"expert on the methodology"*, guide in the application of the methodology; and help when *"we were getting a bit lost...and you* [the facilitator]*...kind-of kick started it again"* (Stakeholder 5). One stakeholder thought that the facilitator influenced the change process and that the facilitation process was *"very powerful."* The difficulty of a *"clear dividing, line between... process and content"* was also highlighted.

Neutrality of Facilitation: The neutrality of the facilitator was regarded as important by several stakeholders; *"Anybody who tried to do it...from within the organization has got baggage... external objective facilitation role tied up with the methodology was absolutely crucial"* (Stakeholder 16). However, Stakeholder 7 suggested that *"When* (colleague X) *came...it was quite clear that, you might well think that you see yourself as neutral but his interjection would question that."*

6   Phase 4: Post SSM Application Evaluation (12 Months)

The following categories emerged from the semi-structured interviews carried out 12 months after the SSM application was complete, shown in Table 2.

6.1   Contribution of SSM Activity to Organizational Change Process

It was evident during these interviews that there had been what could be described as an attitudinal shift within the problem environment towards a more tangible partnership ethos, though the degree of shift was perceived as small. The partnership still did not have an effective IM&T strategy and SSM had not, in the perception of many of the stakeholders, contributed significantly to any such shift. Comments regarding contribution of SSM focussed on three factors.

Created Organizational Insight: The SSM modelling work had shown that the strategic direction had to be resolved before the IM&T strategy itself could be developed. Yet, it appears that the group had reverted back to grappling with the technical problems once the SSM application had ended.

Facilitated Move Towards Partnership Culture: Most stakeholders felt that the MBC had perhaps moved closer to a genuine partnership culture, *"a culture where people are mindful that we are trying to work together...there is a consciousness that there's more to be gained by working together"* (Stakeholder 13).

Contribution of SSM Difficult to Quantify: Whilst acknowledging that SSM had contributed to a sense of change within the partnership, stakeholders found this contribution difficult to quantify. Stakeholder 12 explained *"I don't think it's possible to attribute it to one thing because life isn't like that"* however, *"up to that point* [the

SSM activity] *everybody was all over the place...Now, we're all marching behind the same things, so something has changed.*"

6.2   Contextual Factors Inhibiting Organizational Change

The initial interviews had raised factors that were not caused by or connected to SSM, but were considered to be influential to the process of change. In the second round of interviews they constituted a much larger part of the narrative of concerns articulated, suggesting potential reasons for the lack of momentum.

Persistent Silo Culture: SSM "*got people thinking differently*" and provided the opportunity "*to break out of the silos*" but there had been a return to silo working. Stakeholder 13 reported that "*we still have silos, and some of them are new silos, actually.*"

Espoused Partnership Culture: Although "*there's a lot of excellent lip service paid to it* [partnership working]" issues of "*resources*", "*budgets*" and different "*priorities*" remain. Stakeholder 15 explained that "*how we turn partnership into real operational outputs*" has not been addressed.

Tenacious Political Culture: The impact of the political culture on the ability of the Partnership to make any further progress towards an IM&T strategy was referred to, either directly or indirectly, by most of the stakeholders. The competitive and macho culture of the MBC, one of the consequences of which was a jockeying for the position to lead the IM&T strategy, referred to in the initial interviews, had halted the appointment process. It was suggested that "*people see opportunities in things, especially if they're part of developing them. They get attached and they can muddy the waters.*"

Strategic Events: Substantial changes concerning the Primary Care Trusts were still ongoing and there was a merger between three health services. Some stakeholders had visited a comparable situation in Scandinavia, earlier in the year. From this visit Stakeholder 14 concluded that there was a need to "*create a structure in which you have to hold the IM&T* [strategy]." This was also reached as an outcome of the SSM application, yet it was presented as a fresh insight from the Scandinavian experience. This "*helped us to see...not only what was necessary but how it could actually be done in practice and that's helped raise the awareness and the profile and the level of commitment.*"

Different Priorities: The Partnership struggled as "*Where people have got to make choices about putting time into partnership working or into delivering and managing their own internal organization's demands, nearly all of it's going to internal demands.*"

Lack of Momentum: Although "*everyone agrees that it* [the SSM activity] *was a very good approach*" the work begun during the application needed to be continued. Several stakeholders held the view that "*there has been nobody pulling people together to get together to actually use the methodology...it sowed a seed and that it needed some continuation and some nurturing.*" Stakeholder 10 suggested that

"...had we had the resolve and made the investment...it [SSM] *would have had a directly traceable impact. We just lost the plot."*

Lack of Ownership: Several stakeholders referred to a lack of *"a full-time resource to push this* [IM&T strategy] *forward."* There was no *"champion or... a designated lead officer whose job it is to lead that strategy."* Stakeholders made the point that *"all of us were busy"* and *"It's not our job"*.

Lack of Resources: Finance hindered the appointment of an executive to lead the IM&T strategy, *"The money we were prepared to pay wasn't going to get you a* (names colleague) *sort of person."*

Change of Personnel: Over the year there had been changes in personnel, which had then appeared to shift the structure of power at a senior level; *"the core group who met and...went through the SSM stuff really hadn't been able to influence direction with the* [new] *main players."*

Lack of Alignment of Strategy and Processes: Stakeholder 5 agreed *"there was a lot of coming together and mutual understanding"* but *"practically, on the ground not much has changed."* One stakeholder suggested there was a widespread belief that the IM&T strategy was not a priority and not sufficiently grounded in the reality of the everyday concerns of the MBC, for example: *"What's that* [IM&T strategy] *going to deliver to so and so who doesn't have a council house...who's struggling to feed her kids... there are tremendous benefits in progressing this information society agenda...but they're quite long-term and...the nature of politicians, they're always looking for quick wins."*

7 Discussion

Analysis of the interviews revealed a causal connection between the ultimate effectiveness of SSM and the tenacity of the existing politics and culture of the problem context. The SSM application was seen by stakeholders as episodic, and although it may have contributed to a small attitudinal shift towards partnership working, other organizational factors also contributed to this shift. The immediate outcomes of the application were promising, and if the post of Executive Lead to the IM&T strategy had been appointed it is likely that deep structure change could have been achieved which would have demonstrated a causal relationship to the SSM application. The failure of the appointment can be attributed, in large part, to organizational politics and the interplay of power and influence amongst stakeholders.

SSM gave stakeholders the creative space and confidence to share different views, a process of strengthening in the common purpose of the Partnership. This resonates with long-established theorizing on partnership working, which talks of a shift from organization to environment focus [21]. Additionally, some of the comments suggest that totally candid participation in SSM was not achieved and that there was, in fact, *"unequal power"* in the debate. In spite of the espoused willingness of stakeholders to engage in the non-hierarchical and egalitarian approach, it clearly carried less credibility as a strategy for real survival than the prevailing political culture. Further, the neutral role of the facilitator was also compromised by the prevailing political ethos. The SSM application, could not maintain political independence in the prevailing macho culture of the environment.

Power was manifest both within the SSM application process and in the wider structures that framed the case study context, where these preceded the application and shaped its implementation and subsequent fate. What is at issue here is the substantive capacity of SSM to address tenacious political cultures which appear to be inimical to the participative and non-hierarchical functioning of SSM. This is in spite of the will of many of the individuals in the problem situation to adopt such a participative approach, also manifest in their very selection of SSM as the approach of choice. The findings are discussed in four categories: the process of stakeholder selection; the structure of power underpinning the stakeholder analysis; the ensuing power structure within the problem situation; the role of SSM and systemic change.

7.1 Stakeholder Selection

Stakeholders are key in implementing change in public organizations [27]. SSM models do not prescribe when or how the process of stakeholder selection is done, or who does it. The implication is that the selection of stakeholders is a negotiated process regarding whom should take part between the facilitator and client. White [35] believes that the question of who is involved in problem structuring method applications and the reasons for this involvement are crucial. Shaw et al. [25] consider that the widest possible selection of stakeholders in problem structuring method interventions is important. These arguments suggest a high degree of ephemerality and partiality in stakeholder selection. Given that stakeholder selection needs to be done at the beginning of the application, there is a likelihood that the facilitator may not know enough about the organization and client views may predominate in that selection process. Political and cultural factors may militate against a truly representative or otherwise appropriate stakeholder group. Data analysis from this study suggests that stakeholders can be problematic and be greatly influenced by cultural and political factors in the problem situation.

There is no formalized process for assembling or inserting the political and cultural knowledge of context within SSM's structures of problem-solving. Torlak and Müceldili [31] suggest that a preliminary diagnosis is made at the start of the SSM application; this approach was adopted in phase 1; however, unless the facilitator is extremely politically astute, it seems inevitable that knowledge about cultural and political issues within the problem situation may to some degree be incomplete. In any case, making this knowledge overt or explicit may undermine the facilitator's role as a culturally independent agent and unleash potentially disruptive cognitions within the problem situation. The findings of this research indicate that the process of stakeholder or stakeholder selection in SSM must be informed fully by these issues in an attempt to mitigate the negative influences of organizational power in the ensuing analysis. In highly politicized environments, however, this may not actually be possible.

7.2 Power Structure of the Stakeholder Group

The Partnership as an organizational entity carried political weight and it became clear that some stakeholders attempted to use the SSM application to consolidate or achieve personal power and influence.

For example, during the application process, a number of stakeholders referred to a "*jockeying for position*". The political dominance of the "*quick win*" culture was such that it substantially countered the long term achievement of an information strategy, the SSM application appeared to have made very little impact on the existing power structure.

Flood and Jackson [10] have contended that SSM is in practice managerialist, serves dominant (manager) groups, while worldviews reflect existing social inequalities. The case has demonstrated that Jackson's [12] 'framework of domination', whereby powerful stakeholders are seen to drive the process, is an observable phenomenon in highly politicized situations. SSM was not transferred as a methodology and the single application was not sufficient to change organizational culture and politics. The SSM application appears to have become an instrument of political power in itself; it was captured by a dominant coalition of agents. This only served to distort its impact on the change process. It could be concluded that the egalitarian, participative and non-partisan requirements of SSM posed a challenge or threat to the environment. Given the evidence, it is equally possible that it may have been too weak to affect the tenacious political culture. These findings confirm Callo and Packham's [2] observation to the effect that genuine debate is difficult to achieve in corporations with strong hierarchies of power.

7.3 Power Structure of Problem Domain

The problem situation implied potential outcomes that were equally concerned with process and attitudinal change. The prevailing organizational culture was tenacious; this tenacity affected a host of process outcomes and also appeared to impede progress towards breaking down the traditional silos that blocked integrated working approaches. Silos form from different tribes of government workers in specialized functions, which should not be eliminated as the distinct culture, language and processes within a silo are needed by the specialism [30]. However, silos can become entrenched when competing for resources [30]. Ruijer and Huff [24] propose a networks strategy to overcome the boundaries in bureaucratic organizations by overlaying horizontal openness across functional boundaries, to share information and facilitate collaboration. Creating cultural change requires new shared systems of meaning to be formed, accepted and internalized [23]. The formation of the Civic Partnership established a network to facilitate openness at a strategic level, however, there was a lack of shared meaning in the system of the partnership. Flood [9] suggests that Checkland's SSM seeks to reach an accommodation of views, however, individual needs can re-emerge [27].

Tuan and Shaw [32] suggest that participation in "systemic thinking promotes toleration". At the start of the case study the different stakeholders represented different partner organizations with disparate, polarized and fragmented viewpoints. Through the SSM workshop a way forward was agreed through an accommodation of the different views. When the stakeholders returned to their individual organizations the accommodation of viewpoints started to fragment within the tenacity of the silo culture, the pressures upon individual stakeholders and procedural uncertainty. Steane et al. [27] suggest that stakeholders may come to a temporary agreement, perhaps out of political necessity but there can be lack of substantive agreement; it is a "momentary convergence with provisional closure". Although there was some movement towards partnership working, the silo culture prevailed; there was a failure to "institutionalise a culture of openness" [24].

7.4 SSM and Systemic Change

The aim of this research has been to examine the effectiveness of SSM in the process of organizational change. This section examines the problems associated with establishing causal links between the SSM application and the organizational events taking place during, or subsequent to the analysis. Malinova et al. [22] describe organizational change as emerging from organizational learning processes. In this case, there was a modest change in the organizational culture which may partly be attributed to the learning processes offered within SSM. Several stakeholders referred to the difficulty of attributing, a marginal movement towards a greater partnership culture to the use of SSM. This was because other events were also happening at the same time, which could have contributed to this cultural shift. There were also some stakeholders that did not perceive that any change had taken place.

Checkland refers to the flux and transformation of organizational life. Situations are continually changing and the behaviour of people within those situations undoubtedly contributes to this fluidity. SSM applications are capable of changing or transforming the belief systems of stakeholders, through the creation of insight, clarity and exposure to the logically expressed and interpretable worldviews of others. The results of the evaluation interviews demonstrate that use of the methodology had created insight and had enabled the problem situation to be perceived more clearly. It is possible that the organizational behaviour of some stakeholders changed as a consequence of this, although this change may not have been a radical one. It may have manifested itself only in a psychological or attitudinal change, which was not immediately obvious within the everyday working life of the organization.

These observations confirm Beeson and Davis [1] central emphasis on the human element in their reading of soft approaches to systems analysis. Though change is constitutive of organizational life, its direction and terminus is not pre-figured, automatic or teleological. Instead, it involves processes of negotiation, invention, perception and participation. Similarly, the lack of tangible process outcomes may confirm Flood and Jackson's [10] contention that the cultural feasibility of change is in fact bounded by conformance to the dominant culture and the dominant coalition (of power). Jackson [12] also alludes to this in his claim that facilitators may be forced to abandon radical systems which do not reflect the social and cultural realities of the situation. Radical change could not be said to have been achieved. The express wish to move towards seamless, integrated working could be interpreted as a radical departure from the MBC's silo culture.

8 Conclusion

This case study has demonstrated that two fundamental, underlying principles of SSM cannot be assured. These are:

- That the open and candid participation of stakeholders cannot be assumed, nor evaluated, and
- The absolute neutrality of the facilitator is compromised by the methodology itself, which requires active facilitator involvement and cultural and political knowledge.

Section 5.3 refers to some of the factors affecting stakeholder engagement. Additionally, the facilitator observed the dynamic between herself and participants throughout the application. It is perhaps not surprising that it was observed that the physical presence of the facilitator helps to mitigate the consequences of inconsistent levels of understanding and participation noted above, and that this influence was lost somewhat when the facilitator left the organisation. Most importantly, participants' perceived SSM as a 'means to an end' (i.e. an approach which could help them to resolve the IM&T issue), rather than an organisational modus operandi. In this sense, participants clearly did not regard SSM as a permanent feature in their organisational world.

The study has contributed to the wider understanding of the specific contributions of SSM to facilitate organizational change and highlighted contextual factors that can impede both participation in SSM activity and cultural change. Specifically, these factors may limit the capacity of SSM to address powerful political cultures, particularly where SSM is episodic. The principles of cultural change need to become institutionalized to drive organizational change reflected in an alignment between strategy and supporting processes.

A limitation of the study is that it is reliant on a single case in one country. The 16 stakeholders were at senior levels of their organizations, each representing an individual agency within the MBC; their views may not have been shared by others in their organizations. Further studies are needed to determine the extent to which the factors influencing and inhibiting the role of SSM in organizational change are exhibited in other organizations, and to seek ways to strengthen the capability of SSM to affect change in dominant organizational cultures. Yet, the overarching contentions remain: that SSM is an attractive method for addressing inchoate problems. Its functioning in practice needs to be strengthened by greater understanding of the strength of the political organizational context and an awareness of its influence on the sanctity of the SSM activity.

References

1. Beeson, I.A., Davis, C.: Emergence and accomplishment in organisational change. J. Organ. Change 13(2), 178–189 (2000)
2. Callo, V.N., Packham, R.G.: The use of soft systems methodology in emancipatory development. Syst. Res. Behav. Sci. 16(4), 311–319 (1999)
3. Checkland, P.: Soft Systems. Methodology in Action. Wiley, Chichester (1981)
4. Checkland, P., Holwell, S.: Information, Systems, and Information Systems. Wiley, Chichester (1998)
5. Checkland, P., Scholes, J.: Soft Systems Methodology in Action. Wiley, Chichester (1999)
6. Connell, N.A.: Evaluating Soft OR; some reflections on an apparently 'unsuccessful' implementation using a soft systems methodology (SSM) based approach. J. Oper. Res. Soc. 52(2), 150–160 (2001)
7. Crabtree, F, Miller, W.L.: Doing Qualitative Research, 2nd edn. Sage Publications, London (1999)
8. Dowling, B., Powell, M., Glendinning, C.: Conceptualising successful partnerships. Health Soc. Care Community 12(4), 309–317 (2004)
9. Flood, R.L.: Rethinking the fifth discipline: Learning within the unknowable. Routledge, London (1999)
10. Flood, R.L., Jackson, M.C.: Creative Problem Solving: Total Systems Intervention. Wiley, Chichester (1991)
11. Glaser, B., Strauss, A.L.: The Discovery of Grounded Theory. Aldine, New York (1967)
12. Jackson, M.: The nature of soft systems thinking: the work of Churchman, Ackoff, and Checkland. J. Appl. Syst. Anal. 9, 17–27 (1982)
13. Jacobs, B.: Using soft systems methodology for performance improvement and organisational change in the English National Health Service. J. Conting. Crisis Manag. 12(4), 138–149 (2004)
14. Kalim, K., Carson, E., Cramp, D.: The role of soft systems methodology in healthcare policy provision and decision support. Proc. IEEE Int. Conf. Syst. Manag. Cybern. 6, 5025–5030 (2004)
15. Kelliher, C., Parry, E.: Change in healthcare: the impact on NHS managers. J. Organ. Change Manag. 28(4), 591–602 (2015)
16. King, N.: Template analysis. In: Symon, G., Cassell, C. (eds.) Qualitative Methods and Analysis in Organisational Research: A Practical Guide, pp. 118–134. Sage Publications, London (1998)
17. Knight, L., Harland, C.: Managing supply networks: organisational roles in network management. Eur. Manag. J. 23(3), 281–292 (2005)
18. Kotiadis, K.: Using soft systems methodology to determine the simulation study objectives. J. Simul. 1(3), 215–222 (2007)
19. Kuipers, B.S., Higgs, M., Kickert, W., Tummers, L., Grandia, J., Van der Voet, J.: The management of change in public organizations: a literature review. Public Adm. 92(1), 1–20 (2014)

20. Lee, G., Kwak, Y.H.: An open government maturity model for social media-based public engagement. Gov. Inf. Q. **29**(4), 492–503 (2012)
21. Mackintosh, M.: Partnership: issues of policy and negotiation. Local Econ. **7**(3), 210224 (1992)
22. Malinova, L., Bednar, P.M., Welch, C.: Facilitating organizational change: a collaborative, open systems perspective. In: Benson, V., Filippaios, F. (eds.) Proceedings of the 15th European Conference on Research Methodology for Business and Management Studies, 9–10 June 2016, London, UK, pp. 159–166 (2016)
23. Morgan, G.M.: Images of Organizations. Sage Publications, London (2006)
24. Ruijer, E.H.J.M., Huff, R.F.: Breaking through barriers: the impact of organizational culture on open government reform. Transform. Gov. People Process Policy **10**(2), 335–350 (2016)
25. Shaw, D., Edwards, J.S., Collier, P.M.: Quid Pro Quo: reflections on the value of problem structuring group workshops. J. Oper. Res. Soc. **57**, 939–949 (2006)
26. Signoretta, P., Craglia, M.: Joined-up government in practice: a case study of children's needs in Sheffield. Local Gov. Stud. **28**(1), 59–76 (2002)
27. Steane, P., Dufour, Y., Gates, D.: Assessing impediments to NPM change. J. Organ. Change Manag. **28**(2), 263–270 (2015)
28. Stowell, F. (ed.): Information Systems Provision: The Contribution of Soft Systems Methodology. McGraw-Hill, London (1995)
29. Strauss, A., Corbin, J.: Basics of Qualitative Research: Techniques and Procedures for Developing Grounded Theory. Sage Publications, London (1998)
30. Tett, G.: The Silo Effect: The Peril of Expertise and the Promise of Breaking Down Barriers. Simon and Schuster, London (2015)
31. Torlak, N.G., Müceldili, B.: Soft systems methodology in action: the example of a private hospital. Syst. Pract. Action Res **27**(4), 325–361 (2014)
32. Tuan, N.-T., Shaw, C.: Consideration of ethics in systemic thinking. Syst. Pract. Action Res. **29**(1), 51–60 (2016)
33. Wastell, D., Kawalek, P., Longmead-Jones, P., Ormerod, R.: Information systems and partnership in multi-agency networks: an action research project in crime reduction. Inf. Organ. **14**(3), 189–210 (2004)
34. Weber, R.P.: Basic Content Analysis. Sage Publications, London (1985)
35. White, L.: Evaluating problem structuring methods: developing an approach to show the value and effectiveness of PSMs. J. Oper. Res. Soc. **57**, 842–855 (2006)
36. Wilson, B.: Systems Concepts, Methodologies and Applications. Wiley, Chichester (1990)
37. Wilson, B.: Soft Systems Methodology: Conceptual Model Building and Its Contribution. Wiley, Chichester (2001)

The CIO and CDO Socio-technical Roles in the Age of Digital Business Transformation: An Interpretive Study

Angela Locoro and Aurelio Ravarini

Abstract In this paper, a socio-technical perspective on the roles of Chief Information Officer (CIO) and Chief Digital Officer (CDO) is introduced, and a model of interpretation of their respective roles, their potential interplay and idiosyncrasies is presented and discussed. We start our analysis by proposing a socio-technical model based on typologies of CIOs and IT roles, as well as CIOs and Business Visions, and CIOs and Interpersonal roles taken from the literature, and used as a lens for viewing whether and how CDOs may fit into this model, collaborate with CIOs in pursuing the IT-business alignment vision, or should necessarily clash on the same territory. This model is then used to interpret the results of two empirical analysis about the evolution of CIOs and CDOs roles in Digital Business Transformation scenarios. We carried out interviews directly to CIOs of Italian companies, and use transcripts of online interviews to CDOs of American companies. Both materials deal with the themes of Digital Business Transformation and Strategy, of CIO/CDO's profiles, and of attitudes toward tech trends such as Big Data, Internet of Things and 3D Printing. Notwithstanding their differences, these voices helped us understand what are the possible futures and configurations of CIO and CDO roles in organizations, in a fast changing innovation scenario like the one emerging from our analysis.

Keywords Digital business transformation · CIO role · CDO role · Business strategy · Interpretive study

A. Locoro (✉)
Università degli Studi di Milano-Bicocca, Milan, Italy
e-mail: angela.locoro@disco.unimib.it; angela.locoro@unimib.it

A. Ravarini
Università Carlo Cattaneo - LIUC, Castellanza, VA, Italy
e-mail: aravarini@liuc.it

© Springer International Publishing AG, part of Springer Nature 2019
F. Cabitza et al. (eds.), *Organizing for the Digital World*, Lecture Notes in Information Systems and Organisation 28, https://doi.org/10.1007/978-3-319-90503-7_18

1   Introduction

After a couple of decades since what was coined as "the age of the smart machine" [1], digitization is still pervading the main discourses about organizational strategy. In this paper, the words "digital" and "discourse" are not introduced randomly or left separate. *Digital* roots into the word *digit*, meaning both a "number" and an "electronic signal" that represents meaning through *digits* (i.e., interpreted as 0 and 1 numeric signals). In organizations, technology and digitization are associated with a "textualization process" [ibidem.], i.e. the transcription of quite all kind of information in electronic (text) format. Even "informal discourse is absorbed by the textualization process", and many aspects of communication are internalized by people through a process *mediated by "textual interfaces"*.

In this scenario, every activity in organizations, from conceptualization to organization, from process to command and control, from solving problems to define strategies, is done via the (preliminary) mediation of *digital(-izable) discourses*. In the coming age of "Digital Business Transformation" there is no exception. Digital Business Transformation has been defined[1] as "the profound and accelerating transformation of business activities, processes, competencies and models to fully leverage the changes and opportunities of digital technologies and their impact across society in a strategic and prioritized way, with present and future shifts in mind." This (new) concept seems even more pervading than digitization alone, as it encompasses not only internal organizational aspects, but also external customers, seen as individuals and social groups empowered with and deeply influenced by (digital) technology-induced behavioural changes, in each sphere pertaining their life, e.g., from information to consumerism, from free time to decision making activities, and so on. This definition also implies the concept of *shift*, a fast and accelerating change, which involves both an internal movement (a profound organizational transformation) and an external one (a societal push), capable of quaking and even turning around the very foundation of traditional management, strategies, IS, and business-alignment methodologies.

In order to understand how Chief Information Officer (CIO) evolution and Chief Digital Officer (CDO) emerging role are impacted by this transformation, we may borrow the analogy of the Sloan and Durant's leaderships recalled to us by [2]. In the same vein, we may borrow her analogy of water for describing how business and IT are currently intertwined in a movement where "as liquid water builds up to a boil or builds down to freezing [...] organizational change [undergoes] the following phases: unfreezing, transition, freezing. [The (business-IT) alignment] is caught in a phase change. Things are unfreezing and heading into transition". Exploring whether and how things are "unfreezing and heading into transition" is the goal of our research, which we observe from within the midst of this organizational innovation change movements, with the aim to explore and qualitatively interpret the phenomenon of digital business transformation through the lens of a socio-technical approach. This

---

[1]The definition is available at https://www.i-scoop.eu/digital-transformation/, last accessed 24th March 2017.

approach takes into account the social aspects of this phenomenon, e.g., the emerging role of CIO and CDO as leaders of this innovation inside the enterprise, as well as the its technical aspect, e.g., tech trends such as Big Data, Internet of Things—IoT— and 3D Printing, as technologies capable of exerting a pressure on the innovation discourse and influencing the leadership choices in the strategy of enterprises. In so doing, we examined the existing literature on CIO/CDO role theories, and carried out a bottom-up qualitative analysis of interviews partly administered directly to CIOs, partly taken online as a secondary source of knowledge. These different methods helped us frame and explore the complex phenomenon of digital business transformation driven by tech trends in relation to the creation, transformation or deletion of managerial roles such as those of CIO and CDO.

To be best of our knowledge, theories and models for the study of CDO are a few and do not reach the level of maturity of studies about the CIO role (see for example [3, 4], though they do not deal with tech trends). We try to fill a gap in this direction, although a preliminary one. Our research questions are the following:

- What are the differences between CIOs and CDOs in (perceiving) digital business transformation?
- Whether and how tech trends such as big data, IoT and 3D printing influence CIO/CDO roles in digital business transformation and strategy?
- How do CIOs and CDOs coexist and cooperate? Are their roles complementary, overlapping or redundant?

The paper is structured as follows: Sect. 2 is an overview of CIO existing theories and models, and an account of our reconfiguration of them under a socio-technical perspective. Our interpretive method of interviews analysis is also reported, in Sect. 3 we report our findings of the analysis of CIO and CDO interviews related to our research questions and to our socio-technical model; Sect. 4 concludes.

2 Background and Method

2.1 Definitions of CIO and CDO

In our research, we intend as Chief Information Officer a C-level responsible of IS in organizations. The Chief Digital Officer is a newly born and emerging role charged by a municipality, a government or an enterprise to transform analog business into digital business, by exploiting the ultimate technologies (e.g., what we have called tech trends). The latter role is more innate and intertwined with the business strategy and the marketing functions of an organization, whereas the CIO role had an evolution toward the business vision also depending on the organizational structure of the enterprise (from the silo structure to flatter and more flexible business units). According to [5] the CDO is a role responsible for:

- defining a digital strategy shared by the whole organization;
- coordinating the digital harmonization of activities;
- exploiting the opportunities of digital business offered by markets;
- driving an organization through the digital transformation of its business.

Given the broad-minded scope of the above activities, and the heterogeneity of contexts and enterprise models to which the CDO role may apply, the exact positioning of CDOs in the organizational structure is still controversial: MIT experts identify the CDO as the outbound counterpart of the CIO. According to their opinion, the CDO should be responsible of those outbound activities currently carried out by CIOs, who should then totally focus on inbound activities; McKinsey experts[2] identify as the primary responsibility of CDOs to mediate between CIOs and Chief Marketing Officers (CMOs), and to possess the capabilities and skills of both. A recent report from Deloitte[3] foresees three types of CDO: *ex-agency*, i.e., a marketing leader oriented to digital technology; *digital transformation strategist*, i.e., a technology leader driving enterprises toward innovation, especially in the business areas of media and entertainment; *technologist*, i.e., an inbound role, usually subordinate to the CIO.

2.2 Theoretical Models

In this section, we propose an overview of four typologies and models for CIOs Managerial, Interpersonal, IT and Strategy oriented roles. In this way, we introduce the personal characteristics, the skills and the main functions traditionally or currently expected for IS C-levels in organizations.

The first model [6] describes the three Managerial roles of IT (Informational, Decisional, Interpersonal) through six main activities (two for each role). These activities are clearly polarized according to the dyads active/passive or visionary/conservative or proactive/reactive. They are: *spokesperson* and *monitor* for the informational role; *entrepreneur* and *resource allocator* for the decisional role; and *leader* and *liaison* for the interpersonal role. This model was adapted from Mintzberg's conceptualization of managerial roles [7], and was adopted in the above study in order to qualitatively assessing which of these CIO roles was more related with the business technology strategist one. What emerged from the study was that the informational role is the one that best designates and supports business technology strategy in most cases.

The second model [8] deals with Personality Factors, and grounds upon the psychological five factors model of Digman in [9]. In particular, the personal characteristics studied by Li and Tan and designated as the most effective to describe CIOs' strategic behaviour in organizations are: *openness*, i.e., a "broad-minded, fast-adapting and flexible" attitude toward changes, which characterizes a "sensitivity

---

[2]http://www.mckinsey.com/business-functions/digital-mckinsey/our-insights/getting-the-cmo-and-cio-to-work-as-partners.

[3]Available at http://www.deloittedigital.ca/chief-digital-officer.

toward innovation"; *extraversion*, i.e., a proactive tendency for "complex and highly cognitive" challenges, together with the capability of persuading people toward innovation achievements; and *conscientiousness*, i.e., the readiness and strong disposition to pursue innovation goals with a "systematic and committed" determination.

The third model is based on IT Ideal types of Technical Profiles [10], designed according to the typology theory of Doty and Glick [11]. In this model, the five ideal profiles of IT management in organizations are: *partner*, i.e., a role actively involved in digital business transformation; *systems provider*, i.e., an application oriented technical role; *architecture builder*, i.e., a designer role of business integrated and more flexible and agile infrastructures; *technological leader*, i.e., a role strategically oriented to experiment new technology-based business opportunities; and *project coordinator*, i.e., a role aiming at creating business with valuable IT projects. These ideal profiles are described through the following four dimensions: IT activities, relationships, skills and knowledge, and governance.

The fourth and last model is related to how organizations strategically envision IT and CIOs, as this foresight may influence the structural and innovation power of IT and digital technologies toward digital business transformation [12]. There are four main business IT visions in the model: *automate*, i.e., improving cost savings and efficiency; *informate up*, i.e., empowering management; *informate down*, i.e., empowering employees; *transform*, i.e., achieving business transformation.

Although a landscape of the evolutionary roles of CIO in those few decades was already depicted in other frameworks (see for example [13]), our perspective is slightly different. First, our analysis is not historical, rather it is "possibilistic"; second, none of the researches and models reported above do have a special focus on the socio-technical perspective, as our study tries to have instead; as a third factor, none of the models examined so far takes into consideration other roles than the CIO one.

2.3 A Socio-technical Model

Figure 1 collects the four models presented in Sect. 2.2 and places them along an ideal socio-technical plane, where they are assigned one of the dimensions (either social or technical) to which they belong, according to the features (either social or technical) that they express. For example, Managerial roles model as well as Personal characteristics model are put along the social axes. The IT roles model and the IT visions model are put along the technical axes. A Socio-technical perspective aims to investigate and let emerge the relations and dependences between specific social characteristics of an organization and specific technical choices. In this way, while keeping the two aspects separated and their details differentiated, their interactions and reciprocal influences, as well as their past, present and future configurations may result more evident. In our model, both CIO ad CDO roles are represented by circular, partially overlapping areas, characterized and influenced by the four underlying models and by the interplay of social and technical aspects inside them. For example, while managerial properties and personal characteristics are important for both CIO and CDO roles, personal characteristics such as openness and extraversion may influence the success of digital business transformation. For this reason, they are more mappable to CDO characteristics. On the contrary, decisional and informational roles belong to CIOs managerial peculiarities, while interpersonal roles are more often associated with CDO personal skills, in the light of the *mediating* role (between business and IT) that CDO are supposed to play in organizations. In regard to the technical side of the model, IT visions represent broader and more generic orientations than IT roles. IT roles define the present strategy inside organizations; IT visions may describe the more magmatic movements toward the definition of a strategy, well before a crystallized direction could be taken. Furthermore, IT visions are more oriented to interpersonal and transformational strategies (informate, transform), which are supposed to be more related to CDO roles. IT roles may define clear socio-technical configurations of IT functions, relationships and competences, some of which are totally corresponding to CIO functional roles, with the exception of partner role and technological leader, which may resemble more CDO functional characteristics than CIOs' ones. For these reasons, in our model CDOs are mostly mapped to IT visions, so as to highlight the transformative and even *transitional* characteristics of the role (also proved by the above controversial statements about where CDO should place in an organizational chart), while IT roles are mostly mapped to CIOs functional roles. Both CIO and CDO participate in different proportions to all of the four elements depicted in the plane, as motivated above and depicted in Fig. 1.

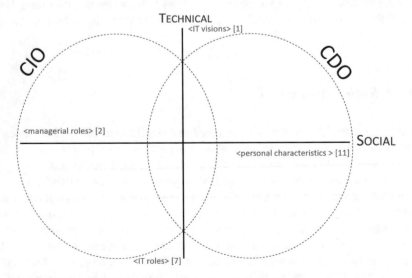

Fig. 1 CIO and CDO models seen from a socio-technical perspective

2.4   Qualitative Analysis

In our study, we analyze interviews we made directly to CIOs of Italian companies in 2016, and interview transcripts that we retrieved from online interviews made to CDOs of American companies,[4] in 2016. Table 1 report the business area, the business size, the role involved in the interviews, and the country where the interviews were made.

We analyzed the interviews transcripts by applying techniques of content analysis [14]. We focus on interviews content where both CIOs and CDOs report about digital business transformation in their enterprise, their opinion on tech trends and whether tech trends influence their activity and the company strategy. To this aim, we adopted a hybrid approach, combining inductive analysis, in order to extract the main, high-level themes, and deductive thematic analysis to reflect on the above themes with respect to our socio-technical model. All of the coding tasks were performed by the present authors iteratively, until a sufficient inter-rater agreement was achieved, and no new piece of interview could be assigned from the available data to the chosen theme and up to aspects of the model. We carried out the content analysis and the coding activity by using NVivo 11 Pro software for Windows.[5]

In the next section, we report and discuss the results of our analysis of the interviews, according to the above themes.

3   Results and Discussion

3.1   Digital Business Strategy and Digital Business Transformation

One of the main differences emerged between CIOs and CDOs is the vision of Digital Business Strategy. For the former, this strategy is oriented to scouting digital business ideas and transform them into solid and valuable products:

> Digital business strategy is not a separate artifact it is a part of top level business strategy, and answers the question – How can our business survive and thrive in an increasingly digital world? – IT strategy is a business question with a technical answer. Digital business strategy is a digital question, with a business answer, which may include non-digital solutions, such as getting into different businesses, or changing strategic posture. A classic example is logistics companies such DHL, UPS, FedEx getting into financial services for their clients, based on digital (informational) capabilities.

For the latter, the continuous transformation process *is* the strategy. In the words of the CDO of "General Electric Power":

---

[4]The online interviews are available at https://www.cxotalk.com/.

[5]http://www.qsrinternational.com/nvivo-product/nvivo11-for-windows.

Table 1 Summary of business sectors, roles, and countries of the interviews

Business sector	# Interviews	Role	Country
Healthcare	2	CIO	Italy
Chemical	2	CIO	Italy
Building	1	CIO	Italy
R&D	1	HR manager	Italy
Optical	1	CIO	Italy
Exhibitions	1	CIO	Italy
Lightning	1	CIO	Italy
Heating	1	CIO	Italy
Software	5	CDO	USA
Food and beverages	2	CDO	USA/Worldwide
Electricity	1	CDO	USA/Worldwide
R&D	2	CEO/Researcher	USA
Consultancy	1	Digital analyst	USA/Worldwide

> That's the right way to say it. Because our customers are facing the same thing, and if you take our customers across all the industries, they are becoming a digital business themselves. And when they become a digital business, that means they have to digitize everything from how they work, […] but how their products, services, and core operations will work is something only a digital industrial company can help them with. And so we want to be customer strategic partner in their own digital transformation and creating new business models for themselves.

The transformation from a technical viewpoint needs a social transformation counterpart, the one related to the CIO and CDO profiles and to a vision that needs to be shared from above. As argued by Gartner digital analysts (italics is our):

> […] digital business model innovation demands specific leadership. Some businesses are treating each opportunity separately, some are asking the CIO to play an extended role, and some are appointing a separate chief digital officer (CDO). In any event, the CIO must actively choose the *ideal leadership position* and then work to influence senior executives and the board to turn that into a reality. A CIO who decides to absorb the digital innovation role - in effect becoming the chief digital officer - must take time to build the necessary capabilities and relationships. This entails introducing the *language of business model innovation to the enterprise dialogue*, investing in education and seeing that digital strategy is integral to business strategy creation, not downstream from it. Unleashing the full potential of digital value means going beyond the *automation* of internal processes to innovating all aspects of the business model.

In this light, our model touching social attitudes such as the interpersonal skills, the technology leadership and the overcoming of the automation tasks for the CDO characteristics, is in line with the view of experts in defining what characteristics the CIO should assume in order to align with the competences and skills required for a CDO. In the words of the CDO of General Electric Power, the CDO is the one thanks to whom the transformation strategy of the company is put in place at all levels:

So a lot of those things are in the environmental setting for the change. When it comes to specifics of how we drove this change, [the answer is] even establishing by bringing people like me. And for the last six quarters that I was in, we established what a digital business in GE is. Now we have Chief Digital Officers across all of the different industries that GE is in, because we ratified the model, and we've created this GE digital as a overall company who drive horizontal [...] if youre thinking about re-imagining and transforming your business, you need believership at the top, and I believe this is the CEO, and some companies would see CDO to become CEOs, just like Im the CEO of the digital business.

For companies which go digital (e.g., media and entertainment companies, as well as food and beverages companies) and were born digital (e.g., software companies, transportation companies such as Uber, and accomodation companies such as AirBnB) the CIO has changed its name and responsibilities, becoming a CDO. As witnessed by the CDO (ex CIO) of Pizza Hut:

The change in title from CIO to CDO represented a pretty substantial shift. As CIO, I had the traditional IT responsibilities for the organization, but with the move to Chief Digital Officer, I've assumed general management responsibilities for the overall digital business.

and by the CDO of SAP, highlighting the tensions and conflicts that a CDO should manage inside the organization:

The Chief Digital Officer role is relatively new and still evolving. Because digital business includes a broad scope with implications for business model, marketing, operations, supply chain, and other basic corporate functions, the CDO role itself has a broad mandate. A key part of the Chief Digital Officer role involves managing tensions because the need for organizational stability and predictability relative to the desire for disruption and change.

One face of the tensions and conflicts that has to be managed inside an organization is related to the radical change of the top-management power logics among peers and in many other directions:

one of the topics accompanying digital disruption is the management adequacy. The CIO role is going to change in this scenario, and what was a power device is going to become something else [...] I do not know whether the CIO generation is ready for this [...] I see many resistances for easier things [...] the impact will be strong enough to challenge the current power assets of many roles, and even the same concept of power.

3.2 The Tech Trends

In the same vein of the business strategy vision, also tech trends are seen differently by CIOs and CDOs. In the lightning sector, for example, the CIO we interviewed does not see the disruptive potential of some tech trends. They express the fact that:

[...] datawarehouse is seen as a prehistoric phenomenon with respect to big data, so that I think that, on one end, we talk of two different things. On the other hand, I realize that enterprises are dealing with advanced business intelligence by exploiting new technology, and in this vein, perhaps big data and BI are quite the same thing [...]

The positive and proactive attitude of CDOs for topics such as big data is well beyond complementarity of visions with respect to tech trends, in several business sectors that we examined (e.g., from food and beverages to software):

> [Big data] is really all about operation staff focusing much more and interpreting data, seeing new ideas as opposed to doing transactional tasks and that sort of thing. And they also need to have real-time applied analytics models, techniques, and insights from big data, and none of this is possible without true business transformation around digital [...]

> I'm a fundamental *believer* that the business world is becoming a big math problem. We have so much data at our fingertips, and how we can target people in a very unique way is becoming fascinating.

> We realized if we could build this big data platform on the data were collecting where we threw away nothing, and we could also go to a specific customer of a subset of customers and see exactly what they were doing [...] to answer business question [...] is powerful and unprecedented.

The perception of how the transformation of business may be profound has emerged when dealing with the theme of Internet of things (IoT). This is seen by some CDOs as a huge paradigm shift in the society and in the business as well:

> Things do need to change and we are moving into an always on environment where the customers are socially connected, their mobile [...] It is always with you, and it is always nearby and *its always on society*. But changing how organizations operate, they dont even know how to operate [...]

The IoT phenomenon is perceived in its turn as a socio-technical ensemble of infrastructural service providers, such as electricity, cars, fuel providers, suggesting how an infrastructure may become a network of networked people and artifacts:

> They can be a network company of things and become a platform company in the digital age controlling everything theyve ever made that everyone of us use. (15:08) *Its people and or things and technology together* [...] And *they need both*, they need the technology infrastructure to connect everyone and everything.

The transformation of business driven by digital tech trends such as IoT seems to most CDOs a fast and easy solution to create value for enterprises:

> [...] we spent the last five years making sure that all our physical products have sensors and are Internet enabled right, Wi-Fi enabled and collecting all this information. [...] I would say a lot of these companies right, they get the Internet of Things, its easy for them to design new products that have sensors that collect information and put it into a cloud-based service, and their first reaction is how do I monetize all these capabilities? But *the profound change that they go to is I can reinvent myself as a customer centric business*.

> This is the first time in human history that we have literally live contact with almost every person on the planet, in the developed world obviously and to everybody. And every resources with things like the Internet of Things, were going to be connected with all value right, directly connected so we can receive value from it, we can transmit value to it as a business, and that is something that is truly unique and has never happened before.

> But others as well, with the Internet of things, where all connected and so the leading digital businesses make the most of all those assets on a network, and channel them and orchestrate them and even control them to some extent to create very high scale business outcomes.

4   Conclusions

In this paper, we explored the phenomenon of Digital Business Transformation from the point of view of the inevitable transitions of visions, assets and mentalities that this brings with it. We focused on a socio-technical model where traditional and emerging roles, such as those of CIO and CDO are are put in relation with technology trends driving the process of business and power transformation. We analyzed interviews in order to understand how tech trends are impacting on digital business strategies and roles in enterprises, where business is going, and what are the challenges, the gaps, and the priorities that need to be discussed in future research.

Acknowledgements This article has been developed under the DiDIY project funded from the European Unions Horizon 2020 research and innovation programme under grant agreement No 644344.

References

1. Zuboff, S.: In the Age of the Smart Machine: The Future of Work and Power. Basic Books (1988)
2. King, J.L.: CIO: concept is over. J. Inf. Technol. **26**(2), 129–138 (2011)
3. Horlacher, A., Hess, T., et al.: What does a chief digital officer do? Managerial tasks and roles of a new C-level position in the context of digital transformation. In: 2016 49th Hawaii International Conference on System Sciences (HICSS), Los Alamitos, CA, USA, pp. 5126–5135. IEEE Computer Society (2016)
4. Horlacher, A,: Co-creating Value—The Dyadic CDO CIO Relationship During the Digital Transformation. Research-in-Progress Papers (June 2016)
5. Westerman, G., Bonnet, D., McAfee, A.: Leading Digital: Turning Technology into Business Transformation. Harvard Business Publishing. Harvard Business Review Press (2014)
6. Carter, M., Grover, V., Thatcher, J.B.: The emerging CIO role of business technology strategist. MIS Q. Exec. **10**(1) (2011)
7. Mintzberg, H.: Mintzberg on Management: Inside Our Strange World of Organizations. Free Press (1989)
8. Li, Y., Tan, C.H.: Matching business strategy and CIO characteristics: the impact on organizational performance. J. Bus. Res. **66**(2), 248–259 (2013)
9. Digman, J.M.: Personality structure: emergence of the five-factor model. Annu. Rev. Psychol. **41**(1), 417–440 (1990)
10. Guillemette, M.G., Paré, G.: Toward a new theory of the contribution of the it function in organizations. MIS Q. **36**(2), 529–551 (2012)
11. Doty, D.H., Glick, W.H.: Typologies as a unique form of theory building: toward improved understanding and modeling. Acad. Manag. Rev. **19**(2), 230–251 (1994)
12. Al-Taie, M.Z., Lane, M., Cater-Steel, A.: The relationship between organisational strategic it vision and CIO roles: one size does not fit all. Australas. J. Inf. Syst. **18**(2) (2014)
13. Chun, M., Mooney, J.: Cio roles and responsibilities: twenty-five years of evolution and change. Inf. Manag. **46**(6), 323–334 (2009)
14. Fereday, J., Muir-Cochrane, E.: Demonstrating rigor using thematic analysis: a hybrid approach of inductive and deductive coding and theme development. Int. J. Qual. Methods **5**(1), 80–92 (2006)

The Dynamics of Complex Sociomaterial Assemblages

The Case of Transcatheter Aortic Valve Implantation

Ole Hanseth, Jasmina Masovic and Bjørn Erik Mørk

Abstract This paper aims to contribute to our understanding of the sociomaterial complexities of information systems. By applying Gilles Deleuze's process ontology, called Assemblage Theory (AT), as interpreted and presented by Manuel DeLanda, we examine the case of a new high-tech medical procedure called transcatheter aortic valve implantation (TAVI). Complex innovations like TAVI evolve as sociomaterial assemblages whose dynamics are seen as driven by the interaction between various stabilizing and de-stabilizing processes. We argue that AT is a very powerful (process) ontology for researching and theorizing the dynamics of increasingly complex information systems.

Keywords Assemblage theory · Process ontology · Sociomateriality · Complexity

1 Introduction

The study of the relationship between the IT systems and their social and organizational context has always been at the center of IS research. Actor-Network Theory (ANT) has since the middle of the '90s been a popular approach while more recently Critical Realism and Agential Realism have received a lot of attention (e.g. [2, 15]). Yet we consider that these theoretical approaches leave the dynamics of socio-material assemblages underexplored. To fill this gap we will in this paper present and draw upon Gilles Deleuze's process ontology [7] labeled Assemblage

---

O. Hanseth (✉) · J. Masovic · B. E. Mørk
University of Oslo, P.O. Box 1072 Blindern, 0316 Oslo, Norway
e-mail: Ole.Hanseth@ifi.uio.no; oleha@ifi.uio.no

J. Masovic
e-mail: Jasminma@ifi.uio.no

B. E. Mørk
e-mail: bemork@ifi.uio.no

© Springer International Publishing AG, part of Springer Nature 2019
F. Cabitza et al. (eds.), *Organizing for the Digital World*, Lecture Notes in Information Systems and Organisation 28, https://doi.org/10.1007/978-3-319-90503-7_19

Theory[1] (AT), as interpreted and presented by DeLanda [3–6]. Our motivation in "for doing so?" is the desire to gain a better understanding of what we call the dynamics of sociomaterial complexities. We find this important because of the rapid growth of the complexity of ICT solutions such as the Internet; the emergence and evolution of platform-based ecologies like those related to iPhone/iOS and Android; and the growth in the number of information systems in organizations. In the latter case, several thousands of various information systems can be found in many large organizations, each integrated with a huge number of other systems across organizational and geographical borders. This makes the understanding of the dynamics of such complex sociomaterial arrangements an urgent issue. These dynamics have been researched under the labels digital and information infrastructures and platform ecosystems (see for instance [16, 17, 25]. This research has drawn extensively upon ANT, Complexity Theory, Reflexive Modernization [11] and recently also Critical Realism [12]. Urry [27] has argued that sociologists should focus more of their research on issues related to globalization and presents a combination of ANT, Complexity Theory and Reflexive Modernization as an ontological foundation for these under the label "global fluids" and suggests that Internet is the paradigm example of such a fluid. The combination of these three theories/ontologies brings us close to AT. However, we see AT as a more coherent and well integrated (process) ontology that helps us better understand how social and material elements are related in addition to two crucial aspects of complex assemblages: firstly, how complexities emerge from simpler elements where AT enables us to focus on both individual elements and larger totalities, and secondly, the dynamics of the unfolding of complex assemblages over time.

The potential of AT will be explored through a case study of the development and evolution of a complex medical procedure called transcatheter aortic valve implantation (TAVI). TAVI is a minimally invasive procedure for treating patients suffering from aortic stenosis. In this case, the aortic valve is replaced by an artificial one and positioned in a patient's heart/aorta by means of digital imaging instruments and catheters inserted through small incisions at the patient's body. TAVI merges the practices of multiple disciplines, foremost cardiovascular surgery, cardiology and radiology. The procedure also involves anesthesiologists in addition to a number of nursing specialists and radiographers. TAVI includes a plethora of digital imaging instruments that are used during diagnostic processes and surgery, numerous interconnected information systems for storing and communicating patient information as well as sophisticated image analysis and presentation tools.

---

[1] Assemblage Theory has so far received almost no attention from the IS research community. Exceptions are [13, 24].

2 Assemblage Theory

Manuel DeLanda presents AT as both a process ontology and a theory of social complexity. Drawing extensively upon the work of Gilles Deleuze, DeLanda [3–6] describes Assemblage Theory as contrary to most social theories which he argues are "organic theories" which form their basis around what he terms *relations of interiority*. In such theories, the component parts of a larger totality are seen as constituted by the very relations they have to other parts of the whole, like the organs that comprise an organism or the different parts of a mechanical watch. DeLanda sees what the philosopher Gilles Deleuze calls "assemblages" as the main alternative to theories of organic totalities. Assemblages are wholes primarily characterized by *relations of exteriority*. This means that he distinguishes the properties defining a given entity from its capacities to interact with (or affect and being affected by) other entities. While its properties are given and may be denumerable as a closed list, its capacities are not given—they may go unused if no entity suitable for interaction is available. In this view, the capacities to interact form a potentially open list since there is no way to tell in advance in what way a given entity may interact with innumerable other entities.

Relations of exteriority mean that a component of an assemblage may be detached from it and plugged into a different assemblage in which its interactions are different. Relations of exteriority also imply that the properties of the component parts can never explain the relations that constitute the whole: "relations do not have as their causes the properties of the [component parts] between which they are established" [5] although they may be caused by and *emerge* from the activation of the component's capacities. These capacities do depend on the component's properties but cannot be reduced to them since they involve reference to other interacting entities.

Assemblages are defined along two dimensions. The first dimension describes the variable roles that an assemblage's components may play and the second dimension defines variable processes in which components become involved. The roles that components engage in range from purely *material* ones at one end to purely *expressive* roles at the other. Thus for example the material components can include individuals, organizations and physical structures such as buildings, networks, computers, and so on. At the other end of the continuum are the expressions about those material entities, which may be expressive or linguistic (e.g., laws, contracts, norms, codes of conduct, rules) and non-linguistic (e.g., bodily expressions, dressing, acts of subordination, the logo of a company, or the design of a smartphone). Most components will at the same time have both material and expressive roles. For instance, an iPhone may play a material role when it is used as a device for communication, but it may also indicate association with a social status (expressive role).

The second dimension refers to the processes of *stabilization* and *destabilization* in which the components become involved. DeLanda discusses some examples of specific processes through which (de-)stabilization takes place. For instance, stabilization may happen through processes that increase the internal homogeneity of an assemblage (making the components more equal to each other) or through those which clarify the boundaries between component parts within and outside the assemblage. On the other hand, there are processes of destabilization that transform the assemblage so that it can express new functions, capacities, forms and boundaries. For instance, adopting social networking technologies like Twitter and Facebook are examples of destabilization processes as they blur the spatial boundaries of social interaction.

Any component of an assemblage may participate in all these processes "by exercising different sets of capacities" [5]. For instance, a member of a political party can stabilize the party by voting in favor of all its issues while at the same time destabilize the party by engaging in scandalous behavior. The combination and interaction of stabilizing and de-stabilizing processes make an assemblage evolve as a continuous process. The dynamics involved in the assemblage's evolution can be explained with many AT terms. Drawing upon Complexity Theory, or what DeLanda calls "the mathematics of dynamic systems", AT may describe the continuous evolution of an assemblage as *path-dependent*, i.e. that it evolves along certain paths. In other cases, de-stabilizing events may sometimes have no apparent effect until a certain *threshold* ("critical mass") is reached. Sometimes the re-stabilization of an assemblage after its destabilization brings the evolution of the assemblage on a new path, i.e. the de-stabilization becomes a *critical juncture* in the assemblage's evolution. After describing our methodology, we will discuss these phenomena through specific examples in the development of the case of TAVI.

Having presented key concepts of AT, we will now briefly compare and contrast AT to the other ontologies popular in IS research.[2] AT has quite a lot in common with Actor Network Theory (ANT). An assemblage is quite similar to an Actor –Network, however, the centrality of emergence in AT implies that there is a significant difference between the two approaches when it comes to multi-level interactions and part-whole relations. If we focus on the stabilization of an assemblage only, this will look pretty much the same as how the stabilization of Actor-Networks through enrolment and alignment has been described. Such stabilization processes were central in the research on the establishment of so-called "immutable mobiles" during the 1980s and 90s. However, more recent ANT research has focused on more complex, unstable, or overlapping networks. Such networks have been described as characterized by "mutable mobiles" and conceptualized as fluids [16]. In our view, however, AT provides us with a richer vocabulary to describe and analyze the "fluid" character of sociomaterial complexities like TAVI and today's ICT solutions more broadly.

Agential Realism (AR) is demonstrated to be a powerful approach in describing the "entanglements" of social and technological aspects of information systems. However, AT and AR are dramatically different in their view on the relations between components of larger totalities. AR claims that components of large wholes are inseparable,[3] that is seeing totalities as based exclusively on relations of interiority, while AT considers relations of exteriority primary. Relations of exteriority between com-

---

[2] Our discussion of AR and CR is based on how these themes are presented and used in IS research, in particular the MISQ Special Issues focusing on each of these [2, 15].

[3] See Faulkner and Runde [8] for an elaborate discussion on this point.

ponents are preconditions for replacing one component with another, i.e. to describe and account for dynamics and change in assemblages. In contrast, the assumption of inseparability implies that AR has been proved to be powerful in describing stable assemblages or their structure at a specific moment. However, in spite of the fact that AR claims that "everything" is "always in the state of becoming," it does not say much about how "things" actually are becoming and change over time.[4] Further, AR provides us with only a limited set of concepts to analyze emergence and the multi-level interactions of complex assemblages. Critical Realism (CR) assumes that social and technological objects are connected and interact, but does not tell us more about how they actually are or may be connected. Emergence is also central to CR, but its terminology for describing how emergence happens is limited, although its concepts for describing and explaining change are more sophisticated. Change is primarily explained as driven by mechanisms triggered by contextual factors.

3 Methodology

Our longitudinal study of TAVI commenced in 2011 and so far spans ten hospitals in Scandinavia (two in Norway, five in Sweden and three in Denmark). Our main site is the Intervention Centre (IVC) at Rikshospitalet (RH) in Oslo. We have observed more than 120 procedures there, each lasting 2–4 hours. We held continuous informal conversations with the practitioners before, during and after the procedures. At the site we conducted over 30 semi-structured interviews of cardiologists, thoracic surgeons, nurses, radiographers, heads of departments and other persons formally and informally involved in TAVI. The key team members have been interviewed several times. The interviews lasted on average 75 min, and were complemented by document analysis and some video recordings.

At each of the other sites we interviewed key practitioners performing TAVI and their respective project or department leaders, altogether comprising another 32 interviews lasting on average 60 min. At three sites we also observed procedures and/or TAVI meetings. We have also interviewed representatives from the two main technology vendors, had field talks with representatives from other two vendors and attended practitioner conferences. Data was coded manually and collaboratively by researchers to include the main on-going concerns expressed by practitioners and critical moments of the TAVI project's development. We went through multiple rounds of analysis, discussed interpretations between researchers to compare and appraise our interpretations and to validate our analytical categories. The results were continuously shared with the practitioners to get their feedback. In other publications [19, 23] we have presented more findings from our study of TAVI.

---

[4]This criticism against AR has been raised, from a Critical Realism perspective, by Mutch [20] and Leonardi [14].

4   Findings

In this section we will describe the elements involved in the TAVI procedure and how
they have evolved and interacted throughout its history. We will begin by describing
the core elements involved when an artificial valve is to be inserted into a heart. We
zoom out to the establishment and evolution of TAVI at the local level, i.e. at RH
and finally we will look at TAVI at national and global levels and the interactions
between the levels. As we are 'zooming out' [21] we will introduce and apply new
aspects of AT for each level.

4.1   The "Core" TAVI Assemblage

TAVI is a procedure that uses advanced technology to treat aortic stenosis, a heart
condition in which the heart's aorta narrows because of increased calcification. This
condition reduces blood flow to the heart and over a period of a few years it significantly weakens the heart muscle. It is commonly treated by open-chest surgery.
Patients offered TAVI are not eligible for open surgery, and have on average only
50% chance of surviving unless they are treated within two years. More recently,
the procedure also began being offered to patients as an alternative to open-chest
surgery.

During the TAVI procedure, the doctors make a small incision in one of the arteries
at a specific location on the patient's body through which they insert thin wires and
catheters. They navigate the catheters through the patient's circulation system guided
by real time digital X-ray videos (fluoroscopy). When the catheter reaches the heart's
aortic valve, the doctors position the new valve, release it, and then retract the catheter.
If all goes well the patient is out of the hospital in a few days. At Rikshospitalet (RH) in
Oslo, TAVI is performed in a hybrid suite at the hospital's Research and Development
department (IVC). This room has various advanced digital X-ray and ultrasound
imaging technologies, other digital instruments linked to numerous monitors placed
around the patient's bed. In addition there are computers for accessing patient records,
X-ray images, and other patient data.

The unique TAVI equipment consists of the replacement valve, catheters and
disposable delivery systems for these catheters (see Images 1 and 2). Depending on
the conditions of the patient the catheter is inserted through one of four possible
access points. The transfemoral TAVI procedure is performed from the groin (the
least invasive) and is generally in the domain of interventional cardiologists (see
Image 3), whereas the three others (central) are performed via small chest incisions
by the surgeons in collaboration with the interventional cardiologists. A TAVI team
typically consists of 2 surgeons, 2(3) interventional cardiologists, an anesthesiologist,
anesthetic nurse, echo cardiographer, radiographers, nurses and crimping nurses. The
producers offer valves in different sizes and capabilities, these again with different

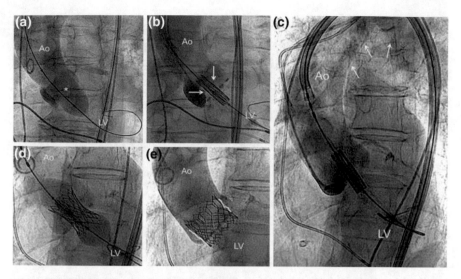

Image 1 X-ray image of the heart's aorta broadcasted from a fluoroscopy robot

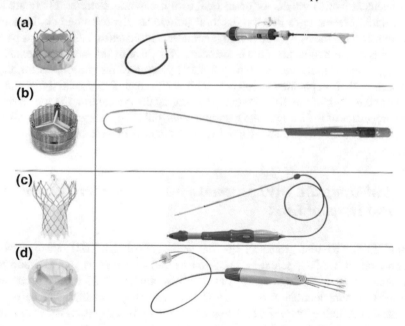

Image 2 Various TAVI valves and accompanying delivery systems [28]

techniques of handling and operating when inside the patient's body. The choice of valve depends on the patient's physical condition.

When looking at TAVI through the lens of AT, we see a number of layers of nested assemblages interacting during a procedure. We find component assemblages

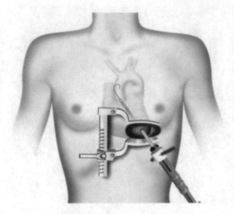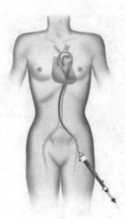

Image 3 The different TAVI procedure access points: the chest and the groin

ranging from material ones like a valve, patient, or a screen to expressive ones such as a statement made by a doctor or an image on the monitor screen. There are also non-material assemblages like the doctors' individual identities and skills or their decisions. Next to these, we find heterogeneous assemblages in the form of a specific task that is performed such as the positioning of a valve or the entire procedure for inserting a replacement valve. During a TAVI procedure the various assemblages are enacting their capacities to interact with each other. The productivity and the quality of the work of the TAVI team in the surgery theatre cannot, then, be reduced to the properties of the assemblage's components, but is an emergent property being a result of the various elements' capacities to interact with each other.

4.2 Stabilizing the TAVI Assemblage at the Surgery Theater and Hospital Level

Around 2006, different groups of doctors at Rikshospitalet (RH) became knowledgeable about TAVI at scientific conferences and in scientific journals and they considered whether to begin using it at their hospital. By 2007 these groups were discussing in more detail how to start TAVI activities. They contacted their respective regional health authority (HSØ) and began working on funding issues. Cardiologists and cardiac surgeons agreed that they should establish a TAVI team where both groups were involved and that TAVI should be performed in the hybrid room at the hospital's Intervention Centre (IVC). Members of the TAVI team were selected, and they decided to use valves from Edwards (one of the two producers of TAVI valves and equipment at that time). Next they attended a course at Edwards' facilities (in Rouen, France) where they trained using simulators. The first two procedures were carried out on the 16th September 2009. Proctors and other support staff provided by

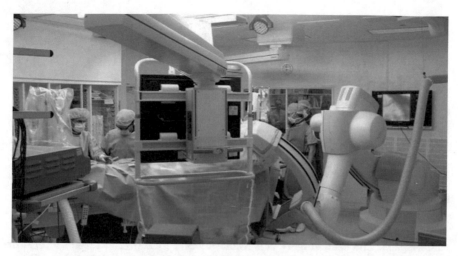

Image 4 The hybrid room during a TAVI procedure. In front is the laparoscopy (live X-ray) robot. (Image is the courtesy of IVC, 2014)

Edwards assisted the first 20 TAVI procedures.[5] The RH team decided to begin with central access procedures (entering the patient's body through their chest) because these were more familiar to them being closer to ordinary open-chest surgery.

Becoming ready to start doing TAVI at RH was primarily a process of defining and stabilizing the assemblage required. This happened through the combination of a number of stabilizing processes. Important among these were the process through which the different elements of the assemblage were "designed" or specified (formally or informally). Equally important were the negotiation and decision-making processes among doctors involved, among doctors and managers at the hospital, between the hospital and health authorities (HSØ), and between the hospital and the TAVI vendors. Another important stabilization process was learning—both individual learning through lectures, observation and rehearsing using simulators, as well as collective learning of how to coordinate various activities (Image 4).

After the first 20 procedures were performed, the focus shifted to establishing TAVI as a regular practice. After a number of central-access procedures they began with transfemoral procedures. The TAVI team wanted to master all available access points and valves to learn under which condition each was most appropriate. Accordingly they eventually purchased the Medtronic valves 9 months after start-up that again included visits to training sites organized by the vendor and supervision of initial procedures by its proctors (Image 5).

As the number of procedures was growing and the TAVI team's experience increased, more organizational structures were gradually established. Some just emerged; others were based on deliberate decisions. Patients were examined by

---

[5] A proctor is a surgeon or an interventional cardiologist who has done at least 50 TAVI procedures. They travel around supervising TAVI practitioners and sharing experiences.

Image 5 The TAVI team in action. (Image is the courtesy of IVC, 2014)

cardiologists. The heart surgery department received the overall responsibility for TAVI patients. This includes keeping a list of patients being considered for TAVI, informing and coordinating with TAVI team members at IVC, doing the measurements of arteries upon which the decisions about access point and valve size should be made, responsibility for pre-and post-operative procedures including coordination with intensive care units, etc. Meetings in the TAVI team before and after each procedure became regular practice where they discussed how the procedure was conducted, if things could or should have been done differently and more general lessons to be learned. After the first start-up period TAVI procedures were carried out two days a month. The number of patients treated rose from about 10–15 patients in 2009, to about 50 in 2010.

All patients considered for heart surgery are discussed by cardiac surgeons and cardiologists at daily "heart meetings." At these meetings they also discuss potential TAVI patients, which are later discussed in a weekly TAVI meeting with 1–2 interventional cardiologists and 1–2 surgeons. During the summer of 2010 a contract specifying the roles and tasks of surgeons and cardiologists was set up and signed. This contract was re-negotiated in 2012. During this process, the TAVI assemblage within the surgery theatre was increasingly stabilized at the same time as the larger TAVI assemblage at the hospital was "designed" and stabilized. Design, learning, negotiation, and decision making were also key stabilizing processes here. The specification and signing of the contract between the surgeons and the cardiologists illustrates one important stabilizing process emphasized by DeLanda [5], namely that of coding.

4.3   Cycles of De- and Re-stabilization

Having described the initial stabilization of TAVI at the surgery theatre and hospital level, we will now turn our attention to the following evolution at TAVI and how this happened through a combination and interaction of different stabilizing and de-stabilizing processes.

Since the early stabilization of the main structure of TAVI at RH, the procedure was undergoing continuous change. For instance, whereas in the beginning a TAVI procedure on average lasted 3–4 h, this was reduced to today 1–2 hours. There has been a change in the choice of access points from central to transfemoral procedures, stabilizing in terms of a 85/15. There has also been a steady progression in terms of offering TAVI to patients with lower surgical risks. The change happened as an outcome of a series of de-stabilizing processes and subsequent re-stabilization where just smaller sub-assemblages of the TAVI assemblage have been modified or replaced by new ones. One important de-stabilizing process has been the entrance into the TAVI market by new vendors offering new valves that RH adopted and used in the treatment of specific groups of patients.

While we above pointed out learning as a stabilizing process, in the evolution of TAVI various learning processes also played a key role as a de-stabilizing force. For example, increased practical experience made the practitioners more skilled in performing the various tasks like preparing the room, crimping the valve and putting it into the catheter, maneuvering the catheter, positioning the valve, etc. The members of the team also became more skilled in coordinating the different activities and tasks in the operation room. Each time, these learning processes caused only very small changes of the TAVI procedure. The TAVI team also improved their practices based on learning from colleagues doing TAVI at other hospitals in Norway and through international communication in informal networks and presentations at research conferences. They have also improved their work based on hints and suggestions provided by the technology vendors.

Finally, the TAVI team learned and modified their practice based on conclusions drawn from the analysis of data they collected about each patient, such as access point, valve type, degree of leakages between the valve and aorta, patient conditions at certain time intervals after surgery, etc. These data were stored together with other patient data in databases. This learning process has improved their competence and changed their practice regarding critical assessments such as criteria for choice also, choice of patients and access point. The change towards more transfemoral procedures and offering TAVI to more low-risk patients are outcomes of this learning. This data analysis also changed the procedure regarding which criteria are used in making decisions about whether a patient is eligible for TAVI or not.

Additionally, the TAVI procedure changed because of conclusions drawn from specific incidents destabilizing the procedure. Such incidents included episodes where the valve inadvertently slipped into the aorta, the collapse of a valve, the breaking of a catheter inside the patient, etc. There have also been occasions of cardiac arrests, which required immediate resuscitations. Incidents such as these lead to an immediate destabilization of the procedure followed by re-stabilization by for example figuring out how to deal with the situation when it happens. This is again followed by discussions and modifications of the procedure to prevent similar incidents and agreeing about how such incidents should be dealt with if they happen again.

Some of the processes mentioned here destabilized only a small part of the overall TAVI assemblage, such as for instance the improvement of individual skills. Other processes de-stabilized larger parts, like for instance the adoption of new valves. Initially, TAVI was offered only to patients diagnosed as inoperable due to extremely high risk for surgery. In this sense, TAVI was a complementary procedure that did not have any direct impact on existing open-chest surgery practices. However as TAVI evolved into a procedure that is also offered to lower risk patients, it de-stabilized the existing open-chest surgery assemblage. It meant that interventional cardiologists and the cardiology department were beginning to take over the treatment of aortic stenosis from surgeons and the surgery department. This was part of a larger movement as the development of other minimally invasive technologies and procedures has caused treatments of other diagnoses, for instance PCI,[6] being transferred from cardiac surgery to cardiology.

4.4 Interacting Processes and Thresholds

Having described the evolution of the TAVI assemblage at RH as cycles of de- and re-stabilization processes, in this section we discuss other forms of interactions between different processes.

Over the years, with growing experience and positive outcomes, TAVI became increasingly considered as a regular treatment of aortic stenosis patients. Accordingly the number of patients treated has constantly been growing. In 2015 more than 150 patients were treated at RH and about 300 in total in Norway [1]. During spring 2014 the cardiologists gave an impetus to the reorganization of TAVI activities. Their proposal was that the transfemoral procedures should be performed in their catheter lab in the cardiology department by a small team of 2 cardiologists and one assisting nurse, an anesthesiology nurse and a radiographer. This would be a significant improvement regarding costs and productivity. The demand for TAVI treatment reached a level where the hybrid room at IVC had become a bottleneck. Doing TAVI in the cath lab would, then, help increase the hospital's capacity to treat patients with aortic stenosis.

After a number of meetings the head of the heart clinic decided to move trans-femoral procedures to the cath labs, and the planning of this transfer started. Nurses working in the cardiology department were selected and the radiographer who was coordinating TAVI at IVC instructed the interventional cardiologists about the prepa-rations that had to be done before the procedures.

The cardiology department started with transfemoral TAVI procedures in one of their cath labs in late 2014. Twelve procedures were performed in the first three weeks. A new contract was negotiated specifying that interventional cardiologists were responsible for patients undergoing transfemoral procedures and surgeons respon-

---

[6]PCI (Percutaneous coronary intervention) is a non-surgical procedure used to treat narrowing (stenosis) of the coronary arteries of the heart found in coronary artery disease.

sible for the central access procedures. However, it turned out that the cath lab was also a scarce resource due to the high number of patients waiting for traditional interventional cardiology procedures (like PCI) and an insufficient number of beds in the post-operative care unit. So after some time and discussions, all the procedures were transferred back to the hybrid room at IVC which was now reserved for TAVI two days every week (only one previously)—one day for interventional cardiologists and transfemoral procedures and one for cardiac surgeons doing central access procedures.

The split of TAVI into two different assemblages or practices was the outcome of the combination of, or interaction between, a number of destabilizing processes: improved skills, improved technologies, growing demand for TAVI, etc. These processes interacted in different ways. First, they all contributed to the de-stabilization of the procedure, i.e. the de-stabilization appeared as an *accumulated effect* of many processes. Second, some of the processes *triggered others*, that is, constituted a *chain or self-reinforcing cycle* of de-stabilizing processes. An example of this is that the growing demand for TAVI was (partially) a consequence of the positive outcome of TAVI for patients, improved technology and learning. All of these were making the transfemoral procedure more applicable, next to the fact that transfemoral was also a less invasive or simpler and less cost effective procedure which implied that HSØ could afford paying for more patients.

Third, destabilizing processes were also unfolding in parallel with the stabilization of the overall procedure. In particular, the performance of more and more procedures and small improvements were making the procedures faster and smoother. These were leading towards the increased stability of the procedures in terms of making the different steps and elements of the procedure increasingly taken for granted by all actors involved. So in this case, there was a kind of *conflict or "competition"* between stabilizing and de-stabilizing processes, and the disruption of the procedure and the split happened when the destabilizing processes got "the upper hand" in this "fight."

The disruption of the TAVI procedure was therefore the outcome of a series of stabilizing and de-stabilizing process unfolding over a long time. The disruption happened when the accumulation of de-stabilizing events reached the *threshold* making the split possible. In such situations, individual de-stabilizing events have no visible effect until the threshold is reached and a small additional event may trigger the change of a large assemblage.

4.5   Path-Dependency and Critical Junctures

We will now look more carefully at how assemblages evolve and how concepts from AT like path-dependency and critical junctures help us in this effort at the same time as we look at how TAVI was performed at other hospitals.

In Scandinavian countries, we see many hospitals where TAVI has evolved and been organized in ways similar to RH. But there are also hospitals where TAVI is organized in a very different ways and has been evolving along very different paths. One example of this is Karolinska Hospital in Stockholm. Lacking a hybrid room, Karolinska immediately started their TAVI procedures in a cath lab within the cardiology department. For this reason they began their TAVI activities doing only transfemoral procedures.

Unfortunately the very first patient died after been given full anesthesia but 'in fact'? before the procedure started. Basis on this they concluded that full anesthesia represented too high of a risk for very sick and old patients (which all TAVI patients were at that time), and that they should try to perform the procedure with local anesthesia and sedation only. This requires a simplification of the procedure so it could be performed without for instance a urine catheter, and within only 2–3 h. These issues in combination brought Karolinska on a "minimalist" specialization path. This included specializing in using valves (and equipment) from one vendor only, using only local anesthesia and percutaneous techniques.

At Skejby Hospital in Denmark they also started the TAVI procedures the cath lab with a team of cardiologists. Here also the very first patient died, in this case during the procedure. However, the TAVI team here drew an almost opposite conclusion from Karolinska. They concluded that TAVI required surgical expertise to be safe, and, accordingly, that cardiac surgeons as well as anesthesiologists had to be included in the TAVI team. Close collaboration among team members was seen as crucial. They also concluded that TAVI should be performed in a hybrid room and not in a cath lab. At the time, they did not have a hybrid room, but a new hospital was being planned. Their cardiologists engaged in the planning process and pushed for the inclusion of a hybrid room in the new hospital. Moreover, they argued that the hybrid room should be located within the surgery department. This, they believed, would make it easier to achieve the surgeons' long-term commitment to TAVI. This strategy was realized and placed their TAVI procedures on a path very different from the one at Karolinska.

These two cases illustrate two important and related aspects of how assemblages evolve. First, there are certain moments that take the evolution of an assemblage in a certain direction—along a specific path. Such moments are called "critical junctures" (or bifurcation or tipping points). The tragic losses of the first patients at Karolinska and Skejby were clearly such critical junctures. In both cases the conclusions drawn from these incidents had a huge impact on how TAVI has evolved ever since at these hospitals. And when an assemblage starts evolving in a certain direction, like the minimalist specialization direction at Karolinska, the evolution along that path becomes progressively stabilized. The future evolution of an assemblage will be increasingly constrained by the path along which it has evolved. It becomes more and more path-dependent.

5   Concluding Discussion

In this section we discuss our research contribution based on the AT analysis of TAVI. We see TAVI as a highly relevant case for discussing the suitability of ontological foundations for IS research. TAVI is clearly a case of high sociomaterial complexity in terms of a dense web of relations between large numbers of different kinds of elements. It exhibits the two aspects of the dynamics we pointed out: the interactions and interdependencies between multiple levels of the case and the "logic" behind how the case is evolving over time. Some, however, may find the case to be primarily about medical instruments and material technologies like the artificial aortic valves and the delivery catheters. These technologies are certainly central to TAVI, but so are the numerous information systems being used during the diagnostic processes and the surgical interventions. Yet others are used to support collaboration between doctors within and across national borders. Many of these systems are also used for the exchange of information between hospitals as related to TAVI patient admission, or are used during the diagnostic processes and planning of the operations. In this way TAVI is a case providing rich illustrations of relations and interdependencies between physical/material and digital objects.

Even though our case narrative does not focus the details of the traditional information systems involved, we do believe that the narrative and our analysis make a contribution related to an important emerging IS research issue: the relations and interactions between technological architecture and governance structures and how these two in combination influence the evolution of the complex sociomaterial assemblages constituting current ICT solutions [10, 24–26]. Our application of AT illustrates how specific technological and organizational arrangements emerge at various levels (surgery theatre, hospital, national, global) and how structures at one level shape the evolution at lower levels which again lead to changes at higher levels in a cyclic pattern, i.e. how stabilizing or destabilizing processes at one level trigger stabilizing or destabilizing processes at other levels. This cyclic process is obviously similar to the ideas of structuration in Giddens' terms. However, an important difference is that Giddens only focuses on social structures ("traces on the mind") while AT helps us to theorize the role of technological/material and organizational structures that are involved in such processes. Importantly, it also enables us to theorize and describe in detail how the structuration processes actually take place based on the activation of components' capacities to interact and the mix of stabilizing and de-stabilizing processes this generates.[7]

In our view AT has proved to be a powerful tool in disclosing and describing the sociomaterial complexity of TAVI. The concepts of capacities to interact (or affect and being affected) and how the enactment of these capacities generates a set of interacting stabilizing and destabilizing processes give a rich picture and capture central aspects of how a sociomaterial assemblage like TAVI evolves. We consider these aspects of AT, and the differences between AT and the other ontologies mentioned in Sect. 2 that make AT a powerful instrument for understanding the structuration processes listed/discussed/outlined above and the development of strategies for making such processes evolve in desired directions.

---

[7]Urry [27] criticizes Giddens for overlooking the role of complexity and demonstrates how Complexity Theory strengthens Structuration Theory.

In this paper we have argued that AT can be a useful and powerful process ontology for understanding, analyzing and theorizing the development, evolution and use of new technologies. We have argued and tried to demonstrate in particular how AT can help us in our research into the overall sociomaterial complexities of current information systems. We see the key contribution that AT can deliver to IS researchers is its concepts for identifying and analyzing the relations between technological and non-technological (humans, organizations, institutions) and how sociomaterial assemblages are unfolding through the interactions between various stabilizing and de-stabilizing processes and how these processes are generated through the enactment of the various assemblages' capacities to interact. AT also sees the components of sociomaterial assemblages not as just entangled and inseparable, but as components having capacities to interact with each other and as separable in the sense that one component can be replaced with another having different capacities and accordingly making the assemblage behave differently. We have in this paper demonstrated how processes are interacting in various ways such as:

- as sequences or cycles of processes where one stabilizing process triggers a de-stabilizing process which again triggers a stabilizing process, and so on;
- parallel processes, either stabilizing or de-stabilizing, strengthening each other; and
- parallel stabilizing and de-stabilizing processes "competing" with each other.

In addition we have demonstrated how some de-stabilizing processes take place through the accumulation of events (for instance enhanced skills through practice) where the change of the assemblage happens only when a certain threshold is reached. There were on the other hand de-stabilizing processes which were more like instant events such as operations going bad or some technological system breaking down. Sometimes when an assemblage is de-stabilized, it may be re-assembled in a way bringing its evolution on a different path and some de-stabilizing processes can then be seen as being *path-creating* [9].

Acknowledgements The research presented here has greatly benefited from discussions with Eric Monteiro, Davide Nicolini, Bendik Bygstad, Margunn Aanestad, Miria Grisot, Kalle Lyytinen, Youngjin Yoo, Per Ingvar Olsen, Olga Mikailova and two anonymous reviewers. In addition, we would like to thank the Research Council of Norway for funding of the project (research grant 210511).

References

1. Aaberge, L., Bendz, B., Beitnes J.O.: TAVI—kateterbasert behandling av aortastenose. In: Forfang, K., Istad, H., Wiseth, R. (eds.) Kardiologi, Klinisk veileder. Gyldendal Akademisk, pp. 265–271 (2015)
2. Cecez-Kecmanovic, D., Galliers, R.D., Henfridsson, O., Newell, S., Vidgen, R. (eds.) The sociomateriality of information systems: current status, future directions. MIS Q. (Special issue) 38(4) (2014)
3. DeLanda, M.: A Thousand Years of Non-linear History. Zone Books, New York (2000)

4. DeLanda M.: Intensive Science and Virtual Philosophy. Continuum, New York (2002)
5. DeLanda, M.: A New Philosophy of Society: Assemblage Theory and Social Complexity. Continuum, New York (2006)
6. DeLanda, M.: Deleuze: History and Science. Atropos Press, New York (2010)
7. Deleuze, G., Guattari, F.: A Thousand Plateaus: Capitalism and Schizophrenia. The Athlone Press, London (1988)
8. Faulkner, P., Runde, J.: On sociomateriality. In: Leonardi, P.M., Nardi, B.A., Kallinikos, J. (eds.) Materiality and Organizing Social Interaction in a Technological World. Oxford University Press, pp. 49–66 (2012)
9. Garud, R., Kumaraswamy, A., Karnøe, P.: Path dependence or path creation? J. Manag. Stud. **47**(4), 760–774 (2009)
10. Grisot, M., Hanseth, O., Thorseng, A.: Innovation of, in, on infrastructures: articulating the role of architecture in information infrastructure evolution. J. Assoc. Inf. Syst. (Suppl. Special Issue Innov. Inf. Infrastruct. **15**(4), 197–219 (2014)
11. Hanseth, O., Jacucci, E., Grisot, M., Aanestad, M.: Reflexive standardization: side effects and complexity in standard making. MIS Q. **30**(2), 563–581 (2006)
12. Henfridsson, O., Bygstad, B.: The generative mechanisms of digital infrastructure evolution. MIS Q. **37**(3), 907–931 (2013)
13. Henningsson, S., Hanseth, O.: The essential dynamics of information infrastructures. In: Paper 14, ICIS 2011 Proceedings (2011). http://aisel.aisnet.org/icis2011/proceedings/projmanagem ent/14
14. Leonardi, P.M.: Theoretical foundations for the study of sociomateriality. Inf. Organ. **23**(2), 59–75 (2013)
15. Mingers, J., Mutch, A., Willcocks, L. (eds.): Critical realism in information systems research. MIS Q. (Special issue) **37**(3) (2013)
16. Mol, A., Law, J.: Regions, networks and fluids: anaemia and social topology. Soc. Stud. Sci. **24**, 641–671 (1994)
17. Monteiro, E., Pollock, N., Hanseth, O., Williams, R.: From artefacts to infrastructures. Comput Support. Coop Work **22**, 575 (2013)
18. Monteiro, E., Pollock, N., Williams, R.: Innovation in information infrastructures: introduction to the special issue. J. Assoc. Inf. Syst. **15**(4) (2014)
19. Mørk, B.E., Greig, G., Masovic, J., Hanseth, O., Nicolini, D.: Controversies as Opportunities for Innovation in the Case of TAVI. In: Hoholm, T., LaRocca, A., Aanestad, (eds.) Controversies in Medical Innovation. Service, Technology and Organization, Palgrave, pp. 75–106 (2018)
20. Mutch, A.: Sociomateriality—taking the wrong turning? Inf. Organ. **23**(1), 28–40 (2013)
21. Nicolini, D.: Zooming in and out: studying practices by switching theoretical lenses and trailing connections. Organ. Stud. **30**(12), 1391–1348 (2009)
22. Nicolini, D.: Practice Theory, Work, and Organization: An Introduction. Oxford University Press, Oxford (2012)
23. Nicolini, D., Mørk, B.E., Masovic, J., Hanseth, O.: Expertise as trans-situated: the case of TAVI. In Sandberg, J., Roulcau, L., Langley, A., Tsoukas, H. (eds.) Skilful Performance: Enacting Expertise, Competence, and Capabilities in Organizations. Oxford University Press, pp. 27–49 (2017)
24. Rodon, J., Silva, L.: Exploring the formation of a healthcare information infrastructure: hierarchy or meshwork? J. Assoc. Inf. Syst. **16**(5) (2015)
25. Tiwana, A.: Evolutionary competition in platform ecosystems. Inf. Syst. Res. **26**(2), 266–281 (2015)
26. Tiwana, A., Konsynski, B., Bush, A.A.: Research commentary-platform evolution: coevolution of platform architecture, governance, and environmental dynamics. Inf. Syst. Res. **21**(4), 675–687 (2010)
27. Urry, J.: Global Complexity. Polity Press, Cambridge, UK (2003)
28. Wenaweser, P., Praz, F., Stortecky, S.: Transcatheter aortic valve implantation today and tomorrow. Swiss Med. Wkly. **146**, w14299 (2016)

Author Index

© Springer International Publishing AG, part of Springer Nature 2019   265
F. Cabitza et al. (eds.), *Organizing for the Digital World*, Lecture Notes in Information
Systems and Organisation 28, https://doi.org/10.1007/978-3-319-90503-7

Printed in the United States
By Bookmasters